MIGRATION AND HUM/

The UN Convention on Migrant Workers' Rights is the most comprehensive international treaty in the field of migration and human rights. Adopted in 1990 and entered into force in 2003, it sets a standard in terms of access to human rights for migrants. However, it suffers from a marked indifference: only forty states have ratified it and no major immigration country has done so. This highlights how migrants remain forgotten in terms of access to rights. Even though their labour is essential in the world economy, the non-economic aspect of migration – and especially migrants' rights – remain a neglected dimension of globalisation.

This volume provides in-depth information on the Convention and on the reasons behind states' reluctance towards its ratification. It brings together researchers, international civil servants and NGO members and relies upon an interdisciplinary perspective that includes not only law, but also sociology and political science.

RYSZARD CHOLEWINSKI was a reader in Law at the University of Leicester from 1992 to 2005. He now works at the International Organization for Migration.

PAUL DE GUCHTENEIRE is Chief of the International Migration and Multicultural Policies Section at UNESCO and director of the *International Journal on Multicultural Societies*.

ANTOINE PÉCOUD is Programme Specialist for UNESCO's International Migration and Multicultural Policies Section. He is also a research associate at the Unité de Recherche Migrations et Société, University of Paris VII, and at Migrations Internationales, Espaces et Sociétés, University of Poitiers (France).

MIGRATION AND HUMAN RIGHTS

The United Nations Convention on Migrant Workers' Rights

Edited by

RYSZARD CHOLEWINSKI

PAUL DE GUCHTENEIRE

ANTOINE PÉCOUD

UNESCO
Publishing

United Nations
Educational, Scientific and
Cultural Organization

CAMBRIDGE
UNIVERSITY PRESS

Published jointly by the United Nations Educational, Scientific and Cultural Organization,
7, place de Fontenoy, 75352 Paris 07 SP, France and Cambridge University Press,
The Edinburgh Building, Cambridge CB2 8RU, United Kingdom

CAMBRIDGE UNIVERSITY PRESS
Cambridge, New York, Melbourne, Madrid, Cape Town, Singapore, São Paulo, Delhi

www.cambridge.org
Information on this title: www.cambridge.org/9780521199469

Published in the United States of America by Cambridge University Press, New York

UNESCO PUBLISHING
www.publishing.unesco.org

First published in 2009

Printed in the United Kingdom at the University Press, Cambridge

A catalogue record for this publication is available from the British Library

Library of Congress Cataloguing in Publication data

ISBN Cambridge University Press 978-0-521-19946-9 hardback
ISBN Cambridge University Press 978-0-521-13611-2 paperback
ISBN UNESCO 978-92-3-104090-0 paperback

The authors are responsible for the choice and the presentation of the facts contained
in this publication and for the opinions expressed therein, which are not necessarily those
of UNESCO and do not commit the Organization.

The designations employed and the presentation of material throughout this publication
do not imply the expression of any opinion whatsoever on the part of UNESCO
concerning the legal status of any country, territory, city or area or of its authorities
or concerning the delimitation of its frontiers or boundaries.

CONTENTS

v

FIGURES

TABLES

NOTES ON CONTRIBUTORS

MARIE D'AUCHAMP is a human rights lawyer and a social anthropologist. She has worked on cases before the European Human Rights Court in Strasbourg (France), and on the UN human rights system in Geneva (Switzerland). For the past few years she has worked with several Geneva-based human rights NGOs, while specializing in migrants' rights. She is currently the Geneva Liaison Officer for December 18.

GRAZIANO BATTISTELLA is Director of the Scalabrini International Migration Institute in Rome. In the 1980s he spent nine years at the Center for Migration Studies in New York, where he was part of the editorial board of the *International Migration Review*. For twelve years he was Director of the Scalabrini Migration Center in Quezon City (the Philippines), where he founded and edited the *Asian and Pacific Migration Journal*. In addition to articles published in specialized magazines, he edited or co-edited *Unauthorized Migration in Southeast Asia, Asian Women in Migration, The Human Rights of Migrant Workers: Agenda for NGOs* and *Philippine Labor Migration: Impact and Policy*.

RYSZARD CHOLEWINSKI holds degrees from the Universities of Ottawa (LL.D.), Saskatchewan (LL.M.) and Leicester (LL.B.) (UK). From 1992 to 2005 he taught in the Faculty of Law at the University of Leicester, where he was a Reader in Law. He has published widely on international and European migration law, including *Migrant Workers in International Human Rights Law: Their Protection in Countries of Employment* (1997); *Borders and Discrimination in the European Union* (2002); *The Legal Status of Migrants Admitted for Employment: A Comparative Study of Law and Practice in Selected European States* (2004); and *Study on Obstacles to Effective Access of Irregular Migrants to Minimum Social Rights* (2005). Currently he works for the Migration Policy and Research Department of the IOM in Geneva (Switzerland).

JONATHAN CRUSH is Director of the Southern African Migration Project, Queen's Research Chair in Migration and Development at Queen's University (Canada), and an honorary professor at the University of Cape Town (South Africa). He has written extensively on a range of migration issues in Africa and is editor of the SAMP Migration Policy Series and African Migration and Development Series.

PAUL DE GUCHTENEIRE is Head of the Programme on International Migration and Multicultural Policies at UNESCO and Director of the *International Journal on Multicultural Societies*. He has worked as an epidemiologist at the Netherlands Cancer Research Foundation, was a past director of the Steinmetz Institute of the Royal Netherlands Academy of Arts and Sciences and was a former president of the International Federation of Data Organizations. His current research focuses on the human rights dimension of international migration and the development of policies for migration management at the international level. His publications include *Democracy and Human Rights in Multicultural Societies* (co-edited with M. Koenig, 2007) and *Migration without Borders: Essays on the Free Movement of People* (co-edited with A. Pécoud, 2007), as well as several works on data collection and analysis in the social sciences.

EUGÉNIE DEPATIE-PELLETIER is Research Associate at La Chaire de recherche du Canada en droit international des migrations, University of Montreal (Canada). She is finishing a Master's degree in demography at the University of Montreal and is specializing in temporary migrant workers in Canada.

GABRIELA DÍAZ is currently a resident researcher at the Center for Inter-American Studies and Programs at the Mexico Autonomous Institute of Technology. During 2005 and 2006, she was a research and writing grantee of the John D. and Catherine T. MacArthur Foundation, for a project entitled *Globalization, International Security and Human Security: Experiences of Women Migrants Detained in Mexico* (together with Gretchen Kuhner). She has done research and outreach work on refugees and migrants in Mexico since 1997, participating in various oral history projects for the National Autonomous University of Mexico and studies on international cooperation for human development for the Centro Latinoamericano de la Globalidad. As Education and Outreach Coordinator of Sin Fronteras, a Mexican NGO, she coordinated the Mexican academic and NGO migration network, Foro Migraciones, and edited the electronic magazine, *Entre Redes*.

CARLA EDELENBOS has been a human rights lawyer with the United Nations since 1991. At present she works for the Office of the High Commissioner for Human Rights as Secretary of the Committee on Migrant Workers. She holds a degree in law from the Erasmus University in Rotterdam and a degree in public international law from the University of Utrecht (the Netherlands). Her recent publications include 'The International Convention on the Protection of the Rights of All Migrant Workers and Members of Their Families' (*Refugee Survey Quarterly*, October 2005) and 'Article 26, the Human Rights Committee's views and decisions: the way of the future' (in G. Alfredsson, J. Grimheden, B. G. Ramcharan and A. de Zayas (eds), *International Human Rights Monitoring Mechanisms*, 2001).

DINA EPALE is Director of Parliamentary Affairs with Action Canada for Population and Development (ACPD), an Ottawa-based human rights advocacy organization. He immigrated to Canada in 1993 and holds a Master's degree in International Relations from McMaster University.

MARIETTE GRANGE is an international human rights advocate. She is experienced in advocacy, campaigning and research work on human rights, with particular emphasis on migrants and refugees. Until recently, she was External Relations Co-ordinator of the International Council on Human Rights Policy in Geneva (Switzerland). She has represented international NGOs before the United Nations in Geneva, including Amnesty International, the World Council of Churches, the International Catholic Migration Commission and Human Rights Watch. She is the author of numerous articles, manuals and papers on human rights and migration-related issues. A board member of December 18, she also acted as an advisor for the Global Commission for International Migration, and has participated in the United Nations High Commissioner for Refugees Global Consultations on International Protection and the Berne Initiative.

FELICITAS HILLMANN is a professor of human geography at the Department of Social Sciences, University of Bremen (Germany). She specializes in migration as well as urban and development studies, with an emphasis on gender issues. Her research has also focused on the role and function of ethnic economies in urban labour markets and on the more general pattern of labour market insertion of immigrants. She holds a Ph.D. from the University of Freiburg (Germany). In 1994 to 2000 she worked as a senior researcher at the Social Science Research

Centre (WZB) in Berlin on the international mobility of highly qualified migrants within the transformation process in eastern Europe. In 2001 to 2006 she lectured at the Free University of Berlin. Recent publications include *Migration als räumliche Definitionsmacht? Beiträge zu einer neuen Geographie der Migration in Europa* (2007); *Asian Migrants and European Labour Markets* (co-edited with E. Spaan and T. van Naerssen, 2005); 'Shifts in the European discourses on migration and development' (*Asian-Pacific Migration Journal*, Vol. 14, Nos. 1–2, 2005, with E. Spaan and T. van Naerssen); 'Gendered landscapes of the ethnic economies: Turkish entrepreneurs in Berlin' (in *Landscapes of Ethnic Economy*, edited by D. Kaplan and W. Li, 2006); 'Migrants care work in private households or: the strength of bilocal and transnational ties as a last(ing) resource in global migration' (in *Care Work in Europe*, edited by B. Pfau-Effinger and B. Geissler, 2005).

AMANDA KLEKOWSKI VON KOPPENFELS is a lecturer in migration studies at the University of Kent at Brussels. She received her Ph.D. from Georgetown University in 1999, focusing on *Aussiedler* migration and implications for German citizenship. In 1999 to 2000, while on a Robert Bosch Foundation Fellowship, she worked for the German Ministry of the Interior and for the International Organization for Migration in Germany. From 2000 to 2002, she worked at the International Organization for Migration Research Department in Geneva (Switzerland), where her research focus was on the trafficking of human beings for sexual exploitation. In 2004 she taught in the Research Group for Migration at the Institute for Political Science at the University of Münster (Germany). She has published on ethnic German migration to Germany, German citizenship, trafficking and regional consultative processes.

GRETCHEN KUHNER has specialized in the human rights of migrants and refugees since 1995. She worked on asylum cases in El Paso and Seattle (USA) while attending law school, and was the legal coordinator of Sin Fronteras, a Mexican NGO, between 1997 and 2005. In this position she established a programme providing direct representation to migrants, as well as the first detention project for migrants in Mexico. She is a member of the Regional Network of Civil Organizations for Migration, a coalition of North and Central American NGOs. Currently she is a resident researcher at the Center for Inter-American Studies and Programs at the Mexico Autonomous Institute of Technology. During 2005 and 2006, she was a research and writing grantee of the John D. and

Catherine T. MacArthur Foundation, for a project entitled *Globalization, International Security and Human Security: Experiences of Women Migrants Detained in Mexico* (together with Gabriela Díaz).

EUAN MACDONALD graduated in law from the University of Edinburgh (UK) in 1999, and also gained a Master's degree from the same university in 2000, focusing on public international law and legal theory. He went on to obtain a Ph.D. in law from the European University Institute in Florence (Italy) in 2006, with a thesis on critical approaches to international legal theory, scheduled for publication in 2009. He has also been a visiting fellow on the Programme for the Study of International Organizations at the Graduate Institute for International Studies in Geneva (Switzerland), and currently works at the Institute for International Law and Justice at New York University (USA), as a researcher on the Global Administrative Law project.

PEGGY NICHOLSON was a student intern with the Institute for Democracy in South Africa in 2005.

HÉLÈNE OGER holds a Master's degree in comparative law from the Sorbonne, Paris, and a Ph.D. in European and comparative immigration law from the European University Institute in Florence (Italy). She is currently a lecturer at Hertfordshire University (UK).

ANTOINE PÉCOUD has been with UNESCO's Section on International Migration and Multicultural Policies since 2003 and is a research associate at the Unité de Recherche Migrations et Société, University of Paris VII and at Migrations Internationales, Espaces et Sociétés, University of Poitiers (France). He holds a B.A. from the University of Lausanne (Switzerland) and a Ph.D. in social and cultural anthropology from the University of Oxford (UK). His research has focused on migration policies, immigrant entrepreneurship in Germany and the human rights implications of international migration. He co-edited *Migration Without Borders: Essays on the Free Movement of People* (with P. de Guchteneire, 2007).

VICTOR PICHÉ is Honorary Professor at the Department of Demography, University of Montreal (Canada) and Senior Advisor on International Migration and Human Rights for Action Canada for Population and Development.

NICOLA PIPER is Senior Lecturer in the Department of Geography and Associate Director of the Centre for Migration Policy Research at

Swansea University (UK). She holds a Ph.D. in Sociology from the University of Sheffield (UK) and has had previous appointments with the Nordic Institute of Asian Studies in Copenhagen (Denmark), the Australian National University in Canberra and the Asia Research Institute in Singapore, a position she occupied during the research and drafting process of her contribution to this volume. Her research interests revolve around international economic migration, governance and policy networks, gender, NGOs and transnational political activism, and migrants' rights. Among her latest publications are the edited volume *New Perspectives on Gender and Migration: Livelihoods, Rights, and Entitlements* (2008) and *Critical Perspectives on Global Governance: Rights and Regulation in Governing Regimes* (with J. Grugel, 2007). She is also the author of numerous journal articles and background papers for international organizations such as the United Nations Economic and Social Commission for Asia and the Pacific, the United Nations Research Institute for Social Development and the Global Commission on International Migration.

BERNARD RYAN is a graduate of University College Dublin (Ireland) and holds a Ph.D. from the European University Institute in Florence (Italy). He is currently a reader in law at the University of Kent (UK), where he teaches British immigration law and international migration law. His principal recent publications and research have concerned labour migration policy, the interrelationship of British and EU immigration law and the development of extraterritorial immigration control. He was the editor of a report on *Labour Migration and Employment Rights* published by the Institute of Employment Rights in 2005.

ISABELLE SLINCKX graduated in international politics at the University of Louvain-La-Neuve (Belgium) and in human rights (Facultés Saint-Louis, Brussels). She worked as Regional Programme Coordinator for December 18 and was the researcher on a joint International Catholic Migration Commission / December 18 project on the UN Treaty Monitoring Bodies and Migrants' Rights.

PATRICK A. TARAN is Senior Migration Specialist with the International Labour Organization in Geneva (Switzerland). Main areas of responsibility include labour migration in Africa, Europe and Commonwealth of Independent States countries; discrimination against and integration of migrant workers; and protection of rights and dignity of migrants. Before joining the International Labour Organization in 2000, he served as Secretary for Migration at the World Council of Churches, Programme Officer for the joint UN Inter-Agency International Migration Policy Program, Director of Migrants Rights International and Coordinator of the Steering Committee of the Global Campaign for the Ratification of the Convention on the Rights of Migrants. Prior to 1990 he directed local and national refugee and immigration programmes in the United States. He has written extensively on topics of migration, discrimination and human rights.

KRISTINA TOUZENIS holds a B.A. and an M.A. law degree from the University of Copenhagen (Denmark). She has focused her research and consultant activities on international public law, especially human rights law and international humanitarian law, with particular attention towards vulnerable groups, such as refugees and migrants, women and children. Her geographical focus has been the Mediterranean region, and she has included Islamic law among her specializations. She teaches human rights law at various Master's courses in Italy. She worked for a time for the Mediterranean Institute for Childhood (Italy), and currently works for the International Organization for Migration as Project Officer. She is the author of *Unaccompanied Minors: Rights and Protection* (2006).

VINCENT WILLIAMS is Project Manager with the Southern African Migration Project based at the Institute for Democracy in South Africa. He has a particular interest in migration policy and human rights, on which he has published a number of articles and reports.

ABBREVIATIONS

AAFQ	Association des Aides Familiales du Québec (Canada)
ACA	Aliens Control Act (South Africa)
ACPD	Action Canada for Population and Development
AETR	Accord Européen sur les Transports Routiers
ANC	African National Congress
APEC	Asia-Pacific Economic Cooperation
APRO	Asian and Pacific Regional Organisation (of the ICFTU)
APWLD	Asia Pacific Forum on Women, Law and Development
ASEAN	Association of Southeast Asian Nations
ATMF	Association des Travailleurs Maghrebins de France
BCEA	Basic Conditions of Employment Act (South Africa)
BSI	Border Safety Initiative (Mexico)
CAB	Citizens Advice Bureau (UK)
CAT	Convention against Torture and Other Cruel, Inhuman or Degrading Treatment or Punishment / Committee Against Torture
CBRD	Committee for Basic Rights and Democracy (Germany)
CCME	Churches Committee for Migrants in Europe
CCPR	Human Rights Committee [of ICCPR]
CEDAW	Convention on the Elimination of All Forms of Discrimination against Women / Committee on the Elimination of Discrimination Against Women
CERD	Convention on the Elimination of Racial Discrimination / Committee on the Elimination of Racial Discrimination
CES	Conseil Économique et Social (France)
CESCR	Committee on Economic, Social and Cultural Rights
CGIL	Confederazione Generale Italiana del Lavoro (Italy)
CHR/HRC	Commission on Human Rights [now Human Rights Council]
CIC	Citizenship and Immigration Canada
CICC	Coalition for the International Criminal Court
CIMADE	Service Oecuménique d'Entraide (France)
CISL	Confederazione Italiana Sindacati dei Lavoratori (Italy)
CMW	Committee on the Protection of the Rights of All Migrant Workers and Members of Their Families

CNCDH	Commission Nationale Consultative des Droits de l'Homme (France)
CNDH	Comisión Nacional de Derechos Humanos (Mexico)
COMMIT	Coordinated Mekong Ministerial Initiative Against Trafficking
COMPAS	Centre on Migration Policy and Society (UK)
CONAPO	Consejo Nacional de Población (Mexico)
CORMSA	Consortium for Refugees and Migrants in South Africa
COSATU	Congress of South African Trade Unions
CPTA	Centro di Permanenza Temporanea e Assistanze (Italy)
CRC	Convention on the Rights of the Child / Committee on the Rights of the Child
CSO	civil society organization
CSVR	Centre for the Study of Violence and Reconciliation (Johannesburg)
CTOC	Convention against Transnational Organized Crime (UN)
DDL	*disegno di legge delega* (authorization to draw up a law) (Italy)
DFID	Department for International Development (UK)
DHS	Department of Homeland Security (USA)
ECHR	European Convention on Human Rights
ECLAC	Economic Commission for Latin America and the Caribbean
ECMW	European Convention on the Legal Status of Migrant Workers
ECOSOC	Economic and Social Council of the United Nations
ECOSUR	El Colegio de la Frontera Sur (Mexico)
EEA	European Economic Area / Employment Equity Act (South Africa)
EESC	European Economic and Social Committee
ELOI	European Legislation Oriented Institutes
EPMWR	European Platform for Migrant Workers' Rights
ETS	European Treaty Series
EU	European Union
FAC	Foreign Affairs Canada
FGTE–CFDT	Fédération Générale des Transports et de l'Équipement–Confédération Française Démocratique du Travail (International Transport Workers Federation)
FIDH	Fédération internationale des ligues des droits de l'Homme / International Federation for Human Rights
G-77	Group of 77
GAO	Government Accountability Office (USA)
GATS	General Agreement on Trade in Services
GCC	Gulf Cooperation Council
GCIM	Global Commission on International Migration
GFMD	Global Forum on Migration and Development
GISTI	Groupe d'information et de soutien des immigrés (France)

GMG	Global Migration Group (UN)
HLD	High-Level Dialogue on International Migration and Development
HRC	Human Rights Council
HRSDC	Human Resources and Skills Development Canada
HRW	Human Rights Watch
IACHR	Inter-American Commission on Human Rights
IADB	Inter-American Development Bank
IAMM	*International Agenda for Migration Management*
ICBL	International Campaign to Ban Landmines
ICCPR	International Covenant on Civil and Political Rights
ICERD	International Convention on the Elimination of All Forms of Racial Discrimination
ICESCR	International Covenant on Economic, Social and Cultural Rights
ICFTU	International Confederation of Free Trade Unions
ICMC	International Catholic Migration Commission
ICPD	International Conference on Population and Development of the United Nations
ICRMW	International Convention on the Protection of the Rights of All Migrant Workers and Members of Their Families
IFRC	International Federation of Red Cross and Red Cresent Societies
IGO	intergovernmental organization
IGWG	Intergovernmental Working Group of Experts on the Human Rights of Migrants
IIDH	Instituto Interamericano de Derechos Humanos
ILC	International Labour Conference
ILO	International Labour Organization
IMRWC/MRI	International Migrants Rights Watch Committee [now Migrants Rights International]
INCMR	Italian National Committee for Migrants' Rights
INM	Instituto Nacional de Migración (Mexico)
IOM	International Organization for Migration
IPMWC	International NGO Platform on the Migrant Workers' Convention
JCWI	Joint Council for the Welfare of Immigrants (UK)
LCP	Live-in Caregivers Program (Canada)
LDH	Ligue des droits de l'Homme (France)
LGP	Ley General de Población / General Population Act (Mexico)
LRA	Labour Relations Act (South Africa)
LSP	Low-Skilled Workers Program (Canada)
MESCA	Mediterranean and Scandinavian countries involved in drafting the ICRMW
MFA	Migrant Forum in Asia
MPG	Migration Policy Group

MRAP	Mouvement contre le Racisme et pour l'Amitié entre les Peuples (France)
MRI	Migrants Rights International
MSF	Médecins sans Frontières
MWF	Migrant Workers Forum
NAALC	North American Agreement on Labour Cooperation
NAFTA	North American Free Trade Agreement
NGO	non-governmental organization
NIC	newly industrialized country
NIE	newly industrialized economy
NNIRR	National Network for Immigrant and Refugee Rights (USA)
NTUC	National Trades Union Congress (Singapore)
NUM	National Union of Mineworkers (South Africa)
OCASI	Ontario Council of Agencies Serving Immigrants (Canada)
OHCHR	Office of the United Nations High Commissioner for Human Rights
OMCT	Organisation Mondiale Contre la Torture / World Organisation Against Torture
PSI	Public Services International
RESF	Réseau Éducation Sans Frontières
SAA	Social Assistance Act (South Africa)
SAARC	South Asian Association for Regional Cooperation
SADC	Southern African Development Community
SAHRC	South African Human Rights Commission
SAMP	Southern African Migration Project
SAWP	Seasonal Agricultural Worker Program (Canada)
SLBFE	Sri Lanka Bureau of Foreign Employment
SRE	Secretaría de Relaciones Exteriores (Mexico)
SSHRC	Social Sciences and Humanities Research Council (Canada)
STPS	Secretaría del Trabajo y Previsión Social (Mexico)
TGWU	Transport and General Workers Union (UK)
THP	The Hague Process on Refugees and Migration
TUC	Trades Union Congress
UDHR	Universal Declaration of Human Rights
UIF	Unemployment Insurance Fund (South Africa)
UIL	Unione Italiana del Lavoro (Italy)
UN	United Nations
UNA-UK	United Nations Association UK office
UNCTAD	UN Conference on Trade and Development
UN-DESA	United Nations – Department of Economic and Social Affairs
UNDP	United Nations Development Programme
UNESCO	United Nations Educational, Scientific and Cultural Organization

UNFPA	United Nations Population Fund
UNHCR	United Nations High Commissioner for Refugees
UNICEF	United Nations Children's Fund
UNITAR	United Nations Institute for Training and Research
UNODC	United Nations Office on Drugs and Crime
WCAR	World Conference against Racism, Racial Discrimination, Xenophobia and Related Intolerance
WCC	World Council of Churches
WGAD	Working Group on Arbitrary Detention
WTO	World Trade Organization

Introduction: The UN Convention on Migrant Workers' Rights[1]

PAUL DE GUCHTENEIRE AND ANTOINE PÉCOUD

The International Convention on the Protection of the Rights of All Migrant Workers and Members of Their Families (ICRMW) is the most comprehensive international treaty in the field of migration and human rights. It is an instrument of international law meant to protect one of the most vulnerable groups of people: migrant workers, whether in a regular or irregular situation. Adopted in 1990 by the United Nations (UN) General Assembly,[2] it sets a worldwide standard in terms of migrants' access to fundamental human rights, whether on the labour market, in the education and health systems or in the courts. At a time when the number of migrants is on the rise, and evidence regarding human rights abuses in relation to migration is increasing,[3] such a convention is a vital instrument to ensure respect for migrants' human rights.

Yet the ICRMW suffers from marked indifference: only forty-one states have ratified it and no major immigration country has done so. Even though it entered into force on 1 July 2003, most countries are reluctant to ratify the treaty and to implement its provisions. This stands in sharp contrast to other core human rights instruments, which have been very widely ratified.[4] This situation highlights how migrants remain

---

[1] We are grateful to Ryszard Cholewinski for his comments on an earlier draft of this chapter.

[2] General Assembly Resolution 45/158 of 18 December 1990.

[3] For recent evidence on the violation of migrants' human and labour rights, see Amnesty International (2006) and Shelley (2007).

[4] These are the International Convention on the Elimination of All Forms of Racial Discrimination (ICERD, 1965, 173 parties); the International Covenant on Civil and Political Rights (ICCPR, 1966, 164 parties); the International Covenant on Economic, Social and Cultural Rights (ICESCR, 1966, 160 parties); the Convention on the Elimination of All Forms of Discrimination against Women (CEDAW, 1979, 186 parties); the Convention against Torture and Other Cruel, Inhuman or Degrading Treatment or Punishment (CAT, 1984, 146 parties); and the Convention on the Rights of the Child (CRC, 1989, 193 parties). Status as at June 2009 (www2.ohchr.org/english/bodies/ratification/index.htm [last accessed 9 April 2009]).

largely forgotten in terms of access to rights; while the need to protect women and children, for example, is – at least on paper – uncontested, granting rights to migrants is not understood as a priority. Even though migrants' labour is increasingly essential in the world economy, the non-economic aspect of migration – and especially the human and labour rights of migrants – remains a neglected dimension of globalization.

This volume provides in-depth information on the ICRMW and on the reasons behind states' reluctance to ratify it. Part I documents the history, content, scope and mode of functioning of the Convention and features chapters by those directly involved in its drafting and implementation, including international civil servants and human rights activists. Part II provides case studies; focusing on major destination countries in four continents (Africa, Asia, Europe and North America), it explores the situation in terms of migrants' rights and the obstacles to and prospects for state ratification of the Convention. This introduction reviews the arguments developed in the contributions[5] and provides an overview of the issues surrounding the Convention.

Migrant vulnerability to human rights violations

Today, one person in thirty-five is an international migrant. In 2005, the number of people who have settled down in a country other than their own was estimated at around 191 million (UN-DESA, 2006). This figure represents 3% of the world's population and has more than doubled since 1975. Nearly all countries are affected by international migration, whether as countries of origin, transit or destination, or as a combination of these. International migration has become an intrinsic feature of globalization, which raises the issue of the protection of the human rights of migrant workers and their families – the *raison d'être* of the Convention. There are at least two characteristics of migrants' position in host societies that expose them to potential human rights violations: as non-nationals or as people of foreign origin, they find themselves in a outsider situation that may increase their vulnerability; moreover, as workers active in what are often underprivileged sectors

---

[5] In addition to the case studies published here, this introduction makes occasional references to UNESCO-sponsored research in central and eastern Europe, North Africa and West Africa. For a more detailed discussion of their findings, see Pécoud and de Guchteneire (2006) and the UNESCO website (www.unesco.org/migration [last accessed 9 April 2009]).

of the economy, they are disproportionately affected by the lack of respect for labour rights.

As outsiders, migrants may not master the language of the host state; they may be unfamiliar with its legal system and administration; or they can be troubled by the exposure to alien cultural and social practices. Of course, this varies greatly according to migrants' specificities: skilled migrants are better off then their less-skilled counterparts; migrants belonging to a large and well-organized minority should be better supported than isolated migrants, and so on. But it remains that, not being nationals, migrants have fewer rights. They have, for example, little input into policy-making processes that affect them directly. Moreover, the fact of crossing borders in search of employment leads migrants to operate in a transnational legal sphere characterized by loopholes, which range from the non-recognition of their qualifications and work experience to difficulties in maintaining connections to their state of origin.

Racism, xenophobia and discrimination are also frequent features of migrants' everyday experiences and they contribute to exacerbating their already fragile situation. While this is partly a matter of tensions between people of different ethno-cultural backgrounds, it is also the product of a general climate of socioeconomic uncertainty and reluctance towards the changes affecting many societies: unemployment, labour market deregulation, decreasing resources for social security and welfare programmes, political populism, as well as fears surrounding globalization and terrorism, all contributing to mistrust between 'natives' and 'foreigners'. As a consequence, migrants' poor living and working conditions rarely inspire solidarity from nationals who rather express scepticism towards their presence and, disregarding their economic, social and cultural contributions, scapegoat them for problems that have little to do with migration (de Varennes, 2002).

In addition, migrant workers see their vulnerability increased by their labour conditions. As Patrick Taran argues in Chapter 6, migrants are among the workers most profoundly affected by global economic trends. In sending regions, free market and neoliberal policies are having disruptive effects on local economies and create human insecurity, hence favouring emigration. In advanced economies, the increasing interconnectedness and competition between countries (heightened by the development of non-Western economies) led, among other things, to deindustrialization and the growth of the services sector, accompanied by a deregulation of labour markets to make them more flexible and competitive. As a consequence, labour markets experience a polarization that sees large numbers of jobs created at their lower end and characterized by conditions unattractive to national workers.

Rich countries are thus ready to look outside their borders for low-skilled workers. Where this enables nationals to enjoy better living and working conditions, it may also create a structural need for migrants who become over-represented in so-called 3-D jobs (dirty, dangerous and degrading). This is particularly visible in sectors such as agriculture, food processing, construction, manufacturing and low-wage services (domestic work, home healthcare) – all characterized by the underdevelopment of workers' protection. The situation is further worsened by migrants' ignorance of their rights: while existing trade unions are increasingly protecting them, this does not happen everywhere, and migrants can count on few other acknowledged institutions (such as civil society groups or migrant organizations) to support them. This makes it easier for cost-conscious and competition-minded employers to provide only minimal protection to migrant workers.

Nowhere is this clearer than with irregular migrants. Even before reaching destination states, they encounter situations of high vulnerability: as media reports show on an almost daily basis, significant numbers of people lose their lives trying to reach destination countries. At least one migrant dies every day at the Mexico-US border, while non-governmental organizations (NGOs) have counted more than 4,000 deaths at European borders between 1992 and 2003 (Cornelius, 2005; Rekacewicz and Clochard, 2004). Irregular migration is now a structural feature of people flows: it is estimated that there are between 11 million and 12 million irregular migrants in the United States, while most European countries are home to several hundreds of thousands of foreigners in an undocumented situation (Battistella, 2008).

Irregular migrants are prone to accept extremely precarious living and working conditions that favour discrimination and exploitation. They constitute a reserve of very flexible and cheap labour, and their status makes it difficult for them to have minimum work standards respected. While this would call for increased protection, in reality they encounter even more barriers to the realization of their rights. The situation is aggravated by the implicit tolerance of governments: despite their harsh discourses on the fight against unauthorized migration, they have limited funds (and political enthusiasm) for combating the employment of irregular migrants through measures such as workplace control.

Another consequence of irregular migration is to put the asylum system under pressure: refugees are suspected of being disguised economic migrants circumventing migration restrictions, which blurs the distinction between refugees and migrants. In principle, refugees' rights are outlined in the 1951 Convention relating to the Status of Refugees and its 1967 Protocol, whereas migrant workers' rights are dealt with by the 1990 ICRMW (as well as by earlier International Labour Organization (ILO) Conventions Nos. 97 and 143, discussed below); article 3(d) of the Convention thus excludes refugees from its scope (along with stateless persons).[6] In practice, however, the boundary is often difficult to establish. Refugee status is granted on the basis of persecutions, and people fleeing other kinds of situations (such as civil disorders, environmental devastation or economic uncertainty) have no access to protection, even if they actually need it, and fall into the 'migrant' category. On the other hand, refugees sometimes avoid presenting themselves as such as claiming this status can be a long and uncertain process. This eventually threatens the very principles of the asylum system, thereby jeopardizing one of the major humanitarian achievements of the last decades (Joly, 2002).

A final obstacle to migrants' access to rights is that of implementation. In Italy, for example, laws do protect migrants but are often not implemented – especially when it comes to irregular migrants, who are *de facto* deprived of many fundamental rights (see Chapter 14). In a recent study, the NGO Médecins du Monde (2007) found that undocumented migrants' access to health services in Europe, which is in principle guaranteed by national laws, was in practice extremely poor; people do not know about their rights, the administrative procedures are complex and some health professionals refuse to treat irregular migrants, who are also afraid of possible denunciations (see also Da Lomba, 2004). This illustrates the 'disjuncture' between rights and their enjoyment in practice, which is particularly visible in the case of non-nationals (Weissbrodt, 2007).

To sum up, migration is today associated with substantial violations of migrants' physical integrity and dignity. This highlights the inability of current policies to address migration in a way that ensures respect for fundamental human rights. These tragic outcomes of migration take place in a context that sees many destination states heavily preoccupied with the surveillance of their borders and with the prevention of

---

[6] The situation of asylum seekers is more complex as the Geneva Convention grants some rights (including right of access to employment) to recognized refugees only.

unauthorized migration, and much less with the protection of (especially irregular) migrants' rights. It is perhaps too optimistic to believe that the Convention would resolve these problems, but it may at least contribute to shifting policies and practices in a different direction.

International migration law and the history of the ICRMW

The mobility of people across international borders, whether for trade, protection or work-related reasons, is as old as borders themselves, and the vulnerability of non-nationals to various kinds of abuse is thus not a new phenomenon. Migration history shows that, already in the nineteenth century, foreign workers were subject to discriminatory rules on the basis of their health, religion, race or economic usefulness. Indeed, non-nationals have historically enjoyed very little legal protection; the dominant idea has long been that rights were connected to nationality and citizenship, thereby granting aliens with very limited protection (Tiburcio, 2001).

The international community's concern with the rights of migrant workers began in the first part of the twentieth century. As Graziano Battistella (Chapter 2) and Patrick Taran (Chapter 6) recall, the 'protection of the interests of workers when employed in countries other than their own' was mentioned in the original Constitution of the ILO, which was drafted at the time of the creation of the League of Nations in 1919. But the beginnings were difficult: the ILO's attempts to create standards in the recruitment and treatment of foreign workers found little support in the pre-Second World War context, characterized by economic crises and strong nationalist/protectionist tendencies (Haseneau, 1991). In the second half of the twentieth century, the development of human rights brought new forms of protection to aliens: by definition, human rights protect all individuals, regardless of their status, and migrants, whether in a regular or irregular situation, thus enjoy their protection. Human rights also introduced the principle of non-discrimination, which permits only reasonable differences in treatment between nationals and non-nationals (if such measures pursue legitimate state objectives and are applied proportionately to those objectives), while granting migrants many civil and political rights (Fitzpatrick, 2003).

In principle, therefore, migrants enjoy the protection of international human rights law. The most important human rights treaties, which are based on the 1948 Universal Declaration of Human Rights (UDHR) – such as the ICCPR and the ICESCR adopted in 1966 – have been widely ratified and extend protection to all human beings, including migrants. Extension of these rights to vulnerable groups turned out to be difficult, however, which motivated the elaboration of more specific international treaties, including the 1979 CEDAW and the 1989 CRC.

At the ILO, the post-war economic boom in Western industrial states led to a renewed interest in migration and to the adoption of the 1949 ILO Convention No. 97 (Convention concerning Migration for Employment (Revised)). Later, when the oil crisis of the early 1970s caused a general economic downturn, the international community became more concerned with irregular migration and the possible associated abuses, which led to the adoption of ILO Convention No. 143 in 1975 (Convention concerning Migrations in Abusive Conditions and the Promotion of Equality of Opportunity and Treatment of Migrant Workers). Yet the stress of the latter on the need to address undocumented migration was met with scepticism by many countries of origin interested in sending their nationals to work abroad. Destination countries were also critical of this convention, as they believed it discouraged temporary migration. These mixed reactions hindered the acceptance of this treaty and paved the way for the ICRMW.

Shortly after the adoption of ILO Convention No. 143, Mexico and Morocco started a campaign for the elaboration of a UN convention on the protection of the human rights of migrants. Apart from their dissatisfaction with former ILO treaties, these countries were reluctant to leave migration issues to the ILO because of this organization's tripartism, which, for many governments, grants unions too important a role (Böhning, 1991). Moreover, UN conventions are, unlike ILO treaties, subject to reservations, which make it possible to accommodate some states' concerns. At that time, developing countries were hoping to seize the opportunity of the oil crisis to promote a new economic order, and the UN was seen as more open to such a developing world majority than the ILO.

An open-ended working group for the drafting of this new Convention was established in 1979 and chaired by Mexico and Morocco. In an account of its work, Graziano Battistella (Chapter 2) stresses how progress was slowed by the difficulty of finding a consensus between states and by the little support coming from some of them. While the less-developed countries of the G-77[7] were prominent in their support for the

---

[7] The 'Group of 77' (G-77) is a coalition of developing nations that was founded in 1964 and designed to promote its members' collective interests, particularly within the UN. The G-77 now has 130 members.

Convention, a group of European states – the so-called MESCA countries (Finland, Greece, Italy, Norway, Portugal, Spain and Sweden) – played a key role in its drafting, to the extent that the Convention is to some extent a European text. Battistella also underlines how humanitarian concerns over migrants' rights and economic interests in their labour were constantly intertwined, both among countries of origin and destination. About half of the UN Member States participated at one stage or another in this drafting process, and on 18 December 1990 the UN General Assembly adopted the ICRMW by consensus.

Content of the Convention

The ICRMW is an attempt to ensure that a broad range of human rights (civil and political, and economic, social and cultural) are accessible to the migrant worker, defined as 'a person who is to be engaged, is engaged or has been engaged in a remunerated activity in a state of which he or she is not a national' (article 2(1)). While the Convention does establish a few new rights specific to the condition of migrants (such as the right to transfer remittances or to have access to information on the migration process), it mostly offers a more precise interpretation of human rights in the case of migrant workers. Most of the rights listed were formulated in earlier conventions, but their application to non-nationals had generally not been specified.

While this may seem a redundant point, it actually represents a major step forward: as Groenendijk (2004, p. xix) recalls,

> it took lawyers and judges in most European countries several decades to accept that 'everyone' in the European Convention on Human Rights… really means every human being, that non-citizens are covered and protected by most of the provisions of human rights instruments, and that these instruments also apply to immigration law…this may appear self-evident today. It surely was not…in the early seventies.

The ICRMW is comprehensive as it applies to the whole migration continuum, such as the recruitment process and the rights of migrants once they have been admitted.

The ICRMW is composed of nine parts. After the definition of the concepts set out in Part I, Part II provides for a general non-discrimination clause. Part III lists the rights that all migrants should enjoy, irrespective of their status, which therefore also apply to undocumented migrants; Part IV then adds rights that are specific to migrants in a regular situation.

Part V deals with the rights applying to specific categories of migrants, while Part VI details the obligations and responsibilities of states. Finally, Parts VII, VIII and IX deal with the application of the Convention as well as with possible reservations and restrictions by states.[8]

Part III, which concerns both documented and undocumented migrants, contains rights such as:

- the right to life (article 9)
- the right not to be subjected to inhuman or degrading treatment such as torture (article 10)
- the right to freedom of thought, conscience and religion, as well as the right to freedom of opinion and expression (articles 12–13)
- the right not to be deprived of property (article 15)
- the right to equality with nationals before the courts and tribunals, which implies that migrant workers are subject to correct judicial procedures, have access to interpreting services and to the assistance of their consulate, and are not sentenced to disproportionate penalties (articles 16–20, 23–24)
- the right not to have identity documents confiscated (article 21)
- the right not to be subject to collective expulsion and to condition individual expulsions to lawful and correct procedures (article 22)
- the right to equality with nationals with respect to remunerations, working conditions and social security (articles 25, 27)
- the right to take part in trade unions (article 26)
- the right to emergency medical care (article 28)
- the right to education for migrants' children (article 30)
- the right to respect for cultural identity (article 31)
- the right to transfer earnings (article 32)
- the right to have access to information on their rights (article 33).

Part IV adds further rights that are reserved for documented migrants. This includes more substantial rights in terms of access to information (article 37), participation in trade unions (article 40); equality of treatment with nationals (articles 43, 45, 54–55); transfer of remittances (article 47); and expulsion procedures (article 56). In addition, this includes:

[8] This section only provides a short overview of the content of the ICRMW. For more detailed discussions, see the contributions to *International Migration Review*'s special issue on the Convention (1991), as well as Cholewinski (1997), de Varennes (2002) and Hune and Niessen (1991, 1994). The text of the Convention is available in Annex 1.

- the right to be temporarily absent from the state of employment (article 38)
- the right to freedom of movement, residence and employment in the state of employment (articles 39, 51–53)
- the right to participate in public affairs in the state of origin, through voting notably (article 41)
- the right to family reunification (article 44).[9]

Part V lists the rights specific to certain categories of migrants, including frontier workers (article 58), seasonal workers (article 59), itinerant workers (article 60), project-tied workers (article 61), specified-employment workers (article 62) and self-employed workers (article 63). Regarding the obligations of states, Part VI of the Convention promotes 'sound, equitable, humane and lawful conditions' for the international migration of workers and members of their families, which includes, for example, cooperation between states (articles 64, 67–68); the establishment of policies on migration, the exchange of information with other States Parties, the provision of information to employers, workers and their organizations on policies, laws and regulations, and assistance to migrant workers and their families (article 65); and the prevention of irregular migration (articles 68–69). It is worth noting in this respect that, even though most obligations concern the countries in which migrant workers are employed, their countries of origin also have obligations. These include: notably providing information on conditions of admission and remunerated activity; giving the right to emigrate and return; regulating and monitoring recruitment agencies; assisting migrants in the resettlement and reintegration process; and providing overseas voting rights.

Finally, the Convention contains a supervision mechanism to monitor the way States Parties abide by their obligations. According to article 73, States Parties must submit to the UN Secretary-General a report on the measures they have taken to implement the Convention. These reports are examined by the Committee on the Protection of the Rights of All Migrant Workers and Members of Their Families (CMW), which is composed of ten independent experts.[10] Given its historic role in

---

[9] Note that this right, which addresses a politically sensitive issue, is formulated in a very careful and qualified way: 'States Parties shall take measures that *they deem appropriate* and that fall *within their competence* to facilitate the reunification of migrant workers with their [family members]' (article 44(2), emphasis added).

[10] Following the ratification of the forty-first country (Niger, in March 2009), the numbers of members will rise to fourteen on 1 January 2010.

protecting migrant workers' rights, the ILO is formally associated with the work of the CMW 'in a consultative capacity' (article 74(5)). In Chapter 4, Carla Edelenbos, Secretary of the CMW, provides an account of the Committee's work so far, showing how – despite the uneven quality of the reports submitted to date and the recurrent non-reporting problem – it has become an actor in international migration law. In principle, states and individuals that believe a state is not fulfilling its obligations can complain to the CMW (articles 76 and 77 respectively). To date, only Guatemala and Mexico have made the necessary declaration under article 77 to recognize the CMW's competence in receiving and considering cases made by other State Parties, while no declaration has been made under article 76. Moreover, a threshold of ten declarations is needed for these articles to become effective, and this option is therefore not available in practice.

The ratification process

After adoption by the UN General Assembly, the ICRMW was open to ratification by states. According to article 86, the Convention is subject to signature by all states, and then to ratification. In addition, it is open to accession. A signature does not establish a state's consent to be bound by the treaty, but it expresses its willingness to continue the treaty-making process; it enables the signatory state to proceed to ratification and is usually done by the executive branch of government. Ratification is the international act whereby a state indicates its consent to be bound to a treaty and usually requires the acceptance of the legislative or law-making branch of government. Finally, accession is the act whereby a state accepts to become a party to a treaty already negotiated and ratified by other states. It has the same legal effect as ratification and usually occurs after the treaty has entered into force. Twenty ratifications were necessary in order for the ICRMW to enter into force. It took thirteen years to reach this threshold in 2003 and, by June 2009, the Convention had been ratified by forty-one states. In addition, fifteen countries have signed it without ratifying.[11]

This ratification record is low in comparison with other UN conventions. For example, the CEDAW was adopted in 1979 and entered into force less than two years later; today, 186 countries are party to the

---

[11] See Annex 2 for the list of signatures and ratifications to the ICRMW as well as to ILO conventions on migrant workers.

CEDAW. Similarly, the CRC was adopted in 1989, entered into force in 1990 and has been ratified by 193 states. This disinterest in migrants' rights affects other migration-related treaties as well as the ICRMW. The two above-mentioned ILO conventions (Nos. 97 and 143) have been ratified by forty-nine and twenty-three states respectively. Eleven developed, industrialized destination countries have ratified one or both conventions, but none of them did so after 1982, indicating a lack of interest in the last two decades.[12] The same applies to the European Convention on the Legal Status of Migrant Workers (ECMW): only eleven states have ratified it (of the forty-seven Member States of the Council of Europe) and all but three did so more than twenty years ago. Finally, states also display reluctance to enter into more liberal commitments in the field of international trade law, notably under Mode 4 of the General Agreement on Trade in Services (GATS), which deals with 'service provision' by natural persons in another World Trade Organization (WTO) member and hence implies the movement of people (Bhatnagar, 2004).

The lack of interest in the ICRMW was not entirely expected. Immediately after the adoption of the Convention, it was believed within the UN that it would enter into force in 1991 or 1992. Even less optimistic observers expected the above-mentioned MESCA countries to ratify; other countries – Argentina, Canada and Venezuela – were also expected to do so (Hune and Niessen, 1991, p. 139), but only Argentina ratified (and only in 2007). States' reluctance became clearer in the late 1990s: a UN survey conducted in 1997 and 1998 revealed that, out of the thirty-eight states that reported on the situation of migrants' rights in their country, thirty-six indicated that they did not intend to ratify either the ILO or the UN conventions on the matter (Bustamante, 2002). At that time, the ICRMW appeared moribund to many, as only a handful of states had ratified it and the threshold for entry into force seemed hard to reach. Governments in industrialized countries in particular discouragingly argued that the Convention was too detailed and ambitious and that states' lack of interest was questioning its relevance and usefulness.

Around that time, however, increased activism around migrants' rights could also be observed. Within the UN, the Commission on Human Rights (CMR) appointed a Working Group of Intergovernmental Experts on the

---

[12] The eleven destination countries that have ratified one or both ILO conventions are Belgium (97), France (97), Germany (97), Italy (97 and 143), the Netherlands (97), New Zealand (97), Norway (97 and 143), Portugal (97 and 143), Spain (97), Sweden (143) and the United Kingdom (97). A number of these countries (Italy, Portugal and Spain notably) had not yet become immigration countries at the time they ratified.

Human Rights of Migrants in 1997 (Bustamante, 2002). It recommended, among other things, a specialized mechanism to follow up the protection of migrants' rights, which led to the appointment of a Special Rapporteur on the Human Rights of Migrants in 1999 (Rodriguez, 2000).[13] In 2000, 18 December – adoption date of the ICRMW – became International Migrants Day. The Global Campaign for Ratification of the Convention on Rights of Migrants was launched in 1998, bringing together international organizations and NGOs to foster ratifications.[14] As Mariette Grange and Marie d'Auchamp argue (Chapter 3), these efforts were crucial in pushing the Convention over the twenty-state threshold so that it could enter into force in July 2003.

So far, nearly all States Parties to the ICRMW are on the sending side of the migration process (with the possible exceptions of Argentina and the Libyan Arab Jamahiriya). Concerned by the situation of their citizens abroad, they view the Convention as part of a strategy to protect their emigrants. For example, major countries of origin, such as Mexico, Morocco and the Philippines, have ratified. By contrast, no major destination country has ratified, which strongly diminishes the impact of the Convention. Its States Parties are home to only a very small percentage of the world's total migrant population, which means that most migrants are currently not protected by the ICRMW. Regardless of the role played by European states in its elaboration, the predominance of less-developed countries among States Parties has led the Convention to be perceived as a 'G-77 treaty' (LaViolette, 2006).

It is worth noting, however, that such neat divides between countries of origin and destination are losing their relevance. Some countries of origin that are parties to the Convention have indeed become transit and destination countries: Morocco, for example, serves as a transit country for migratory flows from West Africa to Europe, a situation that has led to the more or less permanent establishment of undocumented migrants in that country; Mexico is in a relatively similar situation, as migrants from Central America on their way to North America sometimes settle down in that country. Having ratified the ICRMW, these states are, in principle, compelled to follow its recommendations in their treatment of migrants living on their soil.

---

[13] Jorge Bustamante (from Mexico) currently holds the position. From 1999 to 2005, the position was occupied by Gabriela Rodríguez Pizarro (from Costa Rica).

[14] For the activities of this global campaign, see the website (www.migrantsrights.org [last accessed 9 April 2009]).

This is not a straightforward process. Gabriela Díaz and Gretchen Kuhner (Chapter 9) document how Mexico, which was a leading promoter of the Convention and remains a very active state in this field at the international level, used to see the ICRMW as a tool to protect the rights of its citizens living in the United States; the existence of an international standard, even if non-ratified by the United States, could indeed strengthen Mexico's position in relation to its northern neighbour. In the meantime, however, the increasing transit migration from Central and Latin America through Mexico has raised challenges in terms of implementing the Convention, especially as tight control policies (partly designed to ensure cooperation with the United States) have led to increased detention and deportation of irregular migrants – a potential challenge for the respect of their rights. However, Díaz and Kuhner argue that, despite these difficulties, the experience of Mexico shows that countries that are simultaneously countries of origin and transit can ratify the Convention.

As Vucetic (2007, p. 404) notes, 'the non-signature [of the ICRMW] among OECD democracies appears puzzling, bearing in mind that human rights are usually associated with liberal democratic governance and that many liberal democracies vigorously promote human rights internationally'. Little research has been dedicated to the reasons behind states' reluctance to ratify the Convention. A difficulty is that only few states have actually provided reasons for their non-ratification; most have been largely indifferent, and this absence of official reaction makes it difficult to identify the obstacles. Some research has been done on the obstacles to ratification of ILO conventions (for details, see Taran, 2000b). On the basis of the contributions to this volume and of other United Nations Educational, Scientific and Cultural Organization (UNESCO) sponsored research, the following sections outline some of the major difficulties faced by the ICRMW.

Low awareness and misperceptions

A long-standing obstacle to ratification is the low awareness of the ICRMW. As Mariette Grange and Marie d'Auchamp recall in Chapter 3, the Convention was once called the 'best kept secret of the United Nations' by Graziano Battistella. In Germany, Felicitas Hillmann and Amanda Klekowski von Koppenfels report that knowledge of the Convention is low, even among civil society and migration-related actors and institutions (Chapter 13). A similar situation is described in South Africa by Jonathan

Crush, Vincent Williams and Peggy Nicholson (Chapter 10). In Italy, Kristina Touzenis adds that the high uncertainty surrounding ratification by the government discourages interest in the Convention, even among academics concerned with migration, for example (Chapter 14). The UN system itself has not always done all it could to promote the Convention: Taran (2000*a*, p. 18) writes that, until 1996, it was difficult to have access to the text of the ICRMW, and that no single person anywhere in the world was working on it full time; and a key publication such as the 2007–08 *Human Development Report* of the United Nations Development Programme (UNDP) does not mention the Convention in its tables on the status of major human rights instruments (UNDP, 2007, pp. 347–54).

A major consequence of this low visibility is the existence of misunderstandings surrounding the Convention. In Asia, for example, Nicola Piper writes that, if governments at least know of its existence, they are far from fully understanding its implications (Chapter 7). In particular, it is often believed that ratification implies a loss of national sovereignty on admission policies, and that ratification would oblige states to grant large family reunification possibilities for migrants. The first belief is clearly refuted by article 79, which states: 'Nothing in the present Convention shall affect the right of each State Party to establish the criteria governing admission of migrant workers and members of their families';[15] regarding the second, as mentioned above, the Convention recommends family reunification, but in a soft and qualified way that gives States Parties substantial discretionary power. Such misperceptions have harmed the acceptance of the Convention.

While these observations remain valid, there are indications that the situation is changing. In the United Kingdom and France, for example, there have been substantial efforts to promote the Convention, with the result that unions, civil society movements and some politicians are now decently informed about the Convention (Chapters 11 and 12). Similarly, in Canada, while average knowledge of the Convention is weak among parliamentarians, a few political parties have expressed their support for it, even if – being in opposition – they have little influence on the government (Chapter 8). More paradoxical is the situation in Spain, where members of the Socialist Party called for ratification just a few months before coming to power in 2004, but did not follow up once in

---

[15] The relegation of this statement to article 79 is sometimes interpreted as an indication that respect for national sovereignty was not the priority of the drafters of the ICRMW (Vucetic, 2007).

the majority (MacDonald and Cholewinski, 2007, p. 46). MacDonald and Cholewinski thus importantly find that the greater the civil-society engagement in favour of the Convention, the larger the awareness and the more important the political activities surrounding it.

Lack of capacity and resources

Reflecting the cross-cutting nature of migration policy, the Convention is a complex treaty dealing with very different sectors of states' responsibilities: access to health services, labour regulations, the education system, legal procedures, etc. For governments, ratification therefore implies coordinated efforts to implement the standards of the Convention in these different fields of policy. Cholewinski (1997, p. 201) had already noted that 'technical questions alone…may prevent many states from speedily accepting [the ICRMW's] provisions'. Earlier research showed that this is particularly problematic in non-Western states: some countries have little experience in migration policy; they lack trained policy makers to adapt and conform the Convention to existing legal standards, evaluate the possible impact of ratification and prepare the ground for political decisions; and some governments have no coherent political strategy for migration, a situation worsened by the conflicts and competition that sometimes characterize the relationships between concerned ministries. Political orientations thus change frequently, whereas ratification of the ICRMW requires a long-term political commitment (Pécoud and de Guchteneire, 2006, pp. 255–6).

Some of these obstacles may be found in the countries investigated in this volume. In Europe, MacDonald and Cholewinski report that neither Poland nor Norway have historically had much experience with the regulation of immigration, and thus lack the institutional framework and infrastructure that the Convention presupposes; the administration of these countries would find it difficult to manage the incorporation of the provisions of the Convention in their administrative practices (Chapter 15). Even in an important destination country such as Germany, political debates on a comprehensive migration policy are relatively new, as immigration was, until recently, thought of as temporary (Chapter 13). In France, by contrast, administrative experience with migration is well developed and cannot be considered as a major obstacle (Chapter 12).

In South Africa, it is reported that the government approaches migration either as a matter of control or as a brain-drain concern, thus having little expertise and interest in its human rights dimension. The government fears that it would be unable to put in practice the provisions of the Convention: it already experiences difficulties in implementing the current labour legislation because of lack of resources and, as it would be responsible for implementation in the event of ratification, it wants to avoid a situation in which its shortcomings would be publicly highlighted (Chapter 10). In other words, even in the absence of content-related objections to the Convention, its ambitious nature may inspire reluctance.

Finally, financial resources are sometimes mentioned as a problem. Nicola Piper writes that sending states in Asia would find it difficult to finance the costly measures stemming from their obligations under the Convention (Chapter 7). Hélène Oger also reports that, in France, the Ministry of Finance seems reluctant towards the Convention because it calls for facilitating the transfer of remittances from migrants to their home countries, which would reduce the fees charged by banks and contribute to the removal of significant sums of money from the country (Chapter 12). This financial argument is also mentioned in many developing countries, especially when the Convention requires governments to treat migrants in a way that is not even affordable for nationals (Pécoud and de Guchteneire, 2006, pp. 256–7). The weight of these administrative and financial obstacles should be qualified, however: many other international conventions have indeed been widely ratified despite the absence of adequate resources for implementation. If there is a political willingness to ratify, such obstacles are scarcely taken into account, albeit to the detriment of the Convention's impact.

Legal and political obstacles

Legal obstacles refer to situations in which national laws would not be compatible with the Convention's provisions and would therefore need to be changed in the event of ratification. In some cases, legal obstacles are numerous and obvious. Nicola Piper shows, for example, that, in several destination countries in Asia, the rights afforded to migrants are far from matching the Convention's standards. Ratification would thus imply major changes in these countries, which makes it unlikely (Chapter 7). By contrast, in Western countries with a developed human rights tradition, the gap between national laws and the Convention appears relatively minor. This conclusion was, for example, reached by a study done in Belgium, which explored in detail the compatibility of national law with the Convention and found that 'Belgian national law is (in practice) highly compatible with the provisions of the Convention' (Vanheule et al., 2004, p. 320).

The case studies in this volume provide some additional evidence. In France, article 31 of the Convention (which refers to the 'cultural identity' of migrants) is at odds with the French tradition of the indivisibility of the nation (Chapter 12). In the United Kingdom, Bernard Ryan outlines several legal obstacles, pertaining to the legality of irregular migrants' contracts, to the freedom of employment for recently arrived migrants, to the right to remain after employment and to migrants' access to social benefits or family reunification (Chapter 11). In Canada, Victor Piché, Eugénie Depatie-Pelletier and Dina Epale write that the main problem lies in the temporary migration schemes, whose principles are incompatible with the Convention (Chapter 8); indeed, Canada welcomes relatively large numbers of temporary foreign workers, among whom many are low-skilled (notably in seasonal agricultural work and care-giving programmes) and enjoy fewer rights: they are tied to a specific employer, have no possibility for family reunification, are limited in their right to unionize, etc.

It is worth noting here that the compatibility of national laws with the Convention is potentially facilitated by its relative flexibility. Indeed, as the above-quoted article 44(2) on the sensitive issue of family reunification illustrates, the treaty qualifies and softens states' obligations, either by using expressions such as 'states may…', if states 'consider necessary' or if states 'deem appropriate', or by referring to national legislation ('in accordance with national laws'). This leaves margins of discretion to states and reduces the possible contradictions between their laws and practices and the Convention. In addition, States Parties can make reservations, i.e. exclude one or more articles (but not a whole part or an entire category of migrants) that they find incompatible with their laws (article 91). It is therefore difficult to grant too much importance to legal obstacles in developed countries; while they do exist, some of them stem from too strict an interpretation of the Convention, while others could quite easily be addressed by minor reservations.

In a somewhat paradoxical way, the compatibility of the Convention with national laws is put forward by some governments to justify *non*-ratification: given that migrants' rights are already protected by existing laws, the Convention would not improve their situation and would thus be superfluous. This was, for example, explicitly stated in Canada and Germany (Chapters 8 and 13). More specifically, an often-heard argument against the Convention is that migrants are already protected by other international and regional human rights conventions (especially the ICESCR, the ICCPR and the European Convention on Human Rights (ECMR)), which in principle apply to both nationals and non-nationals. Isabelle Slinckx (Chapter 5) critically analyzes this argument and finds that the protection of undocumented migrants is better ensured by the ICRMW than by other treaties; she adds that the Convention enables more careful understanding of migrants' rights and hence their more successful implementation, which is also due to the unique work done by the CMW in interpreting and monitoring the Convention. The different conventions are thus more complementary than redundant.

The relative compatibility of national laws with the Convention would in theory make ratification unproblematic, at least in several developed states. But a wide range of non-legal obstacles make the situation far more complex. These are usually referred to as 'political', 'cultural' or even 'philosophical' obstacles. Broadly speaking, they designate the spirit that guides migration policies in many countries and that diverges substantially from the rights-based approach of the Convention. As MacDonald and Cholewinski argue, these are very real obstacles: regardless of the misunderstandings surrounding the Convention's exact legal implications and of its potential compatibility with current laws in developed industrialized countries, the fact that the philosophy of the Convention is not the one that is prevalent among governments generates an almost structural scepticism towards it that will require important persuasion efforts to be overcome (Chapter 15).

At an immediate level, Kristina Touzenis (Chapter 14) argues, for example, that, if current Italian laws match the Convention's standards, the question of future legal evolution remains open; given the rapid developments in this field (with several new laws having been passed in a few years), one cannot exclude that changes will be introduced that do not respect the Convention. The government may then resist ratifying in order to maintain its freedom. Similarly, Hélène Oger writes that the French Government is concerned with making family reunification more difficult, whereas the Convention rather favours it; it might be that, from a strictly legal perspective, French laws and the Convention are compatible, but the clash between the intentions of the government and those of the Convention cannot be denied (Chapter 12). The following sections examine in greater detail the various ways in which the political priorities of many governments differ from the philosophy of the Convention.

Evolving migration dynamics and divergent political debates

The ICRMW was proposed in the 1970s, drafted in the 1980s and opened to ratification in the 1990s. Migration trends underwent major changes during this period, and so, accordingly, did migration policies. In Europe, for example, the 1970s was a period of transition: the oil crisis put an end to the recruitment of migrant workers, which progressively led to new concerns regarding family reunification and the integration of the second generation. Unemployment concurrently emerged as a major issue, making labour migration no longer a priority (Hune and Niessen, 1994). This ongoing emergence of new dynamics, new debates and new policy concerns represents a challenge for the Convention, which is always at risk of being perceived as outdated and has to establish its relevance in very different contexts.

In Germany, two major issues have been dominating migration debates since the 1990s. The first is the fate of migrants' descendants who, while born and raised in Germany, are perceived as non-integrated in German society. The Convention has little to say on integration matters and is therefore not perceived as an answer to such pressing questions (for a discussion, see Kälin, 2003). The second is the asylum issue, following the wars in the Balkans and consequent increases in the number of asylum seekers. Even though refugees are, as mentioned, outside the scope of the Convention, this issue diverts attention from others such as labour migration or migrants' rights and contributes to the marginalization of the Convention (Chapter 13). Another issue that has emerged is skilled migration. Attracting qualified migrants is now an objective in most developed, industrialized countries, which are thus incited to grant rights to this category of migrants, making human rights abuses less of a concern for them. On the other side of the migration process, South Africa, for example, is reported to be much concerned with the impact of 'brain drain', a matter for which the Convention does not offer clear remedies (Chapter 10).

In a different way, some governments do not adhere to the very matter dealt with by the Convention, i.e. 'migrant workers'. In traditional countries of immigration (Australia, Canada, New Zealand, the United States), the official view is that migrants are not 'migrant workers' but 'settlers' who are, in principle, to become permanent residents and eventually citizens. Victor Piché, Eugénie Depatie-Pelletier and Dina Epale thus highlight the dominant and traditional representation of Canada as welcoming permanent migrants – a migration 'philosophy' that would diverge from the Convention's approach. The government accordingly claims that the very concept of temporary migration for the purpose of work would not apply, making the Convention irrelevant. Yet this largely ignores the reality, as all these countries have experienced temporary work programmes as well. In Canada, the same authors show, for example, that temporary low-skilled migration, while much less known and publicized, is far from negligible and that, as mentioned, the migrants concerned by these temporary schemes are far from enjoying the rights afforded to settlers (Chapter 8).

The Convention also assumes that governments play a key role in the migration process, either by organizing it by themselves (as European states did between the 1950s and the early 1970s) or by carefully regulating the framework within which it takes place. Yet this ignores the growing 'privatization' of the migration process, which sees migrants relying either on various types of brokers and intermediaries or on their own social or family networks to reach destination states. In such cases, states do more to control and restrict migration than to actually organize it. In Asia, for example, Nicola Piper underlines that migration is governed through private actors that largely elude states' attempts to regulate their activities – particularly because of the collusion that often exists between employers, government officials and recruiters (Chapter 7). As Castles (2006) observes, the withdrawal of states from the proactive organization of migration (at least in the low-skilled segment) fits into a general neoliberal context that sees them playing a decreasing role in labour market regulation.

This echoes some claims according to which the ICRMW would be a 'pre-globalization' treaty that would not fully take into account the changes in the world economy that took place in the last decades, including the industrial decline in advanced economies, the growing importance of services, the deregulation of some economic sectors, the withdrawal of the state from large segments of economic activity and the growth of small firms and self-employment. This economic context challenges the successful implementation of labour regulations in general and favours irregularities and abuse, especially when it comes to the low-skilled economic sectors in which many migrants are active.

These observations highlight how the approach of the Convention, along with its rights-based focus, does not fit well into some of the dominant migration-related trends and debates. This would make it difficult to 'sell' the Convention to governments searching for solutions to the challenges now raised by migration. Yet it should not be forgotten that protecting the human rights of migrants has rarely been the primary objective of states' migration policies. Moreover, human and labour rights abuses abound today, irrespective of the new conditions in which migration takes place (see Shelley, 2007, for recent empirical evidence). And as Graziano Battistella (Chapter 2) recalls, the process that led to the Convention was partly initiated after the deaths of twenty-eight irregular migrants from Mali, found in a lorry in the Mont Blanc tunnel in 1972. Today, such deaths occur throughout the world on an almost daily basis. In this sense, the Convention is as relevant as it used to be, and perhaps even more so given the decreasing power of states to impose the conditions in which migrants live and work.

Irregular migration and human trafficking

Among the factors that most strongly influence current migration debates and contribute to marginalizing the ICRMW's rights-based approach, special mention should be made of two: irregular migration and human trafficking. As described above, the Convention explicitly grants rights to irregular or undocumented migrants, a category often ignored by previous treaties. This is one of its most challenging and controversial characteristics (Bosniak, 2004), which has been interpreted by the Convention's detractors as 'encouraging' undocumented migration: migrants would be incited to move without authorization to countries in which they know they will enjoy rights no matter what their status.

Vucetic (2007) argues that the ICRMW's emphasis on undocumented migrants' rights reflects the predominance of G-77 sending countries in the drafting process, which lead destination states to resist ratification. This is indeed a delicate issue; the Convention does not encourage irregular migration, nor does it recommend their regularization;[16] but it does nevertheless call for states to address irregular migration, by preventing it[17] and by putting an end to the existence of irregular migrants.[18] This may be

---

[16] Article 35 states: 'Nothing in the present part of the Convention shall be interpreted as implying the regularization of the situation of migrant workers or members of their families who are non-documented or in an irregular situation or any right to such regularization of their situation.'

[17] Article 68: 'States Parties, including states of transit, shall collaborate with a view to preventing and eliminating illegal or clandestine movements and employment of migrant workers in an irregular situation.'

[18] Article 69: 'States Parties shall, when there are migrant workers and members of their families within their territory in an irregular situation, take appropriate measures to ensure that such a situation does not persist.'

interpreted as an obligation to either expel or regularize undocumented migrants. It is worth adding that the Convention does not allow for reservations that would exclude undocumented migrants (article 88).

This is a major obstacle to the Convention. The report of the Global Commission on International Migration (GCIM) noted that 'a number of countries have stated that they are unwilling to ratify the 1990 Convention because it provides migrants (especially those who have moved in an irregular manner) with rights that are not to be found in other treaties, and because it generally disallows differentiation between migrants who have moved in a regular or irregular manner' (GCIM, 2005, p. 57). Most chapters converge on this point and stress how governments give priority to combating irregular migration; undocumented migrants are predominantly treated as criminals rather than as vulnerable people deserving protection. The very notion of 'illegals', commonly used to designate them, implies *ipso facto* a status of criminality – which is why this notion is discouraged by a 1975 resolution of the UN General Assembly (see Chapter 2) and is absent from the documents of many international and regional organizations (for example ILO, International Organization for Migration (IOM), UNESCO, Council of Europe).[19]

The disagreement over irregular migrants' access to rights is, for example, indicated by Van Krieken (2007): he contests the protection afforded to them, which – he argues – penalizes regular migrants, as the added value of residing and working lawfully in a state would be diminished by the fact that those who are undeclared are also entitled to rights. He adds that, if states are serious and successful in their efforts to prevent irregular migration and to properly integrate regular migrants, they should not become home to undocumented migrants and hence would not need to commit themselves to afford them rights. Indeed, the Convention might appear slightly contradictory, as it calls for preventing irregular migration while at the same time emphasizing the need to protect the rights of irregular migrants. The problem, of course, is that we do not live in an ideal world; a situation in which the issue of the rights of undocumented migrants would not arise because of their non-existence is desirable but unrealistic. Even if states were genuinely doing all they could to manage migration so as to avoid clandestine migration, the presence of irregular migrants would probably persist – and so would the question of their rights.

---

[19] It is worth noting, however, that EU documents still make regular use of terms such as 'illegal immigration' or 'illegal migrants'.

A second concern is the prevention of human trafficking, which has become a priority for the international community. The 1990s have witnessed increasing fears surrounding new forms of migration characterized by coercion, exploitation and the involvement of migration professionals often linked to organized crime. The migratory trajectories of women, in particular, recruited in countries of origin by mafia-type criminal organizations and forced into activities such as prostitution, have been described as modern slavery, raising considerable public emotion and political reactions. Smuggling refers to the act of having a migrant enter a state without authorization, while trafficking concerns not only the displacement (whether across borders or within a country) but also the exploitation of trafficked persons once in the destination country or in the new place of residence. In principle, trafficked or smuggled migrants are understood as victims rather than law-breakers and should therefore benefit from protection. Yet these notions are often difficult to apply in practice, as the distinction between 'smuggled', 'trafficked' or 'irregular' migrants may be tenuous.

The consensus on the need to fight smuggling and trafficking is illustrated by the adoption of the so-called Palermo Protocols to the United Nations Convention against Transnational Organized Crime, adopted in 2000: Protocol against the Smuggling of Migrants by Land, Sea and Air and Protocol to Prevent, Suppress and Punish Trafficking in Persons, Especially Women and Children. Human trafficking has contributed to shedding light on the human rights abuses potentially connected to migration; as a matter of fact, trafficking is often apprehended together with migrants' rights (as was the case at the 2006 High-Level Dialogue on International Migration and Development, which is discussed below). While one cannot negate the human rights violations generated by trafficking, this may nevertheless contribute to a narrow understanding of migrants' rights, to the detriment of the larger issue of the rights of all those migrants who have not been trafficked or smuggled.

Patrick Taran thus regrets that the Palermo Protocols have attracted much of the attention that could have gone to the ICRMW (Chapter 6). Indeed, these have proved much more successful than the Convention, having been ratified by 119 and 131 states respectively. Strictly speaking, however, these are not human rights instruments: while they do provide some protection to migrants, they are embedded in the context of the fight against criminality; they are, indeed, part of the United Nations Convention against Transnational Organized Crime and are monitored not by the Office of the United Nations High Commissioner for Human Rights but by the United Nations Office on Drugs and Crime (UNODC) (see Gallagher, 2001).

The international context

While ratification is a domestic political process, it is strongly dependent on the international context. The low rate of ratification creates an environment in which no government wants to isolate itself by being among the few to ratify. This is particularly the case given the non-ratification of leading developed, industrialized states, which are traditionally prominent human rights advocates. Nicola Piper writes that Asian states do not usually take leadership in terms of ratifying international conventions, and instead wait for Europe to take the lead (Chapter 7). Earlier research similarly showed that European states' negative attitude towards the Convention discouraged the neighbouring countries within its spheres of influence to ratify (in North Africa and central and eastern Europe notably), as their migration policies are strongly influenced by their cooperation with Europe (Pécoud and de Guchteneire, 2006, pp. 258–9). In this respect, it is difficult to overstate the responsibility of developed nations in the current ratification record of the Convention.

Another feature of the international setting is the different kinds of rivalry that exist between states. Destination countries compete on how best to prevent irregular migration through the toughest measures, a climate that is clearly unsupportive of the Convention. Among countries of origin, Nicola Piper reports how Asian states compete with each other to send their workers abroad (to the Gulf States in particular) and fear that ratification would signal an unwelcome rights-consciousness that would jeopardize their success among destination states (Chapter 7). Indeed, the labour migration business is largely demand-driven, and destination countries have more power to dictate the terms of migration. Even a Convention-champion such as Mexico, while quickly signing the Convention, waited until 1999 for ratification, a delay that – according to Gabriela Díaz and Gretchen Kuhner (Chapter 9) – was motivated by the North American Free Trade Agreement negotiations that took place in the 1990s and which deliberately avoided the sensitive migration issue.

In this context, the negative attitude of one often becomes the attitude of all, and there is no incentive and little pressure for states to 'break rank' and ratify. This points to the importance of regional approaches. In Chapter 10, on South Africa, Jonathan Crush, Vincent Williams and Peggy Nicholson argue that ratification should be envisaged at the level of the Southern African Development Community; this would enable cooperation and collaboration, rather than rivalry, and would facilitate implementation, which is more difficult at a single country level. Another regional entity that could play a key role is the European Union (EU). Chapters on European countries emphasize that EU initiatives could substantially increase the acceptance of the Convention, while MacDonald and Cholewinski show how the EU is a key battleground for the Convention (Chapter 15). In France, Hélène Oger reports that the government has used the European argument to justify non-ratification, by stating that – migration being one of the fields in which the EU is competent – Member States cannot ratify in isolation (Chapter 12). But the validity of this argument is questionable: the EU is not a UN Member State and has no authority to ratify a Convention; moreover, individual Member States remain authorized to take measures that go beyond EU minimum standards.

While a coordinated EU approach on the Convention would be highly desirable, Chapter 15 describes how the EU attitude towards the Convention (and to migrants' rights in general) is ambivalent. There have been positive signs: in 2003, the European Parliament supported its ratification,[20] while the European Economic and Social Committee adopted a favourable opinion in June 2004.[21] But these recommendations were not followed, and the Convention is largely ignored in EU policy. The reason for this is that, while there have been superficial engagements in favour of a rights-based approach to migration and of the equal-treatment principle between EU and third-country nationals, human rights are not at the centre of the EU's common migration approach, which is driven by economic concerns as well as by a tendency to criminalize undocumented migrants. Much therefore remains to be done to put the Convention on the European agenda.

---

[20] European Community, Resolution on the EU's rights, priorities and recommendations for the 59th Session of the UN Commission on Human Rights in Geneva (17 March to 25 April 2003), [2003] document No. P5_TA 0034, Sitting of Thursday, 30 January 2003 (*Official Journal of the European Union*, C39/E 70, 2004), at point L5.

[21] European Economic and Social Committee (EESC), SOC/173, Opinion No. 960 of 30 June 2004.

Cultural representations of migration

Ratification of the Convention is frequently complicated by a cultural climate that is unfavourable to migration. Most chapters refer in one way or another to the racist attitudes or discriminatory behaviours that can be found in the relations between nationals and migrants, and report that a large proportion of the citizens of destination countries have a negative perception of migrants. The feeling is that they have too many rights already – obviously not a conducive climate in which to argue for or make commitments to rights for migrants, let alone rights for undocumented migrants. As a result, particularly where the migration issue is a rallying-point for political populism, governments feel that extending further rights and protections to migrants is a political risk.

This rejection of migrants takes place within a larger reluctance to see migrants as a full part of destination societies, and accordingly as deserving of rights. Nicola Piper writes, for example, that several Asian nations, such as Japan or the Republic of Korea, stick to a definition of themselves as homogeneous countries, thereby leaving no space for migrants in the dominant representation of society and ignoring the *de facto* reality of their presence. Others, such as Malaysia or Singapore, are keen on maintaining migrants at the margin of society, by limiting the duration of their stay and their integration opportunities (Chapter 7). On the contrary, ratification implies acknowledging that migrants, even if temporary, are a permanent feature of societies that calls for specific policies.

This representation of migrants as outsiders can also be found in South Africa (Chapter 10), where many stakeholders believe that preference should be given to nationals and permanent residents. Ratification might then give the impression that migrant workers are 'privileged', which – in a context characterized by high levels of xenophobia – is politically (and electorally) difficult. Nicola Piper also writes that, in several Asian countries, migrants' access to rights is not supported because they are not understood as needing protection; rather, migrants are perceived as the lucky ones who have managed to leave their country and enjoy better income opportunities abroad – migrants' status is not perceived as a source of possible exploitation, but as an opportunity (Chapter 7). This was also reported in central and eastern Europe (Pécoud and de Guchteneire, 2006, p. 260).

Underlying this divide between nationals and foreigners is the idea that migrants would be 'less deserving' in terms of access to rights and that only citizens deserve the full protection of human rights (de Varennes, 2002); the human rights standards and expectations that apply to citizens are then put aside when the situation of foreigners is considered. Kristina Touzenis thus refers to what she calls a 'culture of citizenship', i.e. the tacit recognition of migrants' poor living and working conditions as 'normal' (Chapter 14). As Mariette Grange and Marie d'Auchamp (Chapter 3) argue, this would explain the double standards that see Western democracies pride themselves on their human rights record but make an exception when it comes to migrants. Graziano Battistella also argues that the lack of success of the Convention (compared with other core human rights instruments) is not a coincidence but an illustration of the difficulties of addressing the human rights of non-nationals (Chapter 2).

Despite the efforts of international law, migrant workers are thus not recognized as a vulnerable group that should benefit from targeted human rights treaties. This points to an almost ontological characteristic of migrants: while other vulnerable groups (such as women or children) are understood to need protection simply by being, migrants only become troublesome by virtue of being *here*, i.e. in the destination country. It is thus assumed that migration is voluntary and that, if migrants are unhappy with the conditions in the destination country, they can (and should) go back home. In other words, people accepted into another country should be grateful for this privilege and should not claim further rights. Such beliefs not only misunderstand the complexity of the migration process but also negate the very philosophy of human rights (MacDonald and Cholewinski, 2007, p. 64).

The role of civil society and the ICRMW's catalyst function

Most chapters converge on the key role played by civil society and NGOs in promoting ratification of the ICRMW. Yet, as Mariette Grange and Marie d'Auchamp recall in Chapter 3, NGOs were unevenly engaged in the issue of migrants' rights when the Convention was proposed and drafted: in the Cold War atmosphere of the 1970s, their focus was on civil and political rights, and much less on 'soft' economic, social or cultural rights; only a few (mostly faith-based) NGOs accompanied the elaboration of the Convention. Today, it is sometimes reported that NGOs find it difficult to work with the Convention: in Canada, the emergence of civil society campaigning for the Convention has been slowed down by the priority given to on-the-ground support to migrants, as the ICRMW seems too abstract and remote from the most urgent concerns of NGOs

(Chapter 8); in Germany, NGOs are reported to reluctantly use their scarce resources for the Convention, which is perceived as a difficult issue for which investment is uncertain (Chapter 13).

Despite this relatively modest initial engagement and these obstacles, the role of NGOs has been central in promoting the Convention and raising awareness, especially in a context of low support from other stakeholders. Grange and d'Auchamp describe the work done by NGOs, including their international networking within the International NGO Platform on the Migrant Workers' Convention (IPMWC) and their involvement in the International Steering Committee for the Campaign for Ratification of the Migrants Rights Convention, a hybrid structure comprising intergovernmental organizations (IGOs) and NGOs. They add that civil society now has a key role to play in implementing the Convention, for example by getting involved in the examination of States Parties' reports by the CMW (Chapter 3).

The role of NGOs illustrates the catalyst function that can be played by the Convention. Even if non-ratified or incompletely implemented, its very existence may have potentially useful consequences. Bernard Ryan writes that, in the United Kingdom, there is some support for the Convention from civil society, unions and some political parties, and that it has become an authoritative benchmark to evaluate and challenge current migration policies. Ratification by the UK Government is unlikely, but this does not prevent the Convention from spurring debates and indirectly promoting migrants' rights (Chapter 11). Felicitas Hillmann and Amanda Klekowski von Koppenfels are less optimistic but nevertheless note that, in Germany, some of those involved in migration debates see the Convention as useful in that it could highlight some issues; for example, the whole question of undocumented migrants' work is largely taboo in Germany, a situation that a debate on the Convention could help to address in a more satisfactory manner (Chapter 13).

Nicola Piper also underlines the opportunities raised by the Convention, showing how, in the Philippines, ratification has been an element in a wider dynamic in favour of migrants' rights, characterized by strong civil society activism, transnational networks and grass-roots empowerment of migrants (Chapter 7). In a different way, Carla Edelenbos underlines how the CMW has become a promoter of migrants' rights at the international level, through cooperation with other UN agencies, NGOs and other members of civil society (Chapter 4). In other words, thanks (at least partly) to the Convention, the issue of migrants' rights is addressed – among NGOs and IGOs and at the national or international levels. The Convention, regardless of its ratification rate, is an enabling tool that makes it possible for a wide range of actors to discuss the issue of migrants' rights, cooperate with each other and develop coherent strategies for advocacy (see also Leary, 2003, p. 238).

Market forces, sovereignty and security

The obstacles outlined in this introduction refer to three broad themes – market forces, sovereignty and security – that are deeply intertwined and which dominate current migration policies, creating an unfavourable context for the respect of migrants' rights and for ratification of the Convention.

The importance of market forces is difficult to overstate and evident, for example, in the perceived economic usefulness of undocumented migrants without rights or in the competition between states in the global 'labour export' market. Market forces directly challenge the Convention's rights-based logic: they lead to a vertical hierarchization of migrants according to their rarity and economic value, whereas the Convention privileges a horizontal distribution of minimal rights to all migrants, whatever their status and profitability. The contrast between skilled and less-skilled migration illustrates this: highly qualified workers are not numerous and are therefore looked for by destination countries, which compete with one another to attract the brightest; this situation inevitably favours highly skilled migrants, who will be offered attractive living and working conditions (including not only wages but also rights, such as long-term residence permits, access to family reunification, extensive welfare entitlements, etc.).

In contrast, the number of less-skilled workers is virtually unlimited, and destination countries will not need to provide good conditions to attract them: even if offered very limited economic and legal guarantees, migrants are likely to compete to accept extremely poor conditions (such as irregular stay and work). This is reinforced by the context in sending regions, which prompts migrants to accept whatever conditions, as these are likely to already constitute an improvement compared with their home situation. Market forces favour migrants endowed with bargaining power (such as skilled professionals) who can impose respect for their rights on the states they are heading for, whereas less-skilled migrants are unlikely to successfully claim any right. In this logic, rights do not derive from universal norms like the Convention, but rather from the supply-and-demand mechanism that determines migrants' value on the labour market. The current situation in Canada is an example: whereas this country is known for its admission of selected foreigners who are granted permanent settlement, this system coexists with various less-skilled temporary migration schemes involving non-negligible numbers of people, for whom rights are much more limited. As mentioned, this is one of the reasons behind Canada's reluctance to ratify (Chapter 8).[22]

Finally, rights also challenge market forces because of their costs. For employers, migrants' rights make them more expensive to hire: the right to equal treatment with national workers, for example, prevents them from paying lower wages to foreign workers; migrants' other labour rights, such as joining unions or being allowed to change employers, similarly improve their bargaining power with respect to employers. For destination countries too, rights represent costs: migrants' access to welfare or to family reunification make their stay in host countries more expensive for public finances. This is one of the reasons behind irregular migration: undocumented migrants represent the cheapest possible labour force, and governments, unwilling to accept them legally, tolerate them for labour market reasons. A rights-based logic runs directly against such powerful economic interests.

Sovereignty also pervades the obstacles listed above. Following the Universal Declaration of Human Rights (whose article 13(2) states that 'Everyone has the right to leave any country, including his own, and to return to his country'), there is a human right to leave a country but no corresponding right to enter another country. The admission of non-nationals remains a central feature of national sovereignty, and states are keen on maintaining their authority in deciding whom to let in, particularly in a context that sees globalizing trends challenge their sovereignty in several other fields of policy. The argument that migration policy is a matter of national sovereignty is, for example, explicit in Canada and South Africa (Chapters 8 and 10).

International migration law does not dispute this sovereign prerogative, as the above-quoted article 79 of the Convention makes clear. But, contrary to widespread belief, states' authority is not unlimited or

---

[22] This is further illustrated by recent discussions on temporary labour migration schemes, which are increasingly being advocated. As in Canada, such programmes often imply a reduction of migrants' rights (e.g. by tying workers to an employer or by forbidding family reunification). This is often presented as a necessary condition, as increased legal migration flows imply a trade-off between rights and numbers while presenting an improvement compared with irregular migration. Yet this can also be criticized as a relativization of rights, not understood as 'universal, indivisible and inalienable' but as tradable items in the negotiations between governments and migrants (for discussions, see Chapter 6 by Patrick Taran, as well as Ruhs, 2006; Ruhs and Martin, 2008).

unfettered: individuals, including migrants, are protected by a range of international human rights instruments. The tension between states' and migrants' rights is particularly visible when governments use coercive measures to control migration, such as denial of entry, detention of irregular migrants or expulsion – there is, indeed, evidence that such practices are inherently difficult to implement in the full respect of migrants' rights and that, in practice, they do lead to human rights violations (Alonso Meneses, 2003; Vohra, 2007). Irregular migration is the most obvious challenge to sovereignty. By definition, undocumented migrants reside in a destination state without its consent; yet they have rights that should be respected. Their existence thus embodies an extreme case for the universality of human rights and requires states to adopt a 'cosmopolitan' view according to which they are to protect the rights of people whom they did not want to let in. This is straightforward according to human rights logic, but politically very difficult.

In a softer version, sovereignty is also about accountability: even if states realize that their sovereignty is not violated by ratification, they may be reluctant to commit themselves internationally and to have their human rights records in terms of migration scrutinized by other countries. This is reported in the United Kingdom (Chapter 11) and South Africa (Chapter 10), where the issue is made more delicate by the sometimes tense relationships between this country and its neighbours when it comes to migration policy. This is exacerbated, in some cases, by a climate of unease or even suspicion towards the UN, as several states are reluctant to see the UN take initiatives on an issue such as migration (see below).

Finally, contemporary attitudes towards migration are very strongly influenced by a range of factors that usually fall under the 'security' umbrella. Migration issues are almost systematically addressed as a problem of law and order, which is evident in the emphasis placed on border control, irregular migration or trafficking. As Patrick Taran notes in Chapter 6, even though migration is largely about work, it is most often handled by interior or home affairs ministries, and this crime-oriented approach to migration is reported by nearly all contributors. This is reinforced by the growing concerns over terrorism that, since the end of the Cold War (and especially, of course, since the attacks of 11 September 2001 in the United States), have led states to establish new laws, policies and practices to identify people potentially connected to terrorist activities, who often happen to be non-nationals (Bonner, 2004).

In a more diffuse way, migration is also predominantly thought of as a 'threat': migrants would jeopardize social cohesion, employment opportunities, welfare systems, cultural and religious homogeneity, democratic values, etc. – thus representing a diffuse obstacle to the stability of destination states. This forms a general climate of closure, suspicion and scepticism towards migrants and foreigners. The plasticity (or vagueness) of the notion of security facilitates these amalgamations, as it refers both to the classic national security (i.e. the preservation of states from attacks from the outside) and to human or soft security, i.e. the integrity of people rather than of states (Graham, 2000). This is very unsupportive of migrants' rights, as the perception of migrants as a 'threat' is very difficult to reconcile with the perception of migrants as vulnerable people to protect.

These three factors – market forces, sovereignty and security – are very much interconnected. While a thorough analysis of their interconnections is well beyond the scope of this introduction, it may nevertheless be suggested that market forces, especially in a post-industrial context influenced by neoliberal economic thinking, create socioeconomic transformations that affect the wellbeing of large segments of the population – nationals and migrants alike. Such a climate fuels economic insecurity and generates fears and anxieties, surrounding welfare systems, employment or social cohesion. In the absence of successful and comprehensive policies by governments to address these concerns, scapegoats are sought and, regardless of their economic contribution, migrants are all too often blamed for such situations. This encourages a climate of social and cultural intolerance that paves the way for a narrow security-oriented response to much deeper socioeconomic challenges.

Together, market forces, sovereignty and security thus constitute a core obstacle to the Convention, as migrants' rights are understood as threatening these three imperatives: rights would reduce the economic benefits of migration, increase irregular migration by creating attractive conditions in destination states and reduce states' prerogatives to treat non-citizens as they wish. Viewing migrants as full human beings with rights runs contrary to their perception as undeserving outsiders, economic entities or security threats. In this context, the Convention is unlikely to be successful. Even if known to (and properly understood by) all stakeholders, and even in the absence of major legal incompatibilities (at least in developed states), its approach is bound to face reluctance. Yet it is precisely in such a context that the Convention is needed: by establishing legally binding standards for the respect of migrants' rights, it represents a potential counterforce to dominant forces.

Human rights and migration management

In recent years, the international community has started to feel the need for more comprehensive policies that would go beyond the mere control of migration and address, in a cooperative and holistic manner, its multiple facets. 'Migration management', as this process is often called, aims at developing planned and proactive policy measures to the challenges raised by migration. It further relies on the principle that the transnational nature of migration flows call for international cooperation, while acknowledging that migration is a complex issue that demands thoughtful and careful policies to be successfully addressed. The shortcomings of contemporary migration policies further motivate the search for such migration management initiatives, which are expected to more successfully govern the movement of people in a way that respects the interests of both countries of destination and origin, of migrants themselves and of other stakeholders such as the private sector or civil society (for more detailed accounts and discussions, see Ghosh, 2007; Martin et al., 2006). In other words, such initiatives aim, on paper at least, to balance market forces, state sovereignty, security concerns *and* migrants' rights.

Clearly, such an approach to migration is relevant to the ICRMW. This section therefore examines how the Convention (and the human rights of migrants more generally) are addressed in different initiatives, including the GCIM, the High-Level Dialogue on International Migration and Development (HLD), the Global Forum on Migration and Development (GFMD), the Berne Initiative, The Hague Process on Refugees and Migration (THP) and the ILO's *Multilateral Framework on Labour Migration* (ILO, 2006).

The GCIM was established to recommend to the international community a number of principles on how to address international migration, a challenging task given the heterogeneity of states' approaches and their reluctance to discuss such a sensitive topic (Pécoud and de Guchteneire, 2007). Its 2005 report features a broad overview of the issues at stake and a list of recommendations. An entire chapter is devoted to human rights. While the Convention is the subject of a few paragraphs, the report does not recommend ratification (GCIM, 2005, pp. 81–2). Rather, it acknowledges, as mentioned above, states' reluctance towards the Convention and calls for 'complementary' approaches: 'Given the decision of many states not to ratify the 1990 Convention, the Commission considers that there is a particular need for complementary approaches to the issue of migrants' rights' (GCIM, 2005, p. 57). This includes: fully implementing the human rights instruments that have been ratified; implementing the Palermo Protocols; and bridging the gap between norms and practices affecting international migrants. In Chapter 4, Carla Edelenbos reports that the CMW was disappointed with this lack of support for the Convention (see also Grant, 2006, p. 18).

The HLD, which was held by the UN General Assembly in September 2006, was the most important international conference dealing with migration since the issue emerged as central at the 1994 International Conference on Population and Development in Cairo. It devoted one of its four round tables to 'Measures to ensure the respect for and protection of the human rights of all migrants, and to prevent and combat smuggling of migrants and trafficking in persons'. On that occasion, Member States were urged to ratify the Convention, and the summary of the HLD by the President of the UN General Assembly stated that 'governments were called upon to ratify and implement the core human rights conventions and other relevant international instruments, including the [ICRMW]'.[23] As may be expected, the reference to the Convention was made by source countries, while destination states affirmed their long-standing commitment to human rights at large and recalled their ratification of most other major human rights instruments. States agreed, however, that the respect for human rights is a condition for successful migration management and for fostering the migration–development nexus, even if they displayed a reluctance to go beyond dialogue to action and to engage in normative work (Martin et al., 2007).

The GFMD stemmed from a proposition of the UN Secretary-General to establish a consultative mechanism enabling states to regularly share their views on migration and development. The first was organized by Belgium in July 2007 and focused mostly on economic and governance-related issues, such as skilled migration, temporary and circular migration, remittances and policy cooperation, with no specific session on rights-related themes.[24] Carla Edelenbos writes that the CMW was disappointed at not having been invited to the Forum (Chapter 4). However, the 2008 session of the Forum, which took place in

---

[23] UN General Assembly A/61/515, Summary of the High-level Dialogue on International Migration and Development, 13 October 2006.
[24] See www.gfmd-fmmd.org [last accessed 9 April 2009].

Manila, was devoted to the issue of migrants' protection and provided a more favourable context for the promotion of the Convention, the ratification of which was called for in the final statement. It is worth adding that the GFMD is, unlike the HLD, a state-owned process, which means that it is not organized by the UN but by states themselves.

Another 'state-owned' process is the Berne Initiative, launched by the Swiss Government in 2001 with the goal of enabling governments from all over the world to share their priorities and identify common orientations in their migration policies. The main outcome of this initiative is the document *International Agenda for Migration Management* (IAMM), which gathers governments' common views on migration to provide non-binding guidelines on how to manage migration. The IAMM addresses a wide range of migration-related issues, including border control, labour migration, irregular migration, health, asylum, integration, naturalization, etc. A section is devoted to migrants' rights, which emphasizes the need for migration management to respect the human rights of migrants (but without mentioning the ILO or UN conventions).[25] Another initiative is THP, launched in 2000 by the Netherlands Chapter of the Society for International Development. It brings together a wide range of stakeholders to develop proposals for sustainable refugee and migration policies. It notably drafted the 2002 *Declaration of The Hague on the Future of Refugee and Migration Policy*, which mentions the ICRMW as one of the 'key international human rights instruments'.[26]

As far as labour migration is concerned, two other major initiatives are worth mentioning. The first is the ILO's *Multilateral Framework on Labour Migration*, adopted in 2005, which provides a comprehensive rights-based collection of principles, guidelines and best practices on migration policy. Building on a positive understanding of labour migration and its role in development, this document stresses the role of social dialogue and social partners in migration management and thus targets not only governments but also employers' and workers' organizations in an effort to strengthen the coherence of labour migration policies and practices. The *Framework* relies heavily on the principles contained in ILO and UN conventions on migrant workers but, unlike these treaties, is non-binding (ILO, 2006). At the regional level, the Colombo Process, launched in 2003, is a regional consultative process bringing together

---

[25] See www.iom.int/jahia/Jahia/pid/1491# [last accessed 9 April 2009].
[26] See www.thehagueprocess.org [last accessed 9 April 2009].

both origin and destination countries in Asia to address the management of labour migration; one of its purposes is to improve the wellbeing of migrant workers (even though the ICRMW does not appear central therein).[27]

These initiatives clearly show that the need for a comprehensive approach to migration is felt by a wide range of actors; they also demonstrate that governments now display some willingness to exchange views, experiences and effective practices on their policies. Moreover, most of these initiatives incorporate human rights concerns in their approach, which indicates a common understanding on the need for a rights-based perspective on migration. As Kristina Touzenis writes (Chapter 14), they also valuably disconnect migration issues from the emergency situations and crises they are often associated with. Indeed, they imply a kind of public re-education, as the citizens of destination countries, so used to thinking of migration as a 'problem', must be encouraged to view it as a normal feature of their country. Within governments, migration management may also enhance the ability of states to address migration coherently – an important task in light of the capacity problems described above. In principle, this could be beneficial for the ICRMW: it indeed calls for cooperation between states while establishing the standards and definitions that make cooperation possible. Yet these migration management initiatives have not systematically supported the Convention, nor have they led to a decisive increase in its ratification rate.

The Convention seems to be penalized by two of its characteristics. First, it is a binding treaty. As Patrick Taran notes (Chapter 6), the trend today is towards non-binding documents – such as guidelines, codes of practice, etc. – that have in common a reliance on unenforceable (and usually vague) principles. Graziano Battistella argues, for example, that it is the non-binding nature of ILO's *Multilateral Framework on Labour Migration* that made it acceptable to states (Chapter 2). Unsurprisingly, such 'recommendations' are more popular among states and are thus more likely to be adopted (even if one can hope that soft standards 'harden' over time; see Aleinikoff, 2007). Second, the ICRMW is monitored by the UN. With the exception of the HLD, the initiatives described above are state-led, and there is evidence that some governments are reluctant to let the UN play too great a role in migration debates (Martin et al., 2007).

---

[27] See www.colomboprocess.org [last accessed 9 April 2009].

The contributions in this volume often address critically the relation-ship between migration management and human rights. Graziano Battistella (Chapter 2) argues, for example, that the search for a flexible labour force is perceptible in these initiatives; indeed, the use of the word 'management' carries in itself an economic connotation, which may raise inherent tensions with the rights-based approach of the Convention. Mariette Grange and Marie d'Auchamp (Chapter 3) simi-larly view 'migration management' as heavily market-oriented and insuf-ficiently concerned with violations of migrants' rights. They add that an organization such as IOM, which is a key actor in important initiatives such as the former Berne Initiative, the Puebla and Colombo Processes or its own International Dialogue on Migration (for details, see IOM, 2003; Nielsen, 2007), has not always put human rights at the centre of its programmes.[28]

Therefore, in a somewhat paradoxical way, it would seem that, despite the current context that favours exchanges and cooperation on migra-tion, the process initiated in the 1970s that eventually led to the adoption of the Convention would probably meet with strong resistance today. In this sense, the Convention represents a 'heritage' that should be valued – and used in order to put human rights at the centre of migration manage-ment initiatives. This is not only a moral imperative, but also a condition for successful policy making: as Goodwin-Gill (2007) warns, without an emphasis on rights, in both countries of origin and destination, the 'management' of migration may amount to no more than a reorientation of control to accommodate developed industrialized countries' need for labour, and would then likely become another chapter in the history of migration policy failures (Castles, 2004).

Respect for rights is also necessary to ensure people's participation. As illustrated by the migrants circumventing restrictive policies to take 3-D jobs for which they are needed in destination countries, people are unlikely to respect rules that they perceive as ill-defined or too oriented towards destination countries' interests. By committing themselves to the Convention, states have the opportunity to create the necessary climate of confidence and fairness that will ensure the cooperation not only of other states but also of migrants themselves: 'If a regime of "migration management" is to be effective, not only must it be credible

---

[28] More information can be found in the statement by Amnesty International and Human Rights Watch at IOM's Governing Council in 2002 (www.hrw.org/press/2002/12/ai-hrw-statement.htm [last accessed 9 April 2009]).

to states, but it must also be credible to migrants. To achieve this, it must respect the fundamental human rights of migrants, and indeed must actively seek to respect, protect and promote the rights of all migrants' (Amnesty International, 2006, p. 25).

In sum, the migration management initiatives described in this section usefully call for a holistic approach to migration, which would encompass not only the interest in migrant labour or the concerns over security, but also development, human rights, integration, asylum, etc. Arguably, these initiatives so far remain at the level of discussions and publications; this is nevertheless a necessary step in the process, and it is to be hoped that they eventually contribute to shaping actual migration policies. As far as the Convention is concerned, it remains to be seen whether the small role it currently plays therein will grow as migration management initiatives become more ambitious – or whether the current absence of the Convention indicates a structural reluctance to incorporate a binding standard established under the auspices of the UN (Pécoud, 2009).

Conclusion: the way forward

Prospects for ratification of the ICRMW are not encouraging. The obstacles analyzed in this introduction and presented in greater details in the following contributions point to the difficulty of promoting the Convention and of having it accepted and ratified by major destination countries. In addition, the difficulties faced by the Convention are not isolated but embedded in a general international climate that is far from positive: as Graziano Battistella notes, multilateralism and respect for the UN's role are not improving (Chapter 2), while Patrick Taran underlines the worrying relativization of human rights, whose legitimacy is regularly under attack (Chapter 6). In the face of this situation, the question is how to envisage the future of the Convention. As long as destination countries have not ratified it, the Convention will suffer from a severe handicap – as it is meant to protect the world's migrants but has no validity for the vast majority of them. If the current reluctance towards the Convention persists, it is possible to envisage three principal options:

(1) To consider the Convention a 'lost case' and to abandon campaigning for it. As mentioned above, there was a widespread feeling that the Convention was 'dead' at the end of the 1990s, before several

initiatives were launched to promote it again. Since then, many states ratified, which highlights the need to not give up; the current context may be unfavourable and discouraging, but it cannot be excluded that changes in migration policies and discourses – coupled with strong IGO/NGO advocacy – may eventually open new perspectives for the Convention. Moreover, it should be added that, as argued above, a standard is useful, no matter whether it is implemented or not: renouncing resort to the Convention would then imply losing a tool that may be used as a yardstick and a stimulus in migration debates.

(2) To look for alternatives to the Convention. The reluctance towards the Convention has inspired calls for other approaches to the protection of migrants' rights, as illustrated by the emergence of non-binding declarations. Similarly, Van Krieken (2007) suggests amending the Convention to incorporate the concerns of developed destination countries, in order to draft a text acceptable to many more states. In principle, there is nothing wrong in exploring such options; strictly speaking, they are not incompatible with the Convention – more modest agreements could, for example, be understood as paving the way for an ambitious treaty like the Convention. But the risk is that, in a general context of scarce resources for the issue of migrants' rights, the energy put in alternatives may *de facto* relegate the Convention to obscurity. In addition, the existence of less powerful alternative agreements may then be used to further dismiss the usefulness of the Convention.

(3) To continue the efforts to promote the Convention and to convince as many countries as possible to ratify. In light of the preceding discussion, this third option seems to be the most desirable. The very existence of the Convention is in itself an achievement that, as suggested above, would probably be much more difficult to reach in today's context. This calls for using a treaty that, whatever its weaknesses, has the merit of existing. One cannot exclude that a slow increase in the number of ratifications, even from non-destination states, may increase the pressure on major destination states. Moreover, the interest of the international community in migration management is, to a large extent, still in its infancy; states still have to be convinced of the added value of addressing migration in a concerted and multilateral manner. This evolution may ultimately lead to a context more favourable to an international migration agreement such as the ICRMW.

References

Aleinikoff, T. A. 2007. International legal norms on migration: substance without architecture. Cholewinski et al., op. cit., pp. 467–80.

Aleinikoff, T. A. and Chetail, V. (eds). 2003. *Migration and International Legal Norms*. The Hague, Netherlands, T. M. C. Asser Press.

Alonso Meneses, G. 2003. Human rights and undocumented migration along the Mexican-U.S. border. *UCLA Law Review*, Vol. 51, pp. 267–81.

Amnesty International. 2006. *Living in the Shadows. A Primer on the Human Rights of Migrants*. London, Amnesty International.

Battistella, G. 2008. Irregular migration. IOM, *IOM 2008*. Geneva, Switzerland, IOM, pp. 201–32.

Bhatnagar, P. 2004. Liberalising the movement of natural persons: a lost decade? *The World Economy*, Vol. 27, No. 3, pp. 459–72.

Bogusz, B., Cholewinski, R., Cygan, A. and Szyszczak, E. (eds). 2004. *Irregular Migration and Human Rights: Theoretical, European, and International Perspectives*. Leiden, Netherlands, Martinus Nijhoff.

Böhning, R. 1991. The ILO and the new UN Convention on Migrant Workers: the past and future. *International Migration Review*, Vol. 25, No. 4, pp. 698–709.

Bonner, D. 2004. Porous borders: terrorism and migration policy. Bogusz et al., op. cit., pp. 93–113.

Bosniak, L. S. 2004. Human rights, state sovereignty and the protection of undocumented migrants under the International Migrant Workers Convention. Bogusz et al., op. cit., pp. 311–41.

Bustamante, J. A. 2002. Immigrants' vulnerability as subjects of human rights. *International Migration Review*, Vol. 36, No. 2, pp. 333–54.

Castles, S. 2004. Why migration policies fail. *Ethnic and Racial Studies*, Vol. 27, No. 2, pp. 205–27.

2006. Guestworkers in Europe: a resurrection? *International Migration Review*, Vol. 40, No. 4, pp. 741–66.

Cholewinski, R. 1997. *Migrant Workers in International Human Rights Law: Their Protection in Countries of Employment*. Oxford, UK, Clarendon Press.

Cholewinski, R., Perruchoud, R. and MacDonald, E. (eds). 2007. *International Migration Law. Developing Paradigms and Key Challenges*. The Hague, Netherlands, T. M. C. Asser Press.

Cornelius, W. 2005. Controlling 'unwanted' immigration: lessons from the United States, 1993–2004. *Journal of Ethnic and Migration Studies*, Vol. 31, No. 4, pp. 775–94.

Da Lomba, S. 2004. Fundamental social rights for irregular migrants: the right to health care in France and England. Bogusz et al., op. cit., pp. 363–86.

de Varennes, F. 2002. *'Strangers in Foreign Lands' – Diversity, Vulnerability and the Rights of Migrants*. Paris, UNESCO. (MOST Working Paper 9.)

Fitzpatrick, J. 2003. The human rights of migrants. Aleinikoff and Chetail, op. cit., pp. 169–84.

Gallagher, A. 2001. Human rights and the new UN protocols on trafficking and migrant smuggling: a preliminary analysis. *Human Rights Quarterly*, Vol. 23, No. 4, pp. 975–1004.

GCIM. 2005. *Migration in an Interconnected World: New Directions for Action*. Geneva, Switzerland, Global Commission on International Migration.

Ghosh, B. 2007. Managing migration: towards the missing regime? A. Pécoud and P. de Guchteneire (eds), *Migration without Borders. Essays on the Free Movement of People*. Oxford, UK/Paris, Berghahn/UNESCO, pp. 97–118.

Goodwin-Gill, G. S. 2007. Migrant rights and 'managed migration'. V. Chetail (ed.), *Mondialisation, migration et droits de l'homme: le droit international en question* [Globalisation, Migration and Human Rights: International Law under Review]. Brussels, Bruylant, pp. 161–87.

Graham, D. T. 2000. The people paradox. Human movements and human security in a globalising world. D. T. Graham and N. K. Poku (eds), *Migration, Globalisation and Human Security*. London, Routledge, pp. 186–216.

Grant, S. 2006. GCIM report: defining an 'ethical compass' for international migration policy. *International Migration*, Vol. 44, No. 1, pp. 13–19.

Groenendijk, K. 2004. Introduction. Bogusz et al., op. cit., pp. xvii–xxii.

Haseneau, M. 1991. ILO Standards on migrant workers: the fundamentals of the UN Convention and their genesis. *International Migration Review*, Vol. 25, No. 4, pp. 687–97.

Hune, S. and Niessen, J. 1991. The first UN Convention on Migrant Workers. *Netherlands Quarterly of Human Rights*, Vol. 9, No. 2, pp. 130–41.

—— 1994. Ratifying the UN Migrant Workers' Convention: current difficulties and prospects. *Netherlands Quarterly of Human Rights*, Vol. 12, No. 4, pp. 393–404.

ILO. 2006. *ILO Multilateral Framework on Labour Migration. Non-binding Principles and Guidelines for a Rights-based Approach to Labour Migration*. Geneva, Switzerland, ILO.

International Migration Review. 1991. *Special Issue on the Convention: U.N. International Convention on the Protection of the Rights of All Migrant Workers and Members of Their Families*, Vol. 25, No. 4.

IOM. 2003. *World Migration 2003. Managing Migration: Challenges and Responses for People on the Move*. Geneva, Switzerland, IOM.

Joly, D. (ed.). 2002. *Global Changes in Asylum Regimes*. Basingstoke, UK, Palgrave Macmillan.

Kälin, W. 2003. Human rights and the integration of migrants. Aleinikoff and Chetail, op. cit., pp. 271–87.

La Violette, N. 2006. The principal international human rights instruments to which Canada has not yet adhered. *Windsor Yearbook of Access to Justice*, Vol. 24, No. 2.

Leary, V. A. 2003. Labor migration. Aleinikoff and Chetail, op. cit., pp. 227–39.

MacDonald, E. and Cholewinski, R. 2007. *The Migrant Workers Convention in Europe. Obstacles to the Ratification of the International Convention on the Protection of the Rights of All Migrant Workers and Members of their Families: EU/EEA Perspectives.* Paris, UNESCO. (Migration Studies 1.)

Martin, P., Martin, S. and Cross, S. 2007. High-Level Dialogue on Migration and Development. *International Migration*, Vol. 45, No. 1, pp. 7–25.

Martin, P., Martin, S. and Weil, P. 2006. *Managing Migration: The Promise of Cooperation.* Lanham, Md., Lexington Books.

Médecins du Monde. 2007. *Enquête européenne sur l'accès aux soins des personnes en situation irrégulière* [European Survey on Undocumented Migrants' Access to Health Care]. Paris, Observatoire Européen de l'Accès aux Soins de Médecins du Monde.

Nielsen, A.-G. 2007. Cooperation mechanisms. Cholewinski et al., op. cit., pp. 405–26.

Pécoud, A. 2009. The UN Convention on Migrant Workers' Rights and International Migration Management. *Global Society*, Vol. 23, No. 3, pp. 333–50.

Pécoud, A. and de Guchteneire, P. 2006. Migration, human rights and the United Nations: an investigation into the obstacles to the UN convention on migrant workers' rights. *Windsor Yearbook of Access to Justice*, Vol. 24, No. 2, pp. 241–66.

——— 2007. Between global governance and human rights. International migration and the United Nations. *Georgetown Journal of International Affairs*, Vol. 8, No. 2, pp. 115–23.

Rekacewicz, P. and Clochard, O. 2004. Des morts par milliers aux portes de l'Europe [Thousands of deaths at the gates of Europe]. *Le Monde Diplomatique*. Available at www.monde-diplomatique.fr/cartes/mortsauxfrontieres [last accessed 9 April 2009].

Rodriguez, G. 2000. The role of the United Nations Special Rapporteur on the human rights of migrants. *International Migration*, Vol. 38, No. 6, pp. 73–9.

Ruhs, M. 2006. The potential of temporary migration programmes in future international migration policy. *International Labour Review*, Vol. 45, Nos. 1–2, pp. 7–36.

Ruhs, M. and Martin, P. 2008. Number vs. Rights: Trade-offs and Guest Worker Programmes. *International Migration Review*, Vol. 42, No. 1, pp. 249–65.

Shelley, T. 2007. *Exploited. Migrant Labour in the New Global Economy.* London, Zed Books.

Taran, P. A. 2000a. Human rights of migrants: challenges of the new decade. *International Migration*, Vol. 38, No. 6, pp. 7–51.

——— 2000b. Status and prospects for the UN Convention on Migrants' Rights. *European Journal of Migration and Law*, Vol. 2, No. 1, pp. 85–100.

Tiburcio, C. 2001. *The Human Rights of Aliens under International Comparative Law*. The Hague, Netherlands, Kluwer Law International.

UN-DESA. 2006. *International Migration 2006*. New York, UN-DESA.

UNDP. 2007. *Human Development Report 2007/2008. Fighting Climate Change: Human Solidarity in a Divided World*. New York, UNDP.

Vanheule, D., Foblets, M.-C., Loones, S. and Bouckaert, S. 2004. The significance of the UN Migrant Workers' Convention of 18 December 1990 in the event of ratification by Belgium. *European Journal of Migration and Law*, Vol. 6, No. 4, pp. 285–321.

Van Krieken, P. 2007. Migrants' rights and the law of the sea: further efforts to ensure universal participation. *International Migration*, Vol. 45, No. 1, pp. 209–24.

Vohra, S. 2007. Detention of irregular migrants and asylum seekers. Cholewinski et al., op. cit., pp. 49–69.

Vucetic, S. 2007. Democracies and international human rights: why is there no place for migrant workers? *International Journal of Human Rights*, Vol. 11, No. 4, pp. 403–28.

Weissbrodt, D. 2007. The protection of non-nationals in international human rights law. Cholewinski et al., op. cit., pp. 221–35.

PART I

2

Migration and human rights: the uneasy but essential relationship

GRAZIANO BATTISTELLA

Introduction

The ICRMW, one of the seven human rights instruments of the international community, has some notable peculiarities. It is the longest of the UN instruments, it had the slowest progress between adoption and entry into force and it has the smallest number of participating countries (Battistella, 2004). This is no coincidence but is inherently linked to the difficulty the international community has in approaching migration from a human rights perspective and agreeing on standards for its management. To illustrate this position, this chapter retraces the history of the development of international migration standards for migrants before the Convention and then focuses on its preparation, drafting and ratification stages. The various stages show, on the one hand, the close connection between human rights development and protection to migrants, and on the other hand the reluctance to extend agreed principles to migrants as this militates against the flexibility of migration, which no country is willing to renounce. A brief overview of prospects for additional ratifications is also given. After summarizing some reasons for the limited expectations of the role of the Convention, signs of hope for the protection of migrants are indicated.

Human rights and migrants before the ICRMW

Concern for the protection of migrants had been growing for some years before the international community started thinking of an international convention. However, this process was rather slow and limited in the areas involved and the categories of migrants considered. Two major phases of the discussion on the protection of migrants can be identified up to the 1970s, which saw the beginnings of the ICRMW.

Concern without standards

Soon after the First World War, which had stopped the great exodus from eastern and southern Europe to the Americas, migration resumed in great numbers but was quickly restrained by the 1921 and 1924 US immigration acts. The two laws aimed to restrict immigration, introducing national quotas for admission based on the percentage of populations of various origins already present in the United States in the 1910 and 1890 censuses. They had a particular impact on immigration from eastern and southern Europe. The need to regulate international relations in different terms and avoid another disastrous war led the negotiators of the 1919 Treaty of Versailles to set up the League of Nations and led to the creation of the ILO as a specialized agency concerned with the improvement of conditions and living standards of workers throughout the world. The ILO's concern for migrants was identified from the outset, as its Constitution Preamble lists among various purposes the 'protection of the interests of workers when employed in countries other than their own'. Yet any substantive benefits for migrants were more the consequence of the basic principle of equality of treatment. Indeed, migrants benefited from the various conventions and recommendations that the ILO adopted at an early stage for all workers. Migrants were the target of a few specific measures, as they were beneficiaries of conventions relating to maintenance of rights and social security[1] (ILC, 1980, p. 3). But at this initial stage the protection of migrants was strengthened mainly because the conditions of all workers were improved.

As migration from Europe to the Americas remained limited in the 1930s, migration flows from southern to northern Europe intensified. Conditions for migrants were handled through bilateral agreements, but without much coherence among the various accords. The ILO attempted to strengthen the protection of migrants through the 1939 ILO Convention No. 66 (Convention concerning Migration for Employment), which provided a coherent set of measures

---

[1] 1925 Convention concerning ILO Equality of Treatment (Accident Compensation) and its Recommendation, 1925 (Nos. 19 and 25 respectively); 1935 Convention No. 48 (Convention concerning ILO Maintenance of Migrants' Pension Rights).

comprehensively addressing various aspects of labour migration.[2] Unfortunately, the standards remained on paper as Convention No. 66 never entered into force because no country ratified it. The international climate was dominated by nationalism and protectionism. The League of Nations was revealing inherent weaknesses, with limited impact on international relations. Its failure to avoid the tragedy of the Second World War led to its demise. The ILO's efforts were defeated by an unfavourable international environment. Standards found no takers and migrants were left to fend for themselves.

Standards without concern

After the Second World War, migration flows resumed strongly, both from Europe and within Europe, although US restrictions on migration remained in place. A new climate for international relations was established with the creation of the UN, and the great season of human rights recognition flourished. In addition to the protection provided by standards in the human rights instruments, beginning with the Universal Declaration of Human Rights, the protection of the rights of migrants was the object of the 1949 ILO Convention No. 97 (Convention concerning Migration for Employment (Revised)), and of regional treaties. Within the Council of Europe, the 1955 European Convention on Establishment continued in the furrow of an earlier unsuccessful attempt to ensure protection to aliens, while the 1961 European Social Charter provided equality of treatment with nationals on remuneration, union membership and housing benefits.

As significant progress was made in the recognition of the rights of migrants, the real impact was limited either because only a few countries ratified the standards or because ratification was restricted to countries of a specific region. Indeed, with the beginning of the human rights movement, a system of concentric protection circles emerged. The larger the circle, the more universal the human rights application, but also the least specific; the smaller the circle, the more favourable and better enforceable the human rights provisions. This is particularly clear in the case of Europe, where, in addition to the Universal Bill of Rights, there is the 1950 ECHR, and more recently the 2000 European Union Charter of

---

[2] For a more general discussion on the role of the ILO in setting standards for migrants, see Haseneau (1991).

Fundamental Rights. Rights of migrants established in regional systems are normally applicable only to nationals of those regions moving across borders within the regions themselves. Thus, migrants from other regions can only invoke more universal instruments, which might not have been ratified by their country of origin.

To overcome issues created by the stratification of rights, countries began establishing bilateral agreements. In the European experience, this involved, first of all, countries of northern and southern Europe, and was later extended to Turkey and North African countries. Bilateral agreements include a variety of norms, depending on the negotiating countries and their respective interests. To facilitate their negotiation, the ILO included a model as an annex to the 1949 Convention. What bilateral agreements have in common is their effectiveness, because they are established on the principle of reciprocity. In more recent times, countries of destination have become reluctant to enter into such agreements because of the plethora of countries of origin to engage with.

In sum, the whole period before the ICRMW is characterized by a progressive recognition of the rights of migrants, but on the basis of a differential distribution of protection. As migrants from countries party to specific regional agreements receive better protection, to the point that they achieve full incorporation and become citizens (as in the EU), the demand for less-protected migrants seeks workers from regions and countries that are not parties to migrant conventions. While the policies of destination countries are progressively constrained to be based on rights, actual coverage becomes restricted on a portion of the migrant population. Standards are available, but do not concern all migrants in a similar way. This restrictive approach sets the stage for irregular migration and a new demand for protection.

History of the Convention

Beginnings: the 1970s

The 1970s was a period of major change in the world economy, in international migration policies and consequently in international migration flows. Countries of settlement migration, such as Canada and the United States, had lifted restrictions to immigration in the early 1960s, eliminating the quota system based on ethnic origin. The sudden upsurge of immigration from southern and eastern Europe, consisting mostly of family reunification, lasted for about ten years (the time it took to severely reduce the backlog of applications that had accumulated through the years). The decrease of immigration from Europe, motivated largely by the economic improvements achieved by the European Common Market and the shrinking of income differential gaps with North America (in the mid 1970s, a traditional emigration country such as Italy started experiencing more returns than departures), left room for increasing migration from Asia, Mexico and the Caribbean. Australia abandoned its 'white Australia' policy in 1973, setting the stage for a similar diversification of origins of its immigration flows.

The oil crisis, and the consequent economic downturn, following the 1973 war in the Middle East generated two additional major changes. First, immigration countries in Europe decided to stop their labour migration programme and even attempted to reduce the foreign population by providing incentives for return. Integration policies aimed at stabilizing the immigrant population that remained in the territory became the most relevant preoccupation. Second, the Middle East became the new destination for labour migration, mostly from Arab countries and South and South-East Asia.

In this scenario of profound change, the relationship between migration and protection also suffered severe strains. While the traditional migration flows had slowly acquired security, either because of improvements in destination country policies or because of bilateral agreements, policy restrictions accompanied by mounting migration pressure resulted in increasingly widespread irregular migration, with new concerns for the protection of migrants. Although still fettered in the Cold War parameters, international relations were also affected by the human rights discourse (the 1966 ICESCR and the ICCPR entered into force in 1975, also the year of the Final Act of the Helsinki Conference on Security and Cooperation in Europe, which made an explicit reference to the protection of migrants, but most importantly established a monitoring process on the respect of human rights). Thus, while experiencing a deterioration of treatment, migrants became the concern for new protection initiatives, chief among them being the ICRMW.

The beginnings of the Convention may be traced to an episode that occurred in 1972. A sealed truck met with an accident while crossing the tunnel under Mount Blanc. Supposed to be carrying sewing machines, it was in fact transporting twenty-eight workers from Mali, who were travelling from Tunisia to France through Italy and Switzerland (Bertinetto, 1983, p. 189). On the insistence of the representative from Kenya, the United Nations Economic and Social Council (ECOSOC) adopted a resolution in which the CHR was requested to investigate the matter.[3] At about the same time, the ILO began addressing the issue of irregular migration and trafficking of workers. In the same year the UN General Assembly discussed migration and asked the Commission on Human Rights to give priority to the examination of discrimination suffered by migrants. In doing so, the General Assembly was establishing a linkage between discrimination against migrants and racial discrimination.[4] It was also inviting the ILO to continue the study on workforce trafficking. Thus, the issue of special concern for migrants entered the UN system with two different but related perspectives: the human rights perspective and the labour perspective, specifically with preoccupation for the increasing of irregular migration. Attention was called to migrants in general, but particularly on the clandestine traffic of workers.

When it begins to address an issue, the UN asks for specialized reports. In fact, the office of the Secretary-General was asked to prepare a report on migration for the ECOSOC Commission for Social Development, while the Sub-Commission on Prevention of Discrimination and Protection of Minorities was asked to study the issue of trafficking of workers in light of UN instruments on human rights.

The Secretary-General's report was presented in 1975[5] and did not include a recommendation to draft a new convention, but only to proceed to the harmonization of existing instruments concerning migrant workers. The report of the Sub-Commission was also presented in 1975.[6] As the juridical aspects on the topic were scattered throughout various instruments, and in some cases were not very specific, it seemed opportune to prepare a new convention or declaration to render more explicit the rights of migrants that were not sufficiently recognized. It was also indicated that such an exercise should have been the task of the UN, rather than the ILO, as the ILO's approach was considered too concentrated on economic aspects.

Also in 1975, a seminar on the human rights of migrants was organized by the UN in Tunis, within the general climate originated by the demand of the G-77 for a new international economic order. Although the report of the Sub-Commission was available, participants at the seminar did not conclude with the request for a new convention, but

---

[3] Resolution 1706 (LIII) of 28 July 1972.
[4] UN General Assembly Resolution 2920 (XXVII) of 15 November 1972.
[5] UN Doc. E/CN.5/515 of 14 October 1974.
[6] UN Doc. E/CN.4/Sub.2/L.629 of 4 July 1975.

simply with the proposal to prepare a bilateral agreement model to be used by states. It should not be forgotten that some months earlier the ILO had adopted Convention No. 143 on irregular migrants and on the equality of treatment between migrants and national workers. On the issue of correct terminology, the UN General Assembly also adopted in 1975 a resolution inviting countries not to use the term 'illegal migrants', but to speak of 'non-documented or irregular migrant workers'.[7]

The linkage between migrant discrimination and racial discrimination established by the UN General Assembly was also taken by the first World Conference to Combat Racism and Racial Discrimination, held in Geneva in 1978. In its programme of action, it invited states to consider the possibility of an international convention on the rights of migrants.[8] This recommendation, as well as the recommendation that the CHR should continue considering the issue of the rights of migrants not sufficiently recognized, led to UN General Assembly Resolution 33/163 of 20 December 1978, which started the consultation machinery to explore the opportunity to draft an international convention on the rights of migrant workers.

Responses from countries were neither numerous nor favourable. Opposed to a UN convention were Belgium, the United Kingdom and UNESCO, because of concerns on overlapping dispositions or a conflict of measures between human rights instruments. Finland, the Federal Republic of Germany and Sweden also expressed a negative opinion. The ILO was against because it considered a UN convention premature. Italy expressed a favourable opinion on the initiative, but preferred a declaration rather than a convention. Most destination countries either did not answer the inquiry or expressed a negative view. However, a positive opinion was submitted by countries of origin and some countries of the Soviet bloc (Soviet Union, Democratic Republic of Germany, Cuba), who were not much involved in migration flows but were interested in the ideological opportunity that the issue presented.

It is useful to recall the ILO's answer, articulated in four points: (i) a convention on the rights of migrants drafted outwith the ILO constituted a duplication of efforts; (ii) the establishing of a supervising mechanism required additional means, with a waste of resources; (iii) the task to establish standards relating to workers should remain within the

---

[7] UN General Assembly Resolution 3449 (XXX) of 9 December 1975.
[8] UN Doc. A/33/262/Section II, Programme of Action at paragraph 14(V).

competence of the ILO; and (iv) the UN could focus only on those aspects that went beyond the competence of the ILO.[9]

In spite of the lack of widespread consensus, the General Assembly in 1979 adopted a resolution establishing a working group for the drafting of the Convention.[10] Thus, it took approximately ten years to move from a generic preoccupation for the condition of migrants to the establishment of the drafting group. In addition to the previously mentioned events that affected migration in those years, particular importance should be given to the difficult process of adopting ILO Convention No. 143 on irregular migration. In fact, various countries did not support that convention, but for different reasons: some European countries were against the possibility of migrants choosing a different occupation after two years of immigration; some countries of origin (Mexico and Morocco in particular) were reluctant to engage in a reduction of irregular migration; and even in the United States, irregular migration was convenient to the agricultural sector (Böhning, 1991, p. 699). As ILO Convention No. 143 did not achieve immediate widespread support, the door was open for the preparation of a UN convention.

In sum, the initiative to draft a convention on the protection of the rights of migrants converged objectives and preoccupations of a humanitarian nature, which also concealed different economic concerns in countries of destination and origin of migrants. The real concern was irregular migration. By ensuring protection to irregular workers, countries of origin were perhaps aiming at diminishing the unlimited power of repatriation. Conversely, countries of destination were resisting providing protection in order to retain freedom of expulsion. In reality, economic interests were cutting the two sides transversally, as both origin and destination countries were profiting from irregular migration.

Drafting process: the 1980s

Mexico and Morocco, two important sending countries, were particularly active at the diplomatic level to prepare the drafting process. This led to the election of the Mexican ambassador Gonzalez de Leon as

[9] UN Doc. A/34/535 of 18 October 1979.

[10] UN General Assembly Resolution 34/172 of 17 December 1979. Votes were: 118 in favour, none against, and nineteen abstentions, these being: Australia, Austria, Belgium, Burma, Canada, Denmark, Finland, France, the Federal Republic of Germany, Guatemala, Iceland, Israel, Luxembourg, the Netherlands, New Zealand, Norway, Sweden, the United Kingdom and the United States.

chairperson of the working group[11] and to the presentation of a first draft of the Convention.[12] This draft did not find the support of the working group. In particular, it was rejected by countries of western Europe, as it was considered that it would legalize any present and future irregular migration (Bertinetto, 1983, p. 201; Böhning, 1991, p. 701). Instead, a group of Mediterranean and Scandinavian countries (Finland, Greece, Italy, Portugal, Spain, Sweden and later Norway) – all with governments of leftist orientation in the early 1980s – informally converged in a group known as MESCA and submitted an alternative outline of the Convention, which was accepted and which became the definitive structure. The MESCA group kept regular intersession meetings to prepare, with the support of an ILO expert, the text to submit to the discussion of the working group. In the end, the text of the Convention is fundamentally a European text, although modified by the long negotiation process. The MESCA group was also conspicuous for some important absences, as some delegations, such as Belgium and the United Kingdom, played a low-key role or did not participate in the discussions, while the Federal Republic of Germany was often in disagreement, but without hampering the process.

The working group, convened by the Committee on Social, Humanitarian and Cultural affairs of the General Assembly (Third Committee), met for the first time on 8 October 1980 and completed the first draft[13] in autumn 1984, after ten sessions. A brief analysis of the first draft could have led to the conclusion that the whole process was going to be finished relatively soon, because only nineteen articles were left with alternative versions, which required additional negotiation. Instead, ten more sessions were required, and the working group finished its process in June 1990. The ICRMW was then adopted by the General Assembly of the UN on 18 December 1990.[14]

---

[11] Gonzalez de Leon was to maintain this role uncontested until he prematurely passed away one year before the completion of the drafting process. On the other hand, a representative from Morocco, Halima Warzazi, who had prepared in 1974 the influential report of the Sub-Commission on the Prevention of Discrimination and the Protection of Minorities, was designated chair of the working group that drafted the 1985 Declaration on the human rights of individuals who are not nationals of the country in which they live.

[12] UN Doc. A/C.3/35/WG.1CPRP.7 of 11 May 1981. The draft was signed by Algeria, Mexico, Pakistan, Turkey and Yugoslavia, and later by Barbados and Egypt.

[13] UN Doc. A/C.3/39/4 of 11 October 1984.

[14] UN General Assembly Resolution 45/158 of 18 December 1990.

The long drafting process suggests that the initial approach to the Convention did not remain unchanged until the end. Various factors contributed to such change.

The first factor of change has to do with the frequent switch of delegates in the working group. Representatives were mainly of three types: (i) migration experts sent explicitly to participate in the drafting of the text; (ii) experts on human rights; and (iii) officials from the permanent missions to the UN. Only two representatives participated in the entire drafting process (Lönnroth, 1991, p. 715). With the frequent switch of members, knowledge of the history of the text was weakened and interventions presented different nuances.

A second important factor had to do with the margin of flexibility left to delegates. If in the first draft delegates had more freedom to speak their mind, in the second they were more tied to the position of governments, also in view of the possible ratification of the Convention (Lönnroth, 1991, p. 722). Therefore, the first draft presents a general tone more favourable to the protection of migrants, while the final draft is more an expression of the interests of governments, which do not necessarily coincide with those of migrants. The need, true or alleged, to consult with governments often slowed down the drafting process, leading to frequent informal meetings. A more direct supervision of governments also led to a weakened text, to the introduction of reservations and to the transformation of migrants' rights into recommendations to governments (i.e. on family reunification).

Factors not immediately related to the drafting process had an even more decisive role. The change in immigration flows led to changes in the management of migration and in government attitudes towards international agreements. Nations of solid migration tradition, such as the United States and France, were confronted in the 1980s with irregular migration. The two measures they adopted (regularization of immigrants already in the country and sanctions against employers)[15] were influential for the formulation of the approach against irregular migration. Other countries, particularly those of southern Europe, were witnessing the transition from countries of emigration to countries of immigration. This had a profound impact on the attitude towards measures to be included in the Convention. In other traditional European countries of immigration, the process of transforming immigrant communities into minorities was consolidating. This could partially explain the strategy,

[15] See US Immigration Reform and Control Act, 1986.

almost constantly discordant, of the German delegation, keen to empha-size that attention and rights should be limited to immigrants regularly present in the territory. For other countries, such as Japan, immigration was becoming an issue towards the end of the 1980s, explaining the sudden activism of that delegation in the final phase of the drafting process. The composition of migration flows in many countries was also changing, with an increased presence of self-employed migrants and project-tied workers, who were included in the Convention but not without discussion. The typical argument against the inclusion of self-employed workers was the fear that the Convention was to protect wealthy owners of French restaurants abroad, rather than migrant workers.[16]

At the international level, the 1980s were also characterized by a strong impulse towards neoliberalism, under the leadership of Ronald Reagan and Margaret Thatcher, with a consequent reduced emphasis on the protection of workers. In the Soviet Union, the transformation process, initiated with glasnost and perestroika, was taking its course, culminat-ing in the 1989 destruction of the Berlin Wall, although this event occurred too late to have a decisive role on the text of the Convention.

All these aspects help us to understand why the final text ensured that migrants would receive only such protection as traditional labour-receiving countries were already granting them. Thus, the Convention was only marginally innovative over existing standards. Furthermore, a detailed comparison of the first and final drafts would probably lead to the conclusion that the first draft was in some instances more favourable to migrants.

Two examples help to illustrate this. The first concerns the right to family reunification. The second paragraph of article 45 of the text after first reading said: 'Spouses and minor dependent unmarried sons and daughters [of migrant workers] shall be authorized to accompany or join migrant workers and to stay in the state of employment for a duration not less than that of the worker, subject to [procedures prescribed by] the [national] legislation of the state of employment or [applicable] interna-tional agreements.'[17] It was a text that did not contain an alternative version and therefore had obtained consensus in the group. However, in

---

[16] The request for the inclusion of self-employed workers was originally made by the Italian delegation (UN Doc. A/C.3/35/13 Annex IV at paragraph 8 (25 November 1980)), and it was resolved only in 1989.

[17] UN Doc. A/C.3/39/WG.1/WP.1 of 14 June 1984.

the second reading, after lengthy discussion, the paragraph was comple-tely changed, and became what is now article 44.[18] What was originally formulated as a migrant right became a simple recommendation made to states to facilitate the reunification of migrant workers.

A second example concerns the exclusion from the protection of the Convention of 'seafarers and workers on an off-shore installation who have not been admitted to take up residence and engage in a remunerated activity in the state of employment' (article 3(f)). This exclusion was not part of the text after first reading and results in the possibility for a state to give different treatment on salary or social security to seafarers on the basis of their permit of residence (Haseneau, 1990). This constitutes discrimination on the basis of ILO Convention No. 111.[19]

Ratification time: the 1990s

At the end of the drafting process, it was already clear to delegates that the Convention was to face a difficult ratification time. On the one hand, countries of destination in particular had done their best to ensure that the Convention was acceptable to their governments for ratification. In this respect, particularly when a final provision was disappointing, arguments in informal conversations were underscoring that a bland text would ensure ample convergence, and this was considered more relevant than an outstanding text with few ratifications. Even those comments, however, seemed irrelevant in the presence of a diffused impression that no important immigration country was to tie its hands on the management of a sensitive issue such as immi-gration by ratifying an international treaty. Experience has indicated that such an approach is persisting. However, serious analysis should demonstrate that fears for the provisions of the Convention are unjus-tified. It does not diminish the right of states to establish criteria for the admission of migrants; it does not provide escape routes to irregu-lar migrants, as it only gives them humanitarian protection that they already enjoy on the basis of other UN instruments; it does not grant new standards, as it reflects what states were willing to concede in the 1990s.

---

[18] UN Doc. A/C.3/42/6 of 9 October 1987.
[19] The ILO delegate at the working group had indicated this problem. See UN Doc. A/C.3/ 44/4 at paragraph 43 (17 October 1989).

Nevertheless, it took the Convention thirteen years to enter into force.[20] This was achieved mainly because of the need for countries of origin to ensure protection for their migrants, because of civil society lobbying governments and because of the inertia factor of the UN system. A simple glance at the list of countries that have ratified the Convention illustrates the first point. Some of the major countries of origin of migration are included (among them Colombia, Ecuador, Egypt, El Salvador, Ghana, Mexico, Morocco, the Philippines, Senegal, Sri Lanka and Turkey), while only one important destination country is listed, Argentina, which joined the Convention in 2007. Countries of origin have a favourable consideration on the impact the Convention can make for the protection of their migrants, while most countries of destination do not consider it viable to provide protection to migrants through ratification of the Convention. A different conclusion, that countries of destination do not intend to ensure protection to migrants, would be implausible. Most of these countries consider their national system of protection already adequate, if not superior, to the norms included in the Convention. Furthermore, countries of settlement migration have always declared that the Convention is only applicable to migrant workers, not to immigrants, who constitute the majority of their migrants. The distinction between migrant workers and immigrants is based on the admission policy. Migrant workers are admitted for the purpose of employment; immigrants are admitted to settle in the country of destination. There are very few countries with a settlement immigration policy (Canada and the United States, Australia and New Zealand). As the Convention is for the protection of the rights of migrant workers, defined as persons engaged in a remunerated activity, it could be argued that immigrants are not included among the migrants protected by the Convention. On the other hand, most immigrants take up employment after admission and it is possible they could invoke the protection of the Convention. It is true that immigrants are not included among the categories protected, but they are not excluded either. This discussion, which took place mainly during the first draft of the Convention, could find additional reasons in favour or against, but at this point it is largely a moot discussion, as settlement immigration countries do not appear keen to ratify the Convention very soon.

The ratification divide between origin and destination countries reveals that there is always more to politics than meets the eye. The

---

[20] On 14 March 2003, Guatemala deposited the 20th ratification, followed on the same day by El Salvador.

adherence of countries of origin is based on the perception that the protection of migrants is mostly a duty of destination countries, in which case the number of ratifying origin states should be more numerous. Apparently, as every country is both origin and destination of migrations, some are not prepared to ensure in their territory the protection they claim for their migrants abroad. The lack of adherence by destination countries is motivated by the futility of the Convention, as it does not improve on the standards they are already providing. However, futile or not, the Convention is also not dangerous, and the lack of ratification cannot thereby be explained.

NGOs and migrant associations have become particularly active in the 1990s, and ratification of the Convention has proven a fertile ground for various initiatives. An International Migrants Rights Watch Committee was established during the United Nations International Conference on Population and Development (ICPD) held in Cairo in 1994. The Committee was behind the harnessing of some international organizations, such as the ILO, the IOM, the International Catholic Migration Commission (ICMC), Human Rights Watch (HRW) and the International Confederation of Free Trade Unions (ICFTU), to convene a steering committee to launch a global campaign for ratification of the Convention. In Manila in 1997, 18 December was designated as International Migrants Day, and the idea was later taken into the UN system, where the Mexican delegation in Geneva proposed a resolution from the UN CHR, until the General Assembly officially proclaimed it in 2000.[21] It is difficult to evaluate the effectiveness of civil society in harnessing governments towards ratification.[22] After all, NGOs for migrants and migrants' associations are not well known for their cohesiveness or their organization, but they are persistent and vocal. To the extent that migration is a sensitive issue in a country of origin, with the possibility that ensuring migrant protection through a treaty might be high-profile yet low in cost, NGO pressure can be quite effective. This might explain the lack of success of civil society in achieving the same result in countries of destination.

The third relevant factor for the entry into force of the Convention was the slow but constant functioning of the UN system. In fact, every year the General Assembly in New York and the Committee on Human

---

[21] UN General Assembly Resolution 55/95 of 4 December 2000.
[22] Among other initiatives, NGOs have publicized the text of the ICRMW with a view to educating those who can utilise it. See for example ICMC (2006).

Rights in Geneva have adopted resolutions inviting Member States to ratify the Convention. Admittedly, this is routine, with a language that only slightly changes the content of previous resolutions, but it keeps the issue alive. The recommendation to ratify the Convention was also included in the final documents of the various international conferences organized in the 1990s. Among the UN initiatives, special mention should be paid to the institution in 1997 of a group of five experts to gather information on the obstacles to the protection of the human rights of migrants (Bustamante, 2002). The group made the recommendation to establish a Special Rapporteur on the Human Rights of Migrants. The CHR accepted that recommendation,[23] and in August 1999 named the first Special Rapporteur, Gabriela Rodríguez Pizarro of Costa Rica.

Some additional reflection on motivations for not ratifying the Convention[24] helps to explain the lengthy period between adoption and entry into force. A first set of motivations rests with the little enthusiasm for the Convention expressed by various governments before the process started. We have already referred to the countries that did not support the 1979 resolution establishing the working group for the draft Convention, and they comprised most of the traditional destination countries. Two objections were commonly expressed: (i) that if a new Convention was to be drafted, it was to be done by the ILO, the agency competent on migrant workers and equipped with a more efficient supervisory mechanism than the one adopted by UN conventions; and (ii) that destination countries already had in place a protection mechanism or that labour migration was not a specific concern. The latter objection was particularly expressed by the United States, Canada, Australia and New Zealand, the countries with a prevalent settlement migration system, who repeatedly declared that the Convention was not applicable to immigrants. The fact that those same countries took an active role in the drafting process should not be construed as a change of position on adherence to the Convention. The active role was to ensure that the text of the Convention was acceptable in principle to their governments. Events following the adoption of the Convention have not gone in the direction of greater support for it. If anything, support for multilateralism has diminished rather than improved in recent years.

---

[23] CHR Resolution 1999/44 of 27 April 1999.
[24] For a wide-ranging discussion of obstacles to ratification of the ICRMW, see Pécoud and de Guchteneire (2006).

A second set of motivations for not ratifying the Convention concerns the humanitarian principles it contains. As is well known, the third part of the Convention brings together the human rights of migrants, applicable to all, including migrants in an irregular situation. An objection from a technical point of view was raised concerning the possible differences of principles contained in different humanitarian instruments. In case of conflict, which version should prevail? The working group was aware of such an objection and in most cases the text was lifted verbatim from the ICCPR. When changes were made, the general principle stands that the most favourable provision prevails. Therefore, this technical issue did not have an impact on deterring countries from ratifying the Convention. At the same time, as the Convention includes the human rights contained in the covenants, it seems obvious that those countries that have yet to ratify the covenants will find it hard to ratify this Convention.

Other reasons for avoiding ratification are concerns that do not have rational grounds but are based on perceptions of the management of migration. Chief among them is the fear that ratifying the Convention would limit the right of a state to sovereign decisions in admission policies. Article 79 of the Convention reaffirms such a right, but adherence to an international instrument is considered a partial loss of sovereignty, something that many governments are unwilling to do when it comes to migration policies. Proof of this reluctance is given by the refusal of governments to organize an international conference on migration. Considered in General Assembly Resolution 49/127 of 19 December 1994, the Secretariat made three attempts to elicit responses from governments, in 1995, 1997 and 1999. Nevertheless, 110 governments never replied. Of the seventy-eight who did, forty-seven were in favour of an international conference on migration, five indicated partial support, while twenty-six expressed reservations.[25] Thus the idea was abandoned. In its place, a technical symposium on migration and development was convened in The Hague in 1998, but it was not the same thing. Only in September 2006 did countries accept to discuss international migration at a high-profile multilateral event, when the HLO took place in New York. A large number of delegates (140) participated in the two-day event, which did not conclude with an official action plan as in previous international conferences, and where the only relevant decision was to accept the Secretary-General's proposal of establishing a Global

[25] Report A/56/167 of 3 July 2001, paragraph 9.

Forum on Migration and Development, as an opportunity for informal, voluntary, consultative discussion.

Among the most circulated objections to ratification of the Convention is the excessive protection it provides to irregular migrants. We have already indicated how baseless such consideration is. If anything, experts have indicated a key weakness of the effectiveness of the Convention in the inherent difficulty that irregular migrants have in making use of it for fear of being repatriated (Bosniak, 1991, p. 760). An additional criticism of the Convention concerns the uneven responsibility to combat irregular migration that it would impose. Such responsibility would fall mostly on countries of destination (Ahmed, 2000), causing an unfair sharing of the burden. In fact, on the employment of irregular migrants and the sanctions to be imposed on employers who hire them, the Convention mentions only countries of destination (article 68(2)), but this appears logical, as migrants are employed in destination countries. In all other cases, the responsibility to combat irregular migration is given to countries of origin, destination and transit. Nevertheless, destination countries retain the impression that the Convention originated from countries of origin interested in ensuring that irregular migration would not be harshly stamped out.

What prospects for the Convention?

Previous analysis has cast a long shadow on the effectiveness of the Convention as an instrument for the protection of migrants. To be effective, two factors are primarily crucial: ratification by countries of destination and a sufficient number of ratifications to reach the critical mass that would make it easier for other countries to join (Pécoud and de Guchteneire, 2006). We say primarily because the Convention is also to be applied in countries of origin, where countless irregularities are committed against migrants.

Prospects regarding adhesion by destination countries are not very encouraging. It is difficult to see a change of policy among countries that always maintained a critical approach to the Convention. Of the eighteen countries that abstained in General Assembly Resolution 34/172, only Guatemala has modified its position and ratified the Convention. Of course, the situation of Guatemala as a transit country for migration towards 'the north' is greatly different to what it was in 1979. For the other countries, although migration has become an even more sensitive issue than when the drafting process started, the direction on how to face mounting migration pressure is with harsher control measures, at least judging from recent policy discussion and decisions in the United States and Europe.[26]

Countries that did not oppose the Convention and who were even very active in the drafting of the text, such as those of southern Europe, may present a better prospect. Unfortunately, these countries have become, at least in public opinion, the primary gateway for smuggling and trafficking of migrants. In reality, most irregular migration does not consist of irregular entries but of overstayers. Taking the case of Italy, for example, overstayers count for 75% of irregular migrants, while 15% enter through Schengen borders and only 10% are boat people arriving from Africa (Caritas/Migrantes, 2005, p. 121). Nevertheless, it is those 10% that capture the public imagination and dictate the tone of migration policies.

A possible way to crack the current indifference of European countries to the Convention (currently, only Albania and Bosnia and Herzegovina have ratified it) could theoretically come from countries in eastern Europe that have become an important origin for immigration, particularly to Germany, Italy and Spain. However, studies have already indicated the serious difficulties that exist in the region for ratifying this instrument, including unwillingness to be the first to do so and lack of financial support to implement the measures (Zayonchkovskaya, 2004). Pressure can also be exercised through representatives in the European Parliament. In fact, a resolution adopted on 7 February 2002 included a recommendation for EU countries to ratify the ICRMW. A separate evaluation should be made of the possible 'herding' effect that EU membership has on avoiding ratification by individual countries. It should not be very significant, as individual countries continue to establish separate policies. At the same time, the intention to move towards greater harmonization has normally produced among EU Member States the result of aligning on the most restrictive position, which in this case is not to ratify the Convention.

Considering that ratifications are not to be expected in North America and are very doubtful in western Europe, attention has to turn to other regions. In Africa, ratification by Mediterranean countries such as Algeria, Egypt, the Libyan Arab Jamahiriya and Morocco

---

[26] See the discussion on the so-called Sensenbrenner law in the United States and the adoption, although softened by the Sénat, of restrictive measures in the Sarkozy Bill in France.

is important, also for the role they play as transit countries for migrants from sub-Saharan Africa. One important absentee is Tunisia. However, as most North African countries are parties to the Convention, it would be in the best interest of Mediterranean countries in Europe to be part of the same treaty. More cooperation could be established in combating irregular migration in the region, as recommended in article 68 of the Convention. As for sub-Saharan Africa, the best hope might come from West Africa, where eight countries have already ratified the Convention, although Nigeria, the most populous country in Africa, is still missing and does not intend to join the group very soon (Adedokun, 2003).

Prospects for ratification in Asia are no rosier. In a continent characterized by important migration flows in the several sub-systems,[27] most migration is organized as a circular phenomenon of contract workers. Acquisition of rights relating to settlement and integration is practically impossible for labour migrants, and strict emphasis on the economic component relegates the role of the state as supporter of the labour market dominated by employers, recruiters and brokers. If anything, Asia is the region in greatest need of an instrument like the Convention, yet only seven Asian countries have ratified it, and only two are important migration countries (the Philippines and Sri Lanka). Several aspects militate against an expansion of ratifications, including the weak tradition in Asia for ratifying human rights treaties; the fear by countries of origin that ratifying the Convention might lead to loss of competition in the regional labour market; and the fear by destination countries that major changes would have to be undertaken in national migration policy (Piper and Iredale, 2003).

The most interesting geographical area for the implementation of the Convention is Latin America, where thirteen of twenty-two countries have ratified it. Admittedly, some major ones such as Brazil and Venezuela have not yet joined, but ratification by Argentina could have an impact on the undecided countries, and the region already has an important coverage. It may be said that the Convention has already played some role in the revision of national migration legislation, and how it influences regional cooperation should be monitored.

---

[27] Estimates put the number of foreign workers in East and South-East Asia at 6.7 million in 2004 (see Skeldon, 2006, p. 279).

Conclusion

The three phases of the Convention's history have illustrated that it was born to react to the stratification of migrants' rights, in view of ensuring universal protection for all, including irregular migrants, but it has experienced the progressive waning of enthusiasm. Inevitably, enjoyment of rights is proportional to the level of membership, and therefore to stability and duties. Consequently, the Convention is even structured in such a way as to consider only the human rights as universal, while other entitlements are specific to migrants in a regular situation or to specific categories of migrants. Nevertheless, the impression is that even the duty to respect human rights is questioned when it comes to irregular migrants and, although the rate of ratification since 2003 has been more encouraging, the impact of the Convention remains only minimal.

There are at least three reasons for accepting limited expectations of the Convention. The first is related to the tiredness of human rights discourse. After the debate generated by the 1993 Vienna World Conference on Human Rights, the topic has almost disappeared from the international agenda. Western countries are no longer using human rights in international negotiations, as if everyone has accepted the ineffectiveness of such recourse. And countries that protested against the insertion of the human rights clause, such as China, have acquired such economic and political might that they no longer fear it. On the other hand, even the discussion on universality and indivisibility of rights is fading, as it mainly served to reject the human rights clause rather than to pursue an original, non-Western charter of human rights.

A second reason derives from multilateralism fatigue. The little power that the UN ever had has been further weakened by its incapacity to handle crisis situations, and powerful nations no longer feel the need to secure UN consensus before taking international initiatives. The tiredness of multilateralism was accepted also at the 2004 International Labour Conference (ILC), where a multilateral framework for migration was accepted only because it was non-binding. The most encouraging example of multilateralism, the EU, has also received a serious blow with the non-ratification of the EU Constitution by France and the Netherlands, halting a process that was to be completed in October 2006.

But the most important aspect seems inherent in the nature of migration. It appears that migrants are in demand not simply because they supply scarce workforce in economies with a demographic deficit, but because they add flexibility to the system. Unfortunately, flexibility derives from a protection deficit. Increasing protection is perceived as losing competitiveness in the international labour market. It is the sad experience of countries of origin that they rarely fail to agree in winning common conditions for migrants from destination countries. Until the number of migrants (and their negotiators – governments, recruiters and brokers) willing to accept inferior conditions remains larger than the demand for workers, it will be difficult to bring governments and employers to the Convention table.

Facing the impossibility of reaching important results, governments have scaled down their goals and have begun discussions at a lower level, in so-called regional processes. It is difficult to assess the impact of such processes, which at least keep alive the idea of a multilateral approach to migration. But they should not be considered as an alternative to ratifying the Convention.

Together with cautious expectations, there are also signs of hope for increasing relevance and membership of the CMW. The first of such signs is the international community's insistence on the need for migration policies to be based on human rights. This is clearly expressed in the conclusions of the 2004 ILC, in the 2004 International Agenda for Migration Management established by the Berne Initiative and in the 2005 Principles for Action and Recommendations of the Global Commission on International Migration. The latter received a mandate from Kofi Annan to provide policy makers with a 'strong ethical compass' and to help to 'win broad acceptance for a normative framework that has human rights at its heart' (Grant, 2006, p. 15).

A second sign is that protection is not considered detrimental to development. This issue is somehow controversial, as economists tend to frame the discussion with the dilemma 'numbers vs rights', implying that if policies ensure extensive rights, the number of migrants that can be admitted will necessarily be small; and vice versa, if the objective is to ensure a large intake of migrants, protection has to be kept at a lower level. However, it is important that others do not consider protection and development negatively correlated, as it emerges in the UN Secretary-General's report, *International Migration and Development*: 'When there is a legitimate need for workers, providing a legal avenue for their employment and ensuring that their labour rights are protected produces the best results for all.'[28]

---

[28] UN Doc. A/60/871 of 18 May 2006 at 262.

Still missing is articulation of the importance of the linkage between rights-based policies and ratification of the ICRMW. For this to happen, it is necessary to go beyond the declaratory stage into the organizational one. Perhaps the creation of the Global Migration Group[29] might help in that direction. But civil society has to remain vigilant and active because rights are not recognized without claiming them.

References

Adedokun, O. A. 2003. *The Rights of Migrant Workers and Members of Their Families: Nigeria*. Paris, UNESCO. (Country Reports on the Ratification of the UN Convention on Migrants.)

Ahmed, S. R. 2000. *Forlorn Migrants. An International Legal Regime for Undocumented Migrant Workers*. Dhaka, Universal Press Limited.

Battistella, G. (ed.). 2004. *Migrazioni e diritti umani*. Rome, Urbaniana University Press.

Bertinetto, G. 1983. International regulations on illegal migration. *International Migration*, Vol. 21, No. 2, pp. 189–203.

Böhning, R. 1991. The ILO and the new UN Convention on migrant workers: the past and future. *International Migration Review*, Vol. 25, No. 4, pp. 698–709.

Bosniak, L. S. 1991. Human rights, state sovereignty and the protection of undocumented migrants under the International Migrant Workers Convention. *International Migration Review*, Vol. 25, No. 4, pp. 737–70.

Bustamante, J. A. 2002. Immigrants' vulnerability as subjects of human rights. *International Migration Review*, Vol. 36, No. 2, pp. 333–54.

Caritas/Migrantes. 2005. *Immigrazione. Dossier Statistico 2005. XV Rapporto sull'immigrazione*. Rome, Idos.

Grant, S. 2006. GCIM report: defining an 'ethical compass' for international migration policy. *International Migration*, Vol. 44, No. 1, pp. 13–19.

Haseneau, M. 1990. Setting norms in the United Nations system: the International Convention on the Protection of the Rights of All Migrant Workers and Their Families. *International Migration*, Vol. 28, No. 2, pp. 133–58.

—— 1991. ILO standards on migrant workers: the fundamentals of the UN Convention and their genesis. *International Migration Review*, Vol. 25, No. 4, pp. 687–97.

[29] The group, which grew out of the Geneva Migration Group, held its first meeting on 9 May 2006. It includes the ILO, IOM, United Nations Conference on Trade and Development (UNCTAD), United Nations High Commissioner for Refugees (UNHCR), UNODC, United Nations – Department of Economic and Social Affairs (UN-DESA), UNDP, UNESCO, United Nations Population Fund (UNFPA), United Nations Children's Fund (UNICEF), United Nations Institute for Training and Research (UNITAR), UN Regional Commissions and the World Bank.

ILC. 1980. *Migrant Workers. General Survey by the Committee of Experts on the Application of Conventions and Recommendations.* Geneva, Switzerland, ILO.

Lönnroth, J. 1991. The International Convention on the Rights of All Migrant Workers and Members of Their Families in the context of international migration policies: an analysis of ten years of negotiation. *International Migration Review*, Vol. 25, No. 4, pp. 710–36.

Pécoud, A. and de Guchteneire, P. 2006. Migration, human rights and the United Nations. An investigation into the obstacles to the UN Convention on Migrant Workers' Rights. *Windsor Yearbook of Access to Justice*, Vol. 24, No. 2, pp. 241–66.

Piper, N. and Iredale, R. 2003. *Identification of the Obstacles to the Signing and Ratification of the UN Convention on the Protection of the Rights of All Migrant Workers – The Asia-Pacific Perspective.* Paris, UNESCO. (Country Reports on the Ratification of the UN Convention on Migrants.)

Skeldon, R. 2006. Recent trends in migration in East and Southeast Asia. *Asian and Pacific Migration Journal*, Vol. 15, No. 2, pp. 277–93.

Zayonchkovskaya, Z. H. A. 2004. *The Protection of the Rights of Migrant Workers in the Countries of Central and Eastern Europe and the CIS and Perspectives of Joining the 1990 UN Convention.* Paris, UNESCO. (Country Reports on the Ratification of the UN Convention on Migrants.)

3

Role of civil society in campaigning for and using the ICRMW

MARIETTE GRANGE AND MARIE D'AUCHAMP

Introduction

This chapter traces the history and level of NGO and civil society involvement at various key stages in the life of the ICRMW. It studies how, and how effectively, civil society has campaigned for ratification of the Convention and used it as an advocacy tool.

The engagement of NGOs with the Convention has been uneven. Compared with civil society engagement in the development of other key international human rights instruments, its participation in the drafting was minimal, mainly due to the political context and the stage in the evolution of the human rights movement. Nevertheless, there was civil society involvement directly after the adoption of the Convention, including that of some international NGOs, among which were faith-based and women's organizations, as well as trade unions and a number of national and regional NGOs in many regions, primarily in Asia (see Chapter 7). Since the early to mid 1990s, a small-scale but steadily growing group of NGOs has mobilized awareness-raising initiatives and a global ratification campaign. There have been calls for ratification in all regions, and sustained NGO advocacy for the human rights of migrants and towards ratification exist in some thirty countries in Asia, Europe, Latin America, the Middle East and North America, and to a lesser extent in Africa.[1]

The following sections analyse NGO involvement in standard-setting, including the specific context for the drafting and adoption of the ICRMW; review related NGO activities in the period from adoption to entry into force; highlight ongoing NGO ratification campaigns; and detail NGO monitoring of the implementation of the Convention as

[1] National NGO campaigns in favour of the ICRMW may be found on the portal for the Protection of the Rights of Migrants (www.december18.net [last accessed 14 April 2009]).

well as related documenting of violations of the human rights of migrant workers and members of their families. This analysis takes as a constraining backdrop the inherent challenges that arise from the low ratification record of the Convention and the distinct features of contemporary migration-management policies and practices.

NGOs and standard-setting: challenges specific to the ICRMW

The active participation of NGOs in the preparatory work and drafting of a number of core international human rights instruments is well documented. As early as 1947 and 1948, some thirty NGOs participated in the drafting of the Universal Declaration of Human Rights, including trade unions and religious and women's organizations (Nchama, 1991). A number of NGOs presented well-argued input at the Conference of Plenipotentiaries drafting the Convention relating to the Status of Refugees in 1951.[2] In the years leading up to the adoption of the International Convention on the Elimination of All Forms of Racial Discrimination, NGOs held two well-attended international conferences on the issue of racial discrimination in Geneva. Likewise, the women's movement was mobilized for the drafting of the Convention on the Elimination of all Forms of Discrimination against Women, adopted in 1979.

A worldwide Amnesty International landmark campaign on torture, launched in 1973, largely acted as a catalyst for the drafting of the Convention against Torture and Other Cruel, Inhuman or Degrading Treatment or Punishment, adopted in 1984. An Informal Ad Hoc NGO Group for the Drafting of the Convention on the Rights of the Child, supported by UNICEF, was formed in 1983 to provide joint and targeted input during the drafting. More recently, global NGO coalitions such as the International Campaign to Ban Landmines (ICBL) and the Coalition for the International Criminal Court (CICC) actively participated in the respective drafting of the 1997 Convention on the Prohibition of the Use, Stockpiling, Production and Transfer of Anti-Personnel Mines and on Their Destruction (Ottawa Treaty) and the Rome Statute of the International Criminal Court.

A glaring omission in this impressive array of NGO engagement and mobilization is the ICRMW. Only a handful of mostly faith-based

---

[2] See Conference of Plenipotentiaries on the Status of Refugees and Stateless Persons: Summary Record of the First to Thirty-Fifth Meetings, A/CONF.2/SR.1 to A/CONF.2/SR.35.

organizations were involved in the drafting. These were the same organizations that took the lead in raising awareness soon after the adoption
of the Convention, in addition to other NGOs from Asia. Even if both
groups of NGOs were to lay the first building blocks for a worldwide
awareness-raising and ratification campaign, why were the main international human rights NGOs largely absent from the ICRMW drafting
process?

Over 3,000 NGOs currently hold ECOSOC consultative status,
enabling them to formally participate in a number of UN activities. In
1980, when the decade-long drafting of the ICRMW began, NGOs
holding ECOSOC status numbered barely 300. Very few of these were
human rights organizations.[3] Even fewer were directly engaged in issues
relating to migrant workers. The 1970s were pioneering years for international human rights NGOs. Although adopted in 1966, the two international covenants on civil and political rights and on economic, social
and cultural rights only came into force in 1976. During that period, and
the decade when the ICRMW was drafted, existing international human
rights NGOs were mainly focused on civil and political rights or on
combating apartheid. This reflects the Cold War dynamics that gave
prominence to these issues over economic, social and cultural rights or
other 'soft rights' issues such as those of migrant workers.

At the time, the only people on the move who received international
attention and protection were refugees – and even then protection was
seen as humanitarian in character rather than as a human right. Human
rights NGOs concentrated their efforts on denouncing violations of the
human rights of nationals against the exactions of dictators and other
abusive governments, and laying the foundations for effective implementation of international human rights obligations. In contrast, the emergence of migrant-focused NGOs is a much more recent development.
Organizations such as Migrants Rights International and Migrant
Forum in Asia (MFA) only obtained ECOSOC consultative status as
recently as 2001 and 2002 respectively. The absence of such NGOs from
the international policy and advocacy stage during the drafting of the
ICRMW partly resulted from the lack of funding necessary for the mobilization of a migrants' rights movement to coalesce at the international
level. Existing institutional donors have proved very reluctant to fund
migrants' rights activities, in particular advocacy programmes.

---

[3] See list of NGOs in consultative status at the UN Economic and Social Council website
(www.un.org/esa/coordination/ngo/ [last accessed 14 April 2009]).

Lack of NGO involvement in the drafting was not only related to the issue and the overall context (see Chapter 2 for details of the drafting process). Involvement was also hindered by the location of drafting meetings, which took place in New York rather than Geneva. Not only were the rights of migrants – and related economic, social and cultural rights – not an advocacy issue (let alone a priority) for developing and under-resourced human rights NGOs in the 1980s, but the geographical distance created by locating the drafting working group in New York is also likely to have diminished chances for strong civil society involvement. Given that Geneva was the headquarters of the then Centre for Human Rights, which serviced the then CHR and treaty monitoring bodies, existing international NGOs monitoring human rights issues would have been more likely to be alerted to migrants' rights issues and therefore participate in standard-setting.

Possibilities for national or regional NGO participation were even more limited. It was not until the mid 1990s that they became eligible to apply for ECOSOC consultative status.[4] Thus they were automatically disqualified from participation in drafting processes. Furthermore, there was little pressure from civil society at national and regional levels. The countries that were the main supporters of initial studies into the need for a migrant workers' convention (including Algeria, Egypt, Mexico and Morocco) did not have vibrant civil societies at the time. Likewise, civil societies in the group of countries that took the lead in providing one of the initial drafts of the ICRMW, the so-called MESCA group,[5] were either non-existent, weak or did not identify the normative gaps that existed for the protection of migrants as one of their priorities.

Finally, no voluntary NGO support fund was ever established, which could have supported and facilitated the participation of migrant associations in the drafting processes. Such funds have at times been instrumental in enabling civil societies to engage in relevant UN activities and processes. Several examples are illustrative. A United Nations Voluntary Fund on Disability Activities was launched in preparation for the 1981 International Year of Disabled Persons. In 2002, a sub-account of the Voluntary Fund was set up to receive contributions for the participation of NGOs and other experts from developing countries in the work of the drafting Committee for the International Convention on the Rights of

---

[4] ECOSOC Resolution 1996/31 opened access to national and regional NGOs.
[5] Mediterranean and Scandinavian countries, including Finland, Greece, Italy, Portugal, Spain and Sweden, later joined by Norway.

People with Disabilities. In 1995, the General Assembly established a Voluntary Fund for Indigenous Populations, to assist representatives of indigenous communities to attend meetings of the working group to draft the Declaration on the Rights of Indigenous Peoples.

From adoption to entry into force

Despite these initial challenges, a civil society movement in defence of migrants' rights developed throughout the 1990s. Indeed, during the thirteen-year period from adoption to entry into force (1990–2003), NGOs can largely be credited for raising the visibility of the ICRMW. They had to overcome a number of obstacles, including the reluctance of many governments in various parts of the world to ratify the Convention (as Part II of this volume makes clear). These particular circumstances have led NGOs to raise migrants' rights issues in various fora, such as the UN CHR and international conferences and summits, often using the provisions of the ICRMW as a reference and awareness-raising tool. Throughout this period, civil society managed to lay the basis for a global ratification campaign that keeps growing.

Obstacles to strong NGO involvement: specific circumstances of NGO support for ratification

The lack of strong involvement of civil society in the ICRMW drafting process left scars for many years after adoption of the Convention. Historically, ratification drives by civil society have been more forceful when rooted in a high level of activism before or at the drafting stage of a given treaty. For example, after the adoption of the Convention against Torture in 1984, Amnesty International and other NGOs launched a second major campaign that hastened ratification. Likewise, as soon as the CRC had been adopted by the UN General Assembly, the Informal Ad Hoc NGO Group for the Drafting of the CRC decided to continue working as a group focusing on its monitoring and implementation and adopted its current name, the NGO Group for the Convention on the Rights of the Child. By comparison, the lack of possibilities for NGO involvement in the drafting of the ICRMW meant that this was unlikely to happen around migrants' rights. As a consequence, prospects were initially limited for the ICRMW to acquire a strong profile through NGO advocacy work.

NGO advocacy on the need to define the human rights protection framework applicable to migrant workers and members of their families and the pivotal role of the ICRMW has been to a considerable extent hampered by a lack of recognition and support for the Convention by leading migrant-receiving countries in the industrialized world. This is in stark contrast to the traditional stance these countries have taken in support of other core human rights treaties. The demonstrable lack of political will to ratify the Convention within Western countries has been a major hurdle and remains an important paradox.[6] NGOs thus found themselves without the allies on whom they could usually count to champion ratification efforts. Progress has also been constrained by low-level engagement of many grass-roots migrants' associations in the early stages of development of the Convention. Although their primary interest was with the situation of migrant workers and their families, these associations, which provide services and advocacy on the ground, were initially unfamiliar with international human rights standards and how they can be used to protect their constituencies.

NGO advocates have had to grapple with the challenge presented by the high number of governments unwilling to ratify the ICRMW. These governments often argue that the mere fact that the drafting took ten years demonstrates how divisive the issue is. However, lengthy drafting processes have been the hallmark of cardinal human rights treaties. The genesis of the International Bill of Human Rights is particularly salient in this respect. Indeed, 'on the same day that it adopted the Universal Declaration [10 December 1948], the General Assembly requested the CHR to prepare, as a matter of priority, a draft covenant on human rights' (OHCHR, 1996a). The Commission examined the text of the draft covenant in 1949. The General Assembly subsequently decided that the drafting should include two instruments dealing with economic, social and cultural rights on the one hand, and civil and political rights on the other. The exercise continued throughout the 1950s and it was not until 1966 that the preparation of the two covenants was completed. Both the ICCPR and ICESCR entered into force ten years later, in 1976. Yet, while a seventeen-year drafting exercise unquestionably reflects the difficulty in reaching consensus on the terms of many human rights provisions during the ideological stand-off that characterized the Cold War, one

---

[6] This is especially paradoxical given that the ICRMW mainly integrates relevant provisions codified in pre-existing international human rights treaties ratified by Western countries. See International Migration Review (1991) and Cholewinski (1997). For an analysis of its links to the other six core human rights treaties, see Grange (2006) and Chapter 5 of this volume.

rarely comes across the argument that this lengthy drafting period has delegitimized the provisions and thrust of the two final documents.

The uneven progression of civil society in using the ICRMW reflects to a large extent its idiosyncratic drafting history. Although endeavouring to strengthen the international protection framework applicable to migrant workers, protecting the rights of non-citizens remains a complex political challenge. This paradox reflects the imperative of migrant work for both sending and receiving countries as well as a deeply ingrained reluctance to enshrine the rights of non-citizens. While the Convention Relating to the Status of Refugees was adopted more than fifty years ago, the protection needs of migrant workers and members of their families, beyond a number of labour-related rights,[7] was only crystallized in 1990. Since then, many governments and a variety of stakeholders have long entertained mythologies as well as an arguably wilful ignorance about the nature and scope of provisions in the ICRMW. As a consequence, one of the most challenging obstacles to raising awareness about the human rights of migrant workers and members of their families has been persistent invisibility. Graziano Battistella, who participated as an expert in the drafting of the ICRMW, once called it the 'best-kept secret of the United Nations'.[8]

The power of myth and ignorance has been reinforced by the lack of UN publications and educational material on the Convention. After its adoption by the General Assembly on 18 December 1990, there was little official publicity. It took six years for the first UN booklet reproducing the text of the Convention to be published (OHCHR, 1996b). No other UN agency campaigned for ratification in the early to late 1990s, which contrasts with UNICEF putting its full weight behind support of the CRC, which won scores of ratifications in record time. Ever since the ICRMW came into force in mid 2003, it has received little attention. A case in point is the UNDP *Human Development Report 2007/2008*,

---

[7] 1939 Convention No. 66 (Convention concerning Migration for Employment) (withdrawn) (not ratified by any country), 1949 Convention No. 97 (Convention concerning Migration for Employment Convention (Revised)) (ratified by forty-nine countries) and 1975 Convention No. 143 (Migrant Workers (Supplementary Provisions)) (ratified by twenty-three countries).

[8] Oral statement at the founding meeting of the International Migrants Rights Watch Committee (IMRWC), during the UN International Conference on Population and Development, Cairo, 1994 (see also Battistella's account of the history of the ICRMW in Chapter 2).

which fails to list the Convention in its indicator tables listing the 'major international human rights instruments' (UNDP, 2007, pp. 347–50).

Understandably, in a context where the UN could not harness resources to publicize the adoption of its most recent core human rights treaty, and in an environment where the mainstream NGOs have been slow to come on board, NGO advocacy for the human rights of migrant workers has been a very lonely exercise. With neither UN institutional nor broad-based governmental support (beyond the usual supporters, including Mexico and the Philippines) to echo or complement NGO campaigns, it has been extremely hard for civil society efforts to be relayed effectively in influential media and pivotal decision-making fora.

It is worth recalling that, from the outset, there were strong odds against a prompt entry into force. During the deliberations of the UN drafting working group, Australia, Germany, the Gulf States, Japan and the United States indicated that they were unlikely to ratify (Cholewinski, 1997, p. 203). Western European states with strong emigration rates, such as Portugal and other Mediterranean countries, toyed with the idea of ratification for a while. Italy repeatedly flirted with the possibility of ratification but rapid governmental turnover upset parliamentary initiatives to consider it. However, as these countries were sufficiently absorbed into the EU orbit, peer pressure eventually prevailed, and any serious attempt to consider ratification was defeated.[9] The first country to ratify the ICRMW was Egypt in 1993, followed by Morocco in the same year. Ratification proceeded slowly: it took thirteen years to get the requisite twenty States Parties, which triggered the Convention's entry into force in July 2003.

In the face of these obstacles, NGOs, especially those with an operational arm, remained convinced that they needed legal tools to combat specific discrimination and abuse suffered by migrants on account of their particular vulnerabilities. For NGOs, the codification of the ICRMW's provisions into national legislation is the best way to firmly root a rights-based approach to migrant workers and to specifically protect them and members of their families. Over 130 governments have ratified all six other core human rights treaties, yet few actually

---

[9] A number of European institutions have encouraged ratification by EU Member States; see Opinion of the European Economic and Social Committee on the 2004 UN Convention on the Protection of the Rights of All Migrant Workers and Members of Their Families and the European Parliament resolutions on EU rights, priorities and recommendation for the UN Commission on Human Rights for 2002 to 2005. See also Chapter 15 of this volume.

include information on implementation of these treaties to protect the human rights of migrant workers in their reports to relevant UN treaty monitoring bodies (see Chapter 5).[10]

Governments often object to provisions in the ICRMW aimed at protecting undocumented migrants. Yet these largely draw on existing non-discrimination clauses in the other core human rights treaties, which afford minimum protection to all persons, for example access to emergency medical care. Some governments from the North also inaccurately claim that the Convention contains a *right* to family reunification. It remains that many legally resident migrant workers whose labour and social rights are routinely violated in many countries would be protected from exploitative employers and from state discrimination in payment of legally earned retirement rights, for example, through national implementation of the ICRMW. With this Convention, the civil society actors working to defend the rights of migrant workers could build their advocacy on the legal tools offered by the UN set of established international standards.

NGOs have argued that the lack of ratification of the ICRMW by Western states has been instrumental in the perception of double standards when it comes to human rights issues. Negative references to immigration-related issues and the portrayal of immigrants as scapegoats for all sorts of societal ills are increasingly found in election campaigns in many European countries. This has led some decision-makers to fear that any public stance for the protection of migrants could backfire and disqualify them from winning seats in government. This reluctance to ratify the single, core human rights treaty perceived by Western states as imposing a broad implementation framework in their societies is challenged by states in the South. There is a strong paradox in that states with often brittle democracy and weak rule of law are under pressure from the North to ratify the ICCPR, CAT and CEDAW. Many NGOs have argued that this imbalanced attitude has been instrumental in bringing discredit to the system of human rights norms and standards and its perception as a Western concept.[11]

---

[10] There are eight human-rights treaty bodies that monitor implementation of the core treaties: the CAT; the Human Rights Committee (CCPR); the CEDAW; the Committee on the Elimination of Racial Discrimination (CERD); the Committee on Economic, Social and Cultural Rights (CESCR); the CMW; the CRC; and the Committee on the Rights of Persons with Disabilities.

[11] World Council of Churches, oral statement to the Commission on Human Rights at various sessions in the mid 1990s.

Before the ICRMW entered into force, and in an effort to compensate for the absence of a UN strategy for its promotion, NGOs, trade unions, church groups, women's and migrant organizations joined forces to promote the ICRMW and advocate for its ratification during the thirteen years from adoption to entry into force. Advocacy for the Convention developed particularly in Asia. One of the reasons for this strong interest is the absence of any regional human rights mechanism and the limited ratification by Asian states of the other core human rights instruments as well as the ILO conventions. Combined with the vast numbers of migrant workers from and within the region, this provided a strong impetus for advocacy of the ICRMW by MFA, among others.

NGOs and the CHR and its Special Rapporteur on the Human Rights of Migrants

Civil society rolled out awareness-raising activities on the ICRMW in a whole range of arenas where human rights and migrants' rights could be discussed. The UN CHR was an obvious forum. Over the years, NGOs have lobbied to strengthen the relevant CHR resolutions relating to the human rights of migrants and the ICRMW. Time and again, however, NGO representatives lobbying members of the CHR for support for the traditional Mexican-sponsored resolution on the human rights of migrants have met with sceptical Western delegates. These delegates have sought to deflect attention from their failure to ratify by raising in their defence the paradox of governments that had actively supported the drafting of the treaty subsequently failing to ratify it. A case in point was Mexico, which chaired the drafting working group, and yet only ratified the ICRMW in 1999.

Back in the early 1990s, only a small handful of international NGOs made oral statements under the relevant agenda item.[12] After ECOSOC NGO consultative status was opened up to national and regional NGOs in 1996, an increasing number of civil society representatives spoke on the issue of migrants' rights before the Commission, mostly from Asia but also from North and South America, Europe and the Middle East. NGOs also witnessed a growing participation in the Commission's

---

[12] Including the Commission of the Churches on International Affairs of the World Council of Churches, the International Confederation of Free Trade Unions and the Women's International League for Peace and Freedom.

relevant debates by IGOs in the UN family, including the ILO, UNICEF and UNESCO, and the IOM, a non-UN organization.

A critical turning point for raising awareness on violations of the human rights of migrants was the 1994 Preliminary Report submitted to the CHR by Radhika Coomaraswamy, the Special Rapporteur on Violence against Women, its Causes and Consequences. This report included four pages on violence against women migrants, with an additional section on international instruments, which refers to the 1990 ICRMW.[13] The bulk of information on violations of the human rights of migrant women had been submitted to the Special Rapporteur by international NGOs, in particular HRW/Women's Rights Project and Asia Watch. The report was instrumental in firmly anchoring the issue of the human rights of migrants on the CHR agenda. Thanks to this NGO input, four years before the creation of the Special Rapporteur on the Human Rights of Migrants, violations of their human rights were already being recognized by an existing CHR thematic special procedure, a mechanism charged with engaging in independent inquiry and monitoring.

As a result of the increasing number of states co-sponsoring CHR resolutions on migrants' rights, a working group consisting of five intergovernmental experts was established at the 53rd Session of the CHR, in 1997.[14] The working group was given a mandate to gather all relevant information from governments, NGOs and any other relevant sources on obstacles to the effective and full protection of the human rights of migrants, and to elaborate recommendations to strengthen the promotion, protection and implementation of the human rights of migrants. NGOs welcomed the convening of the Intergovernmental Working Group of Experts on the Human Rights of Migrants (IGWG)[15] and actively participated in its meetings. They recommended that the IGWG 'use the definitions and standards elaborated in the Convention' and advocated that it should 'be given broader authority to create a procedure for addressing specific violations'.[16] The IGWG eventually recommended the creation of the mandate of the Special Rapporteur on

---

[13] UN Doc. E/CN.4/199/42 of 22 November 1994, pp. 53–7.

[14] CHR Resolution 1997/15.

[15] Joint oral statement of the Conference of European Churches, the Lutheran World Federation, the World Alliance of Reformed Churches and the World Council of Churches to the 54th session of the CHR (1998) under Item 11.

[16] Written statement submitted by Human Rights Advocates to the 54th session of the CHR, UN Doc. E/CN.4/1998/NGO/43 of 12 March 1998.

the Human Rights of Migrants, which was established in 1999. Importantly, it was the informal meetings between NGOs and IGOs that took place during meetings of the IGWG that paved the way for the creation of the Steering Committee of the Global Campaign for Ratification of the Convention (see below).

Pending the entry into force of the ICRMW, the Special Rapporteur provided a long-awaited mechanism for giving visibility to – and at times providing remedies for – violations of migrants' human rights. Since the creation of the mandate in 1999, NGOs have been providing the Special Rapporteur with information to assist the mandate's monitoring and reporting role. NGOs actively engaged with the first mandate holder, Gabriela Rodríguez Pizarro, during the six years of her mandate, including during country visits. International NGOs, national and regional civil society organizations (CSOs) contributed a wealth of information on violations of the human rights of migrants, as illustrated in the Special Rapporteur's lengthy yearly reports to the CHR entitled 'Communications sent to governments and replies received'.

However, as long as the ICRMW was not in force, it was obvious that the mandate would rest on shaky foundations. This prompted NGOs to keep their focus on organizing ratification activities. Further, the mandate suffered from recurrent shortcomings of the CHR system of special procedures. The Office of the United Nations High Commissioner for Human Rights (OHCHR), responsible for servicing the special procedures, has been chronically under-resourced since its creation. Specifically, the migrants' rights mandate has suffered from a high turn-over of support staff resulting in repeated loss of institutional expertise in the subject matter. The two mandate-holders appointed so far for this thematic special procedure, Gabriela Rodríguez Pizarro and Jorge A. Bustamante, do not have a legal background. A sociological and health-related approach has initially been instrumental in detailing the mechanisms and consequences of marginalization and discrimination against migrant workers and members of their families. However, NGOs supplying information on human rights violations to special procedures often note firmer recommendations from mandate holders with a strong international human rights-law background.

Just as the ICRMW has been treated as a poor relation in the family of core human rights treaties, the Special Rapporteurship also appears to have been a weak mechanism within the system of CHR special procedures. This has been so despite the fact that NGOs have done their utmost to support and publicize the responsibilities of the mandate. After the departure of the former High Commissioner for Human Rights, Mary Robinson, who was a staunch supporter of the human rights of migrants, the issue lost even more visibility and high-level support for a lengthy period (see below for recent OHCHR developments).

In 2000, the CHR agenda item for the human rights of migrants was expanded to include other sub-items on '[m]inorities, mass exoduses and displaced persons and other vulnerable groups and individuals'. This clustering resulted in substantially diminished speaking time for migrants' rights NGOs. Partly in response to this, NGOs kept submitting information to other relevant special procedures, such as the Working Group on Arbitrary Detention (WGAD), which developed a focus on migrants.[17]

Despite the weaknesses of the CHR mechanism on the human rights of migrants, a survey of complaints (referred within the UN as 'communications'), received by the Special Rapporteur since the creation of the mandate and transmitted to relevant governments, is extremely informative. It is obvious that the ICRMW constitutes a unique tool to report violations in relation to detention, the living and working conditions of domestic migrant workers, in particular when they are in an irregular situation, and violence and racism against irregular migrant workers by state officials. This list is matched by respective provisions in the Convention, such as articles 16(4) to 16(9) against arbitrary detention and article 17 on the conditions of detention; articles 25 and 51 to 55 on just and favourable conditions of work; and articles 8 to 35, which ensure respect of the fundamental rights of irregular migrant workers, and particularly articles 10 and 16(2) on protection from physical violence, including from state officials.

NGOs and world conferences and summits

NGOs have also taken part in world conferences and summits, which are distinctive fora to raise awareness on the rights of migrant workers. These have also served as launching pads for the development of various ratification campaigns at international and regional levels.

The first building block for a global campaign started at the time of the 1994 ICPD in Cairo. Already in 1993, the Vienna Declaration had urged all states to guarantee the protection of the human rights of migrant workers

---

[17] Cf. WGAD Deliberation No. 5 on the situation regarding immigrants and asylum seekers, UN Doc. E/CN.4/2000/4 of 28 December 1999.

and their families.[18] The IMRWC was founded at the ICPD as an international civil society group of experts focused on promotion of the ICRMW and the human rights of migrants. Membership was drawn from religious, human rights, migrant and trade union fields. This alliance was instrumental in creating an international 'caucus' around the theme of migration and migrants' rights. The IMRWC evolved and was later renamed, being known today as Migrants Rights International (MRI).

Throughout the 1990s, a small cross-section of members of the Committee from various world regions, including representatives of both international NGOs and grass-roots migrant organizations in Asia, South America and the United States, participated in a range of relevant conferences. These included, in particular, the 1995 World Summit on Social Development in Copenhagen, the 4th World Conference on Women in Beijing also in 1995, and the 2001 World Conference Against Racism, Racial Discrimination, Xenophobia and Related Intolerance (WCAR) in Durban. NGOs organized seminars, held press briefings and distributed material on the ICRMW at parallel events and actively participated in the drafting of outcome documents. Throughout the cycle of world conferences and summits of the 1990s, a small group of dedicated NGOs were instrumental in introducing references to various aspects of migrants' rights into final documents from these world conferences (MFA, 1995). In the preparatory process for Durban, the migration caucus worked in collaboration with refugee-focused NGOs and covered an impressive breadth and depth of geographical and thematic knowledge and expertise. The caucus held regular meetings, issued joint and targeted input and can take substantial credit for the inclusion of migrants' rights language in over fifty paragraphs in the WCAR Declaration and Programme of Action (see ICMC, 2002; NNIRR, 2002).

World conference declarations, programmes of action, platforms and agendas are adopted by consensus. Although they are non-binding, they often contain action-oriented provisions and policy recommendations as well as a number of objectives and strategic goals. A growing number of NGOs have achieved greater impact thanks to their strategic involvement in international conferences. They have developed broad regional and international networks and are able to monitor implementation, publicize action-oriented recommendations and hold governments accountable following public declarations and commitments issued during these conferences.

---

[18] Vienna Declaration and Programme of Action, 2003, Part II, article 33.

NGOs and the Global Campaign for Ratification

The efforts of international NGOs to promote the human rights of migrants gained new impetus in 1998. The IMRWC convened a Steering Committee composed of CSOs and IGOs to establish the Global Campaign.[19] The Steering Committee published a campaigner's handbook (MRI, 1998) that was considered as one of the first popular materials and guide to promoting the ICRMW (Gencianos, 2004). At the same time, the IMRWC was phased out and replaced by the MRI. The organization is primarily directed at securing membership among national and regional migrant groups. International NGOs serviced and moderated the Steering Committee from its inception until the end of 2003. Greater involvement of representatives of the OHCHR, the ILO, UNESCO, and at a later stage the IOM, in the Steering Committee decidedly raised the visibility of migrants' rights issues within UN agencies and among states.

This innovative hybrid IGO and NGO membership gave the Steering Committee a high profile. The multidisciplinary, cross-institutional and cross-sectoral approach has allowed it to reach out to diverse constituencies. The UN Secretary-General made reference to the Steering Committee activities in his migration reports to the General Assembly. It is also likely that the Steering Committee played a role in the increase of ICRMW ratifications between 1998 and its entry into force in 2003.[20] Despite resource constraints, the Steering Committee organized focused public panels at the CHR and for the entry into force of the Convention, which raised its profile and that of migrants' rights. It also organized panel events at the International Conference of the ILO, the World Congress on Human Movements and Immigration (in Barcelona), the Metropolis Conference and the IOM Council (Gencianos, 2004, p. 149).

The Global Campaign has drawn together a collection of loosely connected initiatives, mainly NGO-driven. These have taken place in different

---

[19] The Steering Committee of the Global Campaign for Ratification of the Convention on Rights of Migrants includes December 18, HRW, the ICMC, the ICFTU, the ILO, the International Movement against All Forms of Discrimination and Racism, the IMO, MFA, MRI, the OHCHR, Public Services International (PSI), UNESCO, Women's International League for Peace and Freedom and the World Council of Churches (WCC).

[20] Only nine states had ratified the ICRMW in the eight years since its adoption by the General Assembly in 1990. Over the five years following the creation of the Steering Committee in 1998, eleven states ratified.

regions, and often at the initiative of unrelated actors. They have also been developed as a result of NGO networks connected through common objectives more than common geographical location. NGO activities reflect a firm collective conviction that the ICRMW offers a much-needed consolidation of relevant international norms, as well as being a good educational tool. The major achievement of the NGO community is the relentless documentation of human rights violations and the dissemination of information on the Convention and the rights it protects.

NGOs have had to make up for inadequacies in other sectors. As mentioned above, it was not until 1996 that the UN first produced a booklet publicizing the content of the Convention. Prior to this, faced with the paucity of user-friendly material, NGOs produced their own material to promote its ratification and implementation. A number of primers, NGO manuals and kits were issued, translated and widely disseminated in the 1990s (CCME/WCC, 1991; MFA, 1994; PSI, 1996; MRI, 1998; Scalabrini Migration Center, 1997; APIM, 1998; Asian Migrant Centre, 2000). Only two booklets were issued by the UN during the thirteen years between adoption of the Convention and its entry into force (OHCHR, 1996b; UNESCO, 2003).

One example of the role NGOs played in the dissemination of information on the ICRMW is the multilingual portal developed by the organization December 18.[21] This site was launched in 1999 to fill a significant information gap in publicly available information on the Convention and migrants' rights more generally. The website was developed over several years and offered a platform to CSOs for the promotion and protection of the human rights of migrant workers. Together with the work of the Steering Committee, the impetus the site gave to the issue of migrants' rights stimulated ratification efforts by civil society from 1999 to 2003, as it filled an information gap on existing UN migrants' rights mechanisms. Today, the site provides comprehensive information on governmental and non-governmental, international and regional instruments, mechanisms, activities and organizations relating to the promotion and protection of the human rights of migrant workers and members of their families.

At the regional level, MFA[22] was formalized in 1994. MFA is a regional network of NGOs, associations and trade unions of migrant workers, and

---

[21] The name refers to 18 December 1990, the date the UN adopted the ICRMW. This date was later proclaimed by the UN as International Migrants Day.
[22] MFA has members in Bangladesh, Burma, Hong Kong, India, Indonesia, Japan, Malaysia, Nepal, the Philippines, Republic of Korea, Singapore, Sri Lanka and Taiwan.

individual advocates in Asia committed to the protection and promotion of the rights and welfare of migrant workers. In addition to monitoring and campaigning activities, MFA has been working with the University of New South Wales (Australia) to provide a training programme each year to local and national-level migrant organizations and associations in Asia. A substantial part of the training is devoted to the ICRMW, as well as ILO conventions, CEDAW and other relevant international treaties.

More recently, www.Choike.org [last accessed 14 April 2009], a portal on Southern civil societies located in Uruguay, has also developed a site providing information on the ICRMW, migration and human rights, more specifically at regional level. Initiatives also exist in other regions, such as the Migration Network of the Lebanese NGO Forum and Foro Migraciones in Mexico. These reflect the development and diversification of civil society initiatives around the Convention since its entry into force.

NGO advocacy activities since entry into force

In recent years, civil society advocacy for ratification has gained depth and momentum. International, national and regional coalitions are all at work. Activities at regional and national levels are further strengthened by substantial engagement for the protection of migrant workers by leading international human rights organizations (including Amnesty International, HRW, the International Federation for Human Rights (FIDH) and Anti-Slavery International), worldwide humanitarian organizations (International Federation of Red Cross and Red Crescent Societies (IFRC)[23]) and civil society movements fighting poverty (including Emmaus International[24] and Caritas Internationalis).

Recent global developments and trends have also prompted a number of civil society representatives to become more vocal in defending the rights of migrants, including increased trafficking in human beings; post-9/11 counter-terrorist measures and their impact on specific groups of migrants; growing disparity in the distribution of wealth in the world; widespread immigration-related detention; regional migration-consultative processes and bilateral and multilateral migration-management measures that focus on border control and readmission agreements. The international

---

[23] 'Red Cross and Red Crescent Societies call for greater ratification of migrant and refugee conventions', press release, IFRC, 25 November 2002.

[24] *Pétition pour les droits des travailleurs migrants*, Emmaus International in coordination with Emmaus France, 30 May 2006.

migration policy discourse has resulted in heightened NGO awareness of the need to monitor and document the vulnerability of migrants to serious human rights abuses and advocate for legal tools that define and protect those rights and to provide effective remedies.

National and regional campaigns

To date, the ICRMW has been ratified by forty-one countries. Most of these are described as 'sending countries', such as Mali, the Philippines and Sri Lanka, or 'transit countries'. However, it should not be overlooked that some States Parties, such as Mexico, Morocco and Turkey, are sending, transit and at times recipient countries. Paradoxically, major countries that view themselves as exclusively 'receiving countries' ignore the Convention: to date, no Western country has signed or ratified it, although many of them have widely signed up to the majority of the other UN human rights treaties. Similarly, the Gulf States, where the percentage of migrant workers in the population is significant, show no interest. Argentina could be viewed as a recent exception, as it is a country with a significant immigration history.

In the current political climate, with migration issues making the daily headlines in most world regions, civil society is stepping up campaign activities for ratification of the ICRMW. In Europe, for example, national ratification campaigns have flourished. Pressuring their governments and their parliaments and attempting to shape public opinion, these campaigns bring together traditional human rights NGOs, trade unions and migrant communities and associations. In Belgium and Spain, for example, provincial campaigns have targeted regional and autonomous parliaments and authorities respectively, achieving recognition of the importance of the Convention and the urgent need to ratify it. The International Migrants Day Platform Flanders, a coalition of nine Flemish and Belgian NGOs created in 2003, commissioned a comparative study of the Convention and national legislation. The study, an innovative move, was carried out as a partnership between the International Migrants Day Platform and respected universities in Belgium (Vanheule et al., 2004). It has been used at the political level to campaign for Belgian ratification. Following the International Migrants Day Platform campaign, the Flemish Government decided in April 2004 to officially support Belgian ratification of the ICRMW.

The Catalan civil society campaign Xarxa 18 de Desembre, working in partnership with representatives of the autonomous Catalan Government, was instrumental in the adoption of a resolution by the Parliament of Catalonia that urged its (Catalan) Government to take the necessary steps for the Spanish Government to 'solemnly' sign and ratify the ICRMW in order to complete the legal regulator framework on foreigners' stay in Catalonia.[25]

National campaigns have been launched in France, Germany, Ireland, Italy, Portugal, Switzerland and the United Kingdom. Several organizations have also brought the discussion to the European level, using the Convention to campaign for more attention to migrants' rights within European immigration policies. The European Platform for Migrant Workers' Rights (EPMWR) brings together several national NGOs from European countries and European networks to harmonize and strengthen ratification campaigns at national and European levels. In addition, the EPMWR intervenes whenever appropriate in discussions at EU level, for example in the context of the consultations on the Commission's Green Paper on economic migration (EPMWR, 2005). In other regions, civil society groups and coalitions campaigning for the rights of migrants are active in Bangladesh, Brazil, Hong Kong (MFA), Indonesia, the Middle East, Sri Lanka and the United States.

In other countries, local, national and regional NGOs without long-term campaigning strategies use relevant occasions to remind their governments of the ICRMW and the rights it protects. International Migrants Day, the official UN human rights day celebrated each year on 18 December, has been widely used to advocate for the ratification and effective implementation of the Convention.[26] In 2008, the International Migrants Day was celebrated in some forty countries around the world, with various activities, shows and events promoting

---

[25] 'El Parlament de Catalunya insta el Govern a fer les gestions que convingui amb el Govern de l'Estat perquè signi ratifiqui solemnement la Convenció de les Nacions Unides per a la protecció dels drets de tots els treballadors migrants i llurs familiars, de manera que complementi el marc legal regulador de l'estada dels estrangers a Catalunya.' [The Catalan Parliament urges the government to make efforts to agree with the State Government to formally ratify the United Nations Convention for the Protection of the Rights of All Migrant Workers and their families, so as to complement the legal framework regulating the stay of foreigners in Catalonia.], Resolució 130/VII del Parlament de Catalunya, sobre la signatura i la ratificació de la Convenció de les Nacions Unides per a la protecció dels drets de tots els treballadors migrants i llurs familiars, BOPC [Official Bulletin], No. 106, 3 November 2004, p. 9.

[26] In 1997, Filipino and other Asian migrant organizations began celebrating and promoting 18 December (adoption date of the ICRMW) as the International Day of Solidarity with Migrants; 18 December was eventually chosen by the General Assembly as International Migrants Day.

migrants' rights. Civil society in countries where human rights activities for migrants are dangerous or highly unpopular has been using this official UN day as a unique occasion for organizing public-awareness activities on the need to protect migrants.[27]

A decision to ratify the ICRMW is usually the result of a multiplicity of factors, of which sustained and well-targeted NGO interventions are an important element. Although the impact of campaigning activities is difficult to document, it is worth mentioning that the growing number of ratification campaigns runs parallel with a steady increase in ratification since the entry into force of the Convention in 2003. While it took thirteen years for the first twenty ratifications, the number of States Parties has doubled in only six years. For NGOs active in campaigning for ratification, its entry into force signalled a new phase in their advocacy and monitoring activities. This also marked the end of the invisibility of the Convention; it was finally included in official UN documents and ratification events at the General Assembly as one of the core international human rights treaties.

NGOs and implementation

In the countries that have ratified the ICRMW, existing ratification campaigns or International Migrants Day celebration networks now develop advocacy efforts towards effective implementation, at times singling out provisions most relevant to the national context. In Sri Lanka, the groups campaigning for the implementation of the Convention used the 2005 International Migrants Day to raise the issue of absentee voting for the many Sri Lankan citizens living abroad. Other existing national coalitions that advocate for migrants' rights might concentrate their efforts on the supervisory mechanism set up by the Convention (articles 72 to 75) to monitor its implementation by the States Parties. The CMW, the seventh treaty monitoring body of the UN human rights system, was established after the entry into force of the Convention and has been examining States Parties' reports since then (see Chapter 4). Civil society has either contributed information to

---

[27] See, for example, 'December 18, International Migrants Day: end the exploitation, violence and abuse, protect and promote the rights of all women migrant workers!', December 2004, a statement from the Asia Pacific Forum on Women, Law and Development (APWLD), a coalition of women from the Asia-Pacific, Africa, Latin America and the Caribbean.

country reports or has produced alternative reports to the state reports to complement official information received by members of the CMW.

The ten initial independent members of the Committee were elected in December 2003, from a list of candidates drawn up by States Parties to the ICRMW. International NGOs mobilized to alert national civil society in States Parties on the need to lobby for strong and independent experts as candidates for the Committee. Unfortunately, many elected members did not meet these requirements, and a high proportion are employed in their government administrations or foreign services.

When the ICRMW entered into force in 2003, some NGOs that had actively participated in the Steering Committee of the Global Campaign decided to develop a project to facilitate NGO monitoring of the implementation of the Convention. December 18 took the lead in drafting a project that focused on NGO participation in the work of the CMW. Following the example of the NGO Group on the Convention on the Rights of the Child, a coalition of NGOs sharing interest, activities and expertise on the human rights of migrant workers was created to facilitate and support the involvement and input of NGOs to the CMW. The IPMWC[28] was launched in April 2005, at the 3rd Session of the Committee. The added value of the Platform is that it reaches out to local, national and regional NGOs that are unaware or unable to keep abreast of the activities and calendar schedule of the supervisory mechanism of the CMW and other human rights treaty bodies, in order to involve them in the work of the Committee. At the same time, it fosters a broader NGO awareness on issues relevant to migrants' rights, and creates a proactive environment that benefits all stakeholders. CMW members have expressed their support for this initiative, welcoming the availability of specific, accurate and reliable information necessary for the monitoring of the implementation of the Convention in States Parties. Likewise, the Platform has received the support of the Committee's Secretariat.

Networking links between local and international NGOs facilitated by the Platform are essential to the work of the Committee and the UN human rights system in general. International human rights NGOs are

---

[28] As of June 2009, the members of the IPMWC were: Action Canada pour la population et le développement, Amnesty International, Anti-Slavery International, December 18, FIDH, Franciscans International, HRW, the ICMC, International Centre for Migration, Health and Development, Jesuit Refugee Service, Kav La'Oved Israel, Migrant Care Indonesia, MRI, National Employment Law Project, Organisation Mondiale Contre la Torture, International Movement Against All Forms of Discrimination and Racism, PSI, the English International Association of Lund, WARBE Development Foundation and the WCC.

broadly familiar with the work of UN human-rights treaty monitoring bodies and know how to submit information to independent experts, as they examine States Parties' reports. International NGOs obtain information on local and national situations through their membership[29] or through their own research on specific countries.[30] In order to facilitate more direct involvement by national NGOs with the CMW and other treaty bodies, some members of the Platform decided to develop a guide for NGOs (IPMWC, 2005). It provides practical information on these and other relevant human rights mechanisms. The guide enables NGOs to strengthen their involvement with the UN human rights system, and more particularly their work with the ICRMW.

Since its launch in 2005, the Platform has already achieved some success. It has worked closely with the Committee and its Secretariat in defining the modalities of its interaction with NGOs, based on other supervisory committees' best practices. Further, the Platform was instrumental in the development of the NGO alternative report on the situation in Mexico submitted to the Committee during the examination of the report from Mexico, prepared by Foro Migraciones (2005), a network of Central American NGOs working on the issue of migration and human rights, based in Mexico City, and December 18 as a member of the IPMWC. The report was then presented directly to members at the 4th Session of the CMW in April 2006 as they began the examination of the Mexican report and prepared a list of issues. The report, as well as oral information delivered by a representative of Foro Migraciones, has been largely taken into consideration by the Committee when drafting the list.

The submission of the Mexican report to the CMW was an opportunity for joint efforts by civil society, UN human rights mechanisms and state representatives to strengthen the role of the Committee and raise the profile of migrants' rights. Representatives of the three stakeholders took part in an event organized in parallel to the CMW session in April 2006, to discuss their respective approaches to the reporting process under the CMW. The impact of NGO work on the implementation of the ICRMW directly benefited from the established collaboration of NGOs in the work of the UN treaty monitoring bodies. This mobilization is further supported by migrant workers, who are often well organized at national level, thus facilitating the documentation of human rights violations.

---

[29] This is the case of several IPMWC members, for example the World Organisation Against Torture (OMCT), the FIDH, Franciscans International and the WCC.

[30] In particular, Amnesty International and HRW.

NGO advocacy and international migration policy discussions

In addition to their involvement in the Platform, a number of international, regional and national NGOs also endeavour to follow international developments with respect to regional migration-consultative processes and migration policy developments. Intergovernmental bodies and processes increasingly focus on the 'migration phenomenon', primarily due to new trends in international migration flows and attempts by migrant receiving states to 'manage' them. As migration becomes an urgent and important issue, several regional, bilateral and international multi-state bodies have been participating in 'management approaches'.

While NGOs and civil society tend to be excluded from regional migration-management initiatives, there are exceptions, such as the Puebla Process in Central America and the involvement of the Red Regional de Organizaciones Civiles para las Migraciones (Grange, 2004). This is a useful model: the generalized international interest in migration indeed often neglects the human side, including human rights. As a consequence, many NGOs chose to actively participate in the activities of the Global Commission on International Migration throughout 2005 and in preparation for the UN General Assembly HLD held in September 2006.

Promoting 'humane and orderly migration for the benefits of all', the IOM, an IGO outside the UN family, has spearheaded many migration-management activities and programmes and shows remarkable growth (in contrast to many UN agencies that are registering budgetary shortfalls). An increasing number of NGOs have applied for observer status with the IOM in recent years, including Amnesty International and HRW. At the IOM Council in December 2002, the two organizations made a joint statement and declared that 'in coming to this Council meeting, Member States cannot leave their other obligations at the door'. Many NGOs around the world are indeed concerned that the IOM should not implement programmes that violate the human rights obligations of its members, even if their members so request (HRW, 2002; 2005).

Even though NGOs have welcomed the IOM's recent public stance in favour of the ICRMW, as demonstrated by its membership of the Steering Committee of the Global Campaign for Ratification, they still note that the IOM 'has no formal protection mandate or any responsibility to supervise an international treaty to protect migrants' (Amnesty International, 2006). More generally, NGOs are concerned that migration is not addressed from a human rights perspective in many IGO initiatives. An entire set of activities and reports arising out of the 'international migration and development' focus consider migration as an economic phenomenon outwith its human dimension, or as a demographic and statistical phenomenon. That 'human rights' was not a cross-cutting theme in the UN HLD (see below) illustrates this paradox.

NGOs have played a crucial role in maintaining a minimum standard for migrants' rights in various migration-management documents or processes, even though they were granted very little space. NGOs actively contributed to the UNHCR Global Consultations in International Protection (UNHCR, 2003).The Agenda for Protection endorsed by the UNHCR Executive Committee in 2002 contains a recommendation that 'in the broad context of migration management, states [are encouraged] to consider acceding to the 1990 United Nations Convention on the Protection of the Rights of All Migrant Workers and Members of Their Families, and relevant ILO conventions (notably Nos. 97 and 143)'. In contrast, the outcome document of the Swiss-led 'states-owned' Berne Initiative, the International Agenda for Migration Management, does not refer to the ICRMW.

MRI and the ICFTU played a powerful advocacy role in the rights-based approach of the 2004 Action Plan on Migrant Workers adopted by the ILO. The MRI brought a strong delegation[31] to the ILC (the ILO's annual policy-making assembly) and worked closely with trade unions. The ILC Action Plan includes the development of a non-binding multi-lateral framework for a rights-based approach to labour migration (ILO, 2006).

The launch of the GCIM in December 2003 coincided with the entry into force of the ICRMW. Its nineteen independent Commissioners were mandated to 'provide the framework for the formulation of a coherent, comprehensive and global response to the issue of international migration' (GCIM, 2005). At the same time, the General Assembly decided to devote an HLD during its 61st Session in 2006.[32] The purpose of the HLD was to discuss the multi-dimensional aspects of international migration and development in order to identify appropriate ways and means to maximize its development benefits and minimize its negative impacts.

---

[31] 'Putting the migrants at the center', International Migrants Day press release from MRI, 18 December 2004.
[32] UN General Assembly Resolution A/58/208 of 13 February 2004.

These international developments prompted the OHCHR to create an internal task force on migration at the end of 2005. NGOs welcomed this regained momentum and the assertive voice of the High Commissioner in relation to the human rights of migrant workers.[33] One of the recommendations of the GCIM has been implemented with the creation of the Global Migration Group (GMG).[34] In this context, the role of the OHCHR is to promote 'a human rights approach to migration throughout its work'. This approach has been elaborated upon by the Office in a series of documents in preparation for the HLD.[35] The ICRMW and the importance of migrants' rights were at least acknowledged by these recent processes. The GCIM report refers to the Convention as one of the core UN human-rights treaties that form the 'legal and normative framework affecting migrants' (GCIM, 2005, p. 55). The HLD held one round table on 'measures to ensure respect for and protection of the human rights of all migrants, and to prevent and combat smuggling of migrants and trafficking in persons'.

The various processes, however, did not clearly support wider ratification of the Convention. Instead, the GCIM opted for alternative or 'complementary approaches', such as better implementation of existing international human-rights obligations and adaptation of national laws and practices to these obligations (GCIM, 2005, pp. 57–8). NGOs are concerned that although all fourteen member agencies of the GMG have established respective systems of consultative and observer status for NGOs, the GMG has never invited NGOs to take part in its activities. The former UN Secretary-General, Kofi Annan, in his report[36] for the HLD, mentioned the Convention as one of the core UN human-rights treaties, but omitted to call on states to ratify it. A number of NGOs participating in the HLD preparatory process noted this clear shift in the message of the Secretary-General to states about the ICRMW, as he had called for its ratification on several occasions in the past.[37] Some

---

[33] High Commissioner oral update to the 2nd Session of the Human Rights Council on 18 September 2006.

[34] Membership includes the ILO, IOM, OHCHR, UNCTAD, UNDP, UNESCO, UNFPA, UNHCR, UNICEF, UNITAR, UNODC, UN-DESA, UN Regional Commissions and the World Bank.

[35] In particular, the OHCHR developed a document entitled *Migration and Development: A Human Rights Approach*. Available at www.ohchr.org/english/bodies/cmw/HLMigration.htm.

[36] UN General Assembly A/60/871, International Migration and Development, 18 May 2006.

[37] See UN General Assembly A/61/187, Summary of informal interactive hearings of the General Assembly with representatives of non-governmental organizations, civil society organizations and the private sector, 27 July 2006, paragraph 29.

government representatives also noted this shift.[38] Many NGOs highlighted the lack of reference to human rights in the HLD debate in their position papers[39] or comments to the Secretary-General's report.[40] NGOs organized a parallel event to the HLD in New York to highlight this and the scant opportunity given to migrant groups and civil society in general to actually take an active part in these debates.[41]

Until now, the ICRMW has not been given much visibility in these processes. Nor has the rights-based approach to migration been central in migration policy making, where the focus is on economic growth and facilitating remittances. NGOs have been concerned about a trend in self-censorship about the Convention in some UN-related activities and welcome renewed attention to it as voiced by the High Commissioner for Human Rights and documented in the UNESCO research that has led to the present volume. In this context, NGOs have a fundamental responsibility to campaign for more states to ratify the ICRMW, to hold them accountable to implement the human rights treaties they have adhered to and to monitor violations of the human rights of migrant workers and members of their families.

The recent states-led initiative for a yearly GFMD, as a follow-up to the UN HLD, almost excluded civil society actors from the debate. The Governmental Meetings of the first Global Forum took place on 10 and 11 July 2007 in Brussels, and civil society had only a very limited role, even if a separate Civil Society Day was scheduled. In addition, NGOs organized parallel civil society events. While the 2007 Forum did not focus on human rights, NGOs hope that the forthcoming fora on migration and development will give human rights the central place they deserve, even more so if they are hosted by sending countries. In this respect, the 2008 Forum, hosted by the Philippines, focused on the protection of migrants and constituted a more favourable opportunity to place human rights at the centre of discussions and to recall the importance of the ICRMW.

---

[38] Cf. oral comment to the authors by Ambassador Prasad Karyawasam, chairman of the CMW.

[39] See www.december18.net/web/general/page.php?pageID=574&menuID=36&lang=EN# two [last accessed 14 April 2009] and the NGO press release 'Human rights are essential to migration discussion', 12 July 2006.

[40] A/60/871, International Migration and Development, 18 May 2006.

[41] Global Community Dialogue on Migration, Development and Human Rights, MRI, MFA and NNIRR, 13–15 September 2006, Queens College Worker Education Centre, New York.

Conclusion

Civil society mobilization in favour of the ICRMW has been slow but steady and substantial. NGOs have developed an expert understanding of the provisions of the Convention and have become strong advocates of its use as a pivotal element of the international human rights framework for migrants. They have produced and disseminated a wealth of related material since its adoption. Civil society endeavours for ratification are now well established in many countries, as well as at regional and international levels. A growing number of NGOs have been using the Convention to advise on draft legislation, and as an education, training and awareness-raising tool. Together with a handful of States Parties to the Convention, they have mainstreamed some of its provisions into the outcome documents of the major international conferences and summits of the 1990s. They have used it to monitor violations of the human rights of migrants and to supply information to the former UN CHR and its thematic special procedures as well as to human-rights treaty monitoring bodies. NGOs have also demonstrated foresight in getting involved in migration management and relevant intergovernmental initiatives at the UN and beyond.

The role of civil society in working for the promotion and defence of migrants' rights has been crucial in giving the issue the attention it deserves. For several years after the adoption of the ICRMW, NGOs advocating for migrants' rights have been very lonely. Throughout their campaigning and advocacy work, NGOs have been confronted with a unique situation: the human rights of migrant workers and migrant children and women are *not* popular, even with states that have traditionally championed the drafting and implementation of other human rights norms and standards. For many years after its adoption, UN bodies failed to publicize the existence and content of the Convention. Only recently did UNESCO, the ILO and the OHCHR begin to parallel civil society initiatives and give impetus to migrants' rights. In particular, a migration focal point was created at the OHCHR in 2009. NGO campaigning and use of the Convention, while sustained at the global level and through many regional and national hubs, has so far not attained the visibility of other much-celebrated campaigns. With rare exceptions, governmental and traditional institutional donors have been reluctant to fund civil-society advocacy activities for the human rights of migrants.

Within the framework of the UN reform process, civil society actors keep promoting the human rights of migrants at the Human Rights Council (HRC). They are monitoring the reform of human-rights treaty monitoring bodies to ensure that it does not result in diminished protection of vulnerable groups such as migrants. NGOs have produced analyses and input into debates on migration and migration management at regional and international levels to ensure the mainstreaming of migrants' rights and the ICRMW into these processes. They have demonstrated remarkable resilience in tackling the non-ratification of the Convention by Western recipient countries, a clear product of lack of political will. The Convention is a complex and at times unwieldy treaty. However, as shown in this publication, ignorance and myths have often characterized the attitude of a number of state officials vis-à-vis the Convention. This is undoubtedly the main challenge for many human rights defenders. Advocacy at the level of law, policy and practice does need to be rooted in widely recognized norms to safeguard the rights of migrant workers and members of their families, whether documented or undocumented, from widespread abuse.

References

Amnesty International. 2006. *Living in the Shadows: A Primer on Human Rights of Migrants*. London, Amnesty International. (POL33/006/2006, September.)

APIM. 1998. *Understanding International Migration: A Source Book*. Kuala Lumpur, Asian Partnership on International Migration.

Asian Migrant Centre. 2000. *A U.N. Road Map: A Guide for Asian NGOs to the International Human Rights System and Other Mechanisms*. Rev. edn 2004. Hong Kong, Asian Migrant Centre/Ateneo Human Rights Centre/Canadian Human Rights Foundation/Asia Pacific Forum on Women, Law and Development.

CCME/WCC. 1991. *Proclaiming Migrants Rights: The New International Convention on the Protection of the Rights of All Migrant Workers and Members of their Families*. New York, Churches Committee for Migrants in Europe / World Council of Churches, in consultation with the Quaker United Nations Office. (Briefing Papers No. 3, May.)

Cholewinski, R. 1997. *Migrant Workers in International Human Rights Law: Their Protection in Countries of Employment*. Oxford, UK, Clarendon Press.

EPMWR. 2005. *Human Rights Key to Economic Migration Policy*. Comments on the Green Paper on an EU approach to managing economic migration. Brussels, European Platform for Migrant Workers' Rights. Available at www.december18.net/web/general/page.php?pageID=568&menuID=36&lang=EN [last accessed 14 April 2009].

Foro Migraciones. 2005. *Informe Alternativo – Aplicación de la Convención Internacional sobre la Protección de los Derechos de Todos los Trabajadores Migratorios y sus Familias*. Mexico City, Foro Migraciones.

GCIM. 2005. *Migration in an Interconnected World: New Directions for Action*. Geneva, Switzerland, Global Commission on International Migration.

Gencianos, G. 2004. International civil society cooperation on migrants' rights: perspectives from an NGO network. *European Journal of Migration and Law*, Vol. 6, pp. 147–55.

Grange, M. 2004. Regional migration consultative processes: where is civil society? MFA, *Asian Migrant Yearbook 2002–2003*. Hong Kong, Asian Migrant Centre, MFA.

— 2006. *Strengthening Protection of Migrant Workers and their Families with International Human Rights Treaties: A Do-It-Yourself Kit*. Rev. edn. Geneva, International Catholic Migration Commission.

HRW. 2002. *By Invitation Only: Australian Asylum Policy*. New York, HRW.

— 2005. *Ukraine: On the Margins – Rights Violations against Migrants and Asylum Seekers at the New Eastern Border of the European Union*. New York, HRW.

ICMC. 2002. *Report on the World Conference against Racism, Racial Discrimination, Xenophobia and Related Intolerance*. Geneva, Switzerland, International Catholic Migration Commission.

ILO. 2006. *ILO's Multilateral Framework on Labour Migration: Non-binding Principles and Guidelines for a Rights-Based Approach to Labour Migration*. Geneva, Switzerland, ILO.

International Migration Review. 1991. *Special Issue on the Convention: U.N. International Convention on the Protection of the Rights of All Migrant Workers and Members of Their Families*, Vol. 25, No. 4.

IPMWC. 2005. *A Guide for Non-Governmental Organisations on the Implementation of the UN Migrant Workers' Convention*. December 18 edn. Brussels, International Platform on the Migrant Workers' Convention. (Available in English, Spanish and French.)

MFA. 1994. *Ratifying UN Convention Protecting Migrant Workers: Migrant Women Quest for Justice*. Hong Kong, MFA.

— 1995. Challenging global structures: migrant women take their struggle to Beijing. Hong Kong, MFA.

MRI. 1998. *Achieving Dignity: Campaigner's Handbook for the Migrants Rights Convention*. Rev. edn 2000. Geneva, Switzerland, International Migrants Rights Watch Committee / Steering Committee for the Global Campaign.

Nchama, E. C. M. 1991. The role of non-governmental organizations in the promotion and protection of human rights. *Bulletin of Human Rights*, Vol. 90, No. 1, p. 50.

NNIRR. 2002. A World on the Move. Report on the 2001 UN World Conference Against Racism, Racial Discrimination, Xenophobia and Related Intolerance. Oakland, Calif., NNIRR.

OHCHR. 1996*a*. *The International Bill of Human Rights (Rev. 1)*. Geneva, Switzerland, Office of the United Nations High Commissioner for Human Rights. (Fact Sheet No. 2.)

 1996*b*. *The Rights of Migrant Workers*. Rev. edn 2005. Geneva, Switzerland, Office of the United Nations High Commissioner for Human Rights. (Fact Sheet No. 24.)

PSI. 1996. *Going Out to Work – Trade Unions and Migrant Workers*. Ferney-Voltaire, France, PSI.

Scalabrini Migration Center. 1997. *Rights of Migrant Workers – A Primer on the UN Convention on the Protection of the Rights of All Migrant Workers and Members of Their Families*. Quezon City, Philippines, Scalabrini Migration Center.

UNDP. 2007. *Human Development Report 2007/2008, Fighting Climate Change: Human Solidarity in a Divided World*. New York, UNDP.

UNESCO. 2003. *Information Kit on the United Nations Convention on Migrants' Rights*. Rev. edn 2005. Paris, UNESCO.

UNHCR. 2003. NGO background paper on the refugee and migration interface. *Protection Policy in the Making: Third Track of the Global Consultations, Refugee Survey Quarterly*, Vol. 22, Nos. 2/3, pp. 373–89.

Vanheule, D., Foblets, M.-C., Loones, S. and Bouckaert, S. 2004. The significance of the UN Migrant Workers' Convention of 18 December 1990 in the event of ratification by Belgium. *European Journal of Migration and Law*, Vol. 6, No. 4, pp. 285–321.

4

Committee on Migrant Workers
and implementation of the ICRMW

CARLA EDELENBOS[1]

Introduction

No country in the world today is untouched by migration. In recent years, migration has become an important topic for international conferences, such as the UN General Assembly's HLD in September 2006. Yet, as the former High Commissioner for Human Rights, Louise Arbour, has said: 'While the debate continues to be centred either on the perceived challenges posed by migration, or on its contribution to development and poverty alleviation, the inextricable connection of migration with human rights has yet to permeate discussions and policy. The vulnerability of migrants to abuse should warrant a better understanding of their rights, as well as more – not less – protection.'[2]

In order to address the special needs of migrants in the protection of their human rights, the General Assembly adopted the ICRMW on 18 December 1990. Almost thirteen years later, on 1 July 2003, the Convention entered into force, and on 1 January 2004, the CMW was established, thereby becoming the seventh UN human-rights treaty monitoring body.

Human-rights treaty monitoring bodies monitor the State Party's compliance with their respective treaties. They do this mainly through the consideration of States Parties' reports. Some treaty bodies also have the possibility of examining inter-state or individual communications that denounce violations by a State Party of any of the rights contained in the treaty concerned. Members of treaty bodies are independent experts, elected periodically by the meeting of States Parties to the treaty

---

[1] Opinions expressed by the author in this article do not necessarily reflect the point of view of the organization(s) she is associated with.

[2] Address by Louise Arbour, former United Nations High Commissioner for Human Rights, to the 2nd Session of the HRC, 18 September 2006.

in question. Most treaty bodies meet two or three times a year. Their mandate is exclusively related to the treaty they are monitoring and only concerns the states that have adhered to the treaty in question.

This distinguishes them from other human rights bodies, such as the Human Rights Council and its predecessor, the CHR. These so-called charter-based bodies were not established pursuant to any specific human rights treaties, but rather by virtue of resolutions adopted by the political organs of the UN, in the case of the HRC by the General Assembly. As the membership of these bodies consists of states, they are political, and not expert, bodies. They may examine human rights questions, either thematic or country-specific, on the basis of all existing international norms, and often take political considerations into account.

The HRC also has a system of independent experts, which it inherited from the CHR. These so-called special-procedures mandate holders were nominated by the chairperson of the then Commission in order to study either the human rights situation in a specific country or questions relating to certain human rights themes. The mandate of the Special Rapporteur on the Human Rights of Migrants, for example, was created by the CHR in 1999 and has since been twice renewed. Under this mandate, the Special Rapporteurs may receive information on violations of migrants' rights. They also undertake visits to countries that are willing to receive them and recommend measures on how to improve the protection of the human rights of migrants. The findings are reported once a year to the Council.

Within the UN human-rights treaty monitoring bodies system, a number of expert committees have been established to monitor state compliance with the respective treaties (see Table 4.1).

While benefiting from the experience of the other treaty bodies, the CMW creates its own approach to its work, in line with the specificities of the ICRMW. Since its creation, the Committee has sought close working relations with other treaty bodies, in particular through the annual Inter-Committee and Chairpersons' meetings. The Chair of the CMW, Prasad Kariyawasam, presided over the annual meeting of treaty monitoring body experts in 2004.

Establishment of the CMW

In accordance with article 72, paragraph 3 of the ICRMW, the first election for membership of the CMW was held on 11 December 2003, within six months of the entry into force of the Convention on 1 July

Table 4.1   *Expert committees monitoring UN human rights treaties*

Treaty monitoring body	Treaty
Committee on the Elimination of Racial Discrimination (1969)	International Convention on the Elimination of All Forms of Racial Discrimination (1965)
Human Rights Committee (1976)	International Covenant on Civil and Political Rights (1966)
Committee on Economic, Social and Cultural Rights (1987)	International Covenant on Economic, Social and Cultural Rights (1966)
Committee on the Elimination of Discrimination against Women (1982)	Convention on the Elimination of All Forms of Discrimination against Women (1979)
Committee against Torture (1987)	Convention against Torture and Other Cruel, Inhuman or Degrading Treatment or Punishment (1984)
Committee on the Rights of the Child (1990)	Convention on the Rights of the Child (1989)
Committee on the Protection of the Rights of All Migrant Workers and Members of Their Families (2003)	International Convention on the Protection of the Rights of All Migrant Workers and Members of Their Families (1990)
Committee on the Rights of Persons with Disabilities (2008)	Convention on the Rights of Persons with Disabilities (2007)

2003. Pursuant to article 72, paragraph 1(b), the Committee consists of ten experts of high moral standing, impartiality and recognized competence in the field covered by the Convention.[3] As is the case with other treaty bodies,[4] committee members are nominated and elected by the States Parties to the Convention. At the December 2003 election, they nominated a total of ten experts, all of whom were elected without necessity of a vote. The distribution of members according to geographical groups was as follows: four from Latin America, three from Africa, two from Asia and one from eastern Europe. By lot, five of the members were chosen to serve for two years; the other five members were elected for a term of four years.

---

[3] Having reached forty-one States Parties, the number of members will rise to fourteen on 1 January 2010. See article 72, paragraph 1(b).

[4] With the exception of the CESCR, whose members are elected by ECOSOC.

The CMW held its inaugural meeting from 1 to 5 March 2004 in Geneva. At this meeting, it adopted its provisional rules of procedure. The rules will be revised once the Committee has gained more experience. At the 1st Session, it set the tone for future work by meeting with the States Parties to the Convention, the Commission on Human Rights' Special Rapporteur for the Human Rights of Migrants, the Sub-Commission's Special Rapporteur on the Rights of Non-citizens, UN agencies and other IGOs, as well as NGOs.

On 6 December 2007, the third meeting of States Parties to the Convention took place in New York in order to elect five members to replace those whose mandates were expiring. According to article 72, paragraph 5(c) of the Convention, members of the Committee are eligible for re-election if re-nominated. Of the five outgoing members, four were re-elected. After the third election, the geographical composition of the membership is as follows: three from Latin America, three from Africa, two from Asia, one from eastern Europe and one from western Europe and others.[5]

Functions of the CMW

Article 74 of the Convention sets out the role of the Committee and its functions, which may be described as follows.

Consideration of States Parties' reports

The primary task of the CMW is to study reports by States Parties on the legislative, judicial, administrative and other measures they have taken to give effect to the Convention's provisions. A State Party is requested to present a first report within one year of entry into force of the Convention for the State Party concerned, and thereafter every five years. So far, the Committee has received the initial reports of Azerbaijan, Bolivia, Bosnia and Herzegovina, Colombia, Ecuador, Egypt, El Salvador, Mali, Mexico, the Philippines, Sri Lanka and Syrian Arab Republic.

---

[5] The Committee's composition is now as follows: Francisco Alba (Mexico), José Brillantes (Philippines), Ana Elizabeth Cubias (El Salvador), Anamaría Dieguez (Guatemala), Ahmad Hassan El Borai (Egypt), Abdelhamid El Jamri (Morocco), Prasad Kariyawasam (Sri Lanka), Myriam Poussi Konsimbo (Burkina Faso), Mehmet Sevim (Turkey) and Azad Taghizade (Azerbaijan).

At its 2nd Session, held in Geneva from 25 to 29 April 2005, the CMW adopted its guidelines for the submission of initial reports by States Parties.[6] The guidelines request the States Parties concerned to provide information of a general nature concerning the framework governing the implementation of the Convention, any agreements entered into with other states concerning migration; the characteristics and nature of migration flows; the practical situation with regard to the implementation of the Convention; the measures taken to promote it; and the cooperation with civil society. As to the information on the implementation of the Convention, in view of its length, the guidelines suggest that reporting states group the information by clusters of articles. Finally, in view of the ongoing treaty monitoring body reform, the Committee encourages states to present their reports in conjunction with the Common Core Document guidelines that have been accepted by the Inter-Committee meeting.[7] At its 8th Session, held in Geneva from 14 to 25 April 2008, the Committee adopted its guidelines for the submission of treaty-specific periodic reports. These guidelines refer both to the guidelines for the common core document and to the guidelines for initial reports and contain a list of questions to be answered by States Parties in addition to a request to provide information on any follow-up to the Committee's earlier concluding observations for the State Party concerned.

The CMW follows closely the working methods of the other treaty bodies when it examines the States Parties' reports. In the session preceding the public consideration of a report, the Committee meets behind closed doors with representatives of interested UN agencies, IGOs and NGOs in order to obtain additional information on the rights of migrant workers and members of their families in the country concerned. Thereafter, it adopts a list of issues to be raised during the consideration of the State Party's report. This list is sent to the State Party concerned, which is requested to reply to the questions in writing before the following session.

---

[6] Compilation of guidelines on the form and content of reports to be submitted by States Parties to the international human rights treaties, addendum (HRI/GEN/2/Rev.2/Add.1), 6 May 2005.

[7] Harmonized guidelines on reporting under the international human rights treaties, including guidelines on a common core document and treaty-specific documents, report of the Inter-Committee Technical Working Group (HRI/MC/2006/3), 10 May 2006. See also the report of the eighteenth meeting of chairpersons of the human rights treaty bodies, A/61/50.

The consideration of the report takes place in two public meetings in the presence of a delegation of the State Party. After the opening of the meeting, the chairperson welcomes the delegation, which then makes an oral statement, followed by comments and questions from committee members. The State Party is given time to prepare the answers to the oral questions and delivers them at the following meeting. The members then make concluding comments before the closure of the meeting.

At the same session, but in a private meeting, the Committee discusses the concluding observations on the State Party's report. After the concluding observations are adopted, they are immediately transmitted to the State Party and made public.

So far, the CMW has considered the reports of Mali (4th Session, April 2006), Mexico (5th Session, October to November 2006), Egypt (6th Session, April 2007), Ecuador (7th Session, November 2007), Syrian Arab Republic (8th Session, April 2008), Bolivia (8th Session, April 2008), El Salvador (9th Session, November 2008) and Azerbaijan, Bosnia and Herzegovina, Colombia and the Philippines (10th Session, April 2009).

Mali

In the case of Mali, the CMW received no information from NGOs and only limited information from UN agencies and other organizations. The report itself was short and very general. Because of this, the Committee's list of issues concentrated on obtaining more specific information from the State Party on questions such as the character and nature of the migration flows in Mali; which authorities are competent to receive complaints from migrant workers about violations of their rights; whether migrant workers, including irregular ones, can freely join trade unions; the procedure on confiscation of identity documents; expulsion procedures; availability of urgent medical care; birth registration of children of migrant workers; access to education of migrant workers' children; the existence of any mechanisms facilitating the transfer of remittances; the measures taken to disseminate information to migrant workers about their rights arising out of the Convention and the conditions of their admission; the assistance provided by the authorities to Malians migrating abroad and the measures taken to address their grievances; whether migrant workers have the right to form trade unions and other associations; steps taken to facilitate the participation in elections of Malians abroad; procedures of family reunification; the state's services dealing with migration and their interaction with other actors; recruitment processes of migrant workers; return programmes; the extent of smuggling and trafficking of migrants and the strategy to fight these phenomena; and cooperation with other states.[8]

The Government of Mali replied in writing to most of these questions[9] and provided further information in the dialogue with CMW members during the session. This allowed the Committee to obtain a better understanding of the main issues at stake concerning Mali's implementation of the Convention. One of the issues that emerged was that Mali, which is mainly a country of origin, has taken measures to assist its migrant workers abroad and consults regularly with its diaspora. In countries where a large number of Malians reside, participation in presidential elections is facilitated. A second issue that became apparent was that, despite government efforts to combat trafficking of children, this continued to be a major problem in the country.

Accordingly, in its concluding observations,[10] the CMW noted with satisfaction the existence of the Ministry for Malians Living Abroad and African Integration, which provides information to Malians about conditions of entry and residence in several countries with a large Malian community. While welcoming the possibility of Malians in several countries to participate in presidential elections in Mali, the Committee recommended that the government consider extending this right to a larger number of Malians living abroad. The Committee also noted with satisfaction that Mali is a party to the Palermo Protocols.[11] On the other hand, it noted the difficulties the State Party faced in controlling its extensive borders and thus clandestine movements of migrant workers and members of their families. It noted the very serious problem of trafficking in children, and recommended that Mali intensify its efforts in this respect, in

---

[8] Written replies by the Government of Mali concerning the list of issues (CMW/C/MLI/Q/1) received by the Committee on the Protection of the Rights of All Migrant Workers and Members of Their Families relating to the consideration of the initial report of Mali (CMW/C/MLI/1), 22 March 2006.

[9] Reply to the list of issues (CMW/C/MLI/Q/1/Add.1)(www.unhchr.ch/tbs/doc.nsf/(Symbol)/CMW.C.MLI.Q.1.Add.1.En?OpenDocument [last accessed 12 May 2009]).

[10] Consideration of reports submitted by States Parties under article 9 of the Convention: concluding observations of the Committee on the Protection of the Rights of All Migrant Workers and Members of Their Families: Mali (CMW/C/MLI/CO/1), 31 May 2006.

[11] Palermo Convention against Transnational Organized Crime, Protocol to Prevent, Suppress and Punish Trafficking in Persons, Especially Women and Children, supplementing the United Nations Convention against Transnational Organized Crime, and the Protocol against the Smuggling of Migrants by Land, Air and Sea.

cooperation with IGOs and NGOs. The Committee regretted the absence of information given on measures to combat trafficking in women.

On other matters, the Committee recommended that the government institute a participatory procedure that would allow NGOs and civil society to be involved in the preparation of Mali's second periodic report. This shows the importance that it attaches to the contribution of civil society in its work.

The CMW's good relations with other organizations and awareness of its place in the broader framework of migrant rights' protection was also borne out by its invitation to Mali to consider acceding to the two ILO conventions concerning migrant workers.[12] On the subject of trafficking of children, the Committee also referred to the observations made by the Committee on the Rights of the Child (CRC) and the HRC and encouraged Mali to implement their recommendations.

Mexico

The situation in relation to the initial report of Mexico was quite different from that of Mali. First, the Mexican report was voluminous and provided detailed information on a number of questions. Second, the interest of NGOs in the Mexican report was remarkable. A coalition of local Mexican NGOs (Foro Migraciones) prepared an alternative report on the situation of migrant workers in Mexico, which was almost as voluminous as the official report. Moreover, several international NGOs also provided information (see Chapter 3). At the meeting with the Committee during the 4th Session, in preparation of the consideration of the report, these organizations were represented and provided additional oral information. The National Human Rights Commission of Mexico also presented information to the Committee. UN agencies and international organizations also provided information, both orally and in writing (see Chapter 9).

As a result, the list of issues that the CMW adopted in relation to the initial report of Mexico is much more detailed than in the case of Mali. The Committee asked, for example, whether Mexico was considering withdrawing its reservation under article 22 of the Convention; what measures had been taken to harmonize federal and state legislation; whether national legislation provided for the application of the Convention to refugees and stateless persons (article 3(d)); what measures were taken to combat discriminatory attitudes towards migrants, in

---

[12] ILO Conventions Nos. 97 (Migration for Employment) and 143 (Migrant Workers).

particular women and indigenous migrants; how irregular migrants can exercise their right to an effective remedy; the procedures surrounding detention of migrants; restrictions of freedom of movement of documented migrant workers; the alleged role of law-enforcement officers in extortion, abuse and ill-treatment of migrant workers; the detention regime of irregular migrants; protection of domestic migrant workers; equal treatment of irregular migrant workers in respect of remuneration and conditions of work, as well as social security; restrictions on migrant workers with regard to participation in the executive of trade unions; facilitation of consultation and participation of migrants in decisions affecting them; conditions of family reunification; the situation of seasonal workers; the extent of the phenomenon of trafficking in persons, and measures taken to avoid criminalization of the victims; possible implication of civil servants in smuggling of migrants; information on the support programme for indigenous migrants; and unaccompanied migrant children.

The Government of Mexico submitted timely written replies to these questions[13] and sent a large and highly knowledgeable delegation to the CMW's 5th Session. This allowed Committee members to obtain meaningful answers to their questions. In its concluding observations, the Committee showed appreciation of the seriousness with which Mexico approaches its obligations under the Convention.[14] However, it notes also that, in practice, many problems still persist, especially with regard to the ill-treatment and abuse of irregular migrant workers, the arrest of irregular migrant workers by public officials not authorized to do so and the precarious situation of seasonal workers, migrant domestic workers and unaccompanied children.

Egypt

The consideration of the initial report from Egypt had its own peculiarities. The report first of all provided detailed information, focused mainly on the contents of legislation and regulations, without

---

[13] Written replies by the Government of Mexico to the list of issues (CMW/C/MEX/Q/1) raised by the Committee on the Protection of the Rights of All Migrant Workers and Members of Their Families in connection with the consideration of the initial report of Mexico (CMW/C/MEX/1), 5 October 2006.

[14] Consideration of reports submitted by States Parties under article 9 of the Convention: concluding observations of the Committee on the Protection of the Rights of All Migrant Workers and Members of Their Families: Mexico (CMW/C/MEX/CO/1), 20 December 2006.

reference to their practical application. At the time that the CMW adopted its list of issues,[15] during its 5th Session, no information had been received from alternative sources such as NGOs. Some input was provided by UN agencies and IGOs, but essentially the Committee adopted its list of issues on the basis of the report and publicly available information.

After the list of issues was published, however, Egyptian and other NGOs reacted by providing the Committee with comments on the report and sharing some of their concerns on the situation of migrants in Egypt. The Egyptian National Council for Human Rights also sent information, and representatives of NGOs and national human rights institutions briefed the Committee orally on the first day of the 6th Session and were present during the public consideration of Egypt's report. The written answers to the list of issues[16] were received on time from the Government of Egypt and significantly assisted the Committee in identifying areas and issues that remained unclear.

As a result, committee members were well prepared for the dialogue with the Egyptian delegation, which was led by the Minister of Manpower and Migration and further consisted of five competent officials from the capital, assisted by several staff members of the Permanent Mission of Egypt in Geneva. Matters raised were, for example, problems with the issuing of birth certificates to children born to migrants in Egypt; the limited possibility of migrant children accessing schools; the alleged persistent practice of requesting approval from the husband or other male relative before a passport is issued to Egyptian women; the lack of possibility for Egyptians abroad to participate in national elections in Egypt; the failure of the government to provide information on the rights of migrants under the ICRMW; the sometimes insufficient consular assistance provided to Egyptian migrants abroad, especially in countries where the *kafalah* system persists;[17] and the non-existence of specific anti-trafficking legislation.[18]

---

[15] Written replies by the Government of Egypt concerning the list of issues (CMW/C/EGY/Q/1) received by the Committee on Migrant Workers relating to the consideration of the initial periodic report of Egypt (CMW/C/EGY/1), 6 February 2007.

[16] Ibid., addendum.

[17] The *kafalah* is a system of sponsorship whereby migrants are controlled by their 'sponsor', which may in some cases even prevent them from returning to Egypt.

[18] See the Committee's concluding observations (CMW/C/EGY/CO/1) (www2.ohchr.org/english/bodies/cmw/docs/cmw_c_egy_co1_fr.doc [last accessed 14 May 2009]).

Non-reporting

The main obstacle the CMW is facing in fulfilling its core function is the delay in the presentation of reports by States Parties. Of the thirty-seven initial reports due on 30 April 2009, only thirteen have been received.[19] The Committee first raised the problem in a meeting with States Parties held during its 2nd Session (26 April 2005), in the course of which several of them mentioned that they were in the process of preparing a report. In light of the absence of reports, the Committee has sent formal reminders to States Parties and publishes a list of overdue reports in its annual report to the General Assembly. At its 6th Session, the Committee held another meeting with States Parties, at which many showed a willingness to submit reports in the near future.

The CMW may nevertheless have to consider other methods that would help it to fulfil its primary function of reviewing the status of implementation of the ICRMW by States Parties. In this respect, the Committee may look at the methods used by other treaty bodies to improve reporting. In fact, most States Parties that are delaying the presentation of their report to the CMW do not have a good reporting record for other treaty monitoring bodies, which have adopted the practice of examining the status of implementation of the relevant treaty by the State Party in the absence of a report, if overdue for a long period (i.e. five years or more).

This strategy was first initiated by the Committee on the Elimination of Racial Discrimination in 1991. In general, the treaty monitoring body notifies the State Party concerned that it intends to examine the state's compliance with a convention in the absence of a report, and specifies the date of this scheduled public meeting. If the State Party responds by submitting a report, the procedure is suspended and the normal process of consideration of a report begins. Where the situation in the State

---

[19] The status of initial reports on 30 April 2009 was as follows: Albania, due 1 October 2008; Algeria, received; Argentina, due 1 June 2008; Azerbaijan, received; Belize, due 1 July 2004; Bolivia, received; Bosnia and Herzegovina, received; Burkina Faso, due 1 March 2005; Cape Verde, due 1 July 2004; Chile, due 1 July 2006; Colombia, received; Ecuador, received; Egypt, received; El Salvador, received; Ghana, due 1 July 2004; Guatemala, due 1 July 2004; Guinea, due 1 July 2004; Honduras, due 1 December 2006; Kyrgyzstan, due 1 January 2005; Lesotho, due 1 January 2007; Libyan Arab Jamahiriya, due 1 October 2005; Mali, received; Mauritania, due 1 May 2008; Mexico, received; Morocco, due 1 July 2004; Nicaragua, due 1 February 2007; Niger, due 1 July 2010; Paraguay, due 1 January 2010; Peru, due 1 January 2007; Philippines, received; Rwanda, due 1 April 2010; Senegal, due 1 July 2004; Seychelles, due 1 July 2004; Sri Lanka, received; Syrian Arab Republic, received; Tajikistan, due 1 July 2004; Timor-Leste, due 1 May 2005; Turkey, due 1 January 2006; Uganda, due 1 July 2004; Uruguay, due 1 July 2004.

Party concerned is examined in the absence of a report, the treaty monitoring body bases its consideration on information available to it, including information submitted by UN partners, national human rights institutions and NGOs. The State Party is also invited to send a delegation to attend the session and may thus provide oral information to the treaty monitoring body. Once the treaty monitoring body agrees to provisional concluding observations, they are confidentially communicated to the State Party concerned. If the State Party still does not present a report, the concluding observations are adopted and made public.

Consideration of communications received under articles 76 and 77

Optional article 76 of the ICRMW provides for the consideration by the CMW of communications from a State Party claiming that another State Party is not fulfilling its obligations under the Convention. Optional article 77 provides for the consideration by the CMW of communications received from or on behalf of individuals who claim that their individual rights as established by the Convention have been violated by a State Party. So far, Guatemala is the only State Party to have made the declaration envisaged under article 76. The declaration under article 77 has been made by Guatemala and Mexico. As the articles require that ten States Parties make the declaration before the procedure enters into force, neither the inter-state complaints procedure nor the individual petitions procedure is in force at the moment, and the Committee is thus precluded from considering any communications under these articles.

Annual reports

In accordance with article 74, paragraph 7 of the Convention, the CMW presents an annual report to the UN General Assembly on the implementation of the Convention, containing its considerations and recommendations. The reports are published as official UN General Assembly documents.[20] The Committee's reports contain information on its working methods; its meetings with States Parties, IGOs, NGOs and other participants; the status of reporting by States Parties; its consideration of their reports; and other issues of relevance to its work.

---

[20]   A/59/48 (1st Session), A/60/48 (2nd Session), A/61/48 (3rd and 4th Sessions), A/62/48 (5th and 6th Sessions), A/63/48 (7th and 8th Sessions) and A/64/48 (9th and 10th Sessions).

Promotion of the ICRMW

The CMW sees one of its tasks as promoting awareness of the ICRMW and encouraging states to become party to it. Members actively take part in conferences and other meetings in order to explain the importance of the protection of the human rights of migrant workers and members of their families. The chairperson of the Committee addressed the UN CHR at its 61st Session (13 April 2005) and called upon all states to take the necessary steps to accede or ratify the Convention. In his speech, he referred to the reluctance and scepticism of many states towards the Convention, expressing as his opinion that this attitude called into question their commitment to apply without discrimination the human rights norms that they have already accepted under other core international human-rights instruments. Every year, on International Migrants Day (18 December), the chairperson issues a statement, reminding the international community of the need to safeguard migrants' rights.

The CMW also looks for active cooperation in its promotional activities. International Migrants Day statements, for example, are issued jointly with the UN Special Rapporteur on the Human Rights of Migrants, and International Migrants Day celebrations were held during the CMW session on 16 December 2005, in the presence of the Special Rapporteur, representatives of UN agencies, IGOs and NGOs.

Ratification of the ICRMW is also promoted by the Steering Committee on the Promotion of the Ratification of the Migrant Workers Convention, which consists of IGOs and UN agencies (IOM, ILO, OHCHR and UNESCO), as well as NGOs (December 18, FIDH, HRW, ICMC, International Trade Union Confederation, MFA, MRI, PSI and the WCC). In April 2009, the Steering Committee published a guide on the ratification of the Convention.[21]

Day of General Discussion

Following the practice of several treaty monitoring bodies, the CMW organized a Day of General Discussion during its 3rd Session, on 15 December 2005, under the title 'Protecting the Rights of All Migrant Workers as a Tool

---

[21] See the International Steering Committee for the Campaign for Ratification of the Migrants Rights Convention, *Guide on Ratification: International Convention on the Protection of the Rights of All Migrant Workers and Members of Their Families*, Geneva, 2009 (www.migrantsrights.org/documents/SCRatificationGuide4-2009Final. pdf [last accessed 3 July 2009]).

to Enhance Development'. The Committee was inspired in its choice of subject by the decision of the General Assembly to organize an HLD, and hoped to bring out the importance of human rights in this context.

The day was well attended, by some twenty representatives of states and sixty representatives of civil society, as well as representatives of UN agencies and IGOs. After opening remarks by the CMW chairperson, the UN Special Rapporteur on the Human Rights of Migrants, the ILO representative and committee member (an expert from Morocco) made the first presentation, focusing on human rights, migration and development in countries of origin. In the afternoon, the subject was human rights, migration and development in countries of destination, introduced by an expert from the United Kingdom. The presentations were followed by a lively debate among the participants.

Contributions and discussions concentrated on the importance of recognizing that migrants should be seen as human beings, not as commodities, and that a human rights-based approach has advantages for the wellbeing of all those involved in international migration. With respect to countries of employment, participants considered that protection of human rights and prevention of discrimination are essential in order to enhance the integration of migrant workers and members of their families, thus enabling them to contribute to the country's socioeconomic welfare. Similarly, participants felt that the contribution of migrants to the development of their country of origin would be enhanced by protecting the rights of migrant workers in their country, both before departure and after return, for example through effective use of their acquired skills and experience on their return. In this context, they highlighted the importance of looking into ways of realizing the portability of social security and pension benefits, as well as improving access to the justice system in the country of employment for migrant workers with unsolved claims for wages or benefits.[22]

The day thus allowed for critical reflections on the use of the ICRMW in order to enhance human rights protection of migrants. Through the attendance of several NGOs from different parts of the world (Asia, Latin America, North America and Europe), it also created opportunities for civil society actors to meet and coordinate their projects. At its 11th Session in October 2009, the CMW is holding a Day of General Discussion on migrant domestic workers, in light of the 2010 International Labour Conference that will discuss the need for drafting an international instrument for the protection of domestic workers.

---

[22] See the Committee's annual report to the General Assembly, 2006, A/61/48.

CMW contribution to the HLD

Following the Day of General Discussion, the CMW decided to adopt a written contribution to the General Assembly's HLD. The text of the contribution was discussed in public meetings during the Committee's 4th Session in April 2006. The draft text was made public, which allowed interested organizations to make comments and suggestions for consideration by the Committee.

In its contribution, the CMW notes that migrants are, above all, human beings with rights, as well as active agents of development. Therefore, for the Committee, the question of migration must be approached from a human rights perspective, in conformity with the Universal Declaration on Human Rights as well as state obligations under core international human-rights treaties. It should be borne in mind that the concept of development encompasses not just economic development, but also entails cultural, social and political development. In this context, the Committee observes that migration stimulates cultural and economic exchanges among nations, which in turn promote peace and understanding in keeping with the goals of the UN.

The CMW made recommendations on the following issues:

- dissemination of reliable information both by the states of origin and of employment about conditions of migration, including by informing the public about positive contributions of migrant workers to host countries in order to counter xenophobic and racist tendencies
- control over recruitment agencies
- equality in remuneration and conditions of employment
- protection of migrants' rights and integration, including through consular protection, enactment of legislation to protect the human rights of migrants, training of government officials, establishment of effective and accessible complaints procedures, facilitation of family reunification or family visits and providing access to education for all children of migrant workers
- remedies for violations of migrants' rights, allowing for payment of outstanding wages and benefits, including through provision of legal services and bilateral agreements on access to justice.
- migrants' contact with the country of origin, for example by providing voting rights, establishing mechanisms that would take the needs of migrants into account and, in pursuing temporary migration projects, ensuring full protection of migrants' rights

- measures linked to the return of migrants, including portability of pensions and social security entitlements.[23]

Cooperation with other stakeholders

International Labour Organization

Before the drafting of the ICRMW began, the possibility was considered of elaborating it as an ILO convention rather than a UN human rights convention. When the General Assembly decided to establish a working group to elaborate the text, nineteen delegations abstained because they felt that the Convention should be developed within the context of the ILO, which, according to its constitution, has a responsibility for migrant workers.[24] During the drafting process, ILO representatives closely monitored developments, and the drafters benefited from their input. In recognition of its expertise, the ICRMW, in article 74, paragraph 5, provides that the ILO shall be invited by the Committee to appoint representatives to participate, in a consultative capacity, in the meetings of the Committee. In accordance with paragraph 2 of the same article, the ILO receives copies of the reports submitted by States Parties concerned, so it could assist the Committee with its expertise.

ILO representatives have participated in all the CMW sessions so far. They were consulted on methods of work and shared with the Committee their experience in examining reports from states under the ILO migration conventions (Nos. 97 and 143). They also took an active part in the Committee's Day of General Discussion and provided it with advice during the drafting of its written contribution to the HLD. The ILO regularly provides the Committee with written information on the situation of migrant workers in the countries whose reports are being considered, and may attend the closed meetings in which the list of issues on the reports are prepared. The ILO is also given the opportunity to provide comments when the Committee is adopting its concluding observations on the States Parties' reports.

---

[23] See note by the Secretary-General transmitting the summary of the discussions of the Committee on the Protection of the Rights of All Migrant Workers and Members of Their Families to the High-Level Dialogue on International Migration and Development, A/61/120.

[24] J. Lönnroth, 1991, The International Convention on the Rights of All Migrant Workers and Members of Their Families in the context of international migration policies: an analysis of ten years of negotiation, International Migration Review, Vol. 25, No. 4, pp. 710–36.

UN agencies and other IGOs

In accordance with article 74, paragraph 7 of the ICRMW, the CMW also invites representatives of other UN specialized agencies and organizations, together with IGOs, to attend its meetings. From the outset, cooperation has been especially fruitful between the Committee and the IOM. IOM representatives attend all sessions of the Committee, present information on country situations and in general provide advice and exchange ideas with the Committee. The UNHCR also cooperates with the Committee in providing information on country situations when relevant to its mandate. Other agencies that occasionally attend CMW sessions and provide information are UNESCO, the World Bank, UNFPA and UNDP.

The Committee has also maintained good contacts with the GCIM, which was established in December 2003 and finished its work in October 2005 with the presentation of its report on new directions for action on migration.[25] During the informal meeting of the Committee in October 2004, as well as during its 2nd Session in April 2005, discussions took place between the Committee and the GCIM representative concerning the importance of the Convention within the context of international migration. One of the committee members, Francisco Alba, was also a member of the GCIM, which, of course, facilitated contact between the two bodies.

Nevertheless, the CMW was disappointed with the final report of the GCIM because it failed to call for universal ratification of the Convention. By way of reaction, the Committee expressed its concern about the focus of the report and criticized it for approaching migration fundamentally from a market perspective and thus increasing the risk that migrants are considered as commodities rather than human beings. The Committee further regretted that the report did not specifically support the Convention and did not call upon all states to ratify or accede to it.

NGOs and national human rights institutions

The CMW would not be able to carry out its work properly without the continuing support of civil society. NGOs have played and continue to play a crucial role in promoting the rights contained in the ICRMW (see Chapter 3). They have also been unwavering in their support for the Committee and its work. From the inaugural session onwards, the Committee has had fruitful cooperation with NGOs, which have

---

[25] GCIM, 2005, *Migration in an Interconnected World: New Directions for Action*, Report of the Global Commission on International Migration.

organized themselves in the International Platform on the Migrant Workers' Convention, now with seventeen members.[26]

According to article 74(4) of the ICRMW, NGOs can submit written information to the Committee, just like UN-specialized agencies and IGOs. So far, NGOs have provided written information in relation to the consideration of state reports as well as in relation to the Day of General Discussion.

Starting at its first session, the CMW has had regular meetings with NGO representatives in order to discuss continuing cooperation and to facilitate the participation of civil society in its work. This has resulted in an active NGO role during committee sessions, be it through providing written information, organizing side-events at the session or dialogue with committee members.

The role of national human rights institutions in committee work has so far been limited to the examination of States Parties' reports. Like NGOs, they are given an opportunity to provide written information and to brief the Committee orally, first during a closed meeting preceding the session at which the State Party's report will be considered, and then in public at the session in which the report is being examined. So far, the Mexican National Human Rights Commission, the Egyptian National Council for Human Rights, the Bolivian Defensor del Pueblo and the Procurador para la Defensa de los Derechos Humanos of El Salvador, the Ombudsman of Bosnia and Herzegovina and the Commission on Human Rights of the Philippines have provided information to the Committee.

At their eighth international conference, held in Santa Cruz (Bolivia) from 24 to 26 October 2006, the national human rights institutions agreed to encourage their states to support the CMW and to call for the ratification and implementation of the Convention.[27]

Special procedures

The CMW has also endeavoured to establish good working relations with the special procedures created by the CHR (and continued by the

---

[26] As of June 2009, members included Action Canada for Population and Development, Amnesty International, Anti-Slavery International, December 18, FIDH, Franciscans International, HRW, ICMC, International Centre for Migration, Health and Development, International Movement against All Forms of Discrimination and Racism, Jesuit Refugee Service, Kav LaOved, Migrant CARE, MRI, National Employment Law Project, Organisation Mondiale Contre la Torture, PSI, the English International Association of Lund, Warbe Development Foundation and the WCC.

[27] Eighth International Conference of National Institutions for the Promotion and Protection of Human Rights, Santa Cruz Declaration, 26 October 2006.

HRC). At its 1st Session, the Committee met with both the Special Rapporteur on the Human Rights of Migrants, Gabriela Rodríguez Pizarro, and the Special Rapporteur on the Rights of Non-citizens of the Sub-Commission on the Promotion and Protection of Human Rights, David Weissbrodt, in order to discuss cooperation in promoting the Convention. The current Special Rapporteur on the Human Rights of Migrants, Jorge Bustamante, participated in December 2005 in the Day of General Discussion on the link between human rights, development and migration, and also joined the Committee in its celebrations of International Migrants Day on 18 December 2005.

Observations for the future

Reform proposals

The human rights-treaty protection system, with its eight core international human-rights instruments and eight separate treaty monitoring bodies, is facing increasing calls for reform in order to enhance its effectiveness and efficiency.[28] Many states perceive the periodic reporting obligation as a burden, as it requires them to present different reports to different treaty bodies at different times. Concerns have also been raised about possible divergent interpretations of human rights norms between different treaty bodies. Other issues raised are lack of reporting by states on the one hand, and delays in the examination by treaty bodies of reports on the other.

In order to enhance the cooperation and coordination among them, the chairpersons of treaty bodies have met regularly since 1984, and on a yearly basis since 1995 (Chairpersons meeting). Since 2002, this is preceded by a meeting where each treaty monitoring body is represented by three members (Inter-Committee meeting). The meetings focus on the harmonization of working methods and enhancing the work of the treaty bodies. This has resulted in the approval of harmonized guidelines for a common core document, which will form the first part of each State Party's report to any treaty monitoring body, followed

---

[28] The International Convention for the Protection of All Persons from Enforced Disappearance is another human rights instrument establishing a treaty monitoring body. It has been adopted but is not yet in force. Moreover, the Optional Protocol to the Convention against Torture entered into force on 22 June 2006; its Sub-Committee on Prevention met for the first time in February 2007. The Sub-Committee's mandate is different to that of the existing treaty monitoring bodies.

by a treaty-specific report. Further harmonization of working methods are being discussed, such as a common approach to reservations.

In 2006, the former High Commissioner for Human Rights, Louise Arbour, published a concept paper entailing a radical approach to treaty monitoring body reform through the creation of a single, unified, standing treaty body that would replace the seven existing committees.[29] Although this approach did not meet with strong support from treaty monitoring bodies nor from many Member States, it gave an impetus and a sense of urgency to the discussions on ways of enhancing the effectiveness and efficiency of the existing system. This is resulting in closer coordination among the different treaty monitoring bodies.

The CMW is perhaps more open than other committees to possibilities of change, as it is not yet firmly rooted in its own methods and approaches. So far, the CMW has supported treaty monitoring body reform proposals, especially those that aim at greater harmonization of working methods. Not rejecting out of hand the suggestion of a unified standing treaty body and seeing an advantage in mainstreaming the issue of human rights of migrants, it has nonetheless expressed concern about the need to secure the specificity of the Convention.

Viability of the ICRMW in the light of stagnating ratifications and non-reporting

The next few years will show whether the CMW can make the Convention a vital instrument for protecting the human rights of migrant workers and members of their families. This does not entirely depend on the Committee, but also on factors beyond its control.

The first, of course, is the slow rate of ratification of the Convention and the absence of any major receiving country among the States Parties. Since the Convention entered into force on 1 March 2003, a further twenty-one states adhered to it. The accession of Niger in March 2009 has brought the number of States Parties to forty-one, the number identified in the Convention as required for expanding the membership of the CMW to fourteen. It is to be hoped that in light of the continuing attention to the phenomenon of migration in international debate, efforts will increase to promote the Convention as the most

---

[29] HRI/MC/2006/2, concept paper on the High Commissioner's proposal for a unified standing treaty body, report by the Secretariat, 22 March 2006.

comprehensive framework to assist states in carrying out their migration policies in full respect of human rights.

A second concern is the consideration of initial reports that have been submitted by States Parties to the Convention. So far, the Committee has examined eleven initial reports, and a further two are pending. Twenty-four initial reports are overdue. The Convention can only be effective in providing protection to migrant workers and members of their families if States Parties report to the CMW in order to allow it to scrutinize compliance with their obligations. Without effective monitoring, the Convention is not a viable instrument. CMW consideration of States Parties' reports also gives it an opportunity to provide interpretations of the provisions of the Convention and to apply these provisions to everyday reality. Without this, the Convention risks remaining an unfulfilled promise. A well-functioning monitoring system may also persuade states that so far have been reluctant to recognize that the Convention and the Committee's assistance may be of practical value when dealing with sensitive migration-related issues, and may help them to respect the human rights of migrant workers and members of their families, to the benefit of all involved, including the society of the country of employment. However, if all States Parties fulfill their reporting obligations, the Committee may well need additional meeting time in order to examine all reports.

Conclusion

The balance of the first years of the CMW's work is rather positive. The Committee has shown great interest in moving the protection of migrant workers' rights forward in the international debate, such as that on migration and development at the General Assembly's HLD in 2006 and beyond. The active cooperation of the CMW with both NGOs and UN agencies and international organizations enhances a broad-based campaign for the promotion of the ICRMW.

Consideration of the first reports has shown the CMW's understanding of the practical problems faced by governments in guaranteeing migrant workers' rights and its desire to assist governments to achieve the highest possible standards. The Committee has succeeded in showing that it is capable of giving concrete guidance to states on how to guarantee migrants' rights in their specific domestic situation. Its practice also shows that it does not shy away from emphasizing the obligations of countries of origin, be it in combating smuggling and trafficking of migrants, in providing consular assistance to their nationals abroad or in facilitating the return of their nationals, thus countering an argument that is sometimes heard that the Convention only imposes obligations on the countries of employment.

However, perhaps because of the antagonism that the Convention creates in governmental circles of certain Western receiving countries, it has taken a while for the Committee to become recognized as a major player in international migration discussions. For instance, the Committee was not invited to contribute to the first Global Forum on Migration and Development that was held in July 2007 in Brussels. The organizers of the second Global Forum, which was held in October 2008 in the Philippines, have, however, not only invited a representative of the Committee to attend the Forum, but have also solicited the Committee's contribution into the background paper for the roundtable on migration, development and human rights.[30] It is to be hoped that this development will continue and that the Committee will be recognized as the expert body on the human rights-based approach to migration, and that its guidance will be accepted also by those states that are not a party to the Convention.

In order for the CMW's potential to be realized, a wider acceptance of the Convention by states of origin, of transit and of employment is required. Although the Committee can assist states in complying with the Convention, only when the rights enumerated therein are supported by a broad basis in society can its implementation be successful and can it provide effective protection to migrant workers and members of their families.

---

[30] The Committee's proposal to the Global Forum is being published as part of the Committee's annual report (A/63/48).

5

Migrants' rights in UN human rights conventions

ISABELLE SLINCKX

Introduction

The UN has developed a number of international human rights conventions that many states have ratified, thus committing themselves to respect the rights these conventions set out. These core human rights conventions derive directly from the Universal Declaration of Human Rights and the rights universally recognized as benefiting 'all human beings'. The last of these, the ICRMW, is the most poorly ratified of all, with only forty-one States Parties. But the many states that have not ratified the Convention to date are bound by some or all of the other six conventions. These states often argue that migrants are sufficiently protected by their provisions and that there is therefore no need to ratify the ICRMW.

To what extent are migrant workers' rights effectively protected by the six other UN human rights conventions? Is the ICRMW really unnecessary in the international human rights framework? What protection does the UN human rights system give to migrants and how is it implemented? What are the gaps? These questions are at the heart of this chapter, which aims to clarify the place of migrant workers' rights in the overall UN human rights framework. It is based on a UNESCO-sponsored research project undertaken jointly by December 18 and the ICMC, which included the study of all country-specific conclusions and recommendations, those issued by the six treaty monitoring bodies supervising the implementation and those by the States Parties, of conventions other than the ICRMW, from 1994 to 2005.[1]

---

[1] The research was conducted electronically through the public UN High Commissioner for Human Rights Treaty Bodies Database. The phrase 'migrant workers' seldom appears as such in treaty monitoring body conclusions, thus broader and related concepts were used, including 'migrant/migration', 'work' (in order to also cover overseas, irregular, foreign or undocumented worker), 'minorities', 'alien', 'unaccompanied', 'national/

Today, analysis of the protection level granted to migrants by the main human rights conventions is even more purposeful. They offer a framework of rights that should be the basis for the numerous migration management processes currently open at regional and UN levels. In September 2006, the HLD took place in New York. It gathered states, UN agencies, funds and programmes and the IOM to discuss the multi-dimensional aspects of international migration and development in order to identify appropriate ways and means to maximize its development benefits and minimize its negative impacts.[2]

While hearings were held to air civil society's views, many NGOs and migrant groups and some trade unions have advocated for a rights-based approach to these debates, criticizing the fact that they would often focus on the positive economic aspects of migration rather than on the human side of it. This view is shared by the OHCHR, which recently developed position papers and forward-looking research documents arguing that a rights-based approach should be at the centre of these discussions.[3] Louise Arbour, former High Commissioner for Human Rights, summarized this need in these words: 'Managing migration flows effectively requires an understanding that migrants are not simply agents of development, but human beings with rights which states have an obligation to protect.'[4]

Applicability of UN human rights system to migrant workers

The human rights contained in the seven main human rights treaties of the UN apply, in principle, to all human beings, given that they apply to all persons under the jurisdiction of States Parties, i.e. on their territory. This is ensured through a reminder in their introduction reiterating that the Universal Declaration of Human Rights proclaims that all human beings are born free and equal in dignity and rights and that everyone is entitled to all the rights and freedoms set out therein, without distinction of any kind, in particular as to race, colour or national origin. There are, however, some exceptions to this principle where rights are restricted to nationals.

citizen' (to identify treatment of 'non-nationals' and 'non-citizens') and 'foreign'. Only relevant entries were retained for the study.

[2] See UN General Assembly Resolution A/60/490/Add.3 of 16 December 2005.

[3] See OHCHR, 2006, *Key OHCHR Messages* Geneva, Switzerland, OHCHR; and OHCHR, 2006, *Migration and Development: A Human Rights Approach*, Geneva, Switzerland, OHCHR.

[4] High-level panel in preparation of the High Level Dialogue of the General Assembly on Migration and Development, comments by the High Commissioner for Human Rights, Louise Arbour, Geneva, 4 July 2006.

Although these do not exclude migrant workers from the protection granted by the UN human rights conventions, they do limit this protection in certain cases. In addition, the committees monitoring the implementation of the UN conventions in the States Parties have developed a 'case-law' explicitly or implicitly including migrant workers in many areas of protection.

Treaties

The core UN human rights treaties are currently the ICERD (1965), the ICCPR (1966), the ICESCR (1966), the CEDAW (1979), the CAT (1984), the CRC (1989) and the ICRMW (1990).

While the ICRMW aims specifically at the protection of migrant workers, the other six apply to migrants as well. This is of particular relevance when looking at the ratification rate: to date, only forty-one countries have ratified the ICRMW; by contrast, 125 states have ratified the other six instruments.[5] One can therefore conclude that the applicability of these treaties to migrant workers and their families offers them protection in states that have not ratified the ICRMW.

Moreover, several treaties explicitly state that the rights recognized are to be applied to non-nationals – and hence to migrants – through the strong non-discriminatory clauses prohibiting distinctions of any kind, including grounds such as race, colour, language, national, ethnic or social origin (articles 2(1) and 26 of the ICCPR; article 2(2) of the ICESCR; article 2(1) of the CRC). Strong language can also be used – such as 'every human being' – to refer to individuals who shall enjoy rights such as the right to life, freedom of association, protection of the family (articles 6, 22 and 23 of the ICCPR) or to state the 'right of everyone' to, for example, social security or adequate standard of living (articles 9 and 11, respectively of the ICESCR). The Convention on the Elimination of Racial Discrimination (CERD) is, of course, devoted to categories that are discriminated against on racial grounds, as stated in its article 1(1) describing racial discrimination.[6] All rights it provides for

---

[5] ICMC, 2006, *Strengthening Protection of Migrant Workers and their Families with International Human Rights Treaties; A Do-It-Yourself Kit*, Geneva, Switzerland, ICMC, p. 22.

[6] Article 1.1 of the CERD states: 'In this Convention, the term "racial discrimination" shall mean any distinction, exclusion, restriction or preference based on race, colour, descent, or national or ethnic origin which has the purpose or effect of nullifying or impairing the recognition, enjoyment or exercise, on an equal footing, of human rights and fundamental freedoms in the political, economic, social, cultural or any other field of public life.'

can therefore clearly be extended to migrant workers as they are to be applied 'without distinction as to race, colour, or national or ethnic origin'.[7]

The conclusions reached by the expert committees on examination of state reports (see below) sometimes mention the article that is the legal basis for the conclusion; this gives an interesting indication of the kind of issues mentioned in relation to violations of human rights of migrants and situations of concern. These issues are:

- equality before the law (article 3 of the ICCPR)
- prohibition of slavery, forced labour and traffic in persons (article 8 of the ICCPR; article 35 of the CRC; article 6 of the CEDAW) and protection against all forms of sexual exploitation and sexual abuse (article 34 of the CRC)
- right to freedom of movement and to leave any country, including one's own, and to return (article 12 of the ICCPR)
- right to work and enjoyment of just and favourable conditions of work (articles 6 and 7 of the ICESCR)
- right to form trade unions and join the trade union of one's choice (article 8(1) of the ICESCR)
- best interest of the child (article 3 of the CRC)
- birth registration and right to acquire a nationality (article 7 of the CRC)
- *non-refoulement* clause[8] (article 3 of the CAT).

The UN Special Rapporteur on the Human Rights of Migrants, who visits countries and is entitled to receive individual complaints and general information for all Member States, should also be mentioned.

---

[7] Examples of rights provided thereby include equal treatment before the tribunals; right to security of person; political rights; right to freedom of movement and residence; right to nationality; right to freedom of thought, to peaceful assembly and association; right to work; right to just and favourable conditions of work and other labour rights; right to housing; right to public health, medical care, social security and social services, etc.

[8] This clause aims at avoiding the danger of being subjected to torture in the country to which the individual concerned is being expelled, returned or extradited. The principle was officially enshrined in the 1951 Convention relating to the Status of Refugees: 'No Contracting State shall expel or return ("*refouler*") a refugee in any manner whatsoever to the frontiers of territories where his life or freedom would be threatened on account of his race, religion, nationality, membership of a particular social group or political opinion.'

Monitoring mechanisms and their working methods

Each treaty provides for the setting up of a committee of independent experts tasked with the supervision of the implementation of the respective treaty. These committees are known as treaty monitoring bodies. The treaty monitoring body system is a unique monitoring mechanism, as governments voluntarily accept to have independent experts scrutinize their human rights records through submitting periodic reports on their performance in the implementation of the provisions of the treaties they are parties to (see Chapter 4, Table 4.1 at p. 104).

The supervision can be done through the reporting procedure described above, but also through other mechanisms such as the examination of individual complaints (with the exceptions of the ICESCR and CRC, which do not provide for it). Even though many complaints have been made regarding non-nationals, they overwhelmingly relate to asylum issues and generally are not specific to migrant workers[9] (such as removal orders for rejected asylum seekers and detention issues under the CAT; discrimination in employment and access to services and racist speech under the ICERD; family issues and ill-treatment by police forces under the ICCPR). The *Karakurt v. Austria* case[10] about participation in work councils for non-EU nationals is a good example of a case that would fall within the remit of the ICRMW. The CEDAW protocol allowing for individual complaints only entered into force in 2000, and none of the few communications made are related to migration issues. Regarding the ICRMW, the mechanism has not yet entered into force as the ten statements by States Parties required have not yet been reached.

This system is under review since the Secretary-General presented the document, *Strengthening of the United Nations: An Agenda for Further Change*. The aim is to simplify reporting by states in order to relieve the reporting burden. The debate has focused on treaty monitoring body working methods and various report models, but no agreement has been reached so far (see Chapter 4).

Each treaty monitoring body has developed guidelines on the drafting of state reports.[11] They rarely specifically refer to reporting on migrants,

---

[9] For research on this issue, see www.bayefsky.com/themes/aliens_general_jurisprudence. pdf; and www.bayefsky.com/themes/work_conditions_jurisprudence.pdf [both last accessed 16 April 2009].

[10] Communication 965/2000, *Karakurt v. Austria*, CCPR/C/74/D/965/2000 (4 April 2002) at paragraphs 3.1–3.2, 3.4, 7.5, 8.2–8.4, 9 and 10.

[11] Compilation of guidelines on the form and content of reports to be submitted by States Parties to the international human rights treaties: report by the Secretary-General (HRI/ GEN/2/Rev.2), 7 May 2004.

mainly using the general language of 'non-nationals' or including migrants in the vulnerable or disadvantaged groups. TMBs also regularly issue 'General Comments' or 'General Recommendations'. These are interpretative comments of the articles of the conventions or of general principles, some of which relate to migrant issues.

- The CCPR, in its General Comment No. 15 on 'The Position of Aliens under the Covenant' (1986), states that 'the enjoyment of Covenant rights is not limited to citizens of States Parties but must also be available to all individuals, regardless of nationality or statelessness, such as asylum seekers, refugees, migrant workers and other persons, who may find themselves in the territory or subject to the jurisdiction of the State Party'. This statement was recalled in General Comment No. 31 (paragraph 10) on 'The Nature of the General Legal Obligation Imposed on States Parties to the Covenant' (2004).
- The CESCR issued General Comment No. 14 on 'The Right to the Highest Attainable Standard of Health' (2000), where it affirms that 'States are under the obligation to *respect* the right to health by, *inter alia*, refraining from denying or limiting equal access for all persons, including prisoners or detainees, minorities, asylum seekers and illegal immigrants, to preventive, curative and palliative health services' (article 34). In its General Comment No. 6 on 'The Equal Right of Men and Women to the Enjoyment of All Economic, Social and Cultural Rights' (2005), it stated that 'refugee or migrant status is one of the grounds of discrimination of women in the equal enjoyment of their human rights' (paragraphs 5 and 10). In General Comment No. 18 on 'The Right to Work' (2005), a special paragraph was dedicated to 'migrant workers and the right to work' (paragraph 18).
- The CEDAW issued General Recommendation No. 21 entitled 'Equality in Marriage and Family Relations' (1994), in which it mentions explicitly the right of migrant women to have their family join them (article 15).
- CRC General Comment No. 3 on 'HIV/AIDS and the Rights of the Child' (2003) insisted on the special vulnerability of some categories of children, including migrant, minority, indigenous and street children. In General Comments Nos. 6 on 'Treatment of Unaccompanied Children' (2005) and 7 on 'Implementing Child Rights in Early Childhood' (2005), the CRC insisted on the need to give particular attention to the most vulnerable groups of young children and to those who are at risk of discrimination, including children from migrant families.

- CERD General Recommendation No. 30 on 'Discrimination against Non-citizens' (2004) gives a special place to migrants, refugees and asylum seekers and considers that any differential treatment based on citizenship or immigration status is discriminatory.
- The CAT adopted only one General Comment on 'Conditions for Filing Complaints With Respect to Implementation of Article 3' (1997), which concerns *non-refoulement*. The text does not mention migrant workers but is obviously applicable to undocumented migrants to be deported.

In conclusion, migrant workers are clearly included in the most vulnerable groups by the treaty monitoring bodies. This is a part of the evolution and the extension of the protection mandate of the UN, with migrant status being added to more classical grounds of discrimination such as race, colour, language, religion, political and other opinion, national or social origin, property, birth, age, ethnicity, disability and marital status. How does this protection, however, relate to the protection that is specifically elaborated in the ICRMW to respond to migrants' specific needs?

Place of migrants' rights in UN human rights system

This section details the migrants' rights issues identified by the various treaty monitoring bodies together with the protection responses they give, including a series of case studies, and then analyzes the gaps in this protection, finally presenting the added value of the ICRMW.

Concerns about human rights of migrants as identified by treaty monitoring bodies

Some cross-cutting issues and clusters of rights are examined by several of the treaty monitoring bodies. The main common concerns are trafficking, discrimination, deportation, working conditions, irregular migrants and post-9/11 anti-terrorist measures. On the other hand, an overlap can be noted in treaty monitoring body conclusions due to the lack of mainstreaming of migrant issues.

International Convention on the Elimination of All Forms of Racial Discrimination

The CERD notes with concern the re-emergence of racist attitudes of host populations towards foreigners in general and asylum seekers and immigrants in particular, such as insulting political speech; ill-treatment and violence; expression of prejudices in the media; violent attacks against ethnic minorities by neo-Nazi gangs, etc. The principles of equality before the law and equality in the exercise of the rights and freedoms between nationals and non-nationals should be ensured. Legislative and law-enforcement actions to be taken are: prohibit discrimination on grounds of colour, racial or ethnic origin and nationality; criminalize violence against members of national, ethnic or racial minorities and religious groups; prohibit racist organizations; consider racial discrimination as an aggravating circumstance for other offences; provide for redress for acts of racial discrimination; set up monitoring centres on racism and xenophobia; and organize education and promotion of multiculturalism. The Committee notes with concern the length of administrative detention and incidents and allegations of excessive use of force, vexatious conduct and ill-treatment by law-enforcement officials. In these cases, the state must ensure that a proper investigation is carried out and accompanied by sanctions. Awareness-raising actions should be undertaken to sensitize the police and the judiciary, eradicate racial prejudices and train them to address complaints of racially motivated crimes. International human rights standards should be respected as regards due process.

Discrimination against migrants is noted in the areas of education, housing, access to public services, land property and social security ben-efits, as well as discrimination between migrants according to the kind of work they perform or their nationality. States should ensure that foreign workers enjoy the same labour protection as national workers especially as regards minimum protection against poor working conditions and low wages and proper representation of ethnic minority groups in the labour market, with special focus on women. The Committee is concerned about the enjoyment of fundamental rights by non-citizens, especially the right to security of person and economic, social and cultural rights. The impact of immigration law, or any legislation having implications for foreigners, should be assessed in the light of the ICERD. The Committee notes that in some cases the large influx of immigrants and refugees from neighbouring countries might result in implementation difficulties.

The Committee is particularly concerned that undocumented workers as well as trainees and domestic workers, do not always enjoy all rights and are more likely to suffer ill-treatment. Generally, states should prohibit retention of passports by employers, control recruitment agen-cies, provide for the possibility for irregular workers to lodge complaints in case of infringement and ensure sanctions for employers who recruit undeclared workers. The Committee encourages regularization of

undocumented migrant workers, in order to facilitate the implementation of ICERD provisions on persons without status.

Even if the Committee recognizes that political rights can legitimately
be limited to citizens, it considers that the right to vote and to stand for
local elections should be granted at least to long-term residents in view of
facilitating integration. States should facilitate the acquisition of citizenship to avoid statelessness, and make sure that even stateless persons
fully enjoy their economic, social and cultural rights. States should also
pursue the effective implementation of measures to facilitate the integration of foreigners, such as services and information in their own language
and financial support to organizations for the integration of immigrants.
The list of occupations restricted to citizens should be reduced.

Regarding family reunification, the right to family life should be guaranteed to all persons without distinction; migrants should have the right to
have their children join them. Access to education for children of undocumented workers is important, as well as the integration of these children
without loss of ties to their culture of origin. Regarding post-9/11 anti-
terrorist measures, the Committee recalls that states should 'ensure that
measures taken in the struggle against terrorism do not discriminate in
purpose or effect on grounds of race, colour, descent or national or ethnic
origin'[12] and should prohibit indefinite detention without charge or trial.
Expulsion of foreigners suspected of constituting a threat to national
security needs to be balanced with human rights obligations.

An example of positive aspects underlined by the CERD is the enactment of Decree Law 251/2002 by Portugal on 22 November 2002 which,
inter alia, establishes the Advisory Board for Immigration Affairs, tasked
with ensuring the participation of associations that are representative of
immigrants, employers' associations and social solidarity institutions in
the elaboration of policies promoting social integration and combating
exclusion.[13] The CERD also welcomed with satisfaction the ratification
of the ICRMW by Bolivia.[14]

International Covenant on Civil and Political Rights

The two most frequent subjects of concern for the CCPR regarding
migrants' rights are detention, especially its duration and conditions,
and deportation of aliens, in particular the use of excessive force. The
Committee has identified obligations for states, such as to allow hearings

---

[12] See CERD General Recommendation No. 20, March 2002.
[13] Portugal, 2004, CERD/C/65/CO/6.   [14] Bolivia, 2003, CERD/C/63/CO/2.

and appeals with clear rules against administrative decisions of deportation (even for migrants in an irregular situation); to allow access to human rights organizations and legal advice; and to respect the principle of *non-refoulement*.

Another focus is ill-treatment or harassment of foreigners by law-enforcement officials. In this respect, recommendations deal with training in human rights for law-enforcement officials; a clearer definition of the powers of control of immigration officers at borders; (prompt) investigations; and independent mechanisms to deal with individual complaints. Women migrants are mentioned almost exclusively in relation to trafficking, with a focus on fighting and prosecution. Migrant children are also mostly mentioned in relation to trafficking and forced labour. The Committee also notes with concern the difficulties for large groups of migrant children, whose parents are non-citizens, to access citizenship and birth registration, which can affect the enjoyment of their political rights and their access to education.

Measures targeting increasing xenophobia and hate speech should be adopted. National legislation and/or the constitution should guarantee equality and prohibit discrimination. Various forms of discrimination in the access to the rights guaranteed in the Covenant affecting non-citizens in general and undocumented migrants in particular are of concern to the Committee: access to civil and political rights; freedom of expression; freedom of association (mostly regarding trade unions) and freedom of movement (restrictive practices regarding residence permits; obligatory exit visa; confiscation of identity documents by employers; long waiting periods for family reunification, etc.).

The examination by the Committee of post-9/11 impacts on immigrants leads it to the reassertion that the fight against terrorism cannot be a source of abuse. A foreigner regarded as a threat to state security because of a suspicion of terrorism must have the opportunity to challenge an expulsion measure if they may be exposed to a violation of their rights in the country of return, and should not be returned to a country where they face a risk of torture. The Committee recalls that the rights to privacy and freedom of expression of foreigners or people of foreign extraction must be guaranteed.

An example of positive aspects in states' behaviour, which the Committee usually 'notes with satisfaction' or 'welcomes', is the fact that children of irregular immigrants are entitled to education and medical care.[15]

---

[15] Belgium, HRC, 1998, CCPR/C/79/Add.99.

International Covenant on Economic, Social and Cultural Rights

The main focus of the CESCR is on terms of employment (minimum wage, health and maternal benefits, pension benefits, unemployment benefits, safe working conditions, access to trade unions and work councils, etc.). States should notably provide for: sanctions for employers who fail to observe the terms of employment and the safety regulations; compensation for victims of violations; prohibition of confiscation of identity documents by employers; freedom for foreign workers to change employer for the legal duration of their stay and to seek new employment on expiration of their contract; regular and independent labour inspections; and trade union rights with access to positions of responsibility. Specific sectors with a high density of undeclared work where legal protection is likely to be incomplete should be targeted, such as domestic work, hotel and catering, agriculture, textile, cleaning and building industries. In this respect, the Committee welcomes bilateral agreements for granting of temporary work permits to seasonal workers in order to give them legal status and to protect them from exploitation. It also recommends that states control whether or not employers treat migrant workers in conformity with ILO standards.

Another issue is discrimination in the enjoyment of economic, social and cultural rights affecting migrant workers in the areas of housing, access to work, employment, education and social security schemes. In that regard, the Committee welcomes the enjoyment by undocumented workers of basic social services, good working conditions, health care and education, but notes that in general the protection they enjoy in the area of welfare is very limited. It therefore welcomes measures taken to regularize their situation. The Committee notes with satisfaction the efforts made in view of the integration of foreign workers and immigrants in general by the adoption of various steps, such as educational measures, to combat the emerging trend of xenophobia and racism; instruction in the mother tongues of immigrants; and support for their cultural associations. Clear legislation providing for naturalization without discrimination for all foreigners is necessary. States should develop indicators for measuring racial discrimination and adopt criminal measures to combat all forms of discrimination, especially by police, law-enforcement officials and employers. The Committee also expresses its concern about the high rates of unemployment in European countries.

The Committee carries out a detailed analysis of the phenomenon of emigration. The causes it identifies include deficient management of the country's economy, growing poverty and unequal distribution of wealth resulting in constraints on the enjoyment of economic, social and cultural rights. It expresses concern at the fact that emigrants are often skilled and semi-skilled workers whose massive emigration can have a constraining influence on the enjoyment of rights in the country of origin. Other consequences of massive emigration on the society of origin can be family disintegration, abandoned children and juvenile delinquency. The feminization of emigration too often means humiliation, hardships and violence for emigrant women. Countries of origin should therefore give pre-departure information to potential migrant workers about their rights and the possible difficulties to be faced abroad.

On trafficking, recommendations specific to the ICESCR regard mainly the protection of victims: avoidance of double victimization owing to the lack of sensitization of officials and the judiciary; possibility of claiming redress; and guaranteeing that no expeditious expulsions without procedural safeguards are carried out. Migrant children are mentioned, on the one hand, in connection with trafficking for purposes of labour, domestic work and sexual exploitation and, on the other hand, in connection with access to education, health services and protection from discrimination when they are undocumented. States should review laws or policies that result in split families.

The positive aspects underlined by the Committee most often concern the ratification of ILO conventions Nos. 97 and 143 or the adoption and enforcement of legislation on trafficking. An example of a positive aspect is the National Sanitary Plan (PSN, 2003–2005) adopted in Italy, whose coverage was extended to irregular immigrants so that they can receive preventive medical treatment as well as urgent and basic treatment.[16]

Convention on the Elimination of All Forms of Discrimination Against Women

Trafficking and sexual exploitation of migrant women are by far the main subjects of concern of the Committee on the Elimination of Discrimination Against Women (CEDAW). The Committee considers the vulnerability of women to traffickers as being mainly rooted in the poor economic situation in countries of origin, and recommends women's economic empowerment as a solution. The measures suggested to combat trafficking include awareness-raising campaigns; definition of sexual exploitation and trafficking in Criminal Codes as a serious

---

[16] Italy, ECSR, 2004, E/C.12/1/Add.103.

offence; international, regional and bilateral cooperation between countries of origin, transit and destination; adoption of comprehensive national strategies covering prevention, prosecution and rehabilitation aspects; and regulation and limitation of the commercial sex trade. There is a focus on the protection of victims with measures for return, rehabilitation and social reintegration; short-term residence permits for the duration of the investigation and proceedings; adequate protection for victims who do not testify; elimination of legislation that penalizes victims or exacerbates their situation in any way; facilitation of entry into other occupations in the formal labour market; training of border police and law-enforcement officials to recognize and provide support to victims; prosecution and punishment of offenders including corrupt officials, etc.

The Committee notes the feminization of migration, whether of high-skilled workers (in the health sector) or low-skilled (entertainers and domestic helpers). The causes of feminine migration are perceived as political instability, economic liberalization and free-trade agreements that lead to general poverty, to the economic marginalization of women and to a deterioration of the structure of society. States of origin should take measures to help ensure the human rights of women migrants, such as making the issue of exit visas conditional on obtaining a proper employment contract; opening consular offices in receiving countries; fighting illegal employment agencies; giving information before departure, notably to reduce the risk of trafficking; providing for the mandatory registration of emigrants and insurance coverage in origin countries; taking action to protect jobless and disabled returnees; seeking bilateral agreements with receiving countries; and keeping data on abuse of nationals abroad and having mechanisms to respond to those abuses.

In order to ensure the full enjoyment by migrant women of their rights under the CEDAW, receiving countries should put in place information programmes about the availability of various social and education services, legal remedies, language classes, etc. Social programmes should be designed to address the needs of vulnerable groups such as migrant women and should include culture- and gender-sensitive measures with assistance targeting especially access to areas where they are faced with discrimination: education, employment, healthcare, housing, administration and social protection. Migrant women are faced with multiple discrimination on the basis of gender and ethnic and religious background both in society at large and in their communities. Effective measures should be taken by receiving countries to promote women's rights over discriminatory cultural practices and patriarchal attitudes such as forced marriage, and to provide access to legal and administrative remedies in cases of violence and abuse. Gender aspects should therefore be included in immigration law in order to eliminate discrimination and gender bias; for example, an independent right of residence should be accessible for foreign spouses in the event of separation, as a residence right depending on their marriage could constitute a deterrent to seeking separation or divorce if they experience domestic violence.

To guarantee the respect of labour rights, minimal conditions should be enforced such as a standard labour contract with minimum wage; protection against abuse; access to social security and employment benefits, including paid maternity leave; and compensation on leave because of criminal proceedings against the employer. Categories of migrant women workers whose working and living conditions are particularly precarious and who are particularly at risk of abuse are undocumented migrant women in general, domestic workers and women working in the tourist industry, free trade zones and *maquiladora* industries.

The positive aspects underlined by the Committee mainly cover ratification of the UN Convention against Transnational Organized Crime and its protocols: Protocol to Prevent, Suppress and Punish Trafficking in Persons, Especially Women and Children; and Protocol against the Smuggling of Migrants by Land, Sea and Air.

Convention against Torture, and Other Cruel, Inhuman or Degrading Treatment or Punishment

The main concern regarding migrant workers of the Committee against Torture is the excessive use of force and discriminatory practices by the police when dealing with foreigners in general. To counter those practices, recommendations are made regarding training on issues concerning human rights and the CAT, an independent mechanism for following up complaints as well as quick investigation, legal assistance for the victims and widely applicable civil procedures for damage. The Committee notes with concern the low rate of prosecution and conviction in ill-treatment cases. Migrant-related issues in CAT conclusions are mostly to be found in concluding observations on European countries. Most are common with other Committees, but they are more detailed under the CAT.

On the specific issue of detention prior to removal, the Committee is concerned about the excessive length of detention – especially for unaccompanied minors and for unenforceable expulsions – and about detention in places such as police stations or prisons that lack adequate facilities, good hygiene and recreational activities to ensure the physical and psychological integrity of all individuals accommodated. Family reception centres should be set up for families with children. Migrants should always be separated from convicted criminals. An independent mechanism is needed to monitor the conditions of detention. Training on issues arising under the CAT should be given to private security companies providing security to certain detention facilities. The State Party should ensure that all individuals under its jurisdiction are guaranteed fair treatment at all stages of the proceedings, including an opportunity for effective, independent and impartial review of decisions of expulsion, return or extradition, as well as official legal representation and consular access.

Regarding removals, the absolute nature of the protection of article 3 of the CAT on the principle of *non-refoulement* (prohibition of deportation for individuals facing torture if returned to their own country) should be recognized in domestic legislation. Other principles to be enshrined in national legislation are the prohibition of ill-treatment and excessive force during enforced expulsion; the prohibition of returns of long-term residents with most of their ties in the receiving country or to a country with which the returnee has no significant ties; the prohibition of involuntary sedation; the provision of appeals with suspensive effect if a fear of torture in the destination country is alleged; the provision of complaint facilities against law-enforcement officers and employees of private security companies; medical examinations before and after removals, etc.

As far as trafficking is concerned, the measures promoted by the CAT regard in particular the adoption of legislation on criminalization, prosecution and punishment of the perpetrators.

An example of positive aspects is the adoption by Austria of the Criminal Procedure Reform Act and the amendments to the Code of Criminal Procedure, with new provisions regarding the right of the defendant to be assisted by an interpreter; the issuing of an information sheet on their rights for detainees in twenty-six different languages; the new measures taken to improve conditions of detention; the new regulations on deportation procedures banning the use of any means blocking the respiratory system; and providing for the medical examination of the alien prior to the flight.[17]

---

[17] Austria, 2005, CAT/C/AUT/CO/3/CPR.1.

Convention on the Rights of the Child

Regarding trafficking, recommendations specific to the Committee on the Rights of the Child are to further study the causes, nature and extent of various forms of trafficking of children (sexual exploitation, domestic service, bonded labour, slavery, use as camel jockey or transnational adoption); access to healthcare and psychological assistance; reunification with families; cooperation and assistance from UNICEF and IOM; training of law-enforcement officials, social workers and prosecutors on how to monitor, receive, investigate and prosecute reported cases of sexual abuse in a child-sensitive manner; and measures to raise awareness of the issue in communities of origin. Poverty or abandonment by parents are the main causes of vulnerability of children to trafficking. The Committee lists the international instruments to be ratified (UN Convention against Transnational Organized Crime (CTOC) and its protocols; Optional Protocol to the Convention on the Rights of the Child on the Sale of Children, Child Prostitution and Child Pornography).

All legislation, political, judicial and administrative decisions and programmes and services that have an impact on non-national children, especially vulnerable groups such as refugee and migrant children, should be in line with the general principle of non-discrimination, on grounds of race, national or ethnic origin, among others. This is even more so for immigration law and expulsion procedures. The Committee generally recommends that the best interest of the child is integrated in all legislation and measures concerning children and that consideration is given to their views. It notes the persisting disparities in the enjoyment of economic, social and cultural rights (social welfare, education and housing) for non-national children, migrant children, especially undocumented, undeclared seasonal workers, minority children and refugee and asylum-seeking children. States should also make education compulsory and should strengthen measures to address the problem of high drop-out and repetition rates of migrant children. Both education and social services are often accessible *de facto* but not *de jure* to irregular immigrant children and unaccompanied children, notably in Europe.

The Committee is concerned with restrictive citizenship laws, the slow pace of naturalization and problems of documentation for non-nationals. States should ensure birth registration for all children, including those of undocumented migrants, even when they are not entitled to nationality, to avoid statelessness and to ensure full enjoyment of rights. Procedures for applying for a residence permit should be short, and family reunification should be dealt with in a positive, humane and expeditious manner. The possession of a residence permit should never be a precondition for access to social services. Concerning child labour and economic exploitation of migrant children, the Committee notes with concern that migrant children are more often employed in clandestine work (mostly agriculture and domestic work) or illegal activities than other children. It recommends that studies on children engaged in hazardous work be carried out and that states ratify ILO Convention No. 138 on Minimum Age for Admission to Employment.

Concerning labour emigration, especially of women, the Committee notes that parents often leave children behind with relatives or in institutions. Children experiencing family breakdown following the emigration of one or both parents are more often subject to abuse and exploitation. In this context, bilateral agreements are an important tool for reciprocal enforcement of maintenance orders or for allowing mothers to take their children, as well as programmes and specialized services to assist caregivers in order to limit the institutionalization of children of migrant workers in orphanages or similar institutions. The Committee also draws attention to the impact of emigration of professionals such as special education teachers or health workers, who are essential to the implementation of the rights of children.

Another subject of concern is detention and deportation, especially of unaccompanied minors. States should make sure that minors are effectively returned to their family or to social welfare agencies in their country of origin. Examples of concerns of the Committee in this area are the lack of adequate structures with health and education facilities; lack of an efficient refugee status determination and of operational guidelines on the return of separated children; absence of legal representation and of possibilities to speedily challenge the detention; insufficient child participation in the procedure; lack of trained personnel for interviews and in the juvenile justice system; no guarantees of physical safety; prolonged detention; and the lack of an independent structure to monitor the conditions of detention.

Case studies

This section reviews migration occurrences in a number of countries, selected according to the importance of the migration issue and to their good reporting record. The examples indicate that, even if migration is undoubtedly a pressing issue in these countries, the range of issues covered over the 1994 to 2005 period is limited.

For Morocco and the Republic of Korea, the main concerns regarding the enjoyment of rights by migrants have been identified, and this is in itself an encouraging sign, although the analysis is certainly not as profound as it would have been if a report had been submitted to and examined by the CMW. In addition, the focus is limited to a few burning issues such as trafficking, labour rights and ill-treatment.

Morocco

Migrant-related issues are:[18]

- trafficking (CEDAW)
- lack of equality in law and access to court for foreigners (CERD)
- police brutality and deportation to Ceuta and Melilla of unaccompanied minors who try to emigrate to Spain (CRC)
- immediate expulsion of an alien deemed to be a threat to state security, even if they may be subjected to torture or ill-treatment or sentenced to death in the receiving country (HRC).

Republic of Korea

Migrant-related issues are:[19]

- new immigration regulations facilitating the attainment of permanent residence status and access to school for undocumented children (CERD)
- persisting vulnerability and discrimination in the enjoyment of rights for undocumented workers, notably security of person, social services (CERD, CRC) and education for children (CRC)
- trafficking of foreign women for prostitution into the state (CERD)
- discrimination in working conditions and safety at work between nationals and non-nationals (CERD and CESCR).

Sweden

For Sweden[20] and, more generally, for Western countries, conclusions tend to focus on detention and expulsion issues, especially taking into

---

[18] CEDAW A/58/38 (Part II), paragraphs 137–83, CERD/C/62/CO/5, CERD/A/49/18, paragraphs 209–31, CRC/C/15/Add.211, CCPR/CO/82/MAR.

[19] CERD/C/63/CO/9, CERD/C/304/Add.65, CERD/C/304/Add.12, ESCR E/C.12/1995/3, ESCR E/C.12/1/Add.59, CRC/C/15/Add.197.

[20] CAT/C/CR/28/6, CCPR/C/79/Add.58, CCPR/CO/74/SWE, CEDAW A/56/38, paragraphs 319–60, CERD/C/64/CO/8, CERD/C/304/Add.103, CERD/C/304/Add.37, A/49/18 paragraphs 181–208, CESCR E/C.12/1/Add.70, CRC/C/15/Add.248, CRC/C/15/Add.101.

account the special procedures post-9/11, but this is done very much from the perspective of asylum seekers, minimizing the reality of the presence of migrant workers on the territory. The conclusions are more complete and detailed as the state has good reporting records and submits very exhaustive reports. Migrant-related issues for Sweden are:

- expulsions to a country with which the returnee has no significant ties or that could pose risks to their personal safety under the act that allows foreigners suspected of terrorism to be expelled under a procedure with no provision for appeal (CAT, CERD); lack of appropriate hearing and review in immigration and asylum procedures; risk of violations of fundamental rights of persons of foreign extraction such as the principle of *non-refoulement* but also freedom of expression and privacy (ICCPR)
- length of detention of irregular immigrants (ICCPR)
- persistent manifestations of racism and xenophobia, discrimination in access to public places or to the job market (ICCPR), to education and employment (CEDAW), to housing and public services (CERD), at the workplace and in the instruction in the mother tongue (ICESCR)
- increase in trafficking (CEDAW, CRC); making the buying and soliciting of sexual services a criminal offence (ICESCR)
- lack of consideration for the best interest of asylum-seeking and migrant children in asylum procedures; no access to education for children without residence permits; very long processing period for asylum application and family reunification procedures (CRC)
- positive aspects: signature of the CTOC; a number of initiatives to combat racial discrimination; the new Act on Citizenship facilitating the acquisition of citizenship for children of foreign background; the right to vote and stand for election in municipal elections for non-nationals (CERD).

United States

The United States is a special case, as only one reference to migrant issues was found. An explanatory factor for this is, of course, that the United States has only ratified four of the seven core UN human-rights conventions. This conclusion adopted in 1995 by the CCPR[21] concerns due process for excludable aliens, police violence and brutality affecting particularly minority groups and foreigners and the high incarceration

[21] CCPR/C/79/Add.50, A/50/40, paragraphs 266–304.

rates of Arab, Hispanic and African American populations. This is not satisfactory given the huge numbers of documented and undocumented migrant workers in the country.

It is interesting to compare the results presented here (i.e. issues mentioned for a specific country by the first six treaty monitoring bodies over the period 1994 to 2005) with the issues that emerged from the examination by the CMW of the same country, which can be done for the three states whose reports had been examined by April 2007 (i.e. until the 6th Session of the CMW): Mali, Mexico and Egypt (see also Chapter 4). This exercise gives a deeper understanding of what the added value of the ICRMW would be.

Mali

Mali was the first country to submit its initial report[22] for consideration by the CMW as required under article 73 of the ICRMW. Note that since 1994 there was hardly any mention of migrant-related issues in the six reports submitted by Mali to the various treaty monitoring bodies.[23] Only two conclusions were retained in our research, and the only issue mentioned was trafficking in children. The state report submitted to the Committee in 2005 was not detailed; it is therefore difficult to draw any conclusion from it. But in spite of the lack of detail, some issues could be raised by the Committee that had not been raised in the past twelve years of supervision by the treaty monitoring body system, such as the lack of training for officials working in the area of migration and the lack of information on the implementation of rights.

Mexico

In the case of Mexico,[24] the aspects mentioned in treaty monitoring body conclusions over the last twelve years have concerned:

- vulnerability to exploitation or trafficking of Mexican women emigrating to other countries (CEDAW); relevance of economic and social difficulties to the departure of many Mexican migrant workers abroad (CEDAW and CESCR)

---

[22] See the report and conclusions on Mali available at www2.ohchr.org/english/bodies/cmw/cmws04.htm [last accessed 16 April 2009].

[23] See report status by country on the OHCHR website available at http://tb.ohchr.org/default.aspx [last accessed 16 April 2009].

[24] CCPR/C/79/Add.32, CEDAW A/57/38, Part III (2002), CEDAW A/53/38, paragraphs 354–427, CERD/C/304/Add.30, A/50/18, paragraphs 353–98, CESCR E/C.12/1993/16, CRC/C/15/Add.112, CRC/C/15/Add.13.

- right to security of person for irregular immigrants (CERD)
- exploitation of children as migrant workers and for prostitution (CRC)
- positive aspects: access to the public service by citizens who are not Mexicans by birth (CCPR); accession to the Convention on the Rights of Migrant Workers and the Reciprocal Programme for Obtaining Maintenance Fees with the United States of America (CRC).

The CMW has identified new and more specifically migrant-related issues in the list, for example specific articles of Mexican legislation (mainly the LGP – General Population Act) that seem to be in conflict with the Convention:

- criminalization of undeclared entry into the territory and restrictions to free transit even for documented migrants
- possibility of starting civil proceedings restricted to regular migrants
- anti-gang measures being prejudicial to migrants, especially children and teenagers
- lack of measures to prevent retention of identity documentation by employers or recruitment agencies
- lack of definition of the authorities in charge of identity controls and of the role of the army in the south of the country
- not investigating claims of ill-treatment and extortion by law-enforcement and migration officials
- detention with convicted prisoners and arbitrary duration of detention
- lack of a programme for improving detention centres and overcrowding
- lack of protection measures for women domestic workers and seasonal agriculture workers
- unequal treatment for irregular migrants in conditions of work and social security
- obstacles to setting up trade unions by non-nationals.

Egypt

Finally, Egypt's report is very complete and therefore a definite improvement with regard to providing information on the situation of migrant workers. This is especially the case given that, although Egypt ratified all the other six core UN human-rights treaties, there was not a single reference to migrant workers' issues in the recommendations issued by the treaty monitoring bodies so far.

Obstacles to protection of migrants' rights by the first six UN human-rights conventions

The general level of ratification of the first six UN human-rights instruments varies from 146 States Parties (CAT) to 193 States Parties (CRC) as of June 2009. This is an element in favour of using the six treaty monitoring bodies, as they represent a strong and wide platform reaching most countries in the world. On average, 50% of the conclusions mention migrant issues, which is quite satisfactory in itself and indicative of the size of the problem, but also distressing as migrants still seem to be considered as a minor or secondary issue although the population concerned is around 200 million.[25]

The work of treaty monitoring bodies over the last ten years has consolidated the applicability of the first six UN human-rights conventions to migrant workers. Through their various working methods, these committees have reaffirmed and specified the protection granted to migrant workers by the conventions. But some gaps can nevertheless be identified in the reporting system regarding migrant workers, as for a number of reasons the content of these conclusions sometimes lacks relevance or applicability.

First, committees with the highest percentage of references to migrants – the CRC and the CEDAW – overwhelmingly focus on trafficking, which in itself is not specific to migrant workers. It is reassuring that trafficking is so much taken into consideration given the seriousness of the phenomenon, but this tends to focus on a single issue, whereas migrant women are faced with many other human rights violations that deserve deeper analysis. Trafficking implies an entirely different legal framework that focuses on prevention and sanctioning and not so much on a large array of rights as in the ICRMW. The conclusion formats used by these two committees are more formalized than the others, and systematically include chapters on trafficking and sexual exploitation, especially since the adoption of the CTOC and its two protocols in 2000. The language used in this kind of reference is too often not very specific to the actual situation in the country. Note, however, that recommendations on this issue are usually of good quality and are satisfactory, especially regarding protection of victims, which is

---

[25] GCIM, 2005, *Migration in an Interconnected World: New Directions for Action*, Report of the Global Commission on International Migration, Geneva, Switzerland, GCIM, p. 83.

often missing in the range of measures developed by states that focus more on areas such as border control and prosecution.

Second, conclusions can vary in their degree of precision. They are logically more specific when they address countries that submit more detailed reports, as they mirror the level of detail in the country report, but also the complexity of the protection afforded to migrants and the mechanisms already in place, the kind of flows (refugees, irregular migrants, etc.), the level of respect of human rights in the country for nationals, etc. Treaty monitoring body conclusions will, for example, usually argue in favour of the application of all relevant treaty provisions to undocumented migrants in European countries, whereas in the Middle East, conclusions tend to recommend a more general and basic protection for legally residing migrants.

Third, the coverage of main issues does not seem to be systematic, and is limited to a few high-profile issues in the country during the reporting period. It generally tends to focus on trafficking and detention, expulsion and integration for receiving countries. Finally, recommendations can in some cases lack applicability due to the vague wording used: '[i]nterest and concern were expressed by the Committee as regards efforts to address the needs of minority groups such as migrant women'[26] or '[t]he Committee is concerned about reports of trafficking of children out of Yemen and of women coming to or through the country, as well as the practice of expelling trafficked persons from the country without appropriate arrangements for their care',[27] for example. Only the CMW with its body of experience and best practices would have the expertise to recommend very specific measures really allowing for an improvement of the protection and enjoyment of migrants' rights.

Another indicative aspect is the terminology used in treaty monitoring body conclusions and in state reports. One finding of our research was that the use of the phrase 'migrant worker' is not frequent.[28] Other designations such as 'alien', 'foreigner', (illegal) 'immigrant' are by far more common. The terminology used varies according to the treaty monitoring body but mainly according to countries and regions, as treaty

---

[26] Belgium, 1996, CEDAW A/51/38, paragraphs 164–96.

[27] Yemen, 2005, CCPR/CO/84/YEM.

[28] Note that this varies from region to region: 19% of the conclusions refer to 'migrant workers' for Asia, 12% for Latin American and the Caribbean and 9% only for western Europe (average 11%): December 18/ICMC, 2004, *The UN Treaty Monitoring Bodies and Migrant Workers: A Samizdat*, Geneva, Switzerland, December 18/International Catholic Migration Commission, p. 11.

monitoring bodies often mirror wording used by the states themselves in their reports. Sending countries such as Sri Lanka or Mexico use the phrase 'migrant worker', thereby recognizing a *de facto* situation where their nationals leave in search of work, although mainly under irregular conditions. Receiving countries in the Middle East or Asia (Israel, Kuwait, Lebanon, Republic of Korea, Saudi Arabia, etc.) also use 'migrant worker'. This quite often reflects the fact that measures have been taken in order to regulate migrant workers' movements as such, at least in Asia. For developed receiving countries (e.g. Australia, Canada, Europe), 'immigrant' is much more common, as well as 'non-citizen', 'alien' and 'foreigner'. Most conclusions deal with asylum issues. As long as these countries follow their own immigration policy, migrant workers are not seen as a specific category, but just as a sub-category of the general group of foreigners.

The terminology used by reporting states can thus be confusing, and makes it difficult to establish a difference between refugees, asylum seekers, rejected asylum seekers, ethnic minorities, stateless persons and immigration of second or third generation, and therefore makes it difficult to know if migrant workers are included in that wording or not in a given situation. The risk is then of neglecting the specificity of the protection needs of migrant workers. Of course, a more general terminology allows the inclusion of several categories that are often intertwined in reality, as migrants can pass from one to the other (rejected asylum seekers will, e.g., start working irregularly and become undocumented migrant workers; deportations regard essentially rejected asylum seekers but possibly include irregular migrants as well; continuing immigration from communities that are already present on the territory blurs the distinction between newly arrived and second or third generations). The definition of 'migrant worker' in article 2 of the Convention is the following: 'A migrant worker is a person who is to be engaged, is engaged or has been engaged in a remunerated activity in a state of which he or she is not a national.' This definition is very broad – even if it excludes refugees – as all aliens resident in a country are likely to have worked or to work in the future and are therefore potentially included.

There seems to be an increased use of the term 'migrant workers' in recent years – even by European states.[29] It is clearly being streamlined in UN vocabulary, especially since the entry into force of the ICRMW in

---

[29] The term 'migrant workers' is used by Italy, Ireland and Spain in the CEDAW, by Belarus, Kazakhstan and Nigeria in the CERD and by Italy in the CESCR.

2003, and always among specific protection groups. Calls for ratification of the Convention have become a frequent feature in their recommendations. It may be that, because of the mainstreaming of migrants' rights, references to migrant workers as a vulnerable group in need of specific protection are starting to be systematically included.

Potential added value of the ICRMW

The ICRMW expands on human rights only partly covered by other treaties. Article 1 also provides broader grounds for discrimination than those initially listed in the Universal Declaration of Human Rights or elaborated upon in subsequent conventions. It includes 'conviction', 'nationality', 'age', 'economic position' and 'marital status'. The Convention also covers categories of migrant workers excluded from other international conventions, such as frontier workers and self-employed workers who are not covered by the two major ILO conventions. The CMW also places particular emphasis on the rights of family members and on protection of the family.

The value of the ICRMW can also be measured by the protection it can offer on issues that are not sufficiently taken into account in other treaties. The protection it provides could be particularly useful for undocumented migrants who are one of the most vulnerable categories and who are more likely to be victims of discrimination in access to rights guaranteed in the other six core conventions, where irregular migrants' issues focus on detention, expulsion and ill-treatment as well as on social aspects such as access to education, healthcare, housing, social services – especially for children – and protection in employment. To give some examples: CEDAW draws attention to the fact that undocumented migrant women are particularly at risk of violation of their labour rights; the ICESCR welcomes measures taken to regularize the situation of clandestine immigrant workers; and the CRC recalls that birth registration procedures are important and should be known by the population and especially irregular immigrant families. But none of these committees makes detailed and practical recommendations that could easily be implemented by states, with the exception of the issue of trafficking, where much legislation has been enacted.

This means that the ICRMW could bring added value, as it expressly includes rights for undocumented migrants, which is quite unique, notably under Part III applying to all documented and undocumented migrant workers and consolidating basic safeguards (right to security of person, protection against torture, etc.). Article 25 is particularly meaningful as it guarantees, under the principle of equality of treatment, that some rights (right to receive remuneration, conditions of work and terms of employment, etc.) cannot be refused by employers by reason of any irregularity in the stay or employment of the migrant. The enjoyment of these rights is, however, often very problematic for undocumented migrant workers because of the very short notice before deportations or because of the fear of being denounced when seeking justice.

Our study has indicated that irregular migrants are referred to under a variety of names, and this sometimes makes it unclear whether persons thus included can be considered as migrant workers (e.g. aliens with irregular status, illegal presence, unlawful non-citizens, aliens without papers, clandestine immigrant workers, illegal workers, residents with no residence permit, irregular situation, undocumented, unregistered, etc.). Using the broad definition of migrant worker (article 2 of the ICRMW) would avoid this confusion and clarify their status and rights.

Another specificity of the ICRMW is its focus on labour rights. These are, of course, at the core of the ICESCR, with special emphasis on unfair terms of employment and access to welfare, while the ICCPR and the ICERD are concerned with discrimination between national and non-national workers, and the CEDAW and the CRC devote their attention to the protection of the most vulnerable workers (women and children). But again, the ICRMW is the only treaty consolidating a number of labour rights and applying them to migrant workers in its articles 25, 43, 45, 49, 51, 52, 53 and 55. Recruitment agencies are mentioned by ICERD but without any detailed recommendations. The CMW could use the basis offered by article 66 and find inspiration in good practices from Asia, where labour emigration is organized by the authorities, in order to develop detailed recommendations.

It must be stressed, however, that some provisions of the ICRMW are weaker than similar ones in other core human rights treaties, such as the right to set up trade unions being limited to documented migrant workers, and only the right to emergency medical care rather than the broader right to healthcare is provided for.

Another weakness consists of the reservations made at the time of ratification to exclude or alter the legal effect of certain provisions of the treaty in their application to a given state. Although these reservations must not be incompatible with the object and the purpose of the treaty, some are quite extensive as they relate to fundamental articles and can therefore endanger the protection granted to migrant workers.

It can therefore be concluded that government reporting on the implementation of treaties that do not contain provisions specific to the situation of migrant workers and members of their families cannot be as complete as reporting under the ICRMW. Migrant workers and members of their families find themselves outside the territory of their country of origin and often beyond the protection afforded to its citizens by that state. The positive effect of having rights consolidated in one single treaty cannot be denied, and will allow for CMW conclusions that will enrich and illustrate certain rights for the other committees. Some categories of rights important for migrants are moreover characterized *only* in the ICRMW, even if these are not new rights.

Conclusion

After analysing the treaty monitoring body conclusions and recommendations we concurred that governments that have not ratified the ICRMW cannot offer migrants, through the other instruments, the protection that would be required given the importance and seriousness of violations of migrants' rights. Whereas some treaty monitoring body recommendations are very specific, they generally remain vague and are not precise enough to be easily put into practice and to allow for real changes. Of course, the Convention needs ratification from receiving countries, and the reasons why this has not happened are well documented in this volume. Obviously, states of employment are reluctant to encourage the full protection of the human rights of migrant workers and members of their families, even more so when they are undocumented and thus more vulnerable.

The need for specific protection of migrant workers is recognized by the UN human rights system. Specific mention of migrants' rights is made in the drafting guidelines by almost all treaty monitoring bodies, general recommendations have been issued by some, and all include recommendations for States Parties to supply more data on the implementation of relevant provisions of human rights treaties in order to protect migrant workers.

Note that specific children's or women's issues are frequently covered in reports under committees other than the CRC or the CEDAW, so why is this not the case for migrants? This is partly being done already, but members of other committees cannot be expected to have expertise on migration issues. These are not streamlined in the UN human rights system and there are therefore gaps and overlaps, as illustrated here.

There is not enough use of the specificity of the treaties to examine the situation of migrants and their families under their own particular perspective. Migrant workers are only one of a number of groups in need of specific protection from the other six UN human-rights conventions.

The ICRMW undoubtedly offers a characterized protection and new perspectives on migrants' rights. In particular, the work of the CMW, which largely remains to be developed, offers an expert understanding of the specificities of the situation of migrants. It could draw inspiration from the treatment of migrant issues, and the gaps therein, by other treaty monitoring bodies. The documentation of states' good practices can provide guidance and information to states on strengthening their capacities. Finally, with renewed assessment of state efforts, it can lead to practice-oriented recommendations and the development of follow-up mechanisms.

A paradoxical argument is put forward by some states as a reason for not ratifying the ICRMW, according to which migrants' rights would be sufficiently covered by other treaties, and ratification of the 1990 Convention would not bring any added value. By the same token, other treaties' provisions represent the only protection available in the 155 countries that have not ratified the Convention. Both protections seem more complementary than contradictory, as using the other conventions to strive for better protection is currently the best tool with which to monitor and implement respect of the human rights of migrant workers and members of their families. The ICRMW should be the core convention, the main international standard of any regulatory framework of migration, and should not be replaced ad hoc by other treaties. Protection of the human rights of migrant workers should be approached in a consistent way throughout the UN system.

6

The need for a rights-based approach to migration in the age of globalization

PATRICK A. TARAN

Introduction

The ICRMW, and the reluctance of some states to ratify it, symbolizes sharpening clashes between the conditions of globalization and a rights-based approach to governance. The question of migrants' rights represents a cutting edge of contention between the consequences of the economic logic of globalization vs the moral values embodied in human rights concepts and law. This contention is marked most dramatically by the conditions that many migrant workers face in host countries around the world. As the 2004 International Labour Conference observed:

> Despite the positive experiences of migrant workers, a significant number face undue hardships and abuse in the form of low wages, poor working conditions, virtual absence of social protection, denial of freedom of association and workers' rights, discrimination and xenophobia, as well as social exclusion. Gaps in working conditions, wages and treatment exist among migrant workers and between migrant and national workers. In a significant number of cases, unemployment rates, job security and wages differ between regular migrant workers and national workers (ILO, 2004).

Widespread abuse and exploitation of migrant workers – often described in terms of forced labour and slavery-like situations – stand in marked contrast to the promises that economic globalization will bring better conditions and social protection to the lives of people around the world.

With increasing competition for resources, markets and capital, downward pressures on incomes and conditions of work appear to be generalized across industrialized countries as well as elsewhere. Small- and medium-size companies and labour-intensive economic sectors do not have the option of relocating operations abroad. For governments, political and economic considerations (e.g. retaining employment, tax bases, national production, export market share, etc.) argue for main-taining economic activity that may be only marginally competitive in the cut-throat competition of liberalized international trade. Responses include the downgrading of manufacturing processes, deregulation and flexibility of employment, with increased emphasis on cost-cutting measures and subcontracting (Lean Lim, 1998, p. 277). In a number of countries, these measures are expanding the number of jobs at the bottom of the employment scale. Such employment needs are met only partially or not at all by available or unemployed national workers, for reasons of minimal pay, degrading and dangerous conditions and/or low status in these jobs and sectors. Moreover, the unemployed in some countries have access to social welfare and unemployment insurance.

On the supply side, as an ILO study put it:

> the evidence points to a likely worsening of migration pressures in many parts of the world...Processes integral to globalisation have intensified the disruptive effects of modernisation and capitalist development...Many developing countries face serious social and economic dislocation associated with persistent poverty, growing unemployment, loss of traditional trading patterns, and what has been termed a 'growing crisis of economic security' (Stalker, 2000).

Slow progress in ratifications and the increasingly explicit opposition to the ICRMW reflect, in particular, resistance to recognition of application of human rights standards to migrants. A minimal or non-existent application of rights would contribute to ensuring that migrant labour remains cheap, docile, temporary and easily removable when not needed. Grasping the fate of the ICRMW therefore requires taking account of the fundamental importance of migrant workers as actors and instruments in a globalized stage of modern capitalist development. These factors may indeed be far more important than – and may underlie – the political and legal arguments often cited in explaining resistance to ratification of the Convention.

Context of contention: roles and importance of migrant labour

Migrant labour has become a key feature in meeting economic, labour market and productivity challenges in a globalized economy. Migration today serves as an instrument to adjust the skills, age and sectoral composition of national and regional labour markets. Migration provides responses to fast-changing needs for skills and personnel resulting from technological advances, changes in market conditions and industrial transformations. In countries of ageing populations, migration offers a potential to replenish declining work forces.

At the beginning of the twenty-first century, some 94 million foreigners were estimated to be economically active: employed, self-employed or otherwise in remunerative activity, across the world (estimates cited in ILO, 2009). This is half of the total 91 million people living outside their country of birth or citizenship in 2005. The foreign-born commonly represent 10% of the work force in western European countries, a proportion set to grow substantially. Proportions in a number of countries in Africa, Asia and the Americas are already higher. As highlighted by the 2006 UN General Assembly HLD, cross-border mobility and internationalization of labour forces are becoming central considerations for governments and economic interests worldwide.

Migrant labour in both developed and developing countries fills '3-D' jobs: dirty, dangerous and degrading. Efforts to fill 3-D jobs and to acquire economic competitiveness through high productivity at low cost produce a continuous demand for cheap and low-skilled migrant labour in numerous sectors of national economies. These sectors commonly include agriculture and food processing, construction, cleaning and maintenance, hotel and restaurant services, labour-intensive assembly and manufacturing and the sex industry.

The resulting demand for migrant workers provides a significant impetus to labour flows and facilitates the incorporation of undocumented migrants (Escobar Latapí, 1997, p. 4). Research in southern European countries demonstrates the extent to which 'the migrants take jobs that the locals refuse. It's simply a matter of substitution' (Reynieri, 2001). The latter study also noted: 'we can conclude that migrants are in competition only with marginal sections of the national labour force... when they are not sufficiently sustained by welfare provisions, in specific sectors, and/or in the less-developed areas inside these countries'. For the less-qualified jobs, employers demand workers who will not exercise pressures on the salary structures. Given that, at least initially, immigrant workers will not challenge the relation between salary and the social status attached to specific occupations, contracting migrant workers avoids the economic risks – particularly structural inflation – that national workers induce when they demand salary increases.

Rights and social protection carry costs, an implication that confronts the logic of globalized economic competition. Limitations in the exercise of rights by migrant workers are directly linked to assuring that their labour remains a competitive advantage. This is especially evident in restrictions on rights to association and collective bargaining. As highlighted by the ICFTU, organizing migrants and immigrants into unions or organizations to defend their interests and rights is often extremely difficult, as it is easily intimidated and disrupted by the threat or actual practice of dismissal and deportation (see, e.g., Linard, 1998). The impediments to unionization are compounded where unemployment rates are high among established or second-generation immigrants, for whom threats of dismissal for organizing or simply complaining about lack of occupational safety and health protections and 'decent' work conditions can also be effective intimidation.

With few options available for legally recognized and protected migration in the face of strong pull-push pressures, irregular migration channels have become the only alternative, one which presents lucrative 'business' opportunities for helping people to arrange travel, obtain documents, cross borders and find jobs in destination countries. The flow of low-skilled migrants to more developed regions is channelled by clandestine means precisely because of the non-existence of legal migration categories that would allow for their legal entry to destination countries. Once they are in host countries, they remain confined to jobs in unstructured or informal sectors, in irregular work and under exploitative conditions of employment (Abella, 2002). In contrast, ILO research underlines that legal labour-migration channels contribute to reducing trafficking of migrants (Taran and Moreno-Fontes, 2002).

Women now comprise half of the total migrant worker population; that is as workers themselves, not dependants. Differential opportunities for legitimate employment affect men and women differently. Demand for migrant workers in receiving countries is defined by the labour market segmentation in these countries: opportunities are available for precisely these low-skilled jobs considered suitable for women. The feminization of international labour migration, together with the fact that most job opportunities for women migrants are in unregulated sectors (agriculture, domestic work, the sex industry) and the existence of gender-disaggregated labour markets contribute to the increase of discriminative labour markets in countries of destination. Female migrants are thus marginalized even further; they are more often left with no option but irregular migration and are exposed to the worst forms of abuse with the least protection.

Evolution of international protection

The need for normative international standards and measures to protect workers outside their countries of citizenship has been formally recognized since the early twentieth century. The concern was explicitly written into the founding constitution of the ILO in 1919, and a first international treaty on treatment of foreign workers was established under ILO auspices in 1937. However, the economic and political turmoil that culminated in the Second World War precluded adoption by more than a handful of states. In 1949, the year after adoption of the Universal Declaration of Human Rights and two years before establishment of the 1951 Convention Relating to the Status of Refugees, the first widely implemented instrument on migrant workers was adopted by the ILO and subsequently ratified by an important number of both host and home states of migrants in the 1950s and 1960s.

The 1949 ILO Convention No. 97 (Convention concerning Migration for Employment (Revised)) established equal treatment between nationals and regular migrants in the areas of recruitment procedures, living and working conditions, access to justice, tax and social security regulations. The 1975 Convention No. 143 (Convention concerning Migrant Workers (Supplementary Provisions)) took international migration law further by establishing norms to reduce exploitation and trafficking of migrants while ensuring protection for irregular migrants, and to facilitate integration of regular migrants in host societies. The content of ILO conventions Nos. 97 and 143 formed the basis for drafting the ICRMW, which expanded and extended recognition of economic, social, cultural and civil rights of migrant workers (see Chapter 2 for additional details on the background of the Convention).[1]

The necessary framework for national law on migration in all countries is amply laid out by these three complementary instruments. Together, the two ILO conventions on migration and the ICRMW comprise an international charter on migration, providing a broad normative framework covering treatment of migrants and inter-state cooperation on regulating migration. Eight major points describe the importance of these three conventions:

(1) They establish comprehensive 'values-based' definitions and legal bases for national policy and practice regarding non-national migrant workers and their family members. They thus serve as tools to encourage states to establish or improve national legislation in harmony with international standards.

---

[1] Texts and related information available respectively at www.ilo.org/ilolex/english/index. htm and www.ohchr.org [both last accessed 17 April 2009].

(2) They lay out a comprehensive agenda for national policy and for consultation and cooperation among states on labour migration policy formulation, exchange of information, providing information to migrants, orderly return and reintegration, etc.

(3) The ICRMW further establishes that migrant workers are more than labourers or economic entities; they are social entities with families, and accordingly have rights. It reinforces the principles in ILO conventions on equality of treatment with nationals of states of employment in a number of legal, political, economic, social and cultural areas.

(4) ILO Convention No. 143 and the ICRMW include provisions intended to prevent and eliminate exploitation of migrants, thus reinforcing the 'decent work' agenda defined by International Labour Standards, nearly all of which apply explicitly or implicitly to all migrant workers.

(5) ILO Convention No. 143 explicitly calls for involvement of key non-state stakeholders (i.e. the social partners: employers and trade unions) in elaborating, implementing and monitoring national migration policy.

(6) ILO Convention No. 143 and the ICRMW explicitly address unauthorized or clandestine movements of migrant workers, and call for resolving irregular or undocumented situations, in particular through international cooperation.

(7) These conventions resolve the lacuna of protection for non-national migrant workers and members of their families in irregular status and in informal work by providing norms for national legislation of receiving states and their own states of origin, including minimum protections for undocumented or unauthorized migrant workers.

(8) The extensive, detailed and complementary text contained in these instruments provides specific normative language that can be incorporated directly into national legislation, reducing ambiguities in interpretation and implementation across diverse political, legal and cultural contexts.

For the record, a total of eighty-two different states had ratified one or more of these three complementary standards as at June 2009: 1949 ILO Convention No. 97 has been ratified by forty-nine countries; 1975 ILO Convention No. 143 by twenty-three countries; and the 1990 ICRMW has been ratified by forty-one countries and signed by fifteen others. A number of states have ratified both ILO conventions; several have ratified one or both ILO conventions plus the ICRMW (see Annex 2). Eleven EU Member States have ratified one or both ILO conventions.[2] With fifteen additional signatories to the UN Convention (signing being a preliminary step to ratification), it can be anticipated that some ninety states will have formally adopted international standards on migrant workers within the next few years.

Contradictions in state policy and practice

Despite this comprehensive set of standards, the contemporary reality of policy and practice in many states remains far from consistent. Political rhetoric about combating irregular migration abounds, yet governments informally tolerate it even while they officially reinforce controls against 'illegal' migrant workers. On the one hand, a continual supply of cheap labour abounds, while on the other hand, irregular migrants are exploited, unable to organize in the workplace to defend their dignity and decent working conditions, as well as being stigmatized and isolated from allies and support. Tolerance of restrictions on freedom of movement, long working hours, poor or non-existent health and safety protections, non-payment of wages, substandard housing, etc. all contribute to expanding a market for migrants who have no choice but to labour in conditions simply intolerable and unacceptable for legal employment. The absence of work-site monitoring, particularly in sectors such as agriculture, construction, domestic service, sex work and others where migrants are concentrated, further expands the space and opportunities in which forced or compulsory labour can thrive.

In a growing number of countries, migration management responsibilities have been shifted from labour ministries to interior or home affairs ministries, thus transforming contexts for policy elaboration and implementation from that of labour market regulation to that of policing and national security. Despite migration being about work to a vast extent, this shift separates administration of an increasingly sizeable portion of the work force from the institution of the state most directly concerned with labour market regulation, along with conditions of work and with the other fundamental areas of its competence. At the level of domestic politics and national government administration, promoting an agenda of migration control rather than rights protection has become

---

[2] These are: Belgium, France, Germany, Italy, the Netherlands, Norway, Portugal, Slovenia, Spain, Sweden and the United Kingdom.

a vehicle to capture political attention and budgetary resources. Pursued to the detriment of other considerations, this focus has subordinated to secondary roles fundamental humanitarian and human rights considerations, as well as economic and developmental factors.

The policy dilemmas in the economic and administrative realm are reinforced in the political discourse and ideological frameworks advanced in host states regarding irregular migrants. The utility of their presence – in undeclared and exploited situations – represents a challenge to the normative and ideological values of most industrialized countries in as much as these persons are denied legal and social protection. A predominant response is banal association of irregular migration with crime, arms, drug trafficking and terrorism, and discussion of draconian measures to 'combat illegal migration'. Social stigmatization and outright violence is encouraged by the language of 'illegality' and by military terms – as if 'illegal migrants' were an enemy in war-like confrontation.

More broadly stated, the contention over the treatment of migrant workers and their families reflects a broader clash between value systems for governance of society at national and supra-national levels. One pole can be characterized as a rights-based approach, with an implicit primacy of individual freedoms, equality of opportunity and concern for social welfare. In contrast, a contending approach argues for emphasis on corporate security, in particular that of often-overlapping structures of economic and political authority, notably those of government and of business enterprises. In day to day reality, this contention makes migration a central and significant arena of dispute and redefinition in relations between labour and capital, in distribution of benefits deriving from economic activity, in the level of protection and regulation of conditions of employment and work and in the extent to which working people – foreign workers in particular – can organize to articulate and defend their interests.

Relativizing rights

Contradictions pitting an amalgam of restriction and control measures against a rights-based approach to regulating migration are further reflected in international political developments. A growing assault on the universality of international principles of human rights has indeed evolved over the last decade; it is now particularly focused on migration and the treatment of non-nationals.

Widespread reductions in allocations of resources to meet human needs and to uphold human rights in countries worldwide are associated with arguments that relativize such rights, particularly economic, social and cultural rights. In 1993, the positions taken by a number of governments at the Vienna World Conference on Human Rights signalled a strong and explicit challenge to the universality and inalienability of human rights. At that time, the most prominent basis cited for these challenges was cultural, historical and regional relativity of human rights; these critiques asserted that human rights notions apply differently and to different degrees in different cultural and regional contexts – they are not fully 'global'.

Arguments are being put forth that human rights are not indivisible, but rather that civil and political rights should be differentiated from economic, social and cultural rights. This discourse asserts that the latter, in contrast to the former, can only be considered as ideals because they are both too expensive and too impractical to implement throughout the world. Furthermore, measures to extend and assure such rights require costly and extensive systems, such as welfare, food subsidies, health, education and social service systems, jobs programmes and effective judicial systems. Due to society-wide and large-scale needs, these systems generally require large tax revenues and management by the state. However, taxation today is often stridently characterized as an impediment to private investment, development and economic growth, in both industrialized and developing countries.

New proposals relativizing human and labour rights are emerging specifically in the arena of international migration, with renewed calls for increasing temporary migration options. A 'utilitarian consequentialist' approach argues for an explicit trade-off of lowered application of rights and unequal treatment for non-national workers in exchange for increased opportunities for employment in potential host countries.[3] Rights are commodified as negotiable bundles that may be traded, sold or renounced in exchange for the economic benefits deriving from access to foreign labour markets. This approach is explicitly based on the premise that certain bundles of rights can be forfeited or traded to 'earn' access in temporary circumstances to employment in developed-country labour markets. It also suggests that trade-offs can be negotiated with organizations representing national workers to address their economic and political concerns.

---

[3] An elaboration of this approach appears in Ruhs and Chang (2004).

These arguments coincide with continuously recycled proposals to establish 'minimum' or 'core' rights applying to migrants. Such initiatives have been articulated in recent years in a draft resolution circulated (but not adopted) at the UN CHR in 1997, in proposals emanating from senior officials of the IOM, EU and Council of Europe forums, and in academic circles. Proposals for delineation of 'minimum rights' appear to have intensified following increased ratifications and entry into force of the ICRMW. A clear risk to this approach is establishment of a set of guidelines or principles that are far more general, vague and unenforceable than the explicit standards and supervisory mechanisms of the ILO and the ICRMW.

In other words, newly articulated ideological and political arguments now challenge the applicability of human rights law and principles to migrants and other non-nationals. On the one hand, post-9/11 doctrines advance the notion that the extent and nature of threats to national and state security posed by 'international terrorism' justify (or even require) restrictions on human, civil and judicial rights of migrants in Western democracies as well as elsewhere. The criminalization of migrants and the securitization of states conveniently dehumanize foreigners, removing the imperative of recognizing and protecting their human rights and precluding solidarity and equality of treatment. Securitization of states also seems to be effective in mobilizing at least a sector of national populations to support repressive measures – impeding, in particular, the access of foreign workers and their families to legal defence, social services and to organizing to defend their interests and participation in host societies.

Opposition to wider ratification of the ICRMW is thus becoming more explicit. Over the last few years, officials and diplomats representing European and other Western governments have consistently remarked that the 1990 Convention is:

- impractical and unrealizable as an international standard in part because it is 'too ambitious' and does not distinguish between 'illegal' and 'legal' migrants
- irrelevant because no host states have expressed willingness to adopt it
- essentially 'dead' as a relevant standard because too few states have ratified it.

The UN itself has ceded ground to the opposition. In an explicit shift from a decade and a half of CHR and General Assembly resolutions and World Conference declarations that consistently called upon states to consider ratifying the ICRMW, the report of the UN Secretary-General for the September 2006 HLD omitted any call for ratification of this fundamental convention. Ironically, it did explicitly call on governments to ratify the protocol to the UN CTOC on trafficking in persons.[4] No outcome or conclusions regarding the ICRMW were formulated by the HLD.

Policy framework for realizing rights of migrants

The ICRMW and related legal standards provide only the foundation for the policy and practical measures necessary to realize migrants' rights. Considerable recent dialogue on migration has therefore focused on identifying common approaches among states in regulating what is by definition a phenomenon requiring international cooperation. A decade ago, delegates of some 160 countries agreed on a comprehensive common agenda in the chapter on migration of the Plan of Action adopted by the 1994 ICPD in Cairo. More recently, regional migration dialogues, the Berne Initiative's IAMM, the GCIM[5] and the GFMD have continued discussions and elaborated common approaches.

A vital contribution was the 2004 International Labour Conference in Geneva, which adopted a Plan of Action on Migrant Workers (ILO, 2004). This document outlines a comprehensive approach to regulating labour migration from a rights-based approach in the context of labour market and employment considerations. Especially significant was its unanimous adoption by ministerial-level government representatives, leadership of trade union and employer federations from the 177 ILO member countries. Eight main components of a migration policy agenda to realize the rights and principles contained in the ICRMW and related instruments derive from the following policy dialogue processes.

Standards-based foundation for comprehensive national migration policies and practices

As noted above, the three instruments comprising an international charter on migration provide the normative framework and specific,

---

[4] The UN CTOC, adopted in Palermo in 2000, comprises two protocols: (i) Protocol against the Smuggling of Migrants by Land, Sea and Air; and (ii) Protocol to Prevent, Suppress and Punish Trafficking in Persons, Especially Women and Children.

[5] See final report of the GCIM (available at www.gcim.org/en/finalreport.html [last accessed 18 April 2009]).

model legislative language for national policy. A major point of establishing legal rights and legislative policy standards is to ensure social legitimacy and accountability, only guaranteed by a policy foundation in the rule of law.

Informed and transparent migration policy and administration

Immigration must respond to measured, legitimate needs, as well as taking into account domestic labour concerns. A viable admissions system must rely on regular labour market assessments to identify and respond to current and emerging needs for workers, high and low skilled. Policy and practice also needs to address awareness-raising, supervision of recruitment, administration of admissions, training of public service and law-enforcement officials, recognition of educational equivalencies, provision of social and health services, labour inspection, rights restoration and recovery for victims of trafficking, among other areas.

Institutional mechanisms for dialogue, consultation and cooperation

Migration policy can only be credible, viable and sustainable to the extent it takes into account the interests, concerns and experience of the most directly affected stakeholders. Key stakeholders are the social partners: the employers and businesses that provide employment as well as the trade unions and worker organizations representing the interests of workers, both migrants and nationals. Labour ministries need to have a central role. Consultation and policy making must also take into account other concerned ministries and agencies within government, as well as concerned civil society bodies – and certainly migrants themselves.

Enforcement of minimum, national employment-condition norms in all sectors of activity

Preventing exploitation of migrants, criminalizing abuse of persons that facilitate trafficking and discouraging irregular employment requires the enforcement of clear, national minimum standards for protection of workers (national and migrant) in employment. ILO conventions on occupational safety and health, against forced labour and on discrimination provide minimum international norms for national legislation. A necessary complement is monitoring and inspection in such areas as agriculture, construction, domestic work, the sex industry and other sectors of 'irregular' employment, to prevent exploitation, to detect forced labour and to ensure minimal, decent working conditions for all.

Gender-sensitive migration measures

The feminization of migration and the predominance of abuse of women migrants require gender equality to be recognized as integral to the process of policy making, planning and programme delivery at all levels.

Plan of Action against discrimination and xenophobia

Discrimination and xenophobic hostility against migrants are serious challenges to governance and social cohesion in every region of the world. ILO research has found discrimination rates of 35% against regular immigrant workers (i.e. unlawful discrimination) across western Europe (see Cediey and Foroni, 2007; Attström, 2007; Allasino et al., 2004; Arrijn et al., 1998; Bendick, 1996; de Prada et al., 1996; Goldberg et al., 1996; Bovenkerk, 1995). The 2001 WCAR in Durban articulated a major component of national policy on migration by defining a comprehensive and viable model plan of action specifically to combat discrimination and xenophobia against migrants at national, regional and global levels, based on common experience from different regions.[6]

Linking migration and development in policy and practice

Migration has long been generating significant contributions to both development and social progress and welfare in home and host countries alike. However, such contributions can only be obtained when migrant workers' rights are protected. The migration-protection-development linkages need to be articulated in order to strengthen advocacy and action by home countries as well as host countries to uphold the rights protections that permit migrant workers to obtain their earnings, live

---

[6] Main elements were established in the Declaration and Program of Action adopted at the WCAR in 2001, which includes forty paragraphs on treatment of migrant workers, refugees and other non-nationals (full text available at www.unhchr.ch/pdf/Durban.pdf [last accessed 18 April 2009]). See also www.unhchr.ch/html/racism/00-migra.html [last accessed 18 April 2009] for related documents and links.

and work in decent conditions and safely remit earnings to support families and communities at home.

International consultation and cooperation

Formalized mechanisms of regular dialogue and cooperation among governments and key stakeholders are essential in all regions. Expanding legal and operational regimes for freer circulation of labour/persons in regional economic integration initiatives is one course that by definition enhances protection and prospects for application of the international legal standards necessary for implementation of legal labour-mobility regimes.

In this context, international law, and the ICRMW in particular, provides a normative structure to ensure protection for migrant workers facing exploitation and abuse fostered by conditions of globalization. Wider ratification of the Convention will have major symbolic as well as practical value in implementing the fundamental protections for migrant workers established in international law. These protections can be characterized in three fundamental notions:

(1) Equality of treatment between regular migrant/immigrant workers and nationals in the realm of employment and work.
(2) The application of core universal human rights to all migrants, regardless of status. This was established implicitly and unrestrictedly in the 1975 ILO Convention No. 143 and later delineated explicitly in the 1990 ICRMW.
(3) The application to all workers of the broad array of international standards providing protection in treatment and conditions at work – safety, health, maximum hours, minimum remuneration, non-discrimination, freedom of association, maternity, etc.[7]

---

[7] This notion was upheld in an advisory opinion issued by the Inter-American Court (*Corte Interamericana de Derechos Humanos: Condición Jurídica y Derechos de los Migrantes Indocumentados. Opinion Consultativa OC-18/03 de 17 de Septiembre de 2003, solicitada por los Estados Unidos de Mexico*). In its conclusions, 'the Court decides unanimously, that...the migrant quality of a person cannot constitute justification to deprive him of the enjoyment and exercise of his human rights, among them those of labor character. A migrant, by taking up a work relation, acquires rights by being a worker, that must be recognized and guaranteed, independent of his regular or irregular situation in the state of employment. These rights are a consequence of the labor relationship.'

Impediments

In the experience of the author, who served from 1998 to 2002 as Coordinator of the Global Campaign for Ratification of the Convention on Rights of Migrants, the most salient obstacle to wider ratification of the ILO and UN conventions on migrant workers' rights remains a lack of political will by states to extend basic human and labour rights protections to foreign workers. However, sustained efforts to promote awareness and ratification of these three conventions have also been sadly lacking. Indeed, given enormous economic and political interest in avoiding implementation of an explicit and accountable normative regime on migration, change will only come about when significant political and social pressure is generated for adoption of a rights-based approach.

Despite the imperative deriving from human rights norms and organizational commitments, work on migrants' rights – particularly relating to irregular migration – has generally been marginal and institutionally unsupported in major international and intergovernmental organizations. The ILO has conducted little promotion of ratification of its own migrant worker conventions since the early 1980s. Until the appointment of the UN Special Rapporteur on the Human Rights of Migrants, there was no official in the UN system with an explicit mandate to address migrants' rights issues or to promote the ICRMW. The UN did not even publish the text of the Convention until 1996! The Special Rapporteur – an unremunerated responsibility – has, however, given it considerable visibility since 1998.

The IOM had no mandate or activity on the subject until the late 1990s. Recently, it set up a department on international migration law, whose activities include training and awareness-raising about relevant UN conventions, but nonetheless it has no formal promotion or monitoring role on legal standards. Lest full responsibility for this lacuna be ascribed to these institutions and their leadership, records show that demands for inaction have been consistently reiterated by powerful member governments in the IOM Governing Council, at the UN CHR (now the HRC), at the ILO and in other fora.

The record of CSOs on promoting the international standards on migrant workers also remains scattered, fragmented and limited in impact. Most CSOs concerned with migration issues are nationally based. Focused regional formations have emerged modestly in Asia, Central America and Europe. Only in the last seven years have major international human rights-monitoring organizations (HRW, Amnesty International, etc.) given substantial attention to migrants' rights. With the notable exception of the concerted effort around the 2001 WCAR and some campaigning for the ICRMW, the centre of gravity of CSO discourse remains the denunciation of conditions and of government action (or inaction), characterized by the lack of protection for migrants' human rights.[8]

In a sad parallel to the resource starvation by governments for migrants' rights-related work conducted by IGOs, little funding has been made available from any public or private source for international CSO initiatives to provide staff and fund publications, communications, networking and advocacy activities specifically addressing the human rights of migrants. Despite a lack of resources, the substantial progress in achieving ratifications of the ICRMW appears to be directly and largely tied to the CSO-led promotional efforts of the last decade, particularly since articulation of a Global Campaign involving church, human rights, trade union and other CSOs, together with several IGOs. Since 1998, an International Steering Committee has sought to enhance visibility and orientation, and considerable effort has been sustained by national organizations and coalitions.[9]

Social partners and CSOs have a fundamental role to play in providing moral, political and practical leadership to assure a rights-based approach to international migration. This role is necessarily expressed through a profile of solidarity and advocacy built on work with migrants and their concerns in explicit association with the promotion of international standards and the values they embody. Social partners and CSOs have a critical role to play in convincing governments to do the 'right thing' for all migrants. Work in local communities is undeniably the necessary operational focus for constituent-based organizations. However, the lack of international coordination and cooperation today in defence of migrants denies civil society efforts the visibility and effectiveness required to assert political and organizational initiative in national and international policy and legislation. This ineffectiveness was, for example, visibly manifested by the marginalization of CSOs at the HLD at the UN General Assembly in September 2006.

---

[8] For ample information on evolving civil society activity worldwide on migrants' rights and around International Migrants Day, see the December 18 network website (www. december18.net [last accessed 18 April 2009]).

[9] See the Global Campaign website (www.migrantsrights.org [last accessed 18 April 2009]).

Conclusion: the way forward

Much more than dispersed campaigns will be needed to defend and advance the protection of the rights and dignity of migrants and non-nationals in the context of today's globalized world, with its polarized accumulation of wealth and power and increasing exclusions. Common approaches, strategies and coordination and the ability to mobilize human resources are needed. All this is required to generate alternative solutions, influence the course of events, contribute to the elaboration of national policies and so on.

Several deliberate 'next steps' are imperative:

- campaigning to promote ratification and application of the ILO and UN conventions on protection of the rights of migrant workers in all world regions
- enhancing cooperation between concerned CSOs and social partners – trade unions in particular – in promotion of migrant worker standards country by country
- strengthening common approaches and joint actions between social partners, CSOs and the key standards-based international organizations (OHCHR, ILO and UNHCR globally and the African Union, the Council of Europe, the EU and the Organization of American States in their respective regions)
- sharing and building on examples of 'good practices' of promoting implementation of these normative instruments.

Today, in the context of increasing inequalities in distribution of wealth and the exclusion of entire populations from the benefits and social welfare promised by globalization, it is clear that greater emphasis is needed on advancing rights-based approaches. To the extent that migration is a central arena for expression of values in law, policy and practice, advancing a rights-based framework for the protection of migrants and the regulation of migration is imperative.

The ICRMW is a singularly symbolic instrument; its adoption is arguably fundamental to advancing the primacy of the rule of law and extension of democratic engagement in the context of expanding international migration. Promotion of the rule of law and of respect for diversity as guarantors of democracy and social peace are shared responsibilities among all stakeholders – government, employers, trade unions, civil society and migrants themselves. Social partners, together with CSOs and IGOs – in concert with migrant associations – have key moral and political leadership roles to play in mobilizing societies and governments to ensure implementation of a rights-based framework for international migration.

References

Abella, M. I. 2002. Mondialisation, marchés du travail et mobilité. *Migrations Société*, Vol. 14, No. 79, January–February, pp. 181–94.

Allasino, E., Reyneri, E., Venturini, A. and Zincone, G. 2004. *Labour Market Discrimination against Migrant Workers in Italy*. Geneva, Switzerland, ILO.

Arrijn, P., Feld, S. and Nayer, A. 1998. *Discrimination in Access to Employment on Grounds of Foreign Origin: The Case of Belgium*. Geneva, Switzerland, ILO.

Attström, K. 2007. *Discrimination in Employment against Second Generation Swedes of Immigrant Origin*. Geneva, Switzerland, ILO. (ILO International Migration Papers.)

Bendick, J. Jr. 1996. *Discrimination against Racial/Ethnic Minorities in Access to Employment in the United States: Empirical Findings from Situation Testing*. Geneva, Switzerland, ILO.

Bovenkerk, F. 1995. *Discrimination against Migrant Workers and Ethnic Minorities in Access to Employment in the Netherlands*. Geneva, Switzerland, ILO.

Cediey, E. and Foroni, F. 2007. *Les discriminations en raison de 'l'origine' dans les embauches en France*. Geneva, Switzerland, ILO.

de Prada, M. A., Actis, W., Pereda, C. and Pérez Molina, R. 1996. *Labour Market Discrimination against Migrant Workers in Spain*. Geneva, Switzerland, ILO.

Escobar Latapí, A., 1997. *Emigration Dynamics in Mexico, Central America and the Caribbean*. 12th IOM Seminar on Migration, Managing International Migration in Developing Countries, Geneva, Switzerland, April 1997.

Goldberg, A., Mourinho, D. and Kulke, U. 1996. *Labour Market Discrimination against Foreign Workers in Germany*. Geneva, Switzerland, ILO.

ILO. 2004. *Resolution and Conclusions on Migrant Workers*. International Labour Conference. 92nd Session. Geneva, Switzerland, ILO. Available at www.ilo. org/migrant/download/ilcmig_res-eng.pdf [last accessed 18 April 2009].

— 2009. Forthcoming. *International Labour Migration: Towards a Rights-based Approach*. Geneva, Switzerland, ILO.

Lean Lim, L. 1998. Growing economic interdependence and its implications for international migration. UN Expert Group Meeting on Population Distribution and Migration. *United Nations: Population Distribution and Migration*. New York, UN.

Linard, A., 1998. *Migration and Globalisation – The New Slaves*. Brussels, International Confederation of Free Trade Unions.

Reynieri, E. 2001. *Migrants in Irregular Employment in the Mediterranean Countries of the European Union*. Geneva, Switzerland, ILO. (International Migration Paper No. 41.)

Ruhs, M. and Chang, H.-J. 2004. The ethics of labor immigration policy. *International Organization*, Vol. 58, No. 1, pp. 69–102.

Stalker, P. 2000. *Workers Without Frontiers – The Impact of Globalisation on International Migration*. Geneva, Switzerland, ILO.

Taran, P. and Moreno-Fontes, G. 2002. *Getting At the Roots: Stopping Exploitation of Migrant Workers by Organized Crime*. Geneva, Switzerland, ILO. (ILO Perspectives on Labour Migration 1E.)

PART II

7

Obstacles to, and opportunities for, ratification of the ICRMW in Asia

NICOLA PIPER

Introduction

To date, among the forty-one States Parties that have ratified the ICRMW, three are situated in those parts of the Asian region under discussion here (South, South-East and East Asia): East Timor (in 2004), the Philippines (in 1995) and Sri Lanka (in 1996); with Bangladesh (in 1998), Cambodia and Indonesia (both in 2004) having signed only. The first two ratifications by Asian countries took place in the 1990s – the decade during which only twelve of the current forty-one ratifications occurred. The other twenty-nine countries have acceded since 2000. The Philippines was among the early signatories (1993) and was the first Asian country to ratify. This is not surprising considering that it participated in the deliberations during the Convention's drafting process in the early 1980s and had been a significant labour exporter since the mid 1970s. When looking at ratification rates from a cross-regional perspective, most of the current States Parties are located in Africa (seventeen ratifications), followed by South America (fourteen ratifications). In this respect, despite its overall population size and migration volume,[1] Asia is surprisingly under-represented among States Parties. This is, however, consistent with Asia's overall low rate of ratifications of all UN conventions and covenants, where it takes bottom position.[2] Yet, one phenomenon consistent with the rest of the world is that, so far, no migrant *receiving* country in Asia has ratified the ICRMW.

From the perspective of the direction of migratory flows, Asia is an interesting case because of the high numbers of intra-regional migration, i.e. many foreign workers stay within Asia in their search for work. This

---

[1] Of the worldwide estimated international migrants, nearly 29% were in Asia as of 2000 (IOM, 2005, p. 1).

[2] This is largely because 'Asia' in these statistics typically includes the Gulf States, well known for their reluctance to ratify any international human rights instruments.

can be in the form of immediate cross-border migration, as between Indonesia and Malaysia, or it can be between countries further apart, such as Bangladesh and Japan (Asis and Piper, 2008). In many Asian sending countries, the fact that labour out-migration has increased in volume only since the late 1980s partly explains the slow interest in the Convention. This is also reflected in the fact that only since the late 1990s can rising civil society activism be witnessed in Asia (which by now hosts a considerable number of migrant worker NGOs and migrant associations, most of which are members of at least one of the several regional networks; see below). NGOs in Asia have played an important role in 'spreading the word' about the Convention, and often it was NGOs that translated it into the local vernacular in the first place to help to disseminate its content among the (potential and actual) migrant population, as well as policy makers (Piper and Iredale, 2003).

As elsewhere, Asian labour-receiving countries, without doubt, have more power to dictate the terms and conditions of employment, as well as the rules or regulations of migration. This situation has worsened in light of increased competition and intensified push factors among the labour exporting countries. In this respect, without the corresponding and reciprocal efforts from labour receiving countries, labour sending countries can only hope to mitigate the negative effects of overseas employment on their workers. This also makes NGO and civil society activism in the labour receiving countries enormously important, and transnational networking crucial. However, considering their limited resources and staff, plus the fact that they advocate on behalf of a highly marginalized group that is 'needed but not wanted' by the host society, NGO success is limited.

There are context-specific explanations as to why only two major sending countries, the Philippines and Sri Lanka,[3] have ratified and why others (such as Bangladesh and Indonesia) have not. Overall, the most important root cause of non-ratification is possibly the lack of political will. The specific politics involved in each case, however, differ slightly. The objectives of this chapter are not only to investigate the obstacles to ratification of the ICRMW, but also the kind of opportunities created by ratifying, from a social and political perspective and to a lesser extent from a purely legal perspective. In addressing these two aspects, I draw on two studies conducted under the auspices of UNESCO (Piper

---

[3] East Timor (now Timor-Leste) does not appear to be a significant migrant source nor destination country and is therefore not included in this study.

and Iredale, 2003; Iredale et al., 2005), for which a wide range of stakeholders were interviewed (senior government officials in relevant ministries, representatives of NGOs and trade unions, recruitment agencies, journalists, academic experts and lawyers).

I begin by outlining the major migration patterns and human rights issues that characterize intra-Asian migratory flows today, discussing the obstacles to ratification, followed by the reasons for ratification under the broader frame of 'opportunities' that lead to and derive from ratification. I.then turn to NGO advocacy and transnational activist networks to promote the rights of migrants.

Migration patterns and protection issues in Asia

Of the worldwide estimated 185 million to 192 million international migrants, nearly 50 million (29%) were in Asia as of 2000 (IOM, 2005, p. 1). The ILO estimates that about 22.1 million were economically active in Asia from among the 86 million migrant workers globally (excluding refugees) (ILO, 2004, p. 7). According to the latest report by the UN Secretary-General (2006, p. 12), between 1990 and 2005, high-income countries as a whole registered the highest increase in the number of international migrants. This is also the case in Asia, where the newly industrialized economies (NIEs – i.e. Hong Kong, Singapore, Republic of Korea and Taiwan) and the Gulf Cooperation Council (GCC) countries constitute the major destinations, as well as Japan.[4]

The Philippines have now surpassed Mexico as the world's largest labour exporting country, and of all newly deployed and land-based overseas migrant workers, women are now as likely to migrate as men.[5] The share of independent women participating in labour migration has increased sharply since the late 1970s (ILO, 2003, p. 9). By 2000, 50.1% of all migrants in South-East and East Asia were women (UNFPA, 2006), and in some cases women clearly dominate over their male counterparts. This has allowed commentators to use the phrase 'feminization of migration', which is most pronounced in South-East Asia and Sri Lanka in terms of out-going female migrants.

---

[4] Japan was the first country in East Asia to embark on fast economic development before the NIEs and is therefore not in this category.

[5] Women represent 61 to 72% of all outgoing migrants for 1998 to 2002, and 69 to 72% for 2000 to 2002. If seafarers and rehires were included, the gender distribution would be roughly equal. I owe this observation as well as the figures to Dr Maruja M. B. Asis from the Scalabrini Migration Center in Manila (personal communication).

By the early 1990s, labour migration had grown to the point that nearly all countries in the region were involved as either origin or destination, and some as both (UN, 2003, p. 2). Some countries in Asia constitute new sources of migrant workers bound for Asian destinations, such as Cambodians and Vietnamese working in Malaysia or Taiwan. Other countries, such as Japan, the Republic of Korea and Taiwan, have completed the transition from being mainly labour exporting countries to becoming labour importing countries. Thailand is an example of a country that continues exporting workers although it also began receiving migrant labour during the 1990s (Asis, 2005). South-East and East Asian countries admit migrants exclusively for temporary labour purposes whereby permanent residence, let alone citizenship, is out of reach for most.

Unlike the government-to-government arrangement in western Europe's guest worker programme, the system that has evolved in Asia involves minimal inter-state discussions. With the exception of government regulation of migration matters, recruitment is left largely in the hands of private recruitment agencies (and their networks of various brokers and intermediaries), and the protection of workers rests on contracts signed between workers and their employers (Asis, 2005). This scheme has given rise to irregularities and abuses at all stages of the migration process, exacting costs on migrants and their families. Abusive practices such as excessive placement fees, contract substitutions, contract violations, low wages and non-payment or delay in the payment of wages are widespread. This is compounded by increasing competition on the 'labour exporting scene' with more countries supplying migrant workers, exceeding demand. 'Salary deduction schemes' do not require payment of high fees prior to departure, allowing the poorer strata of migrants to move across borders within the region (Oishi, 2005; Verité, 2005). Unauthorized migrants and trafficked persons are rendered more vulnerable because they are seen as immigration violators and have limited or no access to support services and redress of grievances.

In the countries studied here, most of the labour exporters have not put any rights-based legislation in place that covers the pre-departure, working abroad and return phases. Labour receiving countries, in theory, should protect the migrants as workers, but because of their immigration status, foreign workers are, in practice, often not covered by existing legislation (i.e. labour or employment laws as well as occupational and health regulations). This is a serious problem for the large number of foreign domestic workers, for example, who are explicitly excluded from the coverage of national employment laws in the countries of destination.

The top violation of labour rights is the non-payment or under-payment of wages, followed by unfair dismissal. Another serious issue is the rampant violation of freedom of association (Piper, 2006). Legal and undocumented migrant workers face the various tactics of employers and contractors to keep them out of trade unions despite their legal entitlement to membership. Extending rights to undocumented workers is generally seen as unacceptable. Likewise, the protection of migrant workers' families tends to be a taboo area.

Until the 1990s, labour migration within Asia mainly involved less-skilled workers. Since then, migration of the highly skilled and of professionals has increased in response to greater demand, especially for IT and care workers (nurses, domestic workers), but also in education. In the past, the highly skilled migrated to countries of settlement, but from the 1990s, non-settlement countries, such as the newly industrialized countries (NICs) in Asia, started vying for these sought-after workers. The offer of permanent residence to attract these prized human resources is particularly remarkable for Asian countries, such as Japan, Malaysia, the Republic of Korea, Singapore and Taiwan, which do not allow settlement to less-skilled foreign workers (and in the case of some, even prohibit marriage between lower-skilled migrants and local citizens) (Asis and Piper, 2006).

Obstacles to ratification in South-East and East Asia

The obstacles to ratification of the ICRMW are complex, and their assessment needs to be approached from a holistic framework whereby the protection of migrant labour via international human rights law is seen in relation to politics and practices at national level (intra-state) as well as at transnational or regional level (inter-state). The specific countries under discussion here are Japan, Malaysia, the Republic of Korea and Singapore as the major countries of destination, and Bangladesh and Indonesia as source countries.[6]

Government level

In both the major exporting and importing countries, the ICRMW is known within government circles, largely due to promotion by very

---

[6] The data and analysis of this section are based on the original UNESCO study by Piper and Iredale (2003). This study also included New Zealand.

active NGOs – usually the ones translating the Convention into local languages. This does not, however, mean that it is fully understood in all its details. At the technical legal level, apart from Japan (which was, together with the Philippines, the only Asian country that joined the working group deliberations at least during the final phase of the drafting process), none of the other countries discussed in this section have gone so far as to investigate clause by clause the exact legal implications of ratifying the Convention. This is also the reason why it was only in Japan that the issues of 'duplication' (of the ICRMW with other human rights instruments already ratified) and 'clashes' with national legislation were raised by government officials as among the various reasons for not ratifying. The Ministry of Foreign Affairs had in fact identified a few clauses in the Convention that clash with the Constitution.[7]

The visibility of the ICRMW has not, however, extended into the wider public sphere. Human rights in general are an accepted and appreciated concept in most countries under study here, but the notion of extending human rights to migrant workers has not been given much attention or sympathy. This is related to the prevailing view that migrants do not share the same entitlements to the full protection of human rights law as citizens (cf. de Varennes, 2002). The media, with their tendency to depict lower and unskilled migrant workers as criminals or as undesirable/undeserving in other respects, are partly responsible for this.

In both sending and receiving countries, there is much confusion as to the gains and losses in the event of ratification, and it is often assumed at either end of the migration process that the losses are bigger than the gains. The overwhelming perception of the ICRMW among receiving countries is as an instrument for liberal immigration policies. There is little understanding that the Convention actually encourages the control of clandestine migratory movements and moreover does not encroach upon the rights of states to establish criteria governing admission of migrant workers and their families (although it does set some minimum standards). Sending countries, on the other hand, fear that they would have to grant migrant workers within their midst (mainly highly skilled professionals from developed countries) rights that are superior to local workers' rights. This would go beyond their means.

---

[7] This refers mainly to article 17(3) and (4) of the ICRMW. Whether the Japanese Government was not aware of the possibility of making reservations, with the above argument then appearing as an 'excuse', is unclear.

In receiving countries, the granting of rights to migrants is dependent on the migration status or type of visa, and only a small minority of highly skilled migrants are given an array of rights. As far as less-skilled migrants (who form the numerical majority) are concerned, the objective is to treat them as temporary workers who will be replaced after a certain number of years. The perception in countries such as Malaysia and Singapore is that migrants coming from less-developed countries are given the chance to earn much higher wages than at home, hence there is no need to give them rights or treatment not available to them in their country of origin. Furthermore, certain labour rights do not exist for home-state workers, hence they cannot possibly be implemented for foreigners. Demanding rights for migrants is, therefore, seen as not legitimate. Also, receiving countries typically want to keep their immigration policies flexible in order to be able to quickly respond to economic fluctuations, changes within the labour market and to public opinion.

Furthermore, there is the issue of taking leadership. Senior officials in Japan and the Republic of Korea stated that their governments rarely take the initiative in the ratification of international instruments and usually follow Western countries. Without this external push, it is unlikely that they will make the move. Thus, among destination countries, a change of government mindset is needed to address the reluctance, if not outright fear, of 'being first' to ratify the Convention.

Last but not least, priorities have changed in the aftermath of 9/11. Many government officials reported at the time of the interview that counter-terrorism conventions took precedence after 9/11, and there were certain deadlines to be met that kept relevant ministries very busy, with little time left to consider other conventions. The current priority given to 'national security' issues is reinforced by the multi-ethnic and/or multi-religious composition of many countries in this region and the (alleged or real) existence of pockets of extremism. This means that considering the ratification of other conventions, including the ICRMW, is further down the line of priorities. In the context of 'national security', anti-trafficking issues are considered more important than conventions dealing with broader migrant workers' rights, which is reflected in the greater ratification record of the 2000 CTOC and its two protocols dealing with smuggling and trafficking of persons.[8]

---

[8] For more detailed information, see the UNODC website (www.unodc.org/unodc/en/treaties/CTOC/index.html [last accessed 21 April 2009]).

Non-ratifier sending countries: Indonesia and Bangladesh

According to the ICRMW, the main obligations for origin countries are: to provide information on conditions of admission and remunerated activity; to give the right to emigrate and return; to regulate and monitor recruitment agencies; to assist migrants in the resettlement and reintegration process; and to provide overseas voting rights. Crucial obligations for Bangladesh and Indonesia would therefore be pre-departure information campaigns and training sessions, monitoring of workers abroad and the imposition of sanctions on brokers and recruiters operating illegally. Under the current institutional arrangements in both countries, this is a difficult task. The ratification and implementation processes of any UN convention are complex undertakings, and the governmental budget and expert staff assigned to such matters are very limited.

With regard to Indonesia's current political situation and its entire bureaucratic system being in the process of decentralization, ratification and subsequent implementation of the ICRMW in the near future is not a priority. In 2004, however, Indonesia signed the Convention. In the longer term, decentralization is potentially conducive to better regulate out-migration, taking pressure off the central government in Jakarta. But in both Indonesia and Bangladesh, the sheer number of private recruitment agencies, and the allegedly high level of collusion between government circles and those involved in the export business (recruitment agencies) obstruct any serious efforts to regulate and monitor out-migration from the perspective of migrants' protection.[9]

Another serious obstacle to ratification, as expressed by government officials, is the fear of losing out on the regional job market (as receiving countries might be disinclined to employ foreign workers who would be perceived as too 'rights conscious') and that other sending countries (non-ratifiers) would pick up their workers' share of the pie. This fear particularly affects source countries such as Bangladesh and Indonesia because they depend highly on the Middle East as the destination of their mostly low-skilled workers. In the case of Bangladesh, anecdotal evidence has it that when the government was about to ratify the ICRMW in 1998, it was informed through diplomatic channels that a particular Gulf state would stop admitting its workers if it proceeded with ratification. Oishi writes in a similar vein that 'many GCC countries have adopted policies to control the origin countries of migrant workers'. The goal is 'to prevent

---

[9] This was mentioned in some of the interviews and is also backed up by Jones' study (1996).

groups of those workers from taking unified action against the state' (Oishi, 2005, p. 41). What both countries have in common is the unbalanced dependence on the Middle East as the major destination of their labour force (in addition to Malaysia). Many GCC countries are notorious for their total intolerance of upholding human or labour rights. Malaysia is scarcely better. Public opinion of Indonesian and Bangladeshi migrant workers is rather negative in Malaysia, based on the former being depicted as 'troublemakers' (causing riots, etc.), and the latter the source of 'social problems' (relationship with local women).

NGOs in both Bangladesh and Indonesia are campaigning for ratification of the ICRMW and also for national legislation to protect migrant workers. A consortium of concerned NGOs in Indonesia drafted a national Migrant Worker Bill modelled on the Convention. The Philippines' Migrant Workers Act of 1995 (Republic Act 8042) was used as a frame of reference, and this resulted in the inclusion of a gender perspective into the Indonesian Bill – an element missing from the ICRMW. At the time of writing, the Bill was still with the parliament. The same consortium of NGOs in Indonesia has also lodged a class action court case (Indonesian citizens vs the government) in connection with the so-called Nunukan tragedy.[10] The High Court has accepted this case but postponed its decision indefinitely.

On the whole, major problems are posed by lack of resources, at government and NGO level, lack of awareness or ignorance on the part of the migrants themselves and the strong interests involved in the 'migration business'. All this needs addressing as part of a promotion campaign for the ICRMW.

Receiving countries

According to the ICRMW, destination countries are obliged to: observe the right to join trade unions for any migrant and the right to form associations and trade unions for legal migrants; provide minimum social welfare (such as medical care); ensure equality of treatment in respect of remuneration and conditions of work and employment; allow documented migrants to be temporarily absent without affecting the

---

[10] Following the 2002 Immigration Act, the Malaysian Government carried out mass deportations of undocumented foreign workers (mostly Indonesians and Filipinos). Almost 400,000 Indonesians were deported to a number of places in Sumatra and to Nunukan in Kalimantan. This was not the first but the largest single deportation undertaken (Ford, 2006).

authorization to stay or work; allow liberty of movement, of choosing the residence and access to alternative employment for legal migrants; give the right to seek alternative employment in case of termination of the remunerated activity for migrant workers not authorized to freely choose their remunerated activity; and work towards providing family reunification and extend to children of migrants the right to education.

Unless destination countries were to redesign their present policies, which revolve around temporary schemes for the lower skilled that tie them to specific employers, in the event of ratification, most of these obligations would be violated.

A close examination of recent studies suggests three broad groups of Asian labour-receiving countries, categorized by their contrasting tolerance for civil activism on behalf of migrants: (i) Malaysia and Singapore; (ii) Japan and the Republic of Korea; and (iii) Hong Kong. Each group is characterized by a distinct range of rights that have evoked their own forms and intensities of civil activism. Malaysia and Singapore are characterized by strict immigration policies, rigid labour contract systems, low degrees of state tolerance for civil activism and few entitlements for unskilled migrants. Japan and the Republic of Korea are characterized by tight immigration controls, absence of contract labour systems (except for the trainee system), large numbers of *de facto* migrant workers with few entitlements and relatively high degrees of tolerance for civil activism. Hong Kong is characterized by a strict immigration policy, a rigid labour contract system, more rights for migrants than in the other four countries and a high degree of tolerance for civil activism (Yamanaka and Piper, 2006).

In Malaysia and Singapore, where human and labour rights are, generally speaking, politically taboo, and which have ratified only two international human rights instruments each (the CEDAW and the CRC), both offer legal migration channels to unskilled migrant workers (policies in Malaysia, however, are more ad hoc and erratic). Policies (albeit not statistics) on immigration in Singapore are transparent. Partly because of these states' multi-ethnic composition, however, migration policy is also linked to concerns with maintaining a specific ethnic/religious balance. Permanent residence status is only given to migrants who are highly skilled or who are married to a citizen, and citizenship extended to those of the 'right' ethnic/religious background.

In Japan and the Republic of Korea, a major obstacle to ratification of the ICRMW is that both countries consider themselves strictly mono-ethnic/mono-cultural and not countries of immigration. Both governments feel that if they ratified, this would result in a large-scale influx and eventual settlement of foreign workers. Unskilled migrants and their families are only allowed in if they are ethnically close (such as the *nikkeijin*[11] in Japan and Korean-Chinese in Korea). Other unskilled foreign workers can enter legally as 'trainees' or are tacitly approved as 'undocumented' migrants. There are, however, no draconian practices to the extent that exist in Malaysia and Singapore, where legal marriage between citizens and lower-skilled contract workers is not permitted. None of the governments under investigation here are prepared to extend rights to irregular migrants, and there is very little acknowledgement of the complex ways in which migrants become 'illegal' (at times beyond their knowledge or control).

Problems with recruitment agencies exist in all countries. States typically protect employers more than foreign workers, and this is usually approved by the public at large, which tends to view foreign workers as 'competitors' or 'criminals'. By excluding trainees and domestic workers from coverage under their employment or labour laws, a substantial part of the foreign migrant-worker population is without protection.

Regional developments

In Asia and the Asia Pacific, regional integration is poorly developed compared with Europe, Africa and South America. Despite the existence of the Asia-Pacific Economic Cooperation (APEC) fora and the Association of Southeast Asian Nations (ASEAN), their Member States are so diverse in terms of political systems and economic development that there is very little commonality at the pan-Asian level in many policy areas.[12] In contrast to other regions, a region-wide human rights body does not exist, which is not surprising considering that, statistically, Asia ranks lowest with regard to ratifications of UN human rights instruments. In 1996, existing national human rights institutions in this part of the world formed the Asia Pacific Forum as a venue to discuss and

---

[11] This term refers to South Americans of Japanese origin (i.e. descendants from Japanese immigrants in the nineteenth and early twentieth centuries), mainly from Brazil and to a lesser extent from Peru.

[12] At the sub-regional level, there has been more integration. The South Asian Association for Regional Cooperation (SAARC) was established when its Charter was formally adopted on 8 December 1985 by the heads of state or government of Bangladesh, Bhutan, India, the Maldives, Nepal, Pakistan and Sri Lanka.

promote human rights standards in Asia, but migrant worker issues have so far not been among its main concerns.

With regard to broader regional agreements, trafficking seems to be the most-covered issue. Unlike temporary contract migration, which has been subject to little regional cooperation in the Asia Pacific, the problem of trafficking has been taken up at the regional level to some extent. A number of initiatives do not directly relate to human trafficking but treat it as a subset of other issues, such as irregular migration. Most of these initiatives deal with the control and prevention of such migratory flows, rather than addressing the root causes leading to trafficking and putting protective measures and victim support mechanisms in place.[13]

A fairly recent and important development in the Asian region is the holding of three ministerial-level consultations (labour ministries) by Asian labour-sending countries – in Colombo (April 2003), Manila (September 2004) and Bali (September 2005) – to discuss issues of common concern, including the protection of migrant workers. Concrete action is yet to be taken, other than the plan for a feasibility study on the establishment of a Common Migrant Resource Centre in the GCC. The final statement of the Bali ministerial consultation, however, directly refers to the need to establish 'orderly labour movement and employment policies consistent with the welfare of workers'. Four areas are highlighted as essential:

(1) Ensuring the welfare and wellbeing of vulnerable overseas workers, especially women, during recruitment and employment.
(2) Optimizing benefits of organized labour flows, including the development of new markets.
(3) Building institutional capacity and interministerial coordination to meet labour movement challenges.
(4) Increasing cooperation between countries of origin and destination countries in ensuring the welfare of overseas workers. More specifically, one area of cooperation is to aim at 'establishing minimum

---

[13] One exception seems to be the Coordinated Mekong Ministerial Initiative against Trafficking (COMMIT). In addition, a number of bilateral agreements on trafficking are at various levels of discussion between Thailand, Lao PDR, Myanmar, Cambodia and Vietnam. Among the specific objectives, agreed standards and procedures on repatriation and victim support are mentioned. In addition, COMMIT is one of the few, if not the only, anti-trafficking initiative that explicitly includes men as potential victims. For more information on policies and progress of this initiative, see the United Nations Inter-Agency Project (UNIAP) website (www.no-trafficking.org/content/COMMIT_Process/commit_process.htm [last accessed 21 April 2009]).

wage levels and ensuring safe and decent conditions of employment for contract workers, particularly women, in low skill and low wage sectors'. This finally constitutes a clear recognition of the rampant abusive employment practices. The challenge that lies ahead is to translate this rhetorical statement into action.

The latest development at the regional level in Asia is a declaration made by ASEAN on the 'Protection and Promotion of the Rights of Migrant Workers' at its summit in January 2007 in Cebu (the Philippines). This declaration was signed by all ASEAN Member States, which comprise major labour importers and exporters in the region. As observed by the Center for Migrant Advocacy Philippines, this Declaration is non-binding and its scope is limited to documented migrants and their families who are already residing with them.[14] Nonetheless, in a region where discourse on workers' rights has been notoriously difficult, this seems an important shift in emphasis.

Opportunities created by ratification: the Philippines and Sri Lanka

When a country ratifies an international treaty, it assumes a legal obligation to implement the rights stipulated in that treaty. The first step is to design legislative measures to incorporate international instruments into the national legal structure. Recognition of rights on paper is, however, not sufficient to guarantee that they will be enjoyed in practice. This is usually done via specific policies and programmes. Governments are service delivery agencies and, by ratifying a convention, they undertake certain obligations: the promotion of understanding, acceptance and public discussion of human rights and actual delivery of a wide range of programmes/policies.

As the ICRMW only came into effect in 2003, far too little time has passed to attempt an assessment of its impact. The improvement in migrants' rights cannot be attributed purely to ratification of the Convention. Rather, complex and ongoing sociopolitical processes are involved at various levels (UN, regional, governmental and non-governmental organizations). The reasons that make a country ratify in the first place have to be seen in a specific context. Both the Philippines

---

[14] Personal communication, 17 February 2007.

and Sri Lanka had already had certain institutional and legal elements in place to formalize the export of labour by the time they ratified.

Broadly, both identify themselves as democratic states and place importance on human rights. The right to emigrate is recognized and the freedom of movement considered a constitutional right for both female and male migrants. The Philippines have the longest history of labour export in Asia. The Philippines Government began to involve itself in labour emigration when President Marcos launched an overseas employment programme in 1974 to address problems of unemployment, among others. Institutions were created to handle recruitment and placement of workers. In Sri Lanka, systematic state-level efforts to promote emigration started in 1976, and in 1978 the Foreign Employment Bureau was set up, together with a legal framework. In both countries, the state agencies and embassies conduct research to identify potential niches in the international labour market and send out missions to higher-income countries to win job contracts for their citizens (as also observed by Oishi, 2005).

The Philippines participated in the deliberations of the draft ICRMW in the early 1980s. The Philippine delegation contributed ideas and avidly supported the approval by the UN General Assembly in 1990. The Philippine Government first signed (in 1993) and then fully ratified the Convention on 5 July 1995 and was, thus, the first Asian country to do so. The most significant piece of legislation in the Philippines that translates the obligations of the ICRMW into national law is Republic Act 8042, also known as the Migrant Workers' Act of 1995, introduced around the time of ratification of the ICRMW. The two pieces of legislation were developed concurrently and so there is a great deal of complementarity. This was also a period of heightened civil society activism, largely in reaction to the execution of Flor Contemplacion in 1995, a domestic worker in Singapore, who became the symbol of the sacrifices that female migrant workers were seen to be making to secure the livelihoods of their families.[15] A wide range of institutional mechanisms have been established since then to ensure the protection of the rights of migrant and overseas workers. Voting rights for overseas Filipinos were also implemented recently.[16] In this respect, the Philippines are unique.

---

[15] For more information, see Hilsdon (2000).

[16] See Philippine Migrants Rights Watch website (www.pmrw.org [last accessed 21 April 2009]) for legislative and other details.

In Sri Lanka, on the other hand, the decision to ratify the ICRMW was not driven or prepared by a vibrant civil society movement. Rather, it seems to have been a 'routine ratification' on the part of a government that happened to be 'pro-labour' at that time. The fact that between 1996 and 2004 no action was taken to implement the Convention supports the argument of a routine ratification. The Sri Lanka Foreign Employment Act was already implemented in 1985 and amended in 1994, when the entire criminal code was being amended. The Sri Lanka Bureau of Foreign Employment (SLBFE) Regulation of 1985 sets out the rules of the recruitment process but does not include rights provisions for migrants. Although the welfare components of the ICRMW were seen as compliant at the time, the gravity of the commitment was not fully understood by the Sri Lankan Government at the point of ratification (according to a ministerial official).

The very large numbers of Filipinos going overseas to work over a sustained period of time makes 'labour export' a very contentious issue within the country; thus there is a much greater level of awareness of these issues in the Philippines. There is considerable opposition to the 'costs' of the overseas employment programme in terms of the loss of skilled workers, the mistreatment of many workers by domestic recruiters, offshore recruiters and employers, the absence (largely of women) from families and problems of reintegration, whereas others realize that the programme is essential due to the lack of domestic opportunities. Many civil society participants have become involved in various aspects of the programme, for example: providing training and pre-departure orientation; raising questions about the 'entertainment' industry; highlighting the problems of absentee parents; emphasizing the rights of all migrant workers, including irregular migrants, as well as the paucity or failure of reintegration programmes, to name but a few. In other words, there has been active engagement with policy makers and the policy-making process. In addition, many NGOs are internationally connected, often via the internet, and operate both 'at home' and in many destination countries (see below).

In contrast, Sri Lankan civil society, and specifically migration NGOs, are less developed. There is still a low level of civil society activism in Sri Lanka, let alone in the destination countries. CSO representation on organizational boards, committees, etc. is minimal. For example, there is, so far, no representative of migrants through trade unions or NGOs on the board of the SLBFE. NGOs and trade unions have not engaged in more forceful lobbying for policies and have not formed any strong alliance. In contrast to the Philippines, NGOs do not seem to target individual senators to speak out on migrants' behalf. The ICRMW was ratified largely in response to pressure from outside rather than inside the country. Generally, people's awareness of their rights seems lower than in the Philippines, resulting in them being less well-informed and active. NGOs have been mainly engaged in service provision in Sri Lanka, and to a much lesser extent in advocacy and lobbying. The migrant NGOs that do exist rally mainly around the issue of voting rights and social security (especially pension rights).

There are no signs that migration has decreased since ratification (in terms of 'losing out' on the regional labour market) in either country. But at the same time it has to be said that there has been little 'external' use of the Convention vis-à-vis receiving countries by government representatives. The changes in statistics that exist seem to be mainly due to different measuring methods or new policies/regulations. Sri Lanka is heavily reliant on a small number of destinations for its overseas labour markets. These are mostly in the Middle East, where 'power' exerted by the Sri Lankan Government to influence the conditions and fulfilment of the rights of migrant workers is very limited. Filipinos, by contrast, constitute a far more diverse migrant labour force in terms of occupation, skill level and geographical destination. Thus, the relatively better protection enjoyed by Filipinos is not the direct result of ratification of the ICRMW but the result of a complex set of issues. The different migration and sociopolitical situation has created far more opportunities for migrant worker protection in the Philippines than in Sri Lanka.

Rights activism and the role of civil society

NGOs and migrant associations

The proliferation of NGO networks in Asia in the past two decades reflects the growing role that NGOs are now playing in response to issues concerning migrant labour (Piper, 2003). Networking and alliance formation is thereby a crucial operating method to generate 'critical mass'. This can take the form of national and/or transnational networks. In the specific context of protecting migrant workers, the meaning of transnational networking and organizing, which reflects the nature of cross-border migration involving at least two countries, refers to: (i) local citizens campaigning on behalf of non-citizens; (ii) activists following their compatriot migrant workers to the destination and campaigning on their behalf from there; (iii) migrants campaigning on their own behalf, challenging the government of origin as well as destination; and (iv) migrant workers or their compatriot activists campaigning on behalf of all migrant nationalities, not only their own nationality group (Piper, 2005*a*).

Due to a lack of political space for certain types of activism and/or the often non-legal status of foreign workers, it is sometimes impossible or difficult for migrants to set up their own organizations. In such circumstances, they depend on local citizens to take up their concerns. This is prevalent in countries such as Singapore and Malaysia, where self-organizing is impossible. In countries where it is difficult but not impossible, such as Japan, the Republic of Korea and Taiwan, migrants have been more actively involved in setting up their own organizations. A particularly well-documented example is Hong Kong (Yamanaka and Piper, 2006; Wee and Sim, 2005).

Availability or lack of political space partly explains the different types of group involved in migrant labour advocacy and service provision. Recent studies on four major countries[17] in South-East Asia – Singapore, Malaysia, Indonesia and the Philippines – have provided a detailed mapping of existing organizations and their strategies for promoting and protecting migrants. These studies have made a clear distinction between migrant worker associations (run by migrants or former migrants) and other NGOs. Self-organizing has been identified as particularly effective, which underpins not only the importance of 'freedom of association', but also 'freedom to form political organizations' (direct and indirect violation of which is widespread, however).

Filipinos have emerged as the most widely and best-organized group of migrants, to the extent that they are even engaged in 'training' other groups of migrants to become good activists (as happens in Hong Kong) (Piper, 2005*b*). This is related to a number of reasons discussed elsewhere (Piper and Uhlin, 2002; Yamanaka and Piper, 2006). The most successful of the networks run by Filipinos, in terms of its widespread grass-roots support as well as overseas networking, is possibly MIGRANTE International, a global alliance of overseas Filipino organizations. Membership-based, staffed by activists who were formerly migrants themselves and supported from the grass-roots level, MIGRANTE International has been vital in organizing Filipino migrants on a large scale. Among its objectives are to strengthen the unity and organization

[17] See Asian and Pacific Migration Journal (2006).

of overseas Filipinos and their families in the Philippines and to defend the rights and welfare of overseas Filipinos. The alliance has ninety-five member organizations in twenty-two countries in all global regions. By trying to address the root causes of migration in the Philippines, the NGO and its networks are addressing migrant workers' rights 'at home'. Another Philippines-based, but clearly more regionally oriented, network is MFA, a 260+ membership organization covering the whole of Asia (West, South, South-East, North-East, East), including NGOs from sending and receiving countries.[18] Its member NGOs support any migrant workers, female and male, of any nationality in Asia. They hold regular regional meetings, exchange information (and also engage in lobbying) via e-mail.

Broadly, the main issues fought for by migrant worker associations and NGOs are employment-related rights and improved working conditions. In the specific case of domestic workers who are locked into informal interactions within the home, much of the activism has appealed to the 'morals' of employers, as reflected in campaigns such as Dignity is Overdue (Singapore, Malaysia), and has called for standard contracts as minimum protection. In Malaysia, the trade union council and NGOs also call for the right of all workers to seek redress to end the under-payment or non-payment of wages and to create a 'culture of payment of wages'. In the Philippines, activism by and for migrants' rights has become particularly broad to include, for example, the rights of family members left behind and rights to economic security 'at home', as well as absentee voting rights – a campaign that resulted in the passing of the Overseas Voting Bill in 2004.

Trade unions

Based on a global survey, Johansson (2005, p. 2) observes that the union movement as a whole considers 'reaching out to the unorganized and vulnerable' as key to ensuring the future relevance of trade unions. He goes on to describe unions as 'one of the most progressive actors in the migration debate' and as 'active in organizing them and defending the rights of migrant workers'. It is debatable whether unions are in fact at the forefront in the migration debate. There might be regional variations. Empirical evidence from Asia, for example, points rather to migrant worker associations and NGOs.

[18] For more details, see the MFA website (www.mfasia.org [last accessed 21 April 2009]).

At the global confederation level, the ICFTU has advocated for migrants' rights in many venues and was a crucial participant at the 2004 International Labour Conference in Geneva. The ICFTU's Asian and Pacific Regional Organisation (APRO) has also organized a few regional consultations on the role of trade unions in protecting migrant workers (ICFTU-APRO, 2003). ICFTU-APRO's Action Plan from 2003 includes two major recommendations: (i) establishing a migrant workers' desk or committee; and (ii) recruiting migrant workers as union members. The first has been realized by some national centres, such as Singapore's National Trades Union Congress (NTUC).[19] Malaysia's Trade Union Congress (TUC) has a sub-committee/section on foreign workers but they do not have the funding for full-time staff to work on migrant labour-related issues, let alone legal assistance (interview, July 2005, Kuala Lumpur). The second recommendation by ICFTU-APRO still constitutes an under-developed aspect of trade union work in South-East Asia (as elsewhere). But, more recently, the Malaysian TUC has reaffirmed its commitment to assist and organize migrant workers, including domestic workers.[20] In Thailand, trade union leaders have formulated the so-called Phuket Declaration, resulting from an ILO workshop on migrant labour in August 2005, in which they declare (among other items) that 'Thai Trade Unions should be committed to organize and recruit migrant workers.'[21]

Part of these new initiatives is the attempt to cooperate transnationally in order to offer better protection to temporary migrant workers. The two declarations mentioned above (Malaysian TUC and Phuket) include in their 'action plan' the promotion of close cooperation with unions in sending and receiving countries. The Malaysian TUC

---

[19] According to a recent questionnaire by the ILO sent out to trade unions around the world (to which forty-two trade unions responded, among them NTUC Singapore), sixteen unions replied affirmatively to the question of whether they have a designated migration officer, two of which were in South-East Asia: Hong Kong and NTUC Singapore. The main responsibilities of such migration officers were mostly (i) training and information, followed by (ii) policy advocacy, (iii) individual assistance, and lastly (iv) recruiting members. NTUC Singapore's designated migration officer is part of the Migrant Workers Forum (MWF) set up in 2002, chaired by Yeo Guat Kwang.

[20] Concluding Resolution, MTUC Conference on Migrant Workers, 18 to 19 April 2005, Petaling Jaya Malaysia. I thank Mr Ragwhan of the ILO Bangkok office for sharing this information.

[21] I am grateful to Mr Ragwhan at the ILO Bangkok office for sharing this document with me.

document recommends that sending countries should 'develop a system for networking and information exchange between sending and receiving countries'. As laudable as these statements are, it remains to be seen whether resources will be made available for such transnational cooperation. Philippines-based trade unions, on the other hand, have sent organizers to Hong Kong to assist with the setting up of domestic worker unions there. This seems the kind of strategy that should be employed more widely by unions in the labour sending countries.

Conclusion

Asia is a hugely diverse region in economic and political terms, as manifested by the different migration policies in East, South-East and South Asia, as well as by the different politicization of migrants' rights and space for civil society activism. The concept of extending rights to migrants is rather new, and there is very little understanding of what this means. Ratification and implementation of a multilateral instrument such as the ICRMW is, therefore, a highly contested and politicized issue.

As elsewhere, destination countries are unlikely to ratify this instrument soon. Origin countries, by contrast, have begun to show more interest in the protection of their workers abroad, to a large extent pushed by civil society activism. The most advanced country in this respect is the Philippines. Filipinos emerge as the best protected and politically most active migrant workforce. This has to do with the social profile of the migrants themselves (skills and education level); duration of the state-driven migration programme; diversification of destinations (not dependent on just a few countries); a vibrant civil society at home; and the most widespread civil society networks resulting in high levels of mobilization. The high awareness of migrants' rights and policies to ensure protection are thus the result of a complex set of issues rather than just the ratification of the ICRMW. For the other origin countries, the Philippines case shows that providing prospective migrants with higher levels of protection has to start at home – with improved education standards and the raising of human capital.

Networking across countries and across various types of CSO is a vital ingredient in the promotion of migrant workers' rights and must expand in order to ensure greater influence on national and regional policy making.

References

Asian and Pacific Migration Journal. 2006. *Special Issue: Migrant Labor NGOs and Trade Unions: A Partnership in Progress?*, Vol. 15, No. 3.

Asis, M. M. B. 2005. Recent trends in international migration in Asia and the Pacific. *Asia-Pacific Population Journal*, Vol. 20, No. 3, pp. 15–38.

Asis, M. and Piper, N. 2008. Researching international labour migration in Asia. *The Sociological Quarterly*, Vol. 49, No. 3, pp. 423–44.

de Varennes, F. 2002. *'Strangers in Foreign Lands' – Diversity, Vulnerability and the Rights of Migrants*. Paris, UNESCO. (MOST Working Paper 9.)

Ford, M. 2006. After Nunukan: the regulation of Indonesian migration to Malaysia. A. Kaur and I. Metcalfe (eds), *Divided We Move: Mobility, Labour Migration and Border Controls in Asia*. New York, Palgrave Macmillan, pp. 228–47.

Hilsdon, A. M. 2000. The Flor Fiasco: the hanging of a Filipino domestic worker in Singapore. A. Hilsdon, M. Macintyre, V. Mackie and M. Stivens (eds), *Gender Politics and Human Rights in the Asia-Pacific Region*. London, Routledge.

ICFTU-APRO. 2003. *Migration Issues Concern Trade Unions*. Singapore, International Confederation of Free Trade Unions, Asian and Pacific Regional Organisation.

ILO. 2003. *Preventing Discrimination, Exploitation and Abuse of Women Migrant Workers: An Information Guide – Booklet 1: Why the Focus on Women International Migrant Workers*. Geneva, Switzerland, ILO.

   2004. *Towards a Fair Deal for Migrant Workers in the Global Economy*. Geneva, Switzerland, ILO.

IOM. 2005. *World Migration Report*. Geneva, Switzerland, IOM.

Iredale, R., Piper, N. and Ancog, A. 2005. Impact of ratifying the 1990 UN Convention on the Rights of All Migrant Workers and Members of Their Family – case studies of the Philippines and Sri Lanka. Unpublished report prepared for UNESCO. Bangkok, UNESCO.

Johansson, R. 2005. Role of TU in respect to migrant workers: summary of responses. Unpublished background paper. Geneva, Switzerland, ILO.

Jones, S. 1996. *Making Money off Migrants – The Indonesian Exodus to Malaysia*. Hong Kong, Asia 2000 Ltd.

Oishi, N. 2005. *Women in Motion – Globalization, State Policies, and Labor Migration in Asia*. Stanford, Calif., Stanford University Press.

Piper, N. 2003. Bridging gender, migration and governance: theoretical possibilities in the Asian context. *Asian and Pacific Migration Journal*, Vol. 12, Nos. 1–2, pp. 21–48.

   2005a. Rights of foreign domestic workers – emergence of transnational and transregional solidarity? *Asian and Pacific Migration Journal*, Vol. 14, Nos. 1–2, pp. 97–120.

2005*b*. Transnational politics and organizing of migrant labour in South-East Asia – NGO and trade union perspectives. *Asia-Pacific Population Journal*, Vol. 20, No. 3, pp. 87–110.

2006. Opportunities and constraints for migrant worker activism in Singapore and Malaysia – freedom of association and the role of the state. *Asian and Pacific Migration Journal*, Vol. 14, No. 9, pp. 359–80.

Piper, N. and Iredale, R. 2003. *Identification of the Obstacles to the Signing and Ratification of the UN Convention on the Protection of the Rights of All Migrant Workers: The Asia Pacific Perspective*. Paris, UNESCO.

Piper, N. and Uhlin, A. 2002. Transnational advocacy networks and the issue of trafficking and labour migration in East and Southeast Asia. A gendered analysis of opportunities and obstacles. *Asian and Pacific Migration Journal*, Vol. 11, No. 2, pp. 171–95.

UN. 2003. *Levels and Trends of International Migration to Selected Countries in Asia*. New York, UN-DESA, Population Division.

2006. *International Migration and Development*. Report of the Secretary-General. New York, UN.

UNFPA. 2006. *A Passage to Hope – Women and International Migration*. New York, UNFPA.

Verité. 2005. Protecting overseas workers – research findings and strategic perspectives on labor protections for foreign contract workers in Asia and the Middle East. Research paper, December 2005, Amherst, Mass., Verité.

Wee, V. and Sim, A. 2005. Hong Kong as a destination for migrant domestic workers. S. Huang, B. S. A. Yeoh and N. Abdul Rahman (eds), *Asian Women as Transnational Domestic Workers*. Singapore, Marshall Cavendish, pp. 175–209.

Yamanaka, K. and Piper, N. 2006. *Feminised Migration in East and Southeast Asia: Policies, Actions and Empowerment*. Geneva, Switzerland, United Nations Research Institute for Social Development. (UNRISD Occasional Paper No. 11.)

Obstacles to ratification of the ICRMW in Canada

VICTOR PICHÉ, EUGÉNIE DEPATIE-PELLETIER
AND DINA EPALE

Introduction

Throughout the twentieth century, international migration policies and principles have been dominated by the nationalist/consequentialist paradigm (Piché, forthcoming; Ruhs and Chang, 2004). This paradigm is based on two fundamental principles: first, international migration policies are the exclusive prerogative of national states (national sovereignty); and second, they are geared towards national interests (immigration must thus have positive economic consequences). One notable breach with respect to national sovereignty is the Geneva Convention (1950) whereby States Parties have accepted international standards and multilateral management of refugee protection.

Although 'virtually all migration policies affect the enjoyment of recognized human rights' (Fitzpatrick, 2003, p. 169), the connection between international migration and human rights is relatively recent and can be traced back to the early work of the ILO and, in particular, the 1949 Migration for Employment Convention.[1] However, the basic instrument in human rights of migrants is the ICRMW, which was adopted by the UN in 1990 and came into force thirteen years later, on 1 July 2003, after ratification by twenty signatory countries. As was the case with women and children, the adoption of this specific convention by the international community targeted the human rights protection of a particularly vulnerable group: non-citizens (workers and members of their families). Since the Convention came into force, twenty-one other states have ratified it (bringing the number of ratifications to forty-one as of June 2009) and campaigns geared towards ratification

---

[1] ILO Convention No. 97 (Convention concerning Migration for Employment (Revised)) came into force in 1952; forty-five countries have signed it (see www.ilo.org/ilolex/ english/index.htm [last accessed 12 May 2009]).

are under way in several countries. Although in 1994 most countries (176) adopted the ICPD's Programme of Action (UN, 1994), urging governments to ratify the ICRMW, no developed country has yet ratified it, including Canada.

Canada has a history based on immigration and systematic colonization of its territory by recent arrivals (1960–2008 annual cohorts of immigrants and refugees), a national culture developed by waves of consecutive immigration and an economy that depends greatly on continuing immigration policy (Hawkins, 1974). Furthermore, thousands of foreign workers are brought into Canada every year, of which an increasing number are deemed not to have any 'specific skills' or are 'unskilled'. But despite Canada's official recognition of the importance of respecting human rights at different levels, and the fact that the Convention is a tool that allows the orientation and critical evaluation of its policies, Canada still refuses to ratify it. This chapter, based on a UNESCO-sponsored study realized between September 2005 and August 2006 by the authors, in cooperation with Action Canada for Population and Development (ACPD), investigates the reasons behind this reluctance.

Several parties could play a significant role in the promotion and protection of the rights of migrant workers in Canada: the federal government, elected provincial and federal members of parliament, federal and provincial human rights commissions, provincial governments, workers unions and community groups/NGOs in support of migrant workers and their families. We focus primarily on the points of view of (i) the federal government, (ii) members of the federal parliament and (iii) community groups/NGOs.

More specifically, we identified, in the federal government's organization chart, the departments most involved in the protection of the rights of migrant workers, i.e. those that deal with human rights issues, migration management and the application of labour standards. Three federal departments were targeted for this study: Citizenship and Immigration Canada (CIC); Foreign Affairs Canada (FAC) and Human Resources and Skills Development Canada (HRSDC). Interviews with senior bureaucrats were conducted in a manner that allowed them to express not only their views regarding past and present obstacles to ratification of the ICRMW, but also their opinion on the future promotion and protection of the rights of migrants in Canada and at the international level. Over twenty civil servants in charge of pertinent programmes were interviewed, as were selected members of the House of Commons of the federal parliament, targeting those assigned to the Standing Committee on Citizenship and Immigration.[2] Finally, interviews of active members and a review of the material published by selected Canadian civil society groups and NGOs involved in the promotion of migrant workers' rights in Canada constitute the basis of our analysis of NGO views.[3]

First we present an overview of the current policy framework of migrant workers' rights recognition and protection in Canada. In the following section, we identify the federal government's official reasons for refusing to ratify the ICRMW, followed by the views of selected MP members of the Standing Committee on Immigration and Integration. The final section offers a brief presentation of NGO/community group evaluations of the federal government's official position towards the Convention.

Immigrants and foreign workers in Canada[4]

Canada's current Immigration and Refugee Protection Act 2002 creates five types of migrant worker:

(1) workers selected for immigration[5] and granted permanent status[6]
(2) visitors authorized to work temporarily (without work permit)

---

[2] Of the fifteen requests for an interview, nine members of parliament agreed: two from the Conservative Party of Canada (Barry Devolin and Ed Komarnicki – the former is also Parliamentary Secretary to the current Minister of Citizenship and Immigration Canada); four from the Liberal Party of Canada (Albina Guanieri, Andrew Telegdi, Blair Wilson and Raymonde Folco); two from the Bloc Québécois (Meili Faille and Johanne Deschamps); and one from the New Democratic Party of Canada (Bill Siksay). See the supplementary bibliography at the end of the chapter for government sources consulted for this section.

[3] The NGOs included in our analysis are the following: Action Canada for Population and Development; Amnesty International Canada; Amnistie Internationale, Section Canadienne Francophone; Association des aides familiales du Québec; Centre d'appui aux Travailleurs et Travailleuses Agricoles; Centre des Travailleurs Immigrants; Coalition d'appui aux Travailleurs et Travailleuses Agricoles; Droits Travailleuses et Travailleurs (Im)migrants; The Inter-Church Committee for Refugees; Justicia for Migrant Worker (Ont.); Justicia for Migrant Workers (BC); Kairos; The London Diocesan Migrant Workers Committee; No One is Illegal (Vancouver); North South Institute; OCASI/ STATUS COALITION; Philippine Women Centre of BC; Personne n'est illégal (Montréal); Philippine Women Centre of Quebec; and Solidarité sans Frontières.

[4] In Canada, 'foreign workers' are migrant workers with temporary status.

[5] Other foreigners are admitted as immigrants under family reunification or humanitarian criteria. These newcomers with permanent status are potential workers but are not admitted into Canada specifically to fulfil this economic requirement.

[6] Note that permanent residents (as well as new citizens) could be considered as a special category of migrant workers (see Clark, 1999): they can lose their status and be deported if they are suspected of criminal activities that could jeopardize national security (see Crépeau and Nakache, 2006).

(3) foreign workers authorized to work temporarily in Canada upon obtaining a work permit from CIC
(4) foreign workers authorized to work temporarily in Canada upon obtaining both an authorization from HRSDC and a work permit from CIC
(5) 'undocumented' migrant workers.

Under the immigration regulations, two departments (CIC and HRSDC) are in charge of managing migrant workers' (permanent and temporary) admission and integration in Canada. Table 8.1 gives general statistics on the annual inflows to Canada of foreign nationals admitted for permanent or temporary residence. Most migrant workers during the last decade were not admitted to Canada as immigrants (row 1), but, on the contrary, as foreign workers (row 8). Moreover, if the number of foreign workers admitted annually with permanent status has not significantly risen since 1997, the annual number of admissions of foreign workers under temporary work permits has increased by almost 50% between 1997 and 2006.

The category 'foreign workers' (row 8 in Table 8.1) covers a range of situations. In order to illustrate this diversity, two critical criteria can be combined to produce the typology in Table 8.2: (i) the type of work permit (tied to specific employer or not); and (ii) qualification requirements associated with the worker's occupation in Canada (high skilled vs low skilled). Table 8.2 shows that workers in low-skilled occupations have increased between 2002 (date of implementation of new Immigration Act) and 2006 (from 27,221 to 37,472). Given the current high levels of education and per capita income, the commercialization of domestic work and family services, the ageing of the population and an immigration policy for foreign workers favourable to business people and professionals, the pool of workers ready to accept dirty, dangerous or degrading (3-D) jobs is seeing a downward trend among the active Canadian population. In this context, the Canadian federal government has decided since 2002 to streamline the admission of 'low-skilled' foreign labour under work permit tied to a specific employer. This explains the systematic increase in the percentage of 'low-skilled' temporary foreign workers as illustrated in Table 8.2. On the other hand, the number of high-skilled workers under temporary work permit seems to have been somewhat constant, but these figures are under-estimated in as much as most foreign workers employed temporarily in the Canadian entertainment sector are authorized since 2002 to work without a work permit (Immigration and Refugee Protection Act 2002, articles 186–89)

Table 8.1 *Annual admissions in Canada of foreign nationals, by administrative category (1997 and 2006)*

Admission programmes		Administrative category of (im)migrant	1997	2006
Permanent settlement	'Economic' immigration	(1) Foreign workers granted permanent status	52,408	55,724
		(2) Spouses, children and parents of selected foreign workers	75,943	82,533
		(3) Subtotal	128,351	138,257
	'Family' immigration	(4) Spouses, children and parents of Canadian citizens and permanent residents	59,940	70,504
	'Humanitarian' immigration	(5) Political refugees and families	24,307	32,492
		(6) Humanitarian cases and other attribution of permanent resident status	3,400	10,394
		(7) Total	215,998	251,647
Temporary stay		(8) Foreign workers	75,560	112,658
		(9) Foreign students	42,160	61,703
		(10) Refugee claimants	24,727	21,380
		(11) Visitors and others	51,936	72,315
		(12) Total	194,383	268,056

Source: Adapted from CIC (2006*a*).

Table 8.2   *Annual admissions of migrant workers under a first work permit, by level of qualification associated with the employment authorization (2002–2006)*

Category of work permit issued	Skill level	2002	2003	2004	2005	2006
Migrant workers admitted under permit tied to a specific employer	Occupations with high qualification requirements ('high skilled')	40,596	32,854	33,260	36,480	40,804
	Occupations with low qualification requirements ('low skilled')	27,221	27,556	29,719	32,770	37,472
Migrant workers admitted under open work permit	Level and type of qualification unknown	27,573	28,094	32,244	33,358	34,382
Total		95,390	88,504	95,223	102,608	112,658

Source: Adapted from CIC (2006a).

and therefore are no longer included in foreign worker statistics. This explains why in Figure 8.1 the number of business and professional people has decreased since 2002 as a result of this policy change. Figure 8.1 shows that the changes in admissions of workers between 2002 and 2006 varied according to skill level associated with the job offer.

Rights of migrant workers and families in Canada

The four different categories of documented foreign worker are granted different rights in Canada, as summarized in Table 8.3. Hence, foreign workers granted permanent residence status upon arrival are protected under civil and socioeconomic laws by the Canadian Constitution and applicable federal and provincial laws (with the exception of the right to vote or to be elected). On the contrary, the 'low-skilled' workers under work permit tied to a specific employer and the undocumented workers are granted very limited rights. Their precarious legal and working

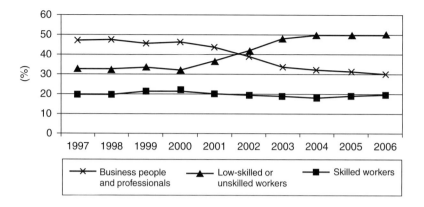

Figure 8.1 Percentage of annual admissions of migrant workers under a first permit linked to a specific employer, by skill level associated with the job (1997–2006).

conditions lead to the conclusion that these are the migrant workers specifically targeted by the ICRMW.

Documented migrant workers vulnerable to rights abuse (placed in Canada under the legal authority of their employer) are admitted through one of three programmes for low-skilled workers currently administered by the federal government (HRSDC and CIC): the Live-in Caregivers Program (LCP), the Seasonal Agricultural Worker Program (SAWP) and the Low-Skilled Workers Program (LSP).

Live-in Caregivers Program

The LCP is geared towards the recruitment of foreign workers to carry out domestic work while living in the home of the employer named on the work permit they have been issued. After having worked for at least twenty-four out of thirty-six months from their initial entry into Canada, the domestic worker can obtain permanent residence status. In December 2006, there were approximately 20,000 workers in Canada under this legal status.

Seasonal Agricultural Worker Program

Several bilateral agreements have targeted citizens from Mexico and the Caribbean who are temporarily employed as agricultural workers in Canada. One of the peculiarities of this programme is the formal involvement, in the recruitment process, of representatives of the federal government, of consular offices and (at least in Ontario and Quebec) of regional Federations of Agricultural Producers. With the official blessing

Table 8.3 *Migrant worker categories and recognition of fundamental rights in Canada*

Migrant worker category	Right to change employer with no risk of deportation	Right to (at least temporary) family reunification	Right to live elsewhere than where chosen by employer	Right to apply for permanent status in Canada upon arrival
Workers selected as immigrants	Yes	Yes	Yes	n.a.
Workers authorized to work without work permit	Yes	Yes	Yes	Yes
Workers authorized to work with work permit	Yes	Yes	Yes	Yes
Workers authorized to work with a HRSDC validation and a work permit; business people, professionals and skilled workers; low-skilled or unskilled workers	Yes / No	Yes / No	Yes / No	Yes / No
Undocumented workers	n.a.	n.a.	n.a.	Only if spouse or parent of a Canadian permanent resident

Source: Adapted from CIC (2006*a*).

of the Department of Human Resources Canada, important constraints to the foreign worker are directly integrated in the standardized agricultural labour contracts annually re-negotiated between representatives of the Canadian producers (employers) and either representatives of the Mexican Government or representatives of the Caribbean governments (governmental labour brokers). In particular, no foreigner associated with this programme can work for any other employer in Canada except the one they were assigned to, unless the employer eventually authorizes a move to a second Canadian employer. Also, after a trial period, which varies between seven and fourteen days, any agricultural producer can terminate the foreign worker's employment, thereby setting the ball rolling for the repatriation to their country of origin. Finally, an agricultural worker is obliged to live in the place chosen by the employer. Between January and December 2006, more than 20,000 Mexican and Caribbean workers have been employed in the Canadian agricultural industry under this programme.

Low-skilled Worker Program

It was not until the coming into force of the new Immigration Law (2002) that standard directives were given for the recruitment of 'low-skilled' foreign workers in economic sectors other than agricultural work and live-in care services. Only then was the recruitment process of this type of foreign worker by Canadian employers normalized. If these new recruitment procedures have significantly simplified and facilitated the admission of 'low-skilled' foreign workers since 2002, these new residents in Canada are not invited to integrate at the community level and, on the contrary, will not be admitted unless they succeed in convincing the Canadian immigration agent that they will leave Canada before the expiration of their (initial or renewed) work permit. If these foreign workers – as opposed to the 'skilled' or 'highly skilled' temporary workers – are authorized to work for only one employer, their socioeconomic integration (and consequently their freedom of movement and their freedom of association) is administratively highly restricted. So, in contrast to the situation of other foreign workers, the federal government has not put into place any options to facilitate obtaining permanent residence status by these 'low-skilled' foreign workers. In 2006, the number of workers placed under this legal framework in Canada amounted to approximately 10,000.

Undocumented workers

As far as undocumented foreign workers are concerned, the geographical and geopolitical situation of Canada makes it difficult for migrants to cross the borders clandestinely or buy falsified Canadian passports on the black market. As a result, it is believed that the majority of 'undocumented' workers in Canada came in legally and are working clandestinely since the expiration of their temporary visas. The number of these undocumented workers cited by politicians, by groups defending the rights of undocumented and non-status people and by the Canadian media in 2006, varies between 200,000 and 800,000, even if in the current context a scientific evaluation of the number of 'undocumented' workers in Canada seems impossible. This group's importance in the Canadian workforce and its contribution to the economy become apparent in the mass media from time to time, when planned deportations would destroy families or community ties, or when workers employed in industries affected by a high level of labour shortage are deported without the implicit consent of the Canadian employer. For example, raids and mass deportations of workers employed occurred in the construction sector in Toronto in 2006 and in the South Ontario agricultural sector at the beginning of 2009.

Obstacles to ratification: the perspective of Canada's federal government

Given the increasing presence of vulnerable migrant workers in Canada, ratification of the ICRMW could appear to Canadian officials as a useful tool for enhancing vigilance at all levels to prevent human and labour rights abuses on Canadian territory. However, an analysis of interviews conducted in 2006 with civil servants in charge of human rights issues allowed us to identify four reasons regularly referred to as a justification of Canada's past refusal to ratify the Convention:[7]

(1) Migration management (including determination of the rights that should be recognized for various groups of migrant workers) lies within the national sovereignty of each nation-state and should not be subjected to multilateral institutions, including UN agencies.

---

[7] At the time of writing, we still had not been able to obtain the legal brief commissioned by the Department of Citizenship and Immigration to the judicial services of the Department of Justice that identifies the legal obstacles to ratifying the Convention.

(2) The spirit of the Convention is not in line with the Canadian political tradition of favouring permanent status upon arrival and access to citizenship for foreign workers and families selected through the Canadian immigration and refugee protection system.

(3) Fundamental rights of all persons, irrespective of their legal status, are sufficiently protected in Canada by other international conventions and the Charter integrated in the Canadian Constitution since 1982 and other human rights and labour legislations applicable in the province of employment.

(4) Signing and ratifying the Convention would force Canada to review its temporary migrants' programmes and deportation procedures in order to make them more respectful of the Convention.[8]

Obstacle 1: migration and national sovereignty

Migration policies are exclusively national sovereignty issues and should not be determined by conventions at multilateral or international levels.

Even if Canada encourages the expansion of bilateral and multilateral dialogue on international migration issues (e.g. in the context of the Commission on Labour Cooperation[9]), its view is that migration policies should be decided exclusively at national level. The opposition to a formal international framework dealing with migrant workers is directly linked to the necessity of reaffirming the rights of states to act contrary to human rights rules in certain cases (e.g. the right not to be deported to a country where there is the risk of being tortured or executed), under the guise of fighting terrorism. Consequently, Canada does not see the legitimacy of setting up migrants' rights in an international convention that will impact on the freedom of countries in terms of their migration policies, rights said to be already enshrined in the 1951 Convention relating to the Status of Refugees and the 1984 Convention against Torture.

This reason for Canada's refusal to ratify the ICRMW has in been part spelled out in the official statement submitted to the GCIM (FAC/CIC, 2005). Moreover, Canada's statement at the HLD (New York, 15 September

---

[8] Other reasons, such as the potential impact on provincial legislations (such as labour legislations), or the cost associated with the training of thousands of Canadian officers in human rights matters related to the Convention, have also been cited as reasons for Canada's reluctance to ratify the Convention (see Clark, 1999).

[9] The Commission on Labour Cooperation is a tri-national consultative body (Canada, United States and Mexico) created in 1993 as a result of the North American Agreement on Labour Cooperation (NAALC).

2006) reaffirms that: (i) the 'new' dialogue on international migration should take place as a stand-alone forum and not within the UN system; (ii) the dialogue process should focus on developing understanding of substantive issues rather than on negotiating resolutions; and (iii) states (not international institutions) should take the leadership role (CIC, 2006b).

Obstacle 2: immigration philosophy

> The spirit of the Convention in terms of migration management is historically in dissonance with Canadian culture and tradition.

The initiative behind the ICRMW arose during the 1970s in an international context that was characterized by an increase in the guest workers' programme, which was geared towards addressing labour shortages in Europe, a concept that was very remote in a Canadian context.[10] Canada was not part of the mobilization around the Convention, but, shortly before the UN adopted it in 1990, last-minute efforts by Canada to change its general philosophy towards a less rigorous approach that would have been more acceptable were in vain.

In the past, the number of temporary workers in Canada was 'negligible' in comparison with the selection of a substantial and ever-increasing number of foreign workers with the goal of permanent residency and complete socioeconomic integration (by having relatively easy access to citizenship). Unlike many European countries, access to citizenship is viewed as a means of integration rather than a reward for those who have integrated 'well'. Basically, Canada does not see why it should sign a Convention that has very little in common with the realities of the country.

Obstacle 3: respect of fundamental rights

> It is unnecessary to sign the Convention as the fundamental rights of all, irrespective of their legal status, are already guaranteed.

---

[10] Although a comparison with the levels of the Europeans cannot be compared, during this era Canada also signed bilateral agreements with several countries to initially frame the migration of guest workers to Canada: Jamaica (1966), Barbados (1967), Trinidad and Tobago (1967) and Mexico (1974). However, as noted above, since the new immigration and refugee protection law came into force in 2002, these bilateral programmes have been transformed into simple contractual agreements between coalitions of Canadian employers and foreign government representatives (except in the case of Mexico, where the Canadian Government remains involved, in theory, in the annual re-evaluation of programmes carried out by agriculture industry representatives and Mexican consulates).

A third justification to non-ratification concerns the effective domestic and international application of legal instruments guaranteeing the respect of human and workers' rights. Canada is already a signatory of the ICESCR and the ICCPR, which encompass a wide range of rights. In addition, it has ratified the CAT, the ICERD, the CEDAW and the CRC, implying that the ICRMW is unnecessary. In other words, migrant workers and members of their families do not constitute a group that requires particular protection mechanisms, unlike, for example, women, children, refugees and ethnic minorities. UN conventions dealing with universal human rights protection are sufficient to guarantee the protection of the rights of migrants.

At the national level, the Canadian Charter of Rights and Freedoms covers the respect of fundamental rights in Canadian law at constitutional level. The protection of the rights of migrant workers/temporary residents is guaranteed by provincial legislation under health and work-safety standards, as well as by municipal housing by-laws. In this view, ratification of the ICRMW for the protection of the rights of migrant workers in Canada would not be necessary.

Obstacle 4: temporary workers

> Given the nature of the type of contract work afforded low or unskilled migrants, by ratifying the Convention, Canada will be forced to restructure its programmes and grant certain rights considered fundamental therein.

Given the tightening of human-capital entry criteria into Canada, only investors, entrepreneurs and highly skilled workers are selected as workers under the current immigration policy. Under pressure by employers to quickly address the problems of low-skilled labour shortages, Canada is increasingly allowing employers to recruit foreign workers for low-wage occupations. However, the federal government does not exercise any implicit or explicit monitoring and enforcement of contractual arrangements under which a worker has accepted to come to Canada. Moreover, the federal government (HRSDC and CIC) explicitly allows the (administrative or contractual) revoking of fundamental rights spelled out in the ICRMW. In this context, the federal government (body with jurisdiction on matters of temporary and permanent integration terms for foreign nationals) is not really interested in accepting the responsibility, through ratification of the Convention, of giving more rights than currently given for low-skilled workers under a temporary work permit, in particular the 'right freely to choose their remunerated activity'[11] spelled out in article 52 of the Convention.

Obstacles to ratification: parliamentarians' point of view

Interviews with nine MP members of the Standing Committee on Citizenship and Immigration revealed that the ICRMW is largely unknown. According to elected officials, this is the most important obstacle. Note, however, that two political parties, the Bloc Québécois and the New Democratic Party of Canada, assured us that they were in favour of Canada ratifying the Convention.[12]

Ratification of the Convention does not feature on the list of seventeen priorities identified by the committee, none of which explicitly address migrants' rights. However, one of the priorities concerns working conditions of vulnerable workers, in particular foreign temporary workers.

Canada's ratification: the NGO perspective

Interviews and meetings with representatives of Canadian CSOs and NGOs working with migrant workers or on related issues show that mobilization for ratification of the ICRMW at non-governmental level is still weak but growing. Even though we are witnessing the emergence of better-coordinated efforts between different provincial and national actors – community groups, workers associations, human rights NGOs, unions, researchers, activists, etc. – currently interested in promoting migrant workers' rights, the majority of the work (i) is still concentrated in the field in order to support abused migrant workers in their fight for reparation under domestic legislation; and (ii) focuses on the review in light of the Canadian Charter of Rights and Freedoms of the current selection point system and temporary recruitment programmes, both discriminating against low-skilled migrant workers.[13]

---

[11] A formal answer by the Canadian Department of Foreign Affairs (responsible for Canada's ratification of international conventions) to Canadian human rights NGOs has been made available to us after the interviews conducted for this study. Some details are given regarding the fundamental rights Canada would *not* be interested in granting to migrant workers (FAC, 2006).

[12] A New Democratic Party of Canada MP has written to the Minister of Citizenship and Immigration requesting that Canada ratify the ICRMW (letter dated 13 June 2006). The minister's response presented the same objections developed during the previous administration and set out in this study.

[13] In Canada, the 'administrative' discrimination of migrant workers made on the basis of their occupation, sex and/or country of origin might not respect the Charter of

With some important exceptions, Canadian civil society does not seem to play a proactive role at international level as regards migrants' rights, and if the promotion of international standards established within the ICRMW is on the agenda of some actors, no group or organization has made ratification of the Convention its primary mission. In their view, however, the official reasons given for the unwillingness to ratify are unfounded. Here are briefly presented the criticisms of the government's position mentioned in civil society statements or by the representatives we interviewed.

Human rights and the limits of national sovereignty

In a context of economic globalization and transnational social networks, the management of migration flows exclusively at the national level displays several shortcomings. The medium- and long-term sustainability of a national migration policy is indeed questionable, as it ignores the socioeconomic interests of the countries of origin, limits the fundamental human rights of temporary residents on the basis of national security concerns and overestimates the capacity of governments to effectively control cross-border movements of people.

In this view, the international mobility of workers is determined by economic, political, demographic, cultural, community and individual forces that operate not only domestically, but also regionally and globally. States should therefore recognize the limits of their sovereignty over the management of migration, which would not only maximize the socioeconomic benefits but would also prevent the development of the social tensions fuelled by social exclusion, especially in the case of migrant workers. Ratification of the ICRMW would not, then, keep Canada from maintaining its unilateral migration policy, but it would help in minimizing the risks of favouring a framework conducive to abuse and violations of the fundamental social rights of workers in Canada.

Permanent immigration vs temporary migration

If Canada can be proud of its migration philosophy's focus on permanent immigration, this does not eliminate the fact that programmes for

Rights and Freedoms integrated in the Canadian Constitution in 1982 (Depatie-Pelletier, forthcoming).

temporary workers exist and are becoming more and more central in hiring unskilled or low-skilled workers to fill jobs for which it is difficult, or even impossible, to find national workers. The rights of these persons thus constitute a real issue, especially because (as immigration is geared towards permanent residence) there is no official body for the management and coordination of temporary migration. Largely at the instigation of employers, temporary foreign workers' contracts strongly limit their rights and social integration. The federal government does not have jurisdiction over their working conditions but nevertheless allows their recruitment despite the absence of control, monitoring mechanisms and agreements with the provinces.

If Canada were to ratify the ICRMW, it would therefore be forced to rethink its legislative and institutional framework relating to the recruitment and use of low-skilled foreign workers. Several NGOs have suggested that, given the Canadian immigration philosophy, the temporary workers' programme should be abolished and replaced by a recruitment system using selection criteria for permanent residency. If the need for low-skilled workers is real, the selection process should be modified to favour this type of economic immigrant. This would eliminate the current double standards in terms of migrant workers' rights, which is one of the major obstacles to ratifying the Convention.

Usefulness of ratification to complement foreign workers' rights in Canada

The argument that migrant workers are covered under other UN conventions implies that temporary workers are not in a specific vulnerable situation. But this is in contradiction to existing cases of exploitation and non-respect of certain rights involving this category of worker in Canada. Ratification of the ICRMW would allow for supplementary rights and would place within the reach of workers a tool specific to the protection of their rights.

This argument is particularly relevant given that several fundamental rights and governmental obligations towards foreign workers, considered 'non-negotiable' in the Convention, are actually not recognized by the government, particularly with respect to programmes geared towards 'low-skilled' foreign workers. There is therefore a clash between the international standards put forward by the Convention and standards established by the Canadian Government. Here are some examples.

Systematically informing foreign workers of their rights

According to article 33 of the ICRMW, the Canadian Government would be held accountable to ensure that employers, governmental organizations, unions, community-based groups and/or foreign consulates systematically inform each and every foreigner of their principal rights as a temporary resident in Canada prior to or upon arrival.

If work contracts associated with low-skilled foreign workers include the responsibility of every Canadian employer to inform foreign workers of their responsibilities and obligations in Canada, as well as any other specific rules to follow in their workplace or place of residence, nowhere is spelt out the right of migrant workers to be informed of their rights in Canada, including the right to refuse to do unsafe work. In the instruction sheet that accompanies the employment contract associated with the new 'low-skilled' workers pilot project, the Canadian Government not only explicitly distances itself from all responsibilities in terms of information on migrant workers' rights, but also avoids recognizing the importance and/or necessity of systematic interventions in this matter by provincial agencies, NGOs or unions.

Despite the number of individual cases that highlight the risks associated with foreign workers' lack of knowledge of their fundamental rights in Canada (in particular those relating to health and safety standards and the procedures to follow in case of workplace injuries), as brought to the attention of the Canadian public by the United Food and Commercial Workers Union and other human rights-based community groups or organizations, the management of the Temporary Workers Programme has until now refused to develop a proactive approach. In the meantime, the federal government appears to limit itself to meeting some representatives from the departments of public works and government services from different provinces in order to secure their future implication in certain aspects of the management of programmes to recruit foreign workers that touch on their relevant jurisdictions, such as the management of work relations and eventually the training of foreign workers on the subject of fundamental rights.

Government responsibility in monitoring the employment of migrant workers

The ICRMW also mentions in explicit terms the necessity for the state not only to oversee the management of foreign workers' programmes by systematically maintaining an active dialogue process with foreign governments of countries from which workers are recruited, but also to offer minimum direct services to foreign workers admitted to their countries (articles 64 and 65).

If the Canadian Government was historically implicated in the management of foreign workers in Canada, its theoretically proactive role[14] appears to have been reduced significantly in recent years to the advantage of well-organized agricultural production corporations.[15] The tendency to 'privatize' the management of the recruitment of migrant workers is not limited to the agricultural sector. The framework, put into place in 2002 by the Department of Human Resources to make it easier for all other Canadian industries to hire 'low-skilled' foreign workers, no longer offers systematic interventions either by the Canadian Government or by representatives of countries of origin, the only exception being the initial authorization of employment. Thus, there is no involvement in contract negotiations or in the supervision of the smooth running of these programmes.

There emerges, from the right of foreign workers to be informed of their rights in the province of employment, and their right to be publicly supported in the event of abuse, another responsibility for the Canadian Government: that of ensuring that every foreign worker upon arrival in Canada is given the contact information of all provincial, federal and non-governmental institutions that are competent in areas relating to health, housing and working conditions and that can be reached by the foreign worker in the event that employer or consular support were lacking in case of illness, accident or abuse during their period of residency in Canada (article 37). In reality, the respective responsibilities of several government agencies in providing services in the areas of health, working conditions, housing, working relations, protection of individuals, etc. have not yet been defined. At the level of several government agencies, such as the federal Department of Citizenship and Immigration, provincial departments of immigration and labour as well as municipal administration, the reason given for the absence of any services adapted for foreign workers is that only the federal Department of Human Resources is legally mandated (according to the Immigration Law) to intervene in the recruitment of foreign workers' programmes by Canadian employers. However, officials in Ottawa, as well as regional directors of the Department of Human Resources working on the temporary workers' programmes, deny having

---

[14] For example, the Canadian Government is officially part of the annual renegotiations of contract work between the Canadian Federation of Agriculture and the Mexican Government.

[15] In particular, Foreign Agricultural Resource Management Services (F.A.R.M.S., Ontario) and F.E.R.M.E. (Quebec) over time have become the main groups in charge of the day-to-day orientation and management of the SAWP.

any jurisdiction in the area of foreign workers' services, thereby limiting their work to servicing Canadian employers and foreign government representatives involved in the sector.

Right of migrant workers to be consulted

Even though the need to systematically consult with representatives of foreign workers during re-negotiations and the re-evaluation of contract work is clearly mentioned in the ICRMW (article 64), and despite the demands of foreign consulates at least in the agricultural sector, the Department of Human Resources has not yet decided to force, or even guarantee, the creation of migrant workers' associations that will be able to democratically identify a number of representatives capable of adequately formulating their different concerns and, where possible, making proposals for improving the employment process based on their own interests. The desire of the United Food and Commercial Workers Union to be seen as a body that represents the interests of migrant and agricultural workers during annual negotiations of minimal working conditions in Canada has until now been systematically ignored by the Canadian Government, with its policy of excluding all union representations or foreign workers' official representatives.

Right of foreign workers to unionize

The right of all foreign workers to join a trade union is clearly recognized by the ICRMW (article 40), as well as the right of any migrant authorized to work in the destination state to create one (article 26). The lack of recognition of the right to unionize by agricultural workers in Ontario and Alberta is in direct contradiction to the spirit of the Convention.[16]

Equal treatment for foreign workers

One of the fundamental principles brought forward by the ICRMW remains the equal treatment between local and foreign workers hired

---

[16] In Manitoba, however, in a decision rendered on 26 June 2007, the Labor Commission has ruled that the sixty-five foreign agricultural workers, hired by a family farm in Portage Manitoba, had the right to form a union. In Quebec, a similar case has been brought before the Labor Relations Commission. The Commission has allowed workers employed in greenhouses to join the union (United Food and Commerce Workers Canada), but has denied the right to collective bargaining to the workers employed in industrial farms (*La Presse*, 25 September 2007). This highly restrictive interpretation of Quebec Labour Code by the Commission has been challenged in the Superior Court by the Union in the hope that agricultural workers will eventually be allowed to unionize under the current legislation. A decision is expected soon (*Le Soleil*, 27 September 2007).

in the same country (article 25). The Canadian Government does not seem to pay much attention to this fundamental principle in its current programming. Furthermore, being bound to a single employer and forced to accept the living arrangements fixed by that employer give rise to a significant disparity between local and foreign workers in terms of having their rights respected by the employer.

Possibility of impartial reconsideration of the reasons for expulsion or exclusion from a programme

According to the ICRMW, the existence of an independent body (article 22) having the role of examining the legitimacy of the decision to expel a migrant worker (article 20) is absolutely necessary in order to avoid the deportation of workers becoming an impediment to the exercise of their rights (article 56), such as access to medical care, financial compensation as a result of a workplace accident, the pursuing of a legal process or the reporting of cases of abuse (article 13).

For the moment, however, by tying the validity of a foreign worker's visa to a specific employer, the Canadian Government implicitly gives all employers the right to deport any migrant worker at will or prevent them from being re-hired by another Canadian employer. In the event that the employer sends a worker back to the country of origin, the reconsideration of the cancellation of the residence permit and/or the expulsion of the worker is actually at the discretion of the consular representative from the worker's country of origin.

In terms of expulsion, note that the Convention also stipulates the obligation of all states to take into consideration humanitarian considerations before authorizing the expulsion of a migrant worker (article 56). The government has never recognized, at least not officially, the value of such an interpretation to consular representatives who have the final say on the expulsion, sometimes called 'voluntary return', of their citizens sent back by employers.

Respect of fundamental principle of family reunification of all residents

The ICRMW recognizes that legal migrant workers have the right to return to members of their family without detriment (article 38): all efforts have to be made to authorize migrant workers and members of their family to be temporarily absent without this affecting residency or work permit, depending on the case. This means that receiving countries are to take into account the obligations and particular needs of migrant workers and members of their family, especially in their country of origin. Workers have the right to be informed of these possibilities. In fact, this article implies the right to vacation without pay for family reasons, accompanied by a right to multiple entries into Canada. If, in the case of seasonal agricultural workers, the right to leave Canada quickly is generally guaranteed by their consular representatives when necessary, workers lose their right to return to Canada to pursue their work and will often not be called back the following season to take part in the SAWP. Prejudices associated with returning to the family in the country of origin for temporary workers in Canada thus exist, thereby affecting the right to family reunification.

Minimizing exploitation of undocumented migrant workers

The ICRMW recognizes that all migrant workers, irrespective of their legal status in the country where they are employed, have the right to ask the employer for any unpaid wages before being sent back to their country of origin by government authorities (article 25). Until now, no protection mechanism for this fundamental right has been put in place by the Canadian Government, constituting an indirect incentive for exploitation of this category of migrant workers in Canada.

Discussion and conclusion

This study suggests five major conclusions on the obstacles to ratification of the ICRMW by Canada. The first concerns the views expressed by elected members of the Canadian Parliament: on the one hand, the lack of knowledge of the existence of the Convention by the majority of elected officials is a significant obstacle; on the other hand, even though two opposition parties have recently decided to express officially their support for ratification (Bloc Québécois and New Democratic Party of Canada), there is still a long road ahead before the other two major parties (Conservatives and Liberals) change their official positions in favour of ratification.

With regard to federal senior bureaucrats working on the protection of human rights, four obstacles were identified. First, migration policy is a country's sovereign right and consequently should not be determined by multilateral or international conventions. Second, the spirit of the Convention is contrary to the Canadian culture and tradition of management of migration, which focuses on the granting of permanent residency. Third, it is unnecessary to sign the Convention given that the fundamental rights of all in Canada are legally guaranteed irrespective of their legal status. Fourth, given the current state of contract work that regulates the stay of skilled or low-skilled migrant workers, by ratifying the Convention, Canada will be forced to re-evaluate its programmes and grant certain rights that are considered fundamental therein. In the light of these obstacles, the Convention is unlikely to be ratified by Canada in the near future.

The point of view of NGOs who work on migrant workers' rights issues calls into question the validity of these official arguments. To begin with, the principle of national sovereignty could apply to all international conventions. Furthermore, national sovereignty is not absolute, and the current context of globalization supports the management of migration policies at the global level. Second, the growing importance of temporary work is in flagrant contradiction to the Canadian philosophy and tradition in terms of immigration. Third, refusing to ratify the ICRMW on the grounds that existing conventions and the Canadian Charter of Rights and Freedoms are sufficient to protect migrant workers is in contradiction to the resolution adopted by the UN General Assembly that considers the migrant population as a vulnerable group; that is, a group insufficiently protected by current conventions. This argument is also contradicted by the many known cases of abuses of the human rights of temporary workers in Canada. In fact, these abuses are so flagrant that the issue was raised in the House of Commons on 21 June 2007: referring to the ACPD study for UNESCO, two MPs, also members of the Standing Committee on Immigration and Integration, urged the government to ratify the Convention (*La Presse*, 21 June 2007, p. A12). Finally, as we have shown earlier, the temporary foreign workers' programmes in Canada display several shortcomings with respect to the rights covered in the Convention. At the beginning of 2006, a Canadian high official confirmed to an NGO representative that the Convention gives rights to temporary foreign workers that the country is unwilling to offer, thus contradicting the argument that migrant workers are already well protected in existing conventions.

Towards recognition and protection of migrant workers' rights in Canada

It should be mentioned that for the first time in 2008, the federal government officially recognized the value of (some) temporary workers for the Canadian economy: their experience could give them a good level of linguistic competency and knowledge of 'Canadian life', and thus foreign workers are now directly selected for permanent residence after twenty-four months of work, if they were employed in an occupation requiring more than a two-year post-secondary diploma. Considering (some) temporary foreign workers as potential future citizens, the Canadian Government might eventually start to fund integration programmes for temporary foreign workers (as this could now be seen as a justified 'investment' for Canada).

This shift by the federal government from the historically clear division between workers recruited on a temporary basis and those recruited for a permanent purpose has, however, yet to be developed for temporary foreign workers employed in the low-skilled occupations. The emergence in 2006 of a national coalition of community groups, NGOs and workers' unions for the defence of migrant workers' rights, the Migrant Justice Network, represented a first important step in the mobilization of resources and of forces favourable to ratification of the ICRMW in Canada. The recent involvement of various Canadian workers' unions within this national coalition, the organization of gatherings in 2007 and 2009 for extensive discussions of collective action proposals and the involvement of the House of Commons Standing Committee on Citizenship and Immigration on the issue of the human rights protection of temporary foreign workers and non-status workers (official recommendations to the federal government released in May 2009) are all concrete indications that migrant workers' rights have become an issue that the federal and provincial governments will eventually have to deal with seriously – hopefully sooner than later.

References

CIC. 2006a. *Facts and Figures 2006*. Ottawa, CIC, Strategic Research and Statistics.
  2006b. Statement by Richard Fadden, Deputy Minister, Citizenship and Immigration Canada, to the High-Level Dialogue on International Migration and Development at the 61st Session of the UN General Assembly, New York, 15 September. Ottawa, CIC.
Clark, T. 1999. *Why It Makes Sense for Canada to Reconsider Ratifying the Migrant Workers Convention*. Available at www.december18.net [last accessed 22 April 2009].
Crépeau, F. and Nakache, D. 2006. Controlling irregular migration in Canada: reconciling security concerns with human rights protection. *Choices*, Vol. 12, No. 1, pp. 1–39.

Depatie-Pelletier, E. (forthcoming). Les travailleurs étrangers temporaires au Canada: questionnements éthiques. F. Piron (ed.), *Éthique des rapports nord-sud*. Quebec, Presse de l'Université Laval.

FAC. 2006. UN Migrant Workers' Convention: response from Foreign Affairs Canada, follow up response to questions asked during the annual human rights consultation between the Canadian Department of Foreign Affairs and Canadian NGOs. Ottawa, Foreign Affairs Canada.

FAC/CIC. 2005. Submission of the Government of Canada to the Global Commission on International Migration, International Policy Coordination, Citizenship and Immigration Canada (11 April). Ottawa, Foreign Affairs Canada/CIC.

Fitzpatrick, J. 2003. The human rights of migrants. T. A. Aleinikoff and V. Chetail (eds), *Migration and International Legal Norms*. The Hague, Netherlands, T. M. C. Asser Press, pp. 169–84.

Hawkins, F. 1974. Canadian immigration policy and management. *International Migration Review*, Vol. 8, No. 2, pp. 141–53.

ILO. 2006. *Multilateral Framework on Labour Migration: Non-binding Principles and Guidelines for a Rights-based Approach to Labour Migration*. Geneva, Switzerland, ILO.

Piché, V. (forthcoming). Migrations internationales et droits de la personne: vers un nouveau paradigme? F. Crépeau (ed.), *La dynamique complexe des migrations internationales*. Montreal Que., Presses de l'Université de Montréal.

Ruhs, M. and Chang, H.-J. 2004. The ethics of labor immigration policy. *International Organization*, Vol. 58, No. 1, pp. 69–102.

UN. 1994. *Report of the International Conference on Population and Development, Cairo, 5–13 September*. New York, UN. (No. E.95.XIII.18.)

Supplementary bibliography

AAFQ. 1998. Mémoire présenté à la ministre de la citoyenneté et de l'immigration, Madame Lucienne Robillard. Montreal, Que., Association des Aides Familiales du Québec. Available at http://bv.cdeacf.ca/CF_PDF/1999_09_0135.pdf [last accessed 10 May 2009].

ACPD. 2006. *Migration and the ICPD Programme of Action*. Ont., Action Canada for Population and Development. Available at www.acpd.ca/acpd.cfm/en/section/Migration [last accessed 10 May 2009].

Amnesty International Canada. 2002. *Without Discrimination: The Fundamental Right of ALL Canadians to Human Rights Protection*. A brief to the UN Committee on the Elimination of Racial Discrimination on the Occasion of the Examination of the Thirteenth and Fourteenth Periodic Reports Submitted by Canada. Available at www.amnesty.ca/canada/un_cerd.pdf [last accessed 10 May 2009].

2004. *Above All Else: A Human Rights Agenda for Canada.* Available at www. amnesty.ca/canada/Human_Rights_Agenda.pdf [last accessed 10 May 2009].

2006. *La traite des femmes, ni ici, ni ailleurs.* Montreal, Que., Section Canadienne Francophone.

GCIM. 2005. *Migration in an Interconnected World: New Directions for Action.* Geneva, Switzerland, GCIM.

Inter-Church Committee for Refugees. 2000. *Migrant Workers in Canada.* Available at www.december18.net/web/docpapers/doc626.pdf [last accessed 10 May 2009].

Interpares Canada. 2006. *The Boundaries of Belonging: Reflections on Migration Policies into the 21st Century.* Ottawa. (Interpares Occasional Papers 7.) Available at www.interpares.ca/en/publications/pdf/boundaries_of_belonging. pdf [last accessed 10 May 2009].

Justicia for Migrant Workers. 2003. *Government Responsible for Unjust Working Conditions for Migrant Farm Workers.* Justicia for Migrant Workers message to new HRDC Minister, Joe Volpe on the International Day for Migrant Workers. Available at lnn.labourstart.org/more.php?id=116_0_1_0 [last accessed 10 May 2009].

2006. *Justice for Migrant Farm Worker: Reflections on the Importance of Community Organising.* Available at www.justicia4migrantworkers.org/ bc/pdf/r12_grez.pdf [last accessed 10 May 2009].

Justicia for Migrant Workers – BC. 2006. *Letter of Protest by Migrant Workers in BC.* Available at http://www.justicia4migrantworkers.org/bc/index.htm#2 [last accessed 10 May 2009].

KAIROS Canada. 2005. *From Economic Fear to Human Development: Short- and Long-term Approaches to Creating Safe, Productive and Meaningful Work in Canada,* submission to the Federal Labour Standards Review Commission. Available at www.kairoscanada.org/e/antipoverty/analysis/submissionLabour Standards050901.pdf [last accessed 10 May 2009].

La Violette, N. 2006. The principal international human rights instruments to which Canada has not yet adhered. *Windsor Yearbook of Access to Justice,* Vol. 24, No. 2.

London Diocesan Migrant Workers Committee. 2004. *Migrant Workers Issues.* Available at www.rcec.london.on.ca/JusticeOffice/MigrantWorkers/issues. html [last accessed 10 May 2009].

No One is Illegal – Vancouver. 2007. *Labour Resolutions to Uphold Dignity of (Im) migrant Workers.* Available at noii-van.resist.ca/?p=440 [last accessed 10 May 2009].

North South Institute. 2006. *Migrant Workers in Canada: A Review of the Canadian Seasonal Agricultural Workers Program.* Available at www.nsi-ins. ca/english/pdf/MigrantWorkers_Eng_Web.pdf [last accessed 10 May 2009].

OCASI/STATUS Coalition. 2004. *The Regularization of Non-Status Immigrants in Canada 1960–2004: Past Policies, Current Perspectives, Active Campaigns.* Available at www.ocasi.org/status/index.asp [last accessed 10 May 2009].

Osmani, F. S. 2000. *Trafic, travail forcé et servitude des femmes migrantes au Québec/ Canada: éléments de diagnostic.* Montreal, Que., Alternatives. Available at www.imadr.org/old/project/petw/trafficking_canada.html [last accessed 10 May 2009].

Philippine Women Centre of BC. 1997. *Trapped: Holding On to a Knife Edge – Economic Violence against Filipino Migrant/Immigrant Women.* Available at http://pwc.bc.tripod.com/research.html [last accessed 10 May 2009].

1999. *Strategizing Action against Violence against Women in the Filipino Community.* Available at http://pwc.bc.tripod.com/research.html.

2001. *Filipino Nurses Doing Domestic Work in Canada: A Stalled Development.* Available at http://pwc.bc.tripod.com/research.html.

Piché, V. 2003. Un siècle d'immigration au Québec: de la peur à l'ouverture. V. Piché and C. LeBourdais (eds), *La démographie québécoise – enjeux du XXIe siècle.* Montreal, Que., Presses de l'Université de Montréal, pp. 225–63.

Solidarity Across Borders. *The Four Demands.* Available at http://solidarityacross borders.org/en/demands [last accessed 10 May 2009].

UNFPA. 2006. *A Passage to Hope: Women in International Migration. State of the World Population 2006.* New York, UNFPA.

9

Mexico's role in promoting and implementing the ICRMW

GABRIELA DÍAZ AND GRETCHEN KUHNER

Introduction

Mexico has been one of the principle promoters of the ICRMW since its conception in the late 1970s. During the drafting of the Convention, Mexico's principle interest was to create an instrument to advocate for the human rights protection of Mexican migrants resident in the United States. While this remains true today, Mexico has since become a major transit country for migrants attempting to reach the United States, and to a lesser extent, a destination country. As such, it is in the complex situation of applying the Convention to different groups of migrants requiring specific forms of protection.

This chapter first reviews Mexico's historical role in the creation and ratification of the Convention. It discusses the dramatic increases of Mexican migrants to the United States in recent years, the development of transit migration through Mexico and the situation for migrants within the country. It reviews some of the principle human rights violations that are specifically covered by the Convention and their relevance to the Mexican situation. Finally, it describes how Mexico plans to move towards compliance with the Convention.

Background

As of 2006, there were approximately 27 million immigrants of Mexican origin resident in the United States, more than 11.5 million of whom were born in Mexico. Each year, this population grows by 400,000 to 485,000 irregular migrants, with an additional 90,000 Mexicans who migrate through work or family visas (Passel, 2005). These migrants sent home almost US$24 billion in 2007, accounting for 3% of gross domestic product and representing the second-largest source of foreign income (Banco de México, 2008).

Protecting the emigrant population is an ongoing challenge for which the Mexican Government has established forty-eight general consulates, career consulates or consular agencies in the United States – the largest consular protection network in a single country. It has been active in submitting cases before regional and international tribunals to ensure consular and labour protection for its nationals. It participates in various regional and bilateral working groups on migration and has signed a range of agreements with the United States regarding Mexican immigrants. It has also established programmes within Mexico to ensure the safe return of nationals who have either been deported or who are returning to visit family members during the holidays.

The Mexican Government is in the difficult position of advocating for its nationals who already reside in the United States, while at the same time addressing the reality that hundreds of thousands more attempt to cross the Mexico-US border in an irregular manner each year – in spite of the increased barriers and enforcement measures implemented since 1994 (Massey, 2005; Passel, 2005). One of the principle concerns is some 3,000 deaths that have occurred along the border between 1998 and 2005 (GAO, 2006).[1] Another issue is the 6.6 million Mexican migrants with irregular status now resident in the United States, as this group is disproportionately affected by human rights violations relating to labour exploitation, as well as access to financial, medical and other social services. In addition, the irregular population is faced with the impossibility of reuniting with or even visiting family members who have remained in Mexico. To address some of these issues, the Mexican Government has and will continue to encourage the United States to pass legislation to regularize part of the population with irregular status, and to establish more opportunities for temporary work.

In addition to protecting the rights of Mexicans in the United States, the Mexican Government must also address the situation of migrant workers resident in Mexico, as well as of the hundreds of thousands of migrants who utilize Mexico as a transit country each year. The extent to which the government has been able to protect these two groups has been taken to task by UN and Inter-American Commission on Human Rights (IACHR) Special Rapporteurs, CSOs, the national and international

---

[1] According to Border Safety Initiative (BSI) reports, since fiscal year 1998 there has been an upward trend in the number of migrant border-crossing deaths annually, from 266 in 1998 to 472 in 2005, with some fluctuations over time.

media and Mexico's National Human Rights Commission, all of which have documented human rights abuses relating to physical integrity and due process.[2] The government is aware of this paradox. Indeed, Mexico's first report to the CMW discusses various challenges and admits that 'the state does not have sufficient material and human resources to respond to irregular migration flows' (UN, 2005). It asserts that Mexico is working on a 'new culture' to recuperate the dignity of those obligated to migrate and identifies the challenge of establishing 'a coherent, long-term policy that creates certainty and facilitates the entry and stay of foreigners in Mexico' (UN, 2005). However, the report goes on to present problems with current legislation and practice, reiterating its commitment to reform legislation where needed, and to change current practices that constitute violations of the Convention.

Involvement in the ICRMW

Mexico's strong participation in the drafting of the ICRMW was motivated by the situation of Mexican migrants in the United States. Towards the end of the 1970s, Mexican immigration to the United States was rising, and there was a corresponding increase in apprehensions and removals. To advocate for their protection, Mexico joined a group of North African countries that had been working for ten years on an international convention specifically dedicated to the protection of the rights of migrant workers, regardless of their immigration status.

As part of Mexico's obligation to protect its nationals abroad, President José López Portillo[3] insisted that it should be a protagonist in the writing and promotion of the Convention (Venet, 2002). As a result, between 1977 and 1979, Mexico sponsored several resolutions that would serve as the basis for the elaboration of the Convention within the UN General Assembly. Mexico maintained a decisive role in the process through the participation of Ambassador Antonio Gonzalez de

---

[2] See UN Doc. E/CN.4/2003/85, Report of the Special Rapporteur, Gabriela Rodríguez Pizarro, on the human rights of migrants, submitted pursuant to Commission on Human Rights Resolution 2002/62; Inter-American Commission, 2003; CNDH, 2005a, 2005b; Foro Migraciones, 2005.

[3] Portillo, a member of the Partido Revolucionario Institucional, was President of Mexico from 1976 to 1982. He believed that revenues from oil would lead to unprecedented economic development. In the international sphere, his government sought economic independence from the United States. However, his actions led to one of Mexico's most severe economic crises.

León, who for some ten years presided over the General Assembly working group in charge of drafting the Convention (SRE, 2006).

Two negotiating positions emerged during the debate on the text. On one side, Mexico and Morocco headed up the developing countries (G-77), composed of migrant-sending countries. On the other side, the Mediterranean-Scandinavian delegations formed the MESCA group, representing migrant-destination countries. These opposing positions caused the negotiations to stall for ten years.

When the ICRMW was finally approved in 1990, Mexico was the first country to sign on 22 May 1991. However, eight years passed before it ratified the Convention on 8 March 1999. The reasons for this delay largely relate to a shift in government priorities: by the mid 1990s, Mexico was in the midst of negotiating the North American Free Trade Agreement (NAFTA) with the United States and Canada, and there was concern that signing the Convention could potentially jeopardize the success of these negotiations.

To encourage the government to ratify the Convention, Mexican civil society organized a national campaign that portrayed migrants as digni-fied workers. In addition, civil society developed a favourable relation-ship with the Mexican Senate, which proved important to ensure that the Convention was ratified with fewer reservations than proposed by the executive branch (Venet, 2002). As a result, the Convention was signed with one reservation to article 22(4), as it contravenes the Mexican Constitution, which takes legal precedence over international instruments.[4]

Today, Mexico remains active at international level in promoting migrants' rights and fostering ratification of the Convention. Examples of this international advocacy include the submission of resolutions on the human rights of migrants before the UN CHR (e.g. Resolutions 2004/53, 2004/56 and 2005/47). Mexico also strongly supported the creation of the UN Special Rapporteur on the Human Rights of Migrants and received two official visits in 2002 and 2008. It has also recently urged States Parties to the Convention to comply with reporting requirements.

---

[4] Article 22(4) contravenes article 133 of the Mexican Constitution and article 125 of the General Population Act. Article 133 of the Constitution of Mexico establishes that international treaties signed by the president of the republic and approved by the Senate will form, together with the Constitution and the laws of the National Congress, the supreme law of the nation. In November 1999, the Supreme Court of Justice of the Nation clarified that all international instruments should be considered secondary or immediately below the Constitution, but above federal and local law.

Now that the Convention has entered into force, the challenge is to achieve implementation. While Mexico was not concerned with destination or transit migrants during the period that it was elaborating and promoting the Convention, today it is faced with the reality that it must apply its terms to migrants within Mexico as well as abroad. The new role that Mexico plays in international migration, as a country of origin, transit and destination, provides an opportunity to demonstrate that destination countries can (and should) ratify the Convention.

Migration patterns

Mexico plays a triple role in international migration: it is at once a receiving, sending and transit country. This is a dynamic position in constant transformation. While in the twentieth century Mexico was viewed as a host country for political refugees, today it is primarily known as a sending country. However, it is also becoming a principle country of transit, with one of the most restrictive migration policies on a global scale.

Mexico as a migrant-sending country

Mexican migration to the United States began towards the end of the nineteenth century during the *Porfiriato*, when more than 5 million Mexican farmers lost their communal lands (*ejidos*).[5] During the same period in the United States, the rapid expansion of agriculture, mining and industry required the recruitment of a large migratory workforce for manual labour (Durand, 1994). The Mexican Revolution and the US entry into the First World War increased Mexican migration to the United States: between 1910 and 1920, 206,000 legal Mexican immigrants and 628,000 Mexican 'temporary workers' were admitted (Loret, 1999). However, the end of the First World War, the Great Depression and drastic unemployment led to a decrease in migration. Furthermore, between 1929 and 1930 there was a massive expulsion of Mexicans from the United States, including US citizens of Mexican origin (Durand, 1994).

---

[5] The government of General Porfirio Díaz is known as the *Porfiriato*. It began in 1876 and ended in 1910 with the beginning of the Mexican Revolution. During this time, the government achieved unprecedented economic development that included the creation of the railroad system, the construction of urban infrastructure and the growth of exports and foreign investment. However, this development went hand in hand with great inequities. For example, the government expropriated the communal lands of more than 5 million farmers to focus on agricultural exports (García, 1981).

Yet, just a decade later, the US entry into the Second World War generated renewed demand for Mexican workers. The Bracero Program for temporary agricultural workers, signed in 1942 as a way to recruit workers through official channels, lasted for over twenty years. In 1964, when the United States unilaterally terminated the Bracero Program for migrant workers, the half million Mexicans who travelled each year to work under this programme continued to migrate, as contacts, networks and travel routes had already been established.

However, by the mid 1970s, the economic crisis in Mexico prompted new increases in migration. By 2004, the Mexican population in the United States was thirteen times greater than that in 1970. In 2006, almost 11.5 million were living in the United States (about 10% of the total Mexican population). Of these, 6.6 million were irregular (Batalova, 2008). In response, increasingly restrictive migration policies and greater controls at the US border were established in the early 1990s, with significant consequences on binational migration. While the number of illegal entries between 1995 and 2005 did not increase (GAO, 2006), the number of apprehensions rose – by 2000, between 1 million and 1.7 million Mexicans were apprehended each year (Alba, 2002) – and new and more dangerous migration routes were established, making the journey perilous. For example, the number of deaths along the border has more than doubled since 1995 (GAO, 2006). In order to diminish these risks and obstacles, irregular migrants increasingly rely on smugglers, who also have raised the fee for their services. Today, a Mexican migrant pays over US$1,500 to cross the US border (Massey, 2005). Finally, restrictive migration policies have promoted greater intolerance towards Mexicans in the United States.

Temporary worker agreements with the United States and Canada

The United States issued 1,709,953 temporary worker visas during fiscal year 2006. Mexican citizens received 184,438 visas, accounting for 10.8% of the total. Of these, 56,427 Mexican workers (58% of the total) participated in the Seasonal Non-agricultural Workers Program (H-2B) and 33,056 in the Returning H-2B Workers Program (90%); 40,283 worked in the United States by acquiring a Seasonal Agricultural Workers visa (H-2A) (87%),[6] 17,654 had Specialty Occupations visas (H-1B) (4%),

---

[6] While most visa programmes received the same percentage of Mexican workers, in 2005 only 1,282 Mexicans acquired a Seasonal Agricultural Workers visa (H-2A).

and 9,247 received the NAFTA Professional Workers visas (TN) (12.5%) (DHS, 2007). The number of Mexicans who received a temporary worker visa during fiscal years 2005 and 2006 represent 16.7% of the Mexican migrants apprehended while attempting to cross the border and work in the United States that same year. Therefore, the majority of migrants do not have access to this legal mechanism to migrate in a safe and orderly manner, and as such are pushed into irregular channels. For example, 'in the period 2001–2003, most [Mexican] temporary migrants were undocumented, 75% did not have authorization to cross the border and 79% did not have permission to work in the United States (compared with 48% and 51%, respectively, in 1993–1997), yet 82% of them were in work during this period' (UN, 2005).

The Mexico-Canada Seasonal Agricultural Workers Program was launched in 1974. In the 2005 season, 11,720 workers participated (Aldrete Valencia, 2006). This is an additional source of regular employment for Mexican migrant workers, but it addresses the needs of only a small number.

Due to the scale and complexity of the phenomenon, the Mexican Government has allowed migration flows to continue with few efforts to manage them (Alba, 2002). In some cases, this 'hands-off' policy creates problems for Mexican migrants even before they leave the country. For example, while the Mexican Federal Labour Law contemplates protection for Mexicans working abroad, in practice the recruiting efforts for temporary worker programmes are often left in the hands of unscrupulous agents who make false promises regarding job offers and visas, and charge exorbitant fees (Caron, 2007).

Mexican migration to the United States today is profoundly rooted in the economic, social and labour interdependence between the two countries (Mohar, 2004). The majority of studies on the phenomenon predict that the economic situation and interdependence will continue to drive migrants out of Mexico for many years to come (Alba, 2002; Mohar, 2004; Papademetriou, 2002; Passel, 2005). For this reason, it is essential to recognize the necessity of a new arrangement that will provide order, security and legality to migration flows, and that will utilize the ICRMW to ensure human rights protection for migrant workers.

Migrants in transit through Mexico

Mexico has become a major transit country for migrants attempting to reach the United States and, to a lesser extent, Canada. Each year, thousands of migrants from Central America, Latin America and other regions pass through Mexico in an irregular manner.

While it is impossible to determine the dimension of irregular migration in Mexico, the Instituto Nacional de Migración (INM–National Migration Institute) estimates that in 2004, over 2 million migrants crossed the Guatemala-Mexico border, approximately 400,000 of whom were Central Americans entering without authorization. Other indicators of irregular migration through Mexico include the number of apprehensions made in Mexico each year, which in 2005 totalled 240,269 according to INM, and 154,994 'Other Than Mexicans'[7] along the Mexico-US border according to the Department of Homeland Security.[8] The Pew Hispanic Centre estimates that approximately 400,000 non-Mexicans enter the United States every year in an irregular manner, mostly through Mexico.

Central America

The majority of migrants passing through Mexico to the United States are from Central America, particularly Guatemala, Honduras and El Salvador. INM detention statistics show that 92.4% of all detained migrants in Mexico in 2005 were from these three countries. Their migration began with the civil conflicts during the 1980s. Once the wars ended, the economies of these Central American countries were devastated, so people continued migrating to the United States through previously established networks.

Later, natural disasters such as Hurricanes Mitch in 1998 and Stan in 2005, and two earthquakes in El Salvador in 2001, spurred new waves of migration. Today, Central American migration is a structural process, embedded in complex economic, social and ethnic networks (Andrade-Eekhoff, 2006; Castillo, 2006; Davy, 2006; Mahler and Ugrina, 2006). In 2007, Central American migrants' remittances accounted for US$12 billion (IADB, 2008). Remittances far outweigh both private capital flows and official development assistance. Particularly remarkable in this regard is Guatemala, where remittances are 21 times greater than

---

[7] Because the vast majority of people apprehended each year by the US Border Patrol are Mexican nationals (87% during fiscal year 2005), the agency categorizes aliens as 'Mexicans' or 'Other Than Mexicans'.

[8] It is important to note the limitations of these statistics. First, they register apprehensions, not persons (a single person may account for more than one apprehension). Second, they do not refer to the same period, as the US statistics run according to fiscal year, October to September.

foreign direct investment and 30 times greater than official development assistance, and represent 10% of its gross domestic product (Agunias, 2006). As a result of their contribution to the Central American economies, migrants are viewed as heroes in their countries (Durand, 2004).

Latin America

Latin American migrants also transit through Mexico. In 2005, Ecuadorians represented the group with the highest rate of detentions from Latin America (3,276, or 1.4% of all detainees), followed by Cubans (2,660, or 1.1% of all detainees), most of whom are trying to reach the United States to seek asylum or to reunite with their families.

The third group was Brazilians, many of whom began to transit through Mexico to enter the United States irregularly in 2000, when Mexico removed the visa requirement for Brazilian tourists. Between 2003 and 2005, the number of Brazilians apprehended in the United States increased by 493%, to over 31,000 apprehensions in 2005 (DHS, 2006). That same year, more than 2,000 Brazilians (the majority with valid tourist visas) were apprehended in Mexico. In addition, Mexican airport immigration officials denied entry to 9,611 Brazilians who did not meet the discretionary criteria to be admitted as tourists (as migration officials believed that the real purpose of their trip to Mexico was to cross irregularly into the United States). As a result of these increases, in mid 2005, Mexico reinstated the visa requirement for Brazilians. This decision reveals the importance of regional cooperation on migration policy.[9]

Other regions

Migrants from other regions of the world make up a small percentage of transit migrants in Mexico. In 2005, 2,580 of them were apprehended, representing only 0.57% of all detainees in Mexico.[10] Migrants from China, Ethiopia, Eritrea, India and the former Soviet Republics, among others, make their way north in search of asylum or better

---

[9] As a result of this policy change, in 2006 the number of apprehensions of Brazilians decreased by 50%, and the number of Brazilians denied entry at the airport was thirty times lower than in 2005.

[10] See Díaz and Kuhner (2008). This estimate is based on an INM comparison of migrants apprehended on a national level and those in the Mexico City Detention Centre. The statistics take into account nationalities other than Latin American, Caribbean and North American. If apprehended migrants from Canada and the United States are included, the figure rises to 1.07%.

economic and social conditions. A major concern here is the highly organized smuggling and trafficking groups that also utilize Mexico as a transit country.

Women and children in transit

Although women migrants living in North America account for 51% of all migrants (Zlotnik, 2003), the presence of women in transit migration flows in Mexico is lower. INM statistics on detainees in the Mexico City Detention Centre show that, in 2005, two of every ten detainees was a woman.[11] However, during 2003 to 2005, the number of apprehensions of female migrants doubled, while apprehensions of male migrants increased by 43%. This could indicate either a growth in women's participation in irregular migration through Mexico or apprehension practices that are having a disproportionate impact on women.

In the same period, the number of apprehensions of girls tripled, while apprehensions of boys increased by 'only' 127%. In 2005, 16% of the almost 3,000 detained women in the Mexico City Detention Centre were minors: 6% were under 12 years of age and 10% were between 12 and 17. Although the statistics do not demonstrate whether or not these girls were travelling alone, the Mexico Report on the Application of the Convention presented to the CMW in 2005 states that 'a third of minors who attempt the crossing do so without the company of relatives or with people smugglers'. In 2004, approximately 17% of the Central Americans who returned to their countries of origin were minors, most travelling unaccompanied (UN, 2005). Research has shown a rise in abuse and exploitation as the number of women and children migrants increases (Oishi, 2002).

Detention and deportation of transit migrants

In 2005, Mexico detained and deported over 240,000 migrants, compared with only 10,000 twenty years ago. Although the numbers are high,

---

[11] In an effort to comply with UN recommendations, in 2003 Mexican migration authorities began to disaggregate information on migrant detainees by sex in two selected districts of the INM: Mexico City and the Tapachula Detention Centres. For this chapter, access to information was limited to the Mexico City Detention Centre statistics, which in 2005 held only 5.7% of all detained migrants in Mexico. In addition, Department of Homeland Security statistics show that women migrants represent 18.5% of all migrants apprehended along the Mexico-US border in fiscal year 2005 (DHS, 2006); and the EMIF GUAMEX survey registered that Guatemalan women accounted for 18% of the migratory flow along the Mexico-Guatemala border in 2004 (CONAPO et al., 2006).

Mexico's concern about the transmigratory flows across its territory (and its policy of detention and deportation of irregular migrants) does not stem entirely from their numerical significance, but rather from two political issues. First, evading migration inspection is both an administrative and a criminal infraction, and the transit of irregular migrants therefore undermines legality and confidence in the government's ability to enforce its own laws. Transit migration flows are also related to increases in organized crime such as smuggling and trafficking. Second, Mexico is concerned with limiting transit migration, particularly of Central Americans, because it believes that this migration may undermine one of the main priorities of its foreign policy, the protection of Mexican migrants in the United States.

These considerations have led Mexico to create one of the world's most restrictive transit migration policies through a comprehensive practice of apprehension and deportation of migrants heading north. As its southern border covers extensive and difficult terrain, and some of the border regions have dynamic transnational communities that are economically and socially interdependent, Mexico has focused its apprehension practices along specific routes in the southern states and more intensively around the Isthmus of Tehuantepec. Although the dynamism[12] of the Mexican southern border facilitates regular and irregular entry into Mexico, once inside the country, the journey is difficult and perilous due to the enforcement scheme.

To ease the effects of a harsher Mexican migration policy, the Mexican Government recently extended the work of its *Grupo Beta*[13] to the border with Guatemala, to help protect migrants from possible abuses and accidents, and in 2001 it created a programme for migratory regularization.[14] However, this humanitarian side of Mexican migration policy remains to be fully implemented in practice.

---

[12] The border between Mexico and Guatemala has more political implications than geographical limitations. The populations in this region are highly connected in terms of social relations, work and culture. As a result, daily crossings are habitual. In addition, much of the border passes through a mountainous jungle with rivers, so there are only ten official crossing points and an infinite number of informal points, making registration and inspection difficult.

[13] The *Grupos Beta* (Beta Groups) are unarmed officers with the sole responsibility of helping and protecting migrants (Mexican and international) from risks along the way.

[14] The Program for Migratory Regulation offers irregular migrants in Mexico the option to process or update their migration documents.

Migrants resident in Mexico

Mexico is known worldwide for its generous asylum policies. In accordance with its humanitarian ideals, Mexico welcomed refugees throughout the twentieth century, including Trotskyites, Spanish Republicans, Nazi resistance and persecuted Jews and, later, South American exiles and Central Americans fleeing civil conflict. Mexico's image as a country of refuge is part of the national identity and of the country's self-presentation at the international level. However, because of its long history of conquests and interventions, Mexico is also a country whose relation with foreigners is one of attraction and rejection.

Hovering around 0.5% of the total population of Mexico over the past three decades, immigrants have never represented a significant proportion of the total population. The census of 2000 accounts for 492,617 foreigners in a total population of 97.4 million. Many of these foreigners are closely related to emblematic cases of refuge (Spaniards, Guatemalans and Argentines). Notable among these are the 25,196 Guatemalan refugees who worked in the country for decades and became naturalized Mexicans between 1996 and 2003 (Castillo, 2006).

The foreign population in Mexico is composed of qualified individuals: 37% hold a Bachelor's degree and 45% are of working age and are economically active, mainly in the services sector (69%) (CONAPO, 2001). Most resident immigrants in Mexico are from the United States (69%): these are principally children of Mexican migrants or people living along the northern border. Guatemalans compose the second most-common nationality but only account for 5.6% of all immigrants (27,636); 55% of all Guatemalans in Mexico live in Chiapas. The rest of the Central American nationalities accounted for 9% of all foreigners in Mexico in 2000 (44,300). Spaniards are the third nationality, followed by other Latin Americans – Cubans, Colombians and Argentines.

In addition to this resident immigrant population, Mexico's foreign population includes a large group of seasonal/temporary workers, mainly from Guatemala, who have a significant impact on the economic life and sociocultural dynamics of the regions in which they live. It is difficult to calculate the number of temporary Guatemalan migrant workers in Mexico, as an unknown portion is irregular: in 2004, the INM documented 41,894 Guatemalan seasonal agricultural workers; however, the combined number of documented and undocumented seasonal agricultural workers may be close to 75,000 per year (Castillo,

2006). Most of them live in Chiapas, particularly in the Soconusco region where they may earn wages up to 50% higher than in Guatemala.

Other migrants in Chiapas, most of whom are irregular, include men and women working in jobs that require little professional training, such as assistants in construction or ambulatory vendors (CONAPO et al., 2006). An increasing number of women and children from Central America also arrive in Mexico, mostly for limited periods. Young women often obtain jobs in the cities as domestic or sex workers (Casillas, 2006). In addition, a growing number of children – a population particularly vulnerable to exploitation – work in informal commerce and services (Rojas et al., 2004).

Migration and human rights

Migrant workers in Mexico, as well as Mexican migrant workers abroad, experience human rights abuses, as defined by the ICRMW and the other main human rights treaties. The most widespread is discrimination based on national and ethnic origin and migration status, which takes place in the workplace, schools and within the justice system.

Mexican migrant workers in the United States

As the Convention applies to migrant workers in their state of origin, transit and destination, Mexico can utilize the principles of the Convention to advocate for Mexican migrant workers' rights in the United States, despite the fact that the latter is not a signatory. The principle concerns for such migrant workers can be grouped in two categories: (i) the right to life, liberty and security, especially while crossing the border and while in detention and deportation proceedings; and (ii) rights relating to residence in the United States, such as non-discrimination in access to employment, healthcare, education and financial services.

Human rights violations against migrants along the US-Mexico border have been well documented. The abuses range from interrogations without translators to dangerous travel conditions and arbitrary shootings. In a report to the UN Human Rights Committee, the Border Network for Human Rights documents how US immigration-enforcement policies have led to violations of life, liberty and security and equality before the law (Border Network for Human Rights, 2006).

This report discusses how current border-enforcement strategies have led to migrant deaths and increased human smuggling, community insecurity and privacy interference. In addition, the report relates that vigilante groups promote racism and that border-enforcement practices include racial profiling.

In addition to the situation along the border, regular as well as irregular Mexican migrant workers may suffer human rights violations while resident in the United States, particularly in the area of employment. Examples include the following:

- Employers avoid the legal hiring of migrant workers, barring them from legitimate employment that would force employers to pay into social security as well as Medicare schemes (Schlosser, 1995; HRW, 2005). In some cases, employers deduct the taxes and pocket the money rather than send it to the government. H-2B (seasonal non-agricultural) workers have their taxes deducted and then have no meaningful way to recover the money (income tax) or simply are not entitled to recover it (social security taxes).
- Domestic workers, and all temporary workers including H-2A/B (seasonal agricultural and non-agricultural), lose their immigration status if they leave an employment situation as their visas are employment-based, making them more vulnerable to exploitation by employers (HRW, 2001).
- Migrant workers are not provided with the appropriate equipment, safety standards and housing, and suffer chronic under-payment of wages.
- Migrant workers do not receive information regarding their rights as migrants and as employees, and often face language and education barriers (HRW, 2005).
- Employers take advantage of the workers' undocumented status – the threat of being deported makes the migrant population less likely to complain or to initiate an employment claim (HRW, 2005).

To address some of these issues, at the request of the Mexican Government, the Inter-American Court of Human Rights ruled in Advisory Opinion OC-18/03 that states have an obligation to respect and guarantee the labour rights of all workers, irrespective of their immigration status. Article 33 of the ICRMW provides that the state of origin as well as the state of employment share responsibility for providing migrants with information regarding their rights.

Policies and programmes to assist Mexicans in the United States

Mexico has implemented several strategies to address the two major challenges mentioned – abuses along the border area and in detention, and for migrant workers resident in the United States. First, along the border, Mexico has employed additional *Grupo Beta* officials to provide information, medical attention and material resources when necessary to migrants. These groups assisted more than 3,000 migrants in 2004.

In terms of removal procedures, Mexico and the United States have signed agreements establishing the locations and conditions of return. One of the ongoing concerns has been the lack of due process rights for minors who are removed from the United States. Mexico has cited the advisory opinion of the Inter-American Court on this issue (Advisory Opinion No. 17, Children's Legal Status and Human Rights), which expressly recognizes that all children have rights that are inherent to their condition, and that the guarantees of due process should apply in every procedure that is initiated for them. In terms of consular protection, Mexico requested Advisory Opinion No. 16 from the Inter-American Court, which discusses the United States' obligation to comply with consular notification. In addition, the International Court of Justice ruled on 31 March 2004 that the United States had deprived fifty-one Mexican nationals of their rights under article 36 of the Vienna Convention on Consular Relations and that those breaches must be reviewed and reconsidered by means of effective judicial mechanisms.[15]

To reduce the discrimination experienced by Mexican migrant workers and to improve their access to financial services to administer remittances, the Mexican Government has issued consular registration certificates in higher volumes to migrant workers in the United States, which they can use in state government offices and police departments, to open bank accounts, join public libraries and, in some states, to obtain a driving licence. Mexico has also taken steps to include Mexican migrant workers in national politics. For example, certain Mexicans residing abroad were able to participate in the presidential election of 2006, and some state laws now allow migrant workers to participate in local politics.

[15] Case Concerning Avena and other Mexican Nationals (31 March 2004, General List No. 128).

Transit migration

Migrants in transit through Mexico experience a range of human rights violations, which may occur during transit, apprehension, detention or deportation. Both the UN and the Organization of American States Special Rapporteurs discuss these violations at length in their country visit reports (UN, 2002; IACHR, 2003). In addition, the National Human Rights Commission and civil society in Mexico have documented violations against migrants in transit, including physical violence, extortion and a series of due process violations (CNDH, 2005a, 2005b; Foro Migraciones, 2005; Frontera con Justicia, 2006). Some of the most pressing issues are discussed below.

Right to life and the prohibition of inhuman and degrading treatment (articles 9 and 10)

While there are no official statistics available on the number of migrants who die each year while in transit through Mexico, Central American consulates report that deaths from train accidents and asphyxiation from riding in closed vehicle compartments are common.[16] Even more common is the loss of limbs and other permanent injuries that migrants sustain as a result of riding on freight trains. For example, in her 2002 report, the UN Special Rapporteur stated that:

> numerous reports have been received of accidents on these trains and on the railway tracks that have resulted in death or the loss of arms or legs. The Special Rapporteur also received many reports about attacks and abuse by private security officers working for the railway companies. Migrants also reported that they had witnessed women being raped by these officers or by other migrants inside of the wagons. (UN, 2002)

One organization states that of the 1,003 migrants interviewed in 2005, 783 reported some type of abuse by train security guards (Fronteras con Justicia, 2006). The National Human Rights Commission issued a recommendation in 2005 concerning the case of two women whose legs had to be amputated after private security guards deliberately pushed them from a moving train (CNDH, 2005b). Other problems include physical and sexual abuse on the part of INM agents and law-enforcement agents, including the Federal Preventative Police, state and municipal police officers (UN, 2002; IACHR, 2003; Foro Migraciones, 2005).

---

[16] Interviews held with consuls of Honduras and Guatemala, April 2006.

In terms of detention conditions, there are also reports documenting verbal and physical abuse of detainees on the part of INM officials in several of the detention centres throughout the country (Sin Fronteras, 2007; CNDH, 2005a, 2005b). The National Human Rights Commission issued a recommendation in April 2006 regarding a case in which a Salvadoran man with pneumonia was handcuffed in an INM office and left to die during the night (CNDH, 2006).

Right to liberty and security of person, safeguards against arbitrary arrest and detention (articles 16 and 17)

During the last five years, Mexico has concentrated efforts to improve and expand its network of detention centres. For example, according to official INM data, in 2002 there were twenty-four migratory centres and one large detention centre in Mexico City. In 2007, the INM has fifty-two detention centres. Under the Dignificación de las Estaciones Migratorias (a programme to improve the detention centres), seven new centres were built between 2000 and 2006, two are under construction and eleven others have been planned. The Mexico City detention centre was remodelled, increasing its capacity from 140 to 400, and in April 2006 the INM inaugurated a new detention centre in Tapachula, Chiapas, which has a capacity for 1,450 detainees – 960 for temporary stay and 490 for longer stays. This new centre serves to document and remove Central Americans through the various return agreements signed between Mexico and Guatemala, El Salvador and Honduras.

The expansion in infrastructure and improvement in conditions has helped to provide some order and uniformity to the detention and deportation process. However, these changes have not met with corresponding improvements in due process for migrants, who are largely detained and deported with minimal information on their situations and rights. In addition, the National Human Rights Commission and civil society have had to continue to pressure the government to ensure that migrant workers are no longer detained in offices, jails or other areas that do not comply with article 17 of the Convention.

Another issue is that because article 123 of the LGP establishes that entering or remaining in Mexico with irregular status is an administrative violation, migrants are vulnerable to extorsion by law enforcement officials who threaten to turn them over to immigration authorities should they fail to pay. Until April 2008, irregular entry or stay was also a crime, allowing all law enforcement to participate in the arrest of migrants whom officials presumed to be undocumented. With the new reforms, only the authorized migration agents and Federal Preventative Police should participate in migrant arrest procedures. While an important step in the legal protection of migrants in Mexico, the impacts of these reforms in practice remain to be seen.

Migrants in Mexico

The LGP and its regulations establish a system for maintaining regular status that is highly bureaucratic and prohibitively expensive. These procedures cause many migrants to remain in or fall back into irregular status. For example, migration documentation is often employment-based. Each time an immigrant changes occupation, they must request authorization from the INM and pay an administrative fee. A document granting legal permanent residence is only issued after ten years of consecutive legal status, during which time the document must be renewed on an annual basis. The effect of these requirements causes discrimination in the workplace, as employers are often hesitant to hire foreigners.[17] In addition, because employers are required to prove compliance with the tax laws in order to hire foreigners, migrants working in the informal sector have difficulty in regularizing their status. Another issue of particular concern is the labour exploitation that occurs among primarily Central American migrant workers in Mexico's southern state of Chiapas. These situations contravene articles 54 and 55 of the Convention, relating to equality of treatment in the exercise of a remunerated activity.

Recognition as a person before the law (article 24)

One of the principle obstacles to obtaining recognition before the law is that article 67 of the LGP establishes that, in order to bring any legal action before a federal, local or municipal authority or a notary public, foreigners must prove that they are in the country legally. This provision makes irregular migrants vulnerable to extortion and arbitrary arrest. In practice, authorities who apply article 67 often turn irregular migrants over to the INM when these migrants attempt to present a complaint before a judicial authority.

Another obstacle is that Mexico made a reservation to article 22(4) of the Convention in that it contravenes article 33 of the Mexican

---

[17] For example, 19.6% of participants in a national survey stated that they would never hire a foreigner (survey by the National Council to Prevent Discrimination and the Ministry of Social Development, 2005).

Constitution. This constitutional article allows the Mexican executive branch to expel foreigners from the country without a prior hearing if it determines that they are participating in 'political affairs'. Although a migrant would have the right to appeal the deportation decision from their country of origin, this rarely occurs. The Mexican Government has indicated that legislators are reviewing the reservations on article 22(4) of the Convention relating to the right of migrant workers with an expulsion order to present a defence or solicit a suspension of the decision of removal (UN, 2005).

Prohibition of slavery and forced labour (article 11)

While slavery and forced labour are prohibited by the Mexican Constitution, the issue of human trafficking within and from Mexico has become an alarming concern in recent years. Mexico has ratified the Protocol to Prevent, Suppress and Punish Trafficking in Persons, Especially Women and Children, Supplementing the United Nations Convention against Transnational Organized Crime. In addition, in November 2007 a comprehensive bill that includes law-enforcement mechanisms for prosecution, and programmes for prevention and protection, was passed by the Mexican Congress.

Studies on the issue have been conducted for trafficking situations involving labour and sexual exploitation in the state of Chiapas, as well as along the Mexican northern-border region, but the phenomenon is still largely misunderstood and under-reported by Mexican law enforcement. Some NGOs, as well as the IOM, have established programmes to identify victims and provide legal and social services, particularly in Cancun, Quintana Roo, Tapachula, Chiapas, Tijuana, Baja California, Tlaxcala and Mexico City, but the number of victims assisted is small in comparison with the estimated number of victims.

Women and children migrants

Women migrants in transit, as well as those living in Mexico, are victims of human rights violations relating to their gender and migration status. For example, women migrants in transit suffer from sexual violence on behalf of authorities who threaten to deport them if they do not acquiesce (UN, 2002; Díaz and Kuhner, 2007). Women living in Mexico whose migration status is dependent on the ongoing support of a spouse often remain in situations of domestic violence because their spouses threaten to have them deported, separating them from their children

(Sin Fronteras, 2004). Other problems concern women migrants sexually exploited by employers who threaten to turn them over to the authorities if they complain. As the LGP grants discretion to deport migrants who have 'participated in activities for which they are not authorized', in many cases, the INM has begun deportation proceedings against women in these situations without screening for domestic violence or sexual exploitation.

Children also suffer inadequate guarantees of the following rights.

Right of a child of a migrant worker to a name, registration of birth and a nationality (article 29)

While these rights are guaranteed by the Mexican Constitution, in practice, many migrants in an irregular situation do not register their children's births. One of the problems is that article 68 of the LGP requires government officials to report irregular migrant parents who register their children later than six months after they are born. This article is sometimes misapplied, and officials report irregular status to migration officials even if registration takes place within six months. As such, many migrant children go unregistered, resulting in a series of other problems such as access to education and healthcare (Foro Migraciones, 2005).

Access to education on the basis of equality of treatment (article 30)

While the Mexican Constitution guarantees primary and secondary education, in practice, school authorities often require proof of regular status in order to enrol children. As legal representation is rarely available or because migrants do not know their rights, many migrant children go without schooling (Foro Migraciones, 2005).

Plans for compliance with the Convention

Mexico does not have an official policy for implementation of the ICRMW. However, it has recently made progress in analyzing the situation of migration in Mexico, identifying gaps and contradictions between national and international law and preparing specific proposals to reform legislation and implementing practices that would improve the situation for migrants of origin, transit and destination, and bring Mexico into compliance with the Convention.

At international level, Mexico has continued to promote the Convention through the various UN mechanisms as described above. Currently, a member of the CMW and the Special Rapporteur for Migrant Workers are Mexican academics, and Mexico was the first country to submit a report to the CMW.

At national level, the Mexican Congress passed a resolution setting out basic principles for a comprehensive migration policy in 2005 that was supported by several prominent academics and CSOs. In addition, the INM held a series of public seminars during 2005 to discuss migration across Mexico's southern border, which resulted in the publication of a proposal for a comprehensive migration policy on the southern border. This proposal contains specific recommendations for programmes and policies in human rights protection, migration management along the border and law enforcement in smuggling and trafficking. These two documents currently constitute Mexican migration policy.

The central principles of this migration policy are based on:

- absolute respect for migrants' human rights, regardless of their legal status
- shared responsibility of sending, receiving and transit countries
- legality, security and order
- combat of drug and human trafficking
- non-criminalization of migrants
- migration as a tool for national development.

At a more technical level, Mexico signed an agreement with the OHCHR in 2003, and began an important process of analyzing its level of compliance with a series of human rights conventions. Migrants' rights were included in both the Diagnostic on the Situation for Human Rights in Mexico and the National Human Rights Plan that derived from the Diagnostic. In order to implement the recommendations contained in the Diagnostic and to make specific proposals for the National Human Rights Plan, Mexico established the Commission on Governmental Policy in Human Rights, involving both government and civil society, on 11 March 2003, with the aim of coordinating national and international activities and directing government policy in human rights. It is headed by the Minister of the Interior, the Minister of Foreign Relations serves as Vice-President and there are several subcommissions.

The Sub-Commission on Migrants' Rights was set up on 14 July 2004 with responsibility for defining the central needs in the development of a migration policy with an understanding of human rights and an emphasis on women, children and youth. It contributed to the section on migrants of the National Human Rights Program, emphasizing the need to: (i) encourage a culture of respect towards those who migrate; (ii) guarantee access to justice and due process to migrants in Mexico and abroad; (iii) harmonize legislation with international instruments for the protection of migrants' rights; and (iv) promote coordination between different institutions involved in migration, including civil society.

For the evaluation of the National Human Rights Program, a mechanism was designed that will ensure ongoing monitoring both by civil society and by the concerned responsible entities of the federal executive branch. Mexico also formally entered into a Program of Cooperation with the EU in February 2004, with the purpose of defining actions and concrete policies for the incorporation of international norms and standards of human rights.

Provisions being analyzed by the government for harmonization with the ICRMW include:

- a court ruling on the legality of depriving migrants of their liberty by detaining them
- the creation of a specific migration category for migrant workers
- legislative provision for giving seasonal workers who have been employed in the country for a significant period of time the possibility of taking up other remunerated activities (UN, 2005).

In addition to consultations and analysis, a specific body to monitor the situation of migrants was created within the National Human Rights Commission at the beginning of 2005. While not a government agency, it is an official voice for the violations of human rights in Mexico. During its first two years, this office issued over fifteen recommendations regarding migrants whose rights had been violated, as well as a special report documenting the inadequate conditions of the detention centres. This new monitoring process has created an additional source of pressure to ensure that the government implements what it has proposed on paper.

In the meantime, the recent recommendations of the CMW summarize some of the principal challenges mentioned in this chapter:

- The Committee recommends that the State Party should consider taking the necessary legislative measures to withdraw its reservation to article 22, paragraph 4 of the Convention, in order to guarantee the right of the persons concerned to explain their reasons for objecting to their expulsion and to submit their case to the competent authority.

- The Committee recommends that the State Party direct its efforts towards the formulation of a migration law that corresponds to the new migration situation in Mexico and is in conformity with the provisions of the Convention and other applicable international instruments.
- The Committee recommends that the State Party should ensure that, in legislation and in practice, migrant workers and members of their families, including those in an irregular situation, have the same rights as nationals of the State Party to file complaints and have access to redress mechanisms before the courts.
- The Committee recommends that the State Party, and more specifically the NIM, should take appropriate steps to ensure that migration control and securing of migrants are carried out exclusively by the competent authorities and that every violation in this regard is promptly reported (UN, 2006).

Let us note that since the examination of Mexico's report by the CMW, Mexico has become the second state (after Guatemala) to make the declaration under article 77 of the Convention.

Conclusion

Mexico is in a position to show the international community that a state which both receives and sends migrants can ratify and comply with the Convention. In terms of protecting Mexican migrants in the United States, Mexico must comply with article 33 to ensure that migrants receive information on their rights; article 41, which grants the right to participate in public affairs of their state of origin; articles 46, 47 and 48, which address the right to transfer belongings, earnings, savings and to avoid double taxation; and ensure that Mexican migrant workers who are returned are able to reintegrate. When necessary, Mexico should also continue with its international and regional advocacy strategies that have resulted in important jurisprudence. In the political arena, Mexico will continue to advocate for improved legislation and practices to protect its nationals in the United States.

Conditions for transit migrants must be urgently addressed due to the extent and gravity of the abuses that occur with impunity each year. The government must allocate the human and financial resources necessary to improve due process guarantees, to ensure that migrants are not arbitrarily detained, to protect migrants from mistreatment on the part of the authorities and civilians, and to prevent the accidents and deaths of migrant workers that occur throughout Mexico. Special measures to protect women and children in transit must be a priority.

Migrants resident in Mexico also face discrimination, much of which could be countered by implementing simple reforms in the documentation procedures, allowing work authorization with fewer conditions, and by offering the option of permanent residence status before spending ten years in Mexico. Reforms must ensure that migrant women and children are protected in situations of domestic violence. Mexico needs to either reform the migration legislation that impedes access to the legal system or ensure that it is properly applied by government authorities, as current practice has caused *de facto* exclusion from the judicial system and birth registration for many migrant workers. In addition, steps need to be taken to grant political rights to migrant workers who are currently barred from membership in senior union positions and all 'political affairs'.

The necessary reforms are clear and have been pronounced at national and international levels. The challenge will be to implement pending proposals that would lead Mexico towards compliance with the Convention. The administration of Felipe Calderón (2007 to 2012) has the opportunity to put these proposals into action – some will require legislative reform at home, but many could be executive directives orienting the application of existing legislation.

References

Agunias, D. 2006. Remittance trends in Central America. *Migration Information Source*, April. Available at www.migrationinformation.org/Feature/display. cfm?id=393 [last accessed 22 April 2009].

Alba, F. 2002. Mexico, a crucial crossroads. *Migration Information Source*, July. Available at www.migrationinformation.org/Profiles/display.cfm?ID=211 [last accessed 22 April 2009].

Aldrete Valencia, H. 2006. *Mexico-Canada Seasonal Agricultural Workers Program*. Workshop on Labour Migration, March 2006. New York, UN. Available at www.unitarny.org/mm/File/Valencia%20Seasonal%20Agricultural% 20Workers%20Programme.pdf [last accessed 22 April 2009].

Andrade-Eekhoff, K. 2006. Migration and development in El Salvador: ideals versus reality. *Migration Information Source*, April. Available at www.migrationinformation.org/Feature/display.cfm?ID=387 [last accessed 22 April 2009].

Banco de México. 2008. *La balanza de pagos en 2007* [Mexico's Balance of Payments in 2007]. Press release, 15 February 2008. Available at www.ime.gob.mx/documentos/remesas_2007.pdf [last accessed 22 April 2009].

Batalova, J. 2008. Mexican immigrants in the United States. *Migration Information Source*, April. Available at www.migrationinformation.org/USfocus/display.cfm?id=679 [last accessed 22 April 2009].

Border Network for Human Rights. 2006. *Behind Every Abuse is a Community*. US/Mexico Border Report to the United Nations Human Rights Committee Regarding the United States' Compliance with the International Covenant on Civil and Political Rights, June.

Caron, C. 2007. Portable justice and global workers. *Clearinghouse Review: Journal of Property Law and Policy*, January–February, pp. 549–57.

Casillas, R. R. 2006. *La Trata de Mujeres, Adolescentes, Niñas y Niños en México: Un Estudio Exploratorio en Tapachula, Chiapas* [Trafficking of Women, Adolescents, Girls and Boys in Mexico: An Exploratory Study in Tapachula, Chiapas]. Mexico City, Inter-American Commission of Women/International Organization for Migration/National Institute for Women, and National Migration Institute.

Castillo, M. A. 2006. *Mexico: Caught Between the United Status and Central America. Migration Information Source*, April. Available at www.migrationinformation.org/Feature/display.cfm?ID=389 [last accessed 22 April 2009]

CNDH. 2005a. *Informe especial de la Comisión Nacional de los Derechos Humanos sobre la situación de los derechos humanos en las estaciones migratorias y lugares habilitados del Instituto Nacional de Migración en la Republica Mexicana* [National Human Rights Commission Special Report on the Human Rights Situation in the Migration Detention Centres and other sites utilized by the National Migration Institute in the Mexican Republic]. Mexico City, Comisión Nacional de Derechos Humanos.

2005b. *Recommendation 045/2005, Sobre el caso de los extranjeros indocumentados que cruzan por el estado de Coahuila* [Regarding the Case of the Undocumented Foreigners that Cross Through the State of Coahuila], *December*. Mexico City, CNDH.

2006. *Recommendation 022/2006, Sobre el caso de Santos Catalino Portillo Funes* [Regarding the Case of Santos Catalino Portillo Funes], *June*. Mexico City, CNDH.

CONAPO. 2001. *La población en México en el nuevo siglo* [Mexico's Population in the New Century]. Mexico City, Consejo Nacional de Población. Prelim pages available at www.conapo.gob.mx/publicaciones/sdm/Lapoblacion/ø.pdf [last accessed 22 April 2009].

CONAPO/INM/STPS/EL COLEF. 2006. *Encuesta sobre migración en la frontera Guatemala – México 2004* [Migration Survey in the Guatemala – Mexico Border 2004]. Mexico City, Secretaría del Trabajo y Previsión Social.

Davy, M. 2006. The Central American foreign born in the United States. *Migration Information Source*, April. Available at www.migrationinformation.org/USFocus/display.cfm?ID=385 [last accessed 22 April 2009].

DHS. 2006. *Fact Sheet. Border Apprehensions: 2005.* Available at www.dhs.gov/immigrationstatistics [last accessed 22 April 2009].

2007. *Yearbook of Immigration Statistics: 2006.* Available at www.dhs.gov/xlibrary/assets/statistics/yearbook/2006/NIMSupTable1DFY06.xls [last accessed 22 April 2009].

Díaz, G. and Kuhner, G. 2007. Women migrants in transit and detention in Mexico. *Migration Information Source*, March. Available at www.migrationinformation.org/Feature/display.cfm?ID=586 [last accessed 22 April 2009].

2008. Women migrants in detention in Mexico: conditions and due process. *Migration Information Source*, June. Available at www.migrationinformation.org/Feature/display.cfm?id=684 [last accessed 12 May 2009].

Durand, J. 1994. *Más allá de la línea: Patrones migratorios entre México y Estados Unidos* [Beyond the Line: Migratory Patterns between Mexico and the United States]. Mexico City, Consejo Nacional para la Cultura y las Artes.

2004. From traitors to heroes: 100 years of Mexican migration policies. *Migration Information Source*, March. Available at www.migrationinformation.org/Feature/display.cfm?ID=203 [last accessed 22 April 2009].

Foro Migraciones. 2005. *Informe Alternativo: Aplicación de la Convención Internacional de los Derechos de los Todos los Trabajadores Migratorios y sus Familiares* [Shadow Report: Application of the United Nations International Convention on the Protection of the Rights of all Migrant Workers and Members of their Families]. Mexico City, December.

Frontera con Justicia, A. C. 2006. *Segundo informe sobre los derechos humanos de los migrantes en transito* [Second Report on the Human Rights of Migrants in Transit], May.

GAO. 2006. *Illegal Immigration. Border-Crossing Deaths Have Doubled Since 1995; Border Patrol's Efforts to Prevent Deaths Have Not Been Fully Evaluated.* Washington, Wash., US GAO. (GAO-06-770.)

García, M. 1981. *Desert Immigrants: The Mexicans of El Paso, 1880–1920.* New Haven, Conn., Yale University Press.

HRW. 2001. *Human Rights Watch World Report 2001: The United States.* New York, HRW. Available at www.hrw.org/wr2k1/usa/index.html [last accessed 22 April 2009].

2005. *Immigrant Workers in the Meat and Poultry Industry.* Submission by Human Rights Watch to the Office of the United Nations High

Commissioner for Human Rights, CMW, December. Available at www.hrw. org/backgrounder/usa/un-sub1005 [last accessed 22 April 2009].

IACHR. 2003. *On Site Visit to Mexico*. Washington, Wash., IACHR, Special Rapporteurship on Migrant Workers and Their Families. Available at www.cidh.org/Migrantes/2003.eng.cap5c.htm [last accessed 22 April 2009].

IADB. 2008. Remittances to Central America to rise to $12.1 billion in 2007, says IDB Fund, Press Release, 6 November. http://www.iadb.org/news/articlede-tail.cfm?language=English&artid=4125.

Loret, D. E. 1999. *The U.S.-Mexican Border in the Twentieth Century*. Wilmington, Del., Scholarly Resources, Inc.

Mahler, S. J. and Ugrina, D. 2006. Central America: crossroads of the Americas. *Migration Information Source*, April. Available at www.migrationinforma-tion.org/Feature/display.cfm?ID=386 [last accessed 22 April 2009].

Massey, D. 2005. *Backfire at the Border: Why Enforcement without Legalization Cannot Stop Illegal Immigration*. Washington, Wash., CATO Institute.

Mohar, G. 2004. Mexico-United States migration: a long way to go. *Migration Information Source*, March. Available at www.migrationinformation.org/Feature/display.cfm?ID=209 [last accessed 22 April 2009].

Oishi, N. 2002. *Gender and Migration: An Integrative Approach*. San Diego, Calif., University of California, Center for Comparative Immigration Studies. (Working Paper 49.)

Papademetriou, D. 2002. *A Grand Bargain: Balancing the National Security, Economic and Immigration Interests of the U.S. and Mexico*. Washington, Wash., Migration Policy Institute. Available at www.migrationpolicy.org/files/bar-gain.pdf [last accessed 12 May 2009]. (Migration Policy Institute Policy Paper.)

Passel, J. S. 2005. *Estimates of the Size and Characteristics of the Undocumented Population*. Washington, Wash., Pew Hispanic Centre, 21 March 2005.

Rojas, M. Ángeles, H., Sánchez Vázquez, J. E., Martínez, F., Molguín, I. F., Castro, V., Sokolov, M. and Tovilla, C. 2004. *Breve diagnostico del Soconusco* [Brief Diagnosis of Mexico's Southern Border]. Tapachula, Chiapas, Mexico, ECOSUR.

Schlosser, E. 1995. *In the Strawberry Fields, The Atlantic Online*. Available at www. theatlantic.com/issues/95nov/strawber.htm [last accessed 22 April 2009].

Sin Fronteras, I. A. P. 2004. *Violencia y mujeres migrantes en Mexico* [Violence and Women Migrants in Mexico]. Mexico City, August.

—— 2007. *Situación de los derechos humanos de la población migrante en las estaciones migratorias de la Ciudad de Mexico y de Tapachula, Chiapas, 2005-2006* [Human Rights Situation of the Migrant Population in the Detention Centres in Mexico City and Tapachula, Chiapas, 2005-2006]. Mexico City, March.

SRE. 2006. *México y la Convención internacional sobre la protección de los derechos de todos los trabajadores migratorios y de sus familiares* [Mexico and the

International Convention for the Protection of the Human Rights of all Migrant Workers and Their Families]. Mexico City, SRE. Available at www. sre.gob.mx/oi/zB01f_Migrat_01.htm [last accessed 22 April 2009].

UN. 2005. Committee on the Protection of the Rights of All Migrant Workers and Members of Their Families, Consideration of Reports Submitted by States Parties Under Article 73 of the Convention: Mexico, November. (CMW/C/MEX/1.)

—— 2006. Committee on the Protection of the Rights of All Migrant Workers and Members of Their Families, Concluding Observations of the Committee on the Protection of the Rights of All Migrant Workers and Members of their Families, December. (CMW/C/MEX/CO/1.)

Venet, F. 2002. *La Convención para la protección de todos los trabajadores migrantes y sus familiares: posibilidades y límites en su aplicación* [The Convention for the Protection of all Migrant Workers and Their Families: Possibilities and Limits of Application]. IIDH, *Primer curso de capacitación para organizaciones de la sociedad civil sobre protección de poblaciones migrantes (Cd. de México, 2 de junio de 1999).* San José, Instituto Interamericano de Derechos Humanos, pp. 267–77.

Zlotnik, H. 2003. The global dimensions of female migration. *Migration Information Source*, March. Available at www.migrationinformation.org/Feature/display.cfm?ID=109 [last accessed 22 April 2009].

10

Migrants' rights after apartheid: South African responses to the ICRMW

JONATHAN CRUSH, VINCENT WILLIAMS
AND PEGGY NICHOLSON

Introduction[1]

South Africa has a long history of abusing migrants' rights. The migrant labour system to the South African mines, for example, was once described as the 'most enduring and far-flung oscillating migrant labour system in history [which] laid the foundations of a particularly ruthless system of racial discrimination' (Crush et al., 1991, p. 3). During the apartheid era, South Africa also failed to accede to any of the major international human rights conventions. In 1994, with the advent of democracy and a new Constitution and Bill of Rights, a rights-based foundation was laid for the protection of all in the country. Over the last decade, South African workers have come to enjoy unprecedented protection through a range of new labour laws (Donnelly and Dunn, 2006). The new South African Government also ratified a significant number of international human rights conventions. However, the ICRMW remains unsigned and unratified. To date, the government has expressed no opinion on the ICRMW, much less voiced opposition to or concerns about its contents. The question addressed in this chapter, then, is whether the failure to ratify is because the government has problems with the Convention itself, like so many other migrant-destination countries (see Taran, 2001; Iredale and Piper, 2003; Piper, 2004; Pécoud and de Guchteneire, 2006).

We argue that the South African failure to ratify is not, in fact, rooted in any principled objection to the ICRMW. To understand the reasons

[1] The authors wish to thank the individuals and organizations that made themselves available for interviews about the Convention. This study was made possible by support from UNESCO. Jonathan Crush also wishes to thank the Social Sciences and Humanities Research Council (SSHRC) of Canada.

for the response to the Convention in the first ten years after apartheid, it is necessary to appreciate the more general context of attitudes to migrants in post-apartheid South Africa. While major progress was made after 1994 in protecting the rights of workers in general through new labour legislation and enforcement of the Bill of Rights, none of these developments was directed at migrants' rights per se (Donnelly and Dunn, 2006). Indeed, popular and official attitudes to foreign migrants became increasingly negative and even xenophobic. Government policy was therefore inimical to the whole concept of special rights for foreign migrants. In such an environment, there was little chance that the Convention would be seen as relevant, much less be signed and ratified.

This chapter first provides an overview of contemporary labour migration to South Africa, showing that the country is the recipient of a significant and growing number of migrant workers in need of protection. Second, the whole question of migrants' rights in post-apartheid South Africa is examined. The apartheid system was premised on the denial of basic rights to all workers, including migrants. The systemic (and now unconstitutional) violation of the rights of migrant workers continued and even intensified after 1994. The ICRMW was clearly at odds with the anti-immigrationist discourse that permeated the first post-apartheid decade and, as such, was always likely to be ignored.

While migrants' rights received short political shrift in the first post-apartheid decade, there has been a marked change in attitude since the 2004 election. This has come about partly as a result of South Africa's changing relations with the rest of Africa, partly because of changes in leadership in the flagship Department of Home Affairs and partly as a result of systematic documentation by researchers, the media and human rights groups of the systemic abuse of migrants' rights by government, employers and citizens. Whether the new rights-aware environment will extend to an open debate and eventual ratification of the Convention remains to be seen. However, the moment has never been more propitious. In that context, it is important to understand what obstacles to ratification are likely to arise. We conclude by arguing that, although the prospects for South Africa's ratification are now much brighter, there are still considerable obstacles that need to be overcome before it becomes a reality.

This chapter is based on a complete review of existing South African labour and human rights legislation and interviews with key informants in government, the private sector, labour unions and NGOs. Interviewees include representatives from the Departments of Labour and Home Affairs, the Parliamentary Portfolio Committee on Labour, the South

African Human Rights Commission (SAHRC), the Congress of South African Trade Unions (COSATU), the National Union of Mineworkers (NUM) and the South African Chamber of Mines.

Labour migration to South Africa

Labour migration to South Africa from the rest of the continent is a long-standing historical reality, dating back to the mid nineteenth century (Crush, 2000a). The exact numbers of migrants in South Africa today are unknown due to the lack of reliable data, but they have certainly increased since the end of apartheid. While South Africa is a favoured destination for skilled and unskilled labour migrants from all over the world, the majority of labour migrants are still from other countries within the Southern African Development Community (SADC) region, specifically: Botswana, Lesotho, Malawi, Mozambique, Swaziland and Zimbabwe (McDonald, 2000). At the same time, South Africa has become a major exporter of (primarily skilled) labour to the developed world (particularly the United States, the United Kingdom, Canada and Australia) (McDonald and Crush, 2002).

The relative importance of labour migration is shown in a five-country survey of migration to South Africa undertaken by the Southern African Migration Project (SAMP) in the late 1990s (see Table 10.1) (McDonald et al., 1998). In the five countries surveyed, 67% of Mozambican migrants were labour migrants. The proportion was much lower in the other countries: 29% of Zimbabweans, 25% of those from Lesotho, 13% of Namibians and only 10% of those from Botswana. In most cases, migration for the purpose of employment was exceeded only by migration for the purpose of visiting family (Botswana, Lesotho and Zimbabwe), shopping (Botswana) and tourism (Botswana and Namibia). Buying and selling goods and shopping both refer primarily to cross-border informal traders who are involved in a very demanding form of self-employment and can also be viewed as labour migrants (Peberdy, 2007). The proportions are particularly high for Zimbabwe (42%), Botswana (26%) and Lesotho (22%).

While the numbers of migrants in South Africa increased after 1994, this has not been through increased opportunities for legal migration and employment. Indeed, legal access to South Africa's labour market by foreign workers became more restricted. Consequently, there was a marked decline in the number of migrants entering South Africa to work, from 118,449 in 1996 to 58,747 in 2002 (see Table 10.2). There are strong signals from the South African Government that it now wishes to reverse

Table 10.1   *Reasons for entry to South Africa (percentage)*

Reason for entry	Botswana	Lesotho	Mozambique	Namibia	Zimbabwe
Employment-related migration					
Work	7	17	45	11	15
Look for work	3	8	22	2	14
Business-related migration					
Business	6	2	2	8	7
Buy and sell goods	2	3	2	2	21
Shopping	24	19	4	1	21
Other reasons					
Visit family	23	34	12	39	13
Medical	5	6	4	4	2
Holiday	14	2	5	19	3
Study	3	1	1	3	2
Other	12	8	2	12	3

Note: Columns do not sum to 100 due to rounding.
Source: SAMP database. Available at www.queensu.ca/samp/sampresources/
Observatory/index.html#data [last accessed 22 April 2009].

this trend, although the bureaucratic and regulatory obstacles to doing so remain strong (Crush and Dodson, 2007). In revising its immigration legislation in 2002, the government introduced or amended several mechanisms through which access to the South African labour market can be obtained. Since 2002, and the passage of the new Immigration Act, the numbers have begun to increase again, particularly from the rest of Africa (up from 16,128 in 2001 to 34,634 in 2005) (see Table 10.2 and Figure 10.1). These numbers are expected to continue rising in future.

The numbers of irregular migrants in South Africa are unknown and probably unknowable. While some sources put the numbers in the millions, an analysis of the methods used to arrive at these figures shows that they are highly suspect (Crush, 2001b). That same study also suggested that the number was probably closer to half a million, an estimate supported by Statistics South Africa.

A recent SAMP survey of five SADC countries shows the major employment sectors for migrants in South Africa (Pendleton et al., 2006; see

Table 10.2 *Legal entry into South Africa for work (1996–2005)*

	1996	1998	2000	2001	2002	2003	2004	2005
Europe	27,126	31,359	26,392	22,900	21,080	24,178	25,239	26,695
North America	7,375	9,449	8,090	6,760	6,070	6,105	6,207	6,527
Central and South America	1,240	1,470	1,252	1,290	1,175	1,420	1,329	1,599
Australia	1,531	1,847	1,535	1,499	1,360	1,329	1,294	1,265
Middle East	1,081	1,185	818	820	942	1,045	1,185	1,362
Asia	8,257	8,279	7,951	8,075	7,140	9,708	13,952	17,590
Indian Ocean islands	307	–	371	306	251	243	202	224
Africa	53,342	23,707	17,562	16,128	16,924	23,155	28,944	34,634
Unspecified	18,190	3,871	4,997	4,652	3,796	4,531	4,912	4,783
Total	118,449	81,442	68,979	62,437	58,747	71,714	83,264	94,679

Source: Statistics South Africa, *Tourism and Migration* reports. Available at www.statssa.gov.za [last accessed 22 April 2009].

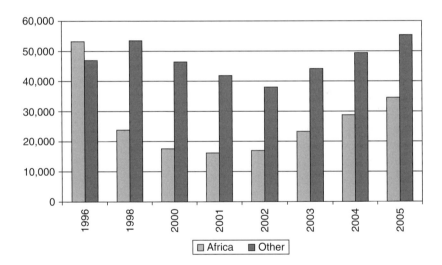

Figure 10.1 Legal entry into South Africa for work (1996–2005).

Table 10.3). Many of these workers (with the exception of those in mining) are probably undocumented migrants who enter the country on a visitor permit or jump borders and then stay on to work. Most informal sector workers also operate across borders using visitor permits.

Table 10.3   *Occupations of SADC migrant workers (percentage)*

Main occupation	Botswana	Lesotho	Mozambique	Swaziland	Zimbabwe	Total
Farmer	1.1	0.3	0.1	0.4	0.7	0.5
Agricultural worker	0.2	2.0	2.2	0.5	1.2	1.3
Service worker	1.1	1.1	1.2	2.5	9.9	3.1
Domestic worker	1.7	9.0	0.9	1.6	1.9	3.2
Managerial office worker	0.3	0.2	0.0	0.8	3.5	0.9
Office worker	1.1	0.3	0.4	1.7	4.6	1.5
Foreman	0.6	0.1	0.5	0.7	0.5	0.5
Mine worker	87.2	68.4	30.5	62.3	3.0	49.5
Skilled manual worker	0.8	6.2	8.0	6.1	4.9	5.6
Unskilled manual worker	0.5	1.5	9.5	7.8	2.1	4.7
Informal sector producer	0.2	2.8	0.8	0.4	4.8	1.8
Trader/hawker/ vendor	0.0	2.0	6.0	0.7	14.7	4.6
Security personnel	0.0	0.2	0.5	1.9	0.1	0.6
Police/military	0.2	0.0	0.1	0.2	0.4	0.1
Business (self-employed)	0.6	1.2	4.0	1.1	4.2	2.2
Employer/manager	0.0	0.0	0.0	0.4	1.3	0.3
Professional worker	1.6	2.9	1.7	3.5	14.7	4.8
Teacher	0.0	0.1	0.1	0.8	7.0	1.5
Health worker	0.6	0.3	0.3	0.5	10.6	2.3
Scholar/student	0.0	0.0	0.0	0.1	1.3	0.3
Other	0.8	0.0	16.9	4.3	2.9	5.3
Don't know	1.1	1.0	16.1	1.7	5.7	5.2
Total	100.0	100.0	100.0	100.0	100.0	100.0

Source: Pendleton et al. (2006), p. 20.

The data show that mining remains the largest employer of labour migrants from these five countries (49.5%) followed by skilled manual workers (5.6%), professionals (4.8%) and unskilled manual labourers (4.7%). Botswana, Lesotho, Swaziland and Mozambique (at over 50%)

in each case are clearly dominated by mine migration (to South Africa). In the Zimbabwean case, mining (at 3%) was relatively insignificant.

The informalization of migrant labour is also evident. Some 6.4% of migrants work in the informal sector and another 2.2% said they are self-employed business people. Somewhat surprisingly, the proportion of commercial farmworkers is relatively low (1.8%). Other sectors in which migrants are employed include domestic work (3.2%), the services sector (3.1%), the health sector (2.3%), teaching (1.5%) and office work (1.5%). In the case of Lesotho, while 68% of migrants are miners, retrenchments have diversified the sources of employment (as well as encouraging more women to migrate). As many as 9% are domestic workers and 6% are skilled manual workers. Mozambican labour migrants are employed in a large array of unskilled and semi-skilled professions. After mining (at 30.5%) comes unskilled manual work (9%), skilled manual work (8%) and trading and hawking (6%).

Zimbabwean labour migrants are employed in an even greater variety of occupations. The single most significant category is informal work and self-employment (at 23.7%), followed by those who identify as professionals (14.7%), health workers (10.6%), service workers (9.9%), teachers (7%), skilled manual workers (4.9%) and office workers (4.6%). Two factors set the Zimbabwean migrant profile apart from that of the other countries: (i) only 30% of migrants work in South Africa compared with over 90% for all the other countries; and (ii) Zimbabwean migration is dominated by skilled and professional people whereas migrants from the other countries are mainly semi-skilled or manual workers (Tevera and Zinyama, 2002). Zimbabwean migration within the SADC is dominated by people working in the informal and services sectors.

The most important form of legal labour migration from the SADC to South Africa is therefore still work in the South African gold mines, as it has been since the late nineteenth century. Table 10.4 shows the numbers and country of origin of migrant mineworkers between 1990 and 2006. In the 1990s, there were widespread mine closures and retrenchments from all areas except Mozambique. The proportion of foreign miners grew to 60% by 1997, when 25% of all mineworkers were from Mozambique. In the first five years of the twenty-first century, with an increasing gold price, there has been renewed expansion in the industry. However, as a result of changes brought about by the Immigration Act of 2002 (see below), new workers are coming primarily from within South Africa (see Figure 10.2). This trend is likely to persist, suggesting that the numbers of foreign migrant mineworkers will continue to fall.

Table 10.4   *Migrant labour in South African gold mines (1990–2006)*

Year	South Africa	Botswana	Lesotho	Mozambique	Swaziland	Foreign (%)	Total
1990	199,810	14,609	99,707	44,590	17,757	47	376,473
1991	182,226	14,028	93,897	47,105	17,393	49	354,649
1992	166,261	12,781	93,519	50,651	16,273	51	339,485
1993	149,148	11,904	89,940	50,311	16,153	53	317,456
1994	142,839	11,099	89,237	56,197	15,892	55	315,264
1995	122,562	10,961	87,935	55,140	15,304	58	291,902
1996	122,104	10,477	81,357	55,741	14,371	58	284,050
1997	108,163	9,385	76,361	55,879	12,960	59	262,748
1998	97,620	7,752	60,450	51,913	10,336	57	228,071
1999	99,387	6,413	52,188	46,537	9,307	54	213,832
2000	99,575	6,494	58,224	57,034	9,360	57	230,687
2001	99,560	4,763	49,483	45,900	7,841	52	207,547
2002	116,554	4,227	54,157	51,355	8,698	50	234,991
2003	113,545	4,204	54,479	53,829	7,970	51	234,027
2004	121,369	3,924	48,962	48,918	7,598	47	230,771
2005	133,178	3,264	46,049	46,975	6,993	43	236,459
2006	164,989	2,992	46,082	46,707	7,124	38	267,894

Source: The Employment Bureau of South Africa (TEBA).

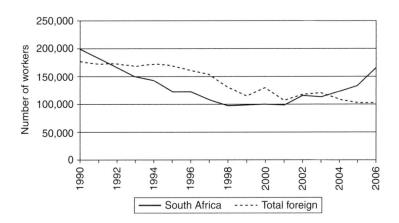

Figure 10.2   Local and foreign migrant labour in South African gold mines (1990–2006).

Historically, labour migration to South Africa from other SADC countries was highly stratified by gender (male-dominated), age (predominantly young) and marital status (predominantly single). The SAMP survey referred to in Table 10.1 revealed that over 60% of men respondents, but only 16% of women, had worked in South Africa. The more recent SAMP survey of migrants in five SADC countries showed that 84.5% of migrants were male and only 15.5% were female (Dodson, 2000). In other words, migration to South Africa continues to be male-dominated. This is very different from the global picture, which shows increasing parity between male and female migration.[2]

The other continuity with the past is that the majority of migrants are unskilled or semi-skilled, with low levels of formal education. As Table 10.5 shows, 15% of the migrant cohort have no formal education, 43% only have primary education and 29% only have secondary education. There are also some significant changes from the past: over half of the migrants are household heads and 68% are married. Migrants are also much older than they used to be (with only 7% under the age of 24 and 41% over the age of 40). Given the new migrant profile, there is some evidence that more migrants (older, married, household heads) are bringing family members with them to South Africa. In other words, the post-apartheid migrant cohort differs in important ways from its apartheid-era predecessor. This means that the range of rights that would have to be protected under the ICRMW will also have shifted.

Migrants' rights beyond apartheid

In the apartheid period, labour migrants were systematically, and with state sanction, subjected to extreme exploitation and human rights violations. South Africa's black union movement made considerable advances in the 1980s and rolled back some of the worst forms of abuse (particularly in the mining industry) (Adler and Webster, 2000). However, sectors such as commercial agriculture were virtually untouched. The exploitation and violations of migrants' rights did not automatically cease in 1994 in sectors such as commercial agriculture, domestic work and construction. Even in mining, some of the gains of the 1980s were lost as the mining companies began to contract out to smaller companies operating outside the bounds of the industry's collective agreements (Crush et al., 2001).

---

[2] According to Zlotnik (2003), in 2000 49% of migrants worldwide and 47% of sub-Saharan African migrants were female.

Table 10.5   *Profile of SADC migrants*

| | | Total | |
		No.	%
Relationship	Head	2,462	52.4
	Spouse/partner	215	4.6
	Son/daughter	1,577	33.6
	Brother/sister	254	5.4
	Other	192	0.4
	Total	4,700	100.0
Sex	Male	3,972	84.5
	Female	731	15.5
	Total	4,703	100.0
Age	15–24	342	7.3
	25–39	2,028	43.2
	40–59	1,758	37.4
	60 and over	169	3.6
	Don't know	398	8.5
	Total	4,695	100.0
Marital status	Unmarried	1,016	21.7
	Married	3,162	67.4
	Cohabiting	203	4.3
	Widowed	152	3.2
	Other	159	3.4
	Total	4,692	100.0
Education	None	689	14.7
	Primary	2,028	43.2
	Secondary	1,350	28.8
	Post-secondary	519	11.1
	Don't know	108	2.3
	Total	4,694	100.0

Source: SAMP database. Available at www.queensu.ca/samp/sampresources/
Observatory/index.html#data [last accessed 22 April 2009].

The continuing disrespect for migrants' rights after 1994 has been extensively documented by the SAHRC (SAHRC, 1999; 2000; 2003; 2006), SAMP (Crush, 1998; McDonald et al., 1998; Danso and McDonald, 2000; Crush, 2001a), human rights groups such as HRW (HRW, 1998) and Lawyers for Human Rights (Handmaker et al., 2001; Lawyers for Human

Rights, 2005), various NGOs and migrant associations (Harris, 2001; CSVR, 2006; CORMSA, 2007) and numerous researchers (e.g. Nyamnjoh, 2006). In addition to documenting the nature and widespread character of these abuses, human rights advocates argued that the failure to afford basic protections to migrants was contrary to the new Constitution and Bill of Rights. In the 1990s, the Minister and Deputy Minister of Home Affairs were generally extremely dismissive of these claims. Every single case brought to court by migrants was fiercely contested by the Department of Home Affairs. Most of these cases were lost by the department, but this did not dissuade it from continuing to attack any and all arguments about the systematic abuse of migrants' rights.

The ongoing abuse of migrants' rights after apartheid has been evident in three main localities. First, at the community level, there was growing intolerance of the presence of non-South Africans. Verbal and physical attacks on migrants and their homes and businesses escalated – and continue today (see e.g. Morris, 1999; McDonald et al., 2000; Dodson and Oelofse, 2002; Sichone, 2003; Landau and Jacobsen, 2004; Landau, 2007). Migrants from neighbouring states who had joined the struggle against apartheid suddenly found themselves ostracized and the object of derogatory labelling and verbal abuse. In some areas, migrants were hounded out of communities and their belongings seized and homes razed. Migrants banded together for protection, intensifying conflict and suspicion between them and locals (who were often themselves internal migrants).

Second, in the workplace, researchers have documented that working conditions for many migrants have improved little since the days of apartheid (e.g. Crush, 1997; Ulicki and Crush, 2000a; Ulicki and Crush, 2000b; Peberdy et al., 2006; Dinat and Peberdy, 2007). Employers were quick to realize that migrant workers were extremely vulnerable and much less likely to report them to the authorities for abuse of South Africa's new labour laws. Many have taken advantage of this situation, particularly in sectors where organized labour is weak (such as commercial agriculture, construction and domestic service).

Third, on the streets of major cities, the police and Home Affairs launched a major assault on 'illegal migration'. Hundreds of thousands of migrants (mainly from neighbouring countries) were rounded up in anti-crime sweeps, railroaded into a notorious holding centre called Lindela near Johannesburg and summarily deported – some only after many months (Klaaren and Ramji, 2001; Madsen, 2004; Masuku, 2006). Such was the enthusiasm of the police that many South Africans (considered too light or too dark to be South Africans or because their pronunciation of Zulu words was poor) were arrested too. The underbelly of these identify and deport campaigns was a major corruption industry in which migrants regularly paid off police not to be arrested or deported. Most black foreigners in South Africa will say that xenophobia remains an everyday reality.[3]

Outside observers were puzzled as to how South Africa could simultaneously be hailed as having one of the most progressive Constitutions and Bill of Rights in the world and be treating migrants with such blatant disregard for their basic rights and freedoms. The ongoing (and intensified) abuse of migrants' rights after 1994 can be attributed to three main factors: (i) the consolidation of a powerful anti-immigration discourse within the state and civil society that portrayed migrants as a threat to the rights of newly enfranchised citizens; (ii) the appointment of a non-African National Congress (ANC) minister to the immigration portfolio and the emphasis placed by him and his advisors on migration control rather than rights; and (iii) the failure of the new government to articulate a clear migration policy and to change inherited apartheid immigration legislation.

First, the anti-immigration discourse that emerged within South Africa in the early 1990s viewed immigration as fundamentally undesirable and tainted by association with the country's racist past. This discourse was reinforced by South Africa's new nation-building project, which was actively redefining the boundaries of inclusion and exclusion (Croucher, 1998; Reitzes, 2000; Peberdy, 2001). As Peberdy argues: 'The development of new and increasingly xenophobic discourses around immigration, particularly undocumented migration from the SADC region, reflects the construction of a new national identity based on citizenship. By using citizenship as a criterion for belonging, the "frontier guards" of South African national identity can abrogate the rights of non-citizens when policing the nation's heartland and borders' (Peberdy, 2001, p. 29).

Central to the new post-apartheid anti-immigrationism was a set of powerful images about migrants and migration. Migration as a process was portrayed in exaggerated and emotive language. Migrants did not enter South Africa or cross its borders; they flooded or poured in on tidal waves from a continent and world in chaos. Simultaneously, the numbers of migrants in the country were highly exaggerated. Officials regularly cited numbers in the millions. All migrants were typecast as 'aliens' without

---

[3] See the personal accounts of female migrants in Lefko-Everett (2007).

Table 10.6 *South African attitudes to rights for citizens and migrants*

	Always (%)	Sometimes*(%)	Never (%)
Should be granted right to freedom of speech and movement			
Citizens	86	13	1
Legal temporary workers	13	43	44
Undocumented migrants	3	13	84
Refugees	3	27	69
*Should be granted right to legal protection***			
Citizens	91	9	1
Legal temporary workers	24	53	23
Undocumented migrants	8	29	62
Refugees	13	44	43
*Should be granted right to police protection****			
Citizens	93	7	1
Legal temporary workers	30	46	24
Undocumented migrants	11	27	61
Refugees	17	41	42
*Should be granted right to social services*****			
Citizens	96	4	0
Legal temporary workers	30	46	25
Undocumented migrants	9	28	63
Refugees	17	41	42

*Literally 'depends on the circumstances'.
**Including not being detained without trial or having a lawyer in court.
***Including freedom from illegal searches and to have property protected.
****Such as education, housing, health care and water.
Source: SAMP database, *South Africa Survey, 1999.* Available at www.queensu.ca/samp/sampresources/Observatory/index.html#data [last accessed 23 April 2009].

any attempt to distinguish between types of migrant. Most were seen as 'illegal' and responsible for South Africa's crime wave. Finally, and very crucially, migrants were seen as a 'threat' to the material interests and rights of newly enfranchised citizens. A survey of South African citizens in 1999 found little support for the idea that migrants should be entitled to certain basic rights (guaranteed in the Constitution).

A nationally representative sample of citizens was asked by SAMP what kinds of rights should be given to the following groups: citizens, (legal) temporary workers, undocumented migrants and refugees. Table 10.6

shows, first, overwhelming support for 'citizen' access to the rights of freedom of speech and movement, legal protection, police protection and access to services. Second, there is a consistent pattern of conditional support for rights for 'legal temporary migrant workers'. While only a quarter of the population thinks that these rights should always be accorded to legal migrants, around half are prepared to see these rights extended in certain circumstances. Only in the case of freedom of speech and movement are people less generous. Third, when it comes to 'undocumented migrants', the picture changes dramatically. Some 85% of respondents feel that these migrants should have no right to freedom of speech or movement. And 60–65% feel that they should not enjoy police or legal protection or access to services. There is clearly a predominant feeling, certainly not confined to South Africa, that by being in a country without official permission, one sacrifices any entitlement to basic rights and protections, even if (as in South Africa) those are guaranteed by the Constitution (Crush, 2000b).

While citizens are prepared to accord more rights to refugees than undocumented migrants, the figures are still sobering. Nearly 70% feel that refugees should never enjoy freedom of movement or speech in South Africa. Around 40% feel that they should never be accorded any of the other basic rights either. Very few (less than 20%) were prepared to grant these rights unconditionally to all refugees.

A second major reason for the lack of attention to migrants' rights after 1994 was that the immigration portfolio was held by a non-ANC minister, Inkatha Freedom Party leader Mangosotho Buthelezi, whom the ANC needed to co-opt and thereby pre-empt civil strife in the province (Kwazulu Natal) where the minister and his political party had a considerable following (Crush and McDonald, 2001). The minister was given considerable latitude to develop and pursue what he considered to be an appropriate post-apartheid migration policy. He received no guidance or direction from the ruling party (which itself was deeply divided on the value of migration to South Africa). His own view, and that of his closest advisors, is best summarized by a submission made to the Cabinet in 1997 in which he argued that undocumented migration was the most significant economic and social threat to transformation in South Africa and that its control required 'draconian solutions'.

The third reason for the sidelining of migrants' rights before the 2004 election (when the minister left office) was the continuation of apartheid-era legislation and bilateral migrant labour agreements with neighbouring states. Until 2002, the law governing migration to South Africa was the Aliens Control Act (ACA) of 1991 and its precursors

(Crush, 1998). The process of rewriting migration policy was not helped by the fact that the ANC was often at loggerheads with the Minister of Home Affairs and his advisors. In addition, there was no articulated government policy to guide the drafters of either the Green or White Papers or subsequent legislation. Draft legislation was modified several times at Cabinet stage and eventually passed into law in a cloud of controversy. Human rights groups and unions expressed considerable concern throughout the process about the proposed new legislation. Even though the ACA had been amended in 1995 to remove the most blatantly racist and discriminatory provisions, the Act remained true to its original intention, which was to restrict and control the movement of persons. For this reason, the minister embarked on a process of not merely amending the existing law, but rewriting it in its totality. The process of redrafting South Africa's immigration law was protracted, controversial and highly politicized (Crush and Dodson, 2007).

Shifting views of migrants' rights

Under the ACA of 1991, legal entry into South Africa for work was through one of two 'gates'. The first gate concerned bilateral agreements between the apartheid government and neighbouring states. These agreements specified the terms and conditions under which migrants could be recruited and employed by the South African mining industry. Long on controls and short on rights, these treaties continued to operate after 1994. Indeed, any suggestion that they should be renegotiated or abolished was rigorously resisted by the mining industry and other South African employers (Crush and Tshitereke, 2001). The second gate (for temporary and permanent skilled immigrants) was via the provisions of the ACA itself. The ACA (as its name implies) was largely devoted to prescribing draconian means and mechanisms for migration 'control'. The ACA was the subject of a systematic legal analysis in 1997, which demonstrated that many of the provisions were unconstitutional and inconsistent with the new South African Bill of Rights (Crush, 1998). The Act continued to licence and encourage enforcement practices that began in the apartheid period and continued thereafter, with added intensity.

The outcome of this highly controversial and lengthy process (which took six years to complete) was legislation (the Immigration Act of 2002) that was not significantly different from the ACA in terms of its core purpose: control of the movement of persons and prevention of 'illegal migration'. The first part of the 2002 Act sets out the following core objectives:

- to facilitate the legal movement of persons to and from, and their sojourn in, South Africa
- to reduce the administrative and bureaucratic requirements associated with the processing and issuing of permits
- to prevent and reduce 'illegal' migration
- to encourage and facilitate cooperation between various organs of government in the implementation of immigration law.

Specifically in relation to labour migration, the intentions of the Act are:

- to prevent and reduce unauthorized access to the South African labour market, particularly of semi-skilled and unskilled workers
- to sanction agencies and employers who are involved in the recruitment and employment of unauthorized workers
- to encourage people with 'much-needed' skills to relocate to South Africa temporarily or permanently
- to ensure that the employment of foreigners does not unduly disadvantage South African citizens and permanent residents, both at the high and low ends of the migration scale (highly skilled and unskilled)
- to make the Department of Labour the primary authority in the implementation and enforcement of immigration law as it pertains to labour migration.

The 2002 Act broke with the ACA in two respects: first, by making reference to the need to encourage skilled persons and investors to migrate to South Africa; and second, by identifying xenophobia as a serious problem that needed to be addressed (although it did not specify how).

However, the bulk of the Act focused on migration control, seeking to involve not only other government departments, but also private and public institutions, in the enforcement of migration law. As with the ACA, the new Act uses the language of migration control and enforcement (as opposed to migration management) and explicitly makes allowance for 'the shifting of resources' away from administration and bureaucracy to enforcement and control. The Act also makes it a legal requirement for various government departments and private institutions to become involved in the implementation and enforcement of immigration law. This is consistent with the view of the drafters of the Act, that immigration policy and law is about entry into and exit from the country, and that other government departments are responsible for formulating and implementing policies and regulations that govern the stay of foreigners in the country. After the 2004 election, the ANC first announced that it would scrap the 2002 Immigration Act. Subsequently, it decided that it could best achieve its objectives through rewriting and amendment. The first set of amendments was legislated in 2004.

In mid 2001, President Thabo Mbeki pointed out that South Africa's 'intimate relationship with the rest of our continent' was being undermined by 'fundamentally wrong and unacceptable' evidence of xenophobia.[4] He called upon all South Africans to revisit their attitude towards fellow Africans. The reasons for this shift in views about the necessity to protect migrants' rights are complex. A key moment was the local and international outcry that accompanied the capture on videotape of the racist physical and verbal abuse of two Mozambican migrants by South African police.[5] This incident was a profound embarrassment to the government, which took harsh punitive measures against the police involved. Cast primarily as an example of racism rather than xenophobia in the South African media, the incident was roundly castigated by senior Cabinet ministers. For Mbeki, though, the incident brought into sharp relief the contradiction between his growing ambition for South Africa to play a leading role in Africa and the reprehensible manner in which his fellow South Africans were treating Africans from other countries. This certainly played a role in his appointment of a leading human and gender rights campaigner as the new Minister of Home Affairs in 2004.

Since 2004, the South African Department of Home Affairs (under a new minister and with new advisors) has begun to introduce a rights-based element into migration discourse. The minister, Nosiviwe Mapisa-Nqakula, whose new personal adviser was a prominent refugee and human rights lawyer, has sought on numerous public occasions to emphasize the constitutional obligation of the South African Government to protect all in the country, including migrants. The relationship between the department and the human rights community thawed considerably as the minister took on board many of their criticisms.

Cognizant of the costliness of the government's deportation policy (in terms of both financial resources and rights abuse), some in government

---

[4] President Thabo Mbeki in *ANC Today*, May 2001.
[5] See www.queensu.ca/samp/migrationresources/xenophobia/press/dogattack/page1.htm [last accessed 23 April 2009].

have begun to look for alternative remedies (particularly since 2004). Ms Mapisa-Nqakula has been particularly proactive in forging a new immigration compact with Lesotho. Under this agreement, signed in June 2007, citizens of Lesotho will find it much easier to move to and work in South Africa. Similarly, to the surprise of many, South Africa is now a signatory to the SADC Draft Protocol on the Facilitation of Movement of Persons in Southern Africa (Peberdy and Crush, 2007).

The Minister also became increasingly concerned about the evidence of xenophobia within her own ranks and explicitly encouraged anti-xenophobia training for officials. In June 2006, the SAHRC and the Parliamentary Portfolio Committee on Home Affairs hosted open hearings on xenophobia in South Africa. The Minister of Home Affairs declared that xenophobia was a scourge that 'needs to be condemned because it is based on prejudice, is frequently violent and most of the time, racist. There is no way that as the South African Government and as a nation we can tolerate or justify xenophobia' (SAHRC, 2006, p. 44). Among numerous recommendations to government was ratification of the ICRMW. At the UN HLD, held in New York in September 2006, Minister Mapisa-Nqakula spoke about the centrality of migrants' rights to development and also mentioned the UN Convention:

> Migrants should be located at the centre of the migration debate. The protection of the human rights of migrants and their families as enunciated in the UN as well as in the ILO conventions is a central component of balanced and comprehensive migration management. Migration facilitation and enforcement must not compromise the rights and dignity of migrants. The exploitation of migrants through mechanisms as trafficking, as well as migrant smuggling, should be criminalized under domestic and international law. Social pathologies such as racism, racial discrimination, xenophobia and other forms of related intolerance, as well as inhuman and degrading treatment, impact negatively on development and must be eradicated.[6]

South Africa, for the first time, seems primed for an open debate about the ICRMW and its ratification. Given this situation, it seems important to proactively identify what kinds of obstacles might exist.

---

[6] Statement on Behalf of the Group of 77 and China, by HE Ms Nosiviwe Mapisa-Nqakula, Minister of Home Affairs of the Republic of South Africa, at the UN High-Level Dialogue on International Migration and Development, United Nations, New York, 14 September 2006.

Possible obstacles to ratification

Common arguments against ratification of the ICRMW are either that it conflicts too much with domestic law or that the rights that it seeks to guarantee are already enshrined in domestic law. South Africa falls into the second category of countries, although it could just as well be argued that this is precisely why it should be ratified. Chapter Two of the South African Constitution of 1996, which contains the Bill of Rights, is phrased in a manner that suggests that all persons are entitled to almost all the rights contained therein. These include rights of equality and non-discrimination, access to education, health, welfare and other social services and housing, among other things. The only rights specifically reserved for citizens are those relating to freedom of movement and residence, occupation and profession and political rights. South Africa's labour and related legislation is drafted in a manner to give effect to the entitlements set out in the Bill of Rights.

At the same time, as many migrants continued to be treated by the state and employers in ways that were disturbingly reminiscent of the situation before 1994, labour and human rights laws in South Africa underwent a major overhaul. Since 1994, a series of laws designed to protect and promote the rights of workers have been passed or amended. None of these laws makes any distinction between workers who are citizens or permanent residents and those who are migrants. It is assumed, therefore, that the laws apply equally to all workers, irrespective of residence status, including temporary, seasonal and permanent migrant workers as well as undocumented workers. However, while this may be true in principle, the manner in which these laws are implemented and enforced often means that migrants are excluded. A brief description of the relevant policies and legislation follows.

The Labour Relations Act of 1995 (LRA) ensures the rights to:

- fair labour practices
- form and join trade unions and employers' organizations
- organize and bargain collectively
- strike and lock-out.

Furthermore, the LRA promotes conciliation and negotiation as a means of settling labour disputes.

The Basic Conditions of Employment Act of 1997 (BCEA), as the title implies, is the primary piece of legislation that establishes and enforces the basic conditions of employment for all workers (with the exception of those employed in the defence, intelligence and security establishments). The BCEA prescribes working hours, including overtime and compensation for overtime work; types of leave; remuneration procedures; termination of service procedures and minimum wages for domestic, farm and seasonal workers. The BCEA also criminalizes child labour and imposes a jail penalty of up to three years for those found guilty of employing children (a child is defined as anyone under the age of 15).

The Employment Equity Act of 1998 (EEA) was written to promote and protect the right of workers to equal opportunities by eliminating unfair discrimination on the grounds of race, gender, sexual orientation and so on, including ethnic or social origin, language and birth. In terms of the EEA, the Department of Labour (2000) has also promulgated a *Code of Good Practice on Key Aspects of HIV/Aids and Employment* that sets out guidelines for employers and workers to implement to ensure that individuals with HIV are not unfairly discriminated against.

The Skills Development Act of 1998 sets out the manner in which employers must take responsibility for ensuring the development of skills in their workforce. This Act functions in conjunction with the affirmative action components of the EEA as well as the Development Levies Act of 1999, which prescribes that all employer organizations have to contribute to a Skills Development Fund that is administered by the Department of Labour.

The Unemployment Insurance Act of 2001 makes it compulsory for employers to register any persons who work for more than twenty-four hours per month with the Unemployment Insurance Fund (UIF). This includes farmers who must register farm workers (since 1997), and since April 2003 domestic workers are also covered by the Act and must be registered for UIF contributions.

The Occupational Health and Safety Act of 1993 makes it the responsibility of both employer and employee to ensure health and safety at the workplace. However, the role of the employer in ensuring the protection of workers is emphasized, including the need to take preventive measures and inform workers of potential threats and hazards.

The Compensation for Occupational Injuries and Diseases Act of 1993 has as its main objective to provide for compensation for disabilities caused by occupational injuries or diseases, or for death resulting from such injuries or diseases. The fund is made up of contributions from employers and, unlike the UIF, no deductions are made from employees as a contribution to the fund.

All the above policies and legislation fall within the jurisdiction of the Department of Labour, which is responsible for the administration, implementation and enforcement thereof. In addition, however, several statutory bodies have been established to advise and provide oversight in terms of the operation and implementation of the above legislation. These are:

- Advisory Council for Occupational Health & Safety
- Commission for Conciliation, Mediation and Arbitration
- Commission for Employment Equity
- Compensation Board
- Employment Conditions Commission
- National Economic Development and Labour Council
- National Productivity Institute
- National Skills Authority
- Unemployment Insurance Board.

The labour laws described above are all designed to give effect to paragraph 23, clauses 1–6 of Chapter Two (Bill of Rights) of the South African Constitution of 1996. In addition to those specific clauses, Chapter Two also explicitly prohibits slavery, servitude and forced labour (paragraph 13). Note, however, that while the above rights are conferred on 'everyone', only citizens have the right to choose their trade, occupation or profession freely (paragraph 22).

In the context of this discussion, migrant workers are specifically excluded from employment equity legislation pertaining to previously or historically disadvantaged groups and affirmative action. Thus, while the law makes provision for preference to be given to 'designated groups' (black people, women and disabled people) in terms of employment, this only applies to citizens and permanent residents, not to migrants.

As noted above, with the exception of the right to choose their trade, occupation or profession freely, migrant workers are entitled to the same levels of protection afforded to citizens. Consequently, the institutions and bodies referred to above should have within their respective mandates the protection and promotion of the rights of migrant workers. However, it remains to be seen whether and how effective these bodies will be in extending their mandate to encompass migrant workers.

As with labour laws, there are several laws that deal with the provision of social and welfare services to citizens and residents. Of these, the most important is the Social Assistance Act (SAA) of 1992, subsequently amended by the Welfare Laws Amendment Act of 1997. In the language of the original draft of the SAA, it is expressly stipulated that persons who wish to apply for social welfare assistance must be able to provide proof of South African citizenship. However, in Chapter Two of the Constitution, there is no such restriction, and every person has the right to all social and welfare services provided by the state. The amendment of the Act in 1997 does not address the question of access by those who are not citizens, but given that the Constitution is the supreme law, it is logical that migrants are entitled to these services, provided that they can prove residence in South Africa.

The Immigration Act of 2002 also makes provision for migrants (documented and undocumented) to have access to these services on the basis that it would be unconstitutional to turn them away on the basis of citizenship or legal status. However, the Act requires that service providers should endeavour to establish the legal status of a person prior to providing the service. In the event of being unable to do so, or if the person is found to be in South Africa without appropriate documentation, it is a legal requirement to report this to the Department of Home Affairs. Failure to report such persons is a punishable offence.

In a recent court case, in which Mozambican migrants applied for court intervention after they were denied access to social welfare on the grounds that they were not South African citizens, judgment was handed down in favour of the migrants.[7] The judge found the denial of grants to be unconstitutional. By extension, this judgment will become established jurisprudence and would apply to all social and welfare services provided by the state.

However, there is evidence that migrants (documented and undocumented) are routinely denied services on the basis that they are not citizens. This is consistent with the perception that migrants place an additional and unsustainable burden on the resources available to provide social and welfare services. So while labour legislation may have changed and in theory should afford protection to migrants, in practice this is often not the case.

All the respondents interviewed for this study agreed that South Africa's labour legislation applies equally to migrant workers and to nationals, and that no distinction or denial of rights can be instituted on the basis of nationality or citizenship. They were also clear that, as with the ICRMW, a distinction should be made between documented

---

[7] Constitutional Court, 2003. *Khoza* v. *Minister of Social Development* (CCT 12/03); Constitutional Court, 2004, *Mahlaule* v. *Minister of Social Development* (CCT 13/03).

and undocumented migrants. But some, particularly the interviewees from the NUM and the COSATU, were adamant that once a person had been employed, they should be entitled to the full protection of South Africa's labour legislation, irrespective of their legal status. As one interviewee noted, 'a worker, is a worker, is a worker'. In this respect, it is not just South Africa's labour law that is applicable, but also the Constitution, which outlaws discrimination on the basis of nationality or origin. All key informants agreed that if it was made clear that the provisions and purpose of the Convention are not substantively different from what is already contained in South Africa's domestic policies and laws, this would overcome the first hurdle.

Another issue raised in the interviews related to the capacity of government to implement not only its own policies and legislation, but also any additional obligations that may emanate from ratifying the Convention – a problem of accountability. It appears that officials do not want to be obligated by international law to do something that they fear they are unable to do. In the overall context of wanting to promote ratification, serious attention has to be paid to what exactly the requirements and obligations might be for the South African Government, and to develop its capacity to meet these requirements and fulfil its obligations.

Third, the question of political sovereignty was raised by some in government. To what extent does the Convention inhibit the right of South Africa to make decisions and formulate its own policies and regulations regarding the entry, sojourn and entitlements of migrants? This question is also related to the debate about the rights of citizens vs the rights of migrants and, as previously noted, is an important political question. While this concern with the impact of the Convention on the sovereignty of states appears to emanate from a misunderstanding or misinterpretation, given that the Convention itself explicitly makes it clear that it shall not affect the right of States Parties to establish criteria governing the admission and stay of migrant workers, it is nonetheless a real concern. Phrased differently, to what extent does political will already exist or need to be created for the South African Government to ratify the Convention? Clearly, this question is also related to how much is known about the Convention and the obligations that it imposes on government.

If the above issues can be addressed satisfactorily, that will provide significant impetus towards ratification of the Convention by the South African Government. However, while the issue of capacity will have to be dealt with in order to effectively implement the Convention, for ratification to even be considered there must first be a renewed focus within government on the rights of migrant workers and their families. The fact that, for the most part, neither government nor civil society institutions have given high priority to migration only facilitates the lack of political will.

One concern was that by promoting the rights of migrant workers and their families in the manner proposed by the Convention, local workers may be (seen to be) disadvantaged. The highly antagonistic environment towards foreign migrants and the widespread feeling that migrants' rights should be curtailed, not expanded, clearly worry elected representatives at all levels of government. In this respect, the 'equality with nationals' provisions of the Convention may indeed pose some difficulties. In commenting about the extension of rights to migrant workers, one interviewee spoke of 'double standards' – implying that, on the surface, migrant workers are supposed to enjoy all the rights that citizens enjoy, but that in practice this is not the case. Another interviewee made a similar point and used the phrase 'government speaks with forked tongue'. He argued that while government seems to implicitly and sometimes explicitly support the extension of workers' rights to migrant workers, this is not directly and clearly reflected in its policy and regulatory frameworks.

Perhaps one of the biggest immediate obstacles to ratification of the Convention is the fact that awareness and knowledge of it in South Africa is very limited. With the exception of two of the interviewees, all the others indicated that they had 'heard of it' but were not familiar with its content. In two cases, interviewees had not heard of the Convention prior to receiving the request for an interview. Again, all the interviewees agreed that, to their knowledge, the Convention had never been formally tabled or discussed in South Africa, and they confirmed that familiarity with it was limited to a few individuals in government who may have had the opportunity to participate in international fora where the Convention had been discussed. A suggestion put forward by the COSATU representative was that a broad-based awareness programme or campaign could be conducted to explain the origin, purpose and contents of the Convention.

One question put to all interviewees was whether they believed that the implementation, reporting and monitoring requirements imposed by the ICRMW would pose an administrative burden on the South African Government that may be regarded as too cumbersome and, therefore, could potentially pose an obstacle to ratification. While most of the interviewees suggested that they did not think that this would be sufficient grounds for non-ratification, the deputy chairperson of the SAHRC made the point that South Africa was already a signatory and has ratified several other international conventions that have similar reporting and monitoring requirements and that, in her view, it was merely a matter of adding an additional convention. She thus firmly expressed the view that this would not be a problem for the South African Government.

Given the significant degree of congruence between South Africa's domestic law and the Convention, there appears to be no substantive reasons (other than those described above) why South Africa should not ratify the Convention. However, as pointed out by one of the interviewees, ratification does introduce an element of international accountability, which means that not only would the South African Government have to report on its progress with implementing the Convention, but other parties to the Convention could also hold it accountable for non-implementation or violation. In this respect, one of the interviewees noted that, in the context of the Southern African sub-region, the South African Government was particularly adept at introducing new or amending its existing applicable migration policies and regulations without consulting or informing the governments of countries whose nationals would be affected by such changes. If South Africa was a signatory to the Convention, any such moves that might constitute a violation of the rights of migrant workers could be challenged.

At a broader level, the issue of international accountability was also linked by one of the interviewees to the question of political sovereignty. He argued that the principles that underpin immigration policies and laws are related to the sovereignty of the nation-state, the integrity of national borders and the sole right of the state to govern entry into its national territory. He suggested that there would be some concern that ratification of the Convention and adherence to its obligations and provisions could be interpreted as government having lost control over its sovereign right to make decisions about who may enter the country, under what conditions and what they would be entitled to once they have been allowed entry.

South Africa's labour legislation and regulations provide for a range of mechanisms to promote and protect the rights of workers, including migrant workers. However, it is clear that the ability and capacity of government to enforce labour law to achieve compliance is lacking. While there have been reported cases of government taking action against employers for contravening the law, these have been inconsistent and sporadic. One of the interviewees reported that a senior official in the

Department of Labour candidly admitted that, until such time as the department had sufficient capacity to enforce labour law, it was unlikely to ratify the ICRMW because doing so would make it liable to taking steps to ensure implementation and that it lacked the capacity to do so. On the basis of this, it appears as if there would be a willingness to ratify, certainly on the part of the responsible department, but that this willingness is constrained by concerns about lack of capacity.

Conclusion

Despite a protracted process of migration policy making, migration policy issues generally, and the rights of migrants in particular, have not received much attention in the post-apartheid policy and public domains. To the extent that migration has been placed on the policy agenda, it has largely been restricted to concerns about control and enforcement and the need to retain or recruit sufficient numbers of skilled personnel in particular sectors of South Africa's economy.

Most government officials, as well as politicians, acknowledge the importance of migration as a 'cross-cutting' issue, but few are willing to take it up and place it firmly on the government policy agenda. In a broad range of policy documents relating to education, health, labour and so on, cursory reference is made to migration as one of the factors to be considered, but none of these documents contain substantive detail. Even the Department of Home Affairs, which is responsible for the development of migration policy and law and the enforcement thereof, treats migration as an administrative and bureaucratic matter, rather than an important policy matter that has implications for the whole of government.

In this respect, it is important to note that the Department of Social Development has identified migration as one of the key components in its projection of anticipated demographic changes, along with mortality and fertility. However, very little substantive research, planning or policy development has taken place.

The first step in promoting ratification in South Africa will be for the government to assess existing legislation in order to see how it compares with the ICRMW. By uncovering areas where the current policy fails, the government will have a better understanding of why a more detailed, comprehensive agreement such as the Convention is necessary. It will also highlight what additional resources would be needed for the implementation of the Convention, as well as where the two overlap. In many respects, the current policy in South Africa already embodies the

Convention's institutions and protections on a much broader scale. A comparison could expose these similarities and show which parts of the existing legislation could be easily extended to migrant workers. While it is unlikely that government will take on such an assessment on its own, CSOs can play an integral role in driving this process by conducting preliminary studies and publicizing the results.

Once South Africa begins to genuinely consider ratification, the capacity of government will ultimately become an issue. However, government does not necessarily have to possess the capability needed to implement the Convention in its entirety before ratification can take place. Once it is ratified, government can work gradually through timelines set for implementation and enforcement, starting with the most certain and straightforward areas. CSOs can also play an important role in helping to develop this capacity through research and training.

Another way in which to promote ratification is to position the Convention in the context of the SADC sub-regional agenda. In the past, South Africa has shown increased receptiveness to policies taken up on a broad, regional scale. Considering the Convention's emphasis on the entire process of migration and its provisions on collaboration, it would be extremely difficult for a country in Southern Africa to effectively implement it on its own. Ratification on a regional scale would serve as a mechanism through which Southern African countries could hold each other accountable to the obligations of the Convention. Existing agreements such as the SADC Protocol on the Facilitation of Movement of Persons and the Social Charter on the Fundamental Rights of Workers could serve as a foundation for this cooperation and enforcement.

Before more technical questions such as the details of implementation can be fully addressed, government must be made aware that ratification of the Convention will not require the adoption of an entirely new set of policies, laws and regulations, but first, a re-interpretation of existing policies, laws and regulations and their applicability to migrant workers and their families, and second, the amendment of existing policies, laws and regulations to the extent required.

References

Adler, G. and Webster, E. (eds). 2000. *Trade Unions and Democratization in South Africa, 1985–1997*. New York, St Martin's Press.

CORMSA. 2007. *Protecting Refugees and Asylum Seekers in South Africa*. Johannesburg, Consortium for Refugees and Migrants in South Africa.

Croucher, S. 1998. South Africa's illegal aliens: constructing boundaries in a post-apartheid state. *Ethnic and Racial Studies*, Vol. 21, No. 4, pp. 639–60.

Crush, J. 1997. *Covert Operations: Clandestine Migration, Temporary Work and Immigration Policy in South Africa*. Cape Town, SAMP. (Migration Policy Series No. 1.)

(ed.). 1998. *Beyond Control: Immigration and Human Rights in a Democratic South Africa*. Cape Town, SAMP.

2000a. Migrations past: an historical overview of cross-border movement in southern Africa. McDonald (ed.), op. cit., pp. 12–24.

2000b. The dark side of democracy: migration, xenophobia and human rights in South Africa. *International Migration*, Vol. 38, pp. 103–34.

2001a. *Immigration, Xenophobia and Human Rights in South Africa*. Cape Town, SAMP. (Migration Policy Series No. 22.)

2001b. *Making Up the Numbers: Measuring 'Illegal Migration' to South Africa*. Cape Town, SAMP. (Migration Policy Brief No. 3.)

Crush J. and Dodson, B. 2007. Another lost decade: the failures of South Africa's post-apartheid migration policy. *Tijdschrift voor Economische en Sociale Geografie*, Vol. 98, No. 4, pp. 436–54.

Crush, J. and McDonald, D. 2001. Evaluating South African immigration policy after apartheid. *Africa Today*, Vol. 48, No. 3, pp. 1–14.

Crush, J. and Tshitereke, C. 2001. Contesting migrancy: the foreign labour debate in post-1994 South Africa. *Africa Today*, Vol. 48, No. 3, pp. 49–72.

Crush, J., Jeeves, A. and Yudelman, D. 1991. *South Africa's Labor Empire: A History of Black Migrancy to the Gold Mines*. Cape Town/Boulder, Colo., David Philip/Westview Press.

Crush, J., Ulicki, T., Tseane, T. and Jansen Van Veuren, E. 2001. Undermining labour: the social implications of sub-contracting on the South African gold mines. *Journal of Southern African Studies*, Vol. 27, No. 1, pp. 5–32.

CSVR. 2006. *Women on the Run: Female Survivors of Torture Amongst Zimbabwean Asylum Seekers and Refugees in South Africa*. Research Report for the CSVR. Johannesburg, Zimbabwe Torture Victims Project/Centre for the Study of Violence and Reconciliation.

Danso, R. and McDonald, D. A. 2000. *Writing Xenophobia: Immigration and the Press in Post-Apartheid South Africa*. Cape Town, SAMP. (Migration Policy Series No. 17.)

Department of Labour. 2000. *Code of Good Practice on Key Aspects of HIV/Aids and Employment*. Government Gazette, No. 21815, 1 December 2000. Available at www.workinfo.com/Free/Sub_for_legres/Data/Regulation%20No_%20390%20of%202000.htm [last accessed 10 May 2009].

Dinat, N. and Peberdy, S. 2007. Worlds of work, health and migration: domestic workers in Johannesburg. *Development Southern Africa*, Vol. 24, No. 1, pp. 187–204.

Dodson, B. 2000. Women on the move: gender and cross-border migration to South Africa from Lesotho, Mozambique and Zimbabwe. McDonald (ed.), op. cit., pp. 110–50.

Dodson, B. and Oelofse, C. 2002. Shades of xenophobia: in-migrants and immigrants in Mizamoyethu, Cape Town. J. Crush and D. A. McDonald (eds), *Transnationalism and New African Immigration to South Africa*. Toronto, Ont./Cape Town, Canadian Association of African Studies/SAMP. pp. 12–48.

Donnelly, E. and Dunn, S. 2006. Ten years after: South African employment relations since the negotiated revolution. *British Journal of Industrial Relations*, Vol. 44, No. 1, pp. 1–29.

Handmaker, J. de la Hunt, L. A. and Klaaren, J. (eds). 2001. *Perspectives on Refugee Protection in South Africa*. Pretoria, Lawyers for Human Rights.

Harris, B. 2001. *A Foreign Experience: Violence, Crime and Xenophobia during South Africa's Transition*. Johannesburg, Centre for the Study of Violence and Reconciliation. (Violence and Transition Series, Vol. v.)

HRW. 1998. *Prohibited Persons: Abuse of Undocumented Migrants, Asylum Seekers and Refugees in South Africa*. New York, HRW.

Iredale, R. and Piper, N. 2003. *Identification of the Obstacles to the Signing and Ratification of the UN Convention on the Protection of the Rights of All Migrant Workers: The Asia-Pacific Perspective*. Paris, UNESCO. (Country Reports on the Ratification of the UN Convention on Migrants.)

Klaaren, J. and Ramji, J. 2001. Inside illegality: migration policing in South Africa after apartheid. *Africa Today*, Vol. 48, pp. 35–48.

Landau, L. 2007. Discrimination and development? Migration, urbanisation, and sustainable livelihoods in South Africa's forbidden cities. *Development Southern Africa*, Vol. 24, No. 1, pp. 61–76.

Landau, L. and Jacobsen, K. 2004. Refugees in the new Johannesburg. *Forced Migration Review*, Vol. 19, pp. 44–6.

Lawyers for Human Rights. 2005. *Crossing Borders, Accessing Rights, and Detention: Asylum and Refugee Protection in South Africa*. Johannesburg, Lawyers for Human Rights. (Forced Migration Studies Programme.)

Lefko-Everett, K. 2007. *Voices from the Margins: Women's Migrant Experiences in South Africa*. Cape Town, SAMP. (Migration Policy Series No. 46.)

Madsen, M. 2004. Living for home: policing immorality among undocumented migrants in Johannesburg. *African Studies*, Vol. 63, pp. 173–92.

Masuku, T. 2006. Targeting foreigners: xenophobia among Johannesburg's police. *ISS Crime Quarterly*, Vol. 15, pp. 19–25.

McDonald, D. A. (ed.). 2000. *On Borders: Perspectives on International Migration in Southern Africa*. Cape Town/New York, SAMP/St Martin's Press.

McDonald, D. A. and Crush, J. (eds). 2002. *Destinations Unknown: Perspectives on the Brain Drain in Southern Africa*. Pretoria, Africa Institute.

McDonald, D., Mashike L. and Golden, C. 2000. The lives and times of African migrants and immigrants in post-apartheid South Africa. McDonald (ed.), op. cit., pp. 168–95.

McDonald, D. A., Gay, J., Zinyama, L., Mattes, R. and de Vletter, F. 1998. *Challenging Xenophobia: Myths and Realities about Cross-Border Migration in Southern Africa*. Cape Town, SAMP. (Migration Policy Series No. 7.)

Morris, A. 1999. *Bleakness & Light: Inner-City Transition in Hillbrow, Johannesburg*. Johannesburg, Wits University Press.

Nyamnjoh, F. 2006. *Insiders & Outsiders: Citizenship and Xenophobia in Contemporary Southern Africa*. London, Zed Press.

Peberdy, S. 2001. Imagining immigration: inclusive identities and exclusive policies in post-1994 South Africa. *Africa Today*, Vol. 48, pp. 15–34.

—— 2007. *Monitoring Small-Scale Cross Border Trade in Southern Africa*. SAMP Report for the Regional Trade Facilitation Project. Johannesburg, SAMP.

Peberdy, S. and Crush, J. 2007. Histories, realities and negotiating free movement in southern Africa. A. Pécoud and P. de Guchteneire (eds), Migration Without Borders. Essays on the Free Movement of People. Oxford, UK/ New York/Paris, Berghahn Books/UNESCO., pp. 175–97.

Peberdy, S., Tjaalard, D. and Msibi, N. 2006. *Construction Workers and Vulnerability to HIV/AIDS in Johannesburg*. SAMP Report for the International Organization for Migration. Cape Town, SAMP.

Pécoud A. and de Guchteneire, P. 2006. Human Rights and the United Nations: an investigation into the obstacles to the UN Convention on Migrant Workers' Rights. *Windsor Yearbook of Access to Justice*, Vol. 24, No. 2, pp. 241–66.

Pendleton, W., Crush, J., Campbell, E., Green, T., Simelane, H., Tevera, D. and de Vletter, F. 2006. *Migration, Remittances and Development in Southern Africa*. Cape Town, SAMP. (Migration Policy Series No. 44.)

Piper, N. 2004. Rights of foreign workers and the politics of migration in South-East and East Asia. *International Migration*, Vol. 42, No. 5, pp. 71–97.

Reitzes, M. 2000. Mindsets and migrants: conceptions of state, sovereignty and citizenship in South Africa. J. Whitman (ed.), *Migrants, Citizens and the State in Southern Africa*. Basingstoke, UK, Macmillan, pp. 62–81.

Sichone, O. 2003. Together and apart: African refugees and immigrants in Cape Town. D. Chidester (ed.), *What Holds us Together: Social Cohesion in South Africa*. Pretoria, Human Sciences Research Council, pp. 120–40.

SAHRC. 1999. *Illegal? Report on the Arrest and Detention of Persons in Terms of the Aliens Control Act*. Johannesburg, SAHRC.

—— 2000. *Lindela at the Crossroads for Detention and Deportation: An Assessment of the Conditions of Detention*. Johannesburg, SAHRC.

—— 2003. *Final Report of the Inquiry into Human Rights Violations in Farming Communities*. Johannesburg, SAHRC.

2006. *Report on Open Hearings on Xenophobia and Problems Related to It.* Johannesburg, SAHRC/Parliamentary Portfolio Committee on Foreign Affairs.

Taran, P. 2001. Status and prospects for the UN Convention on Migrants' Rights. *European Journal of Migration and Law,* Vol. 2, No. 1, pp. 85–100.

Tevera, D. and Zinyama, L. 2002. *Zimbabweans Who Move: Perspectives on International Migration in Zimbabwe.* Cape Town, SAMP. (Migration Policy Series No. 25.)

Ulicki, T. and Crush, J. 2000a. Gender, farmwork and women's migration from Lesotho to the new South Africa. *Canadian Journal of African Studies,* Vol. 34, No. 1, pp. 64–79.

2000b. Poverty, gender and migrancy: Lesotho's migrant farmworkers in South Africa. *Development Southern Africa,* Vol. 24, No. 1, pp. 155–72.

Zlotnik, H. 2003. The global dimensions of female migration. *Migration Information Source,* March. Available at www.migrationinformation.org/Feature/display. cfm?ID=109 [last accessed 23 April 2009].

11

Policy on the ICRMW
in the United Kingdom

BERNARD RYAN

Introduction

This chapter reviews the policy debate in the United Kingdom concerning the ICRMW. The first section argues that non-ratification by the United Kingdom is a consequence both of the Convention's implications for immigration policy and of the United Kingdom's desire to avoid international commitments with respect to immigration policy. The second section shows the growth in support for the Convention among trade unions, NGOs, members of parliament and others. One implication is that the Convention has the potential to influence public policy in the United Kingdom, even in the probable absence of ratification.

The migration context in the United Kingdom helps to explain the interest in the Convention. The years after 2000 saw public policy favour inward labour migration at all skill levels[1] and a significant increase in the number of migrant workers actually admitted.[2] The Highly Skilled Migrants Programme, introduced in January 2002 to enable those with high earnings and qualifications to take employment or self-employment, led to over 6,000 successful applications by June 2004. The total number of work permits issued or extended rose from 54,000 in 1997 to a peak of 153,000 in 2003. Quotas for temporary, low-skilled schemes also increased – from roughly 10,000 places in agriculture from 1997 to 2000, to roughly 45,000 places in 2003, made up of 25,000 in agriculture, 10,000 in hospitality and 10,000 in food processing.

The most significant policy development since 2000 was the opening of the British labour market to nationals of the central and eastern European states that joined the EU on 1 May 2004 (the 'A8'). That policy

---

[1] See in particular these Home Office statements on migration policy: Home Office (2002, 2005a, 2005b).
[2] For statistical information up to mid 2005, see Ryan (2005a).

resulted in 427,000 successful applications for registration as workers by A8 nationals by the end of June 2006 (Home Office et al., 2006, Table 1, p. 6). As was intended, A8 migration led to a reduction in the number of non-EU workers being admitted. The number of work permits fell to 138,000 in 2004; the quota for agricultural workers fell to 16,250 in 2005 and 2006, the hospitality quota was ended in June 2005 and the food processing quota would be reduced to 3,500 per annum.[3] Taken as a whole, however, these falls in non-EU migrant workers amounted to around 45,000 per annum in total, far less than the roughly 200,000 A8 workers registering each year.

The growth in labour migration has been associated with a weak position in the labour market for some migrant workers (see reports from TUC, 2003; 2004a; 2004b; CAB, 2004). Their exposure to forms of exploitation is itself bound up with the general inadequacies of labour law and its enforcement, as well as the limits to collective organization in many sectors.[4] It is also linked to the probable growth in unauthorized employment in the United Kingdom (see Anderson and Rogaly, 2005; Black et al., 2005). The main concrete result of political concern at the treatment of migrant workers was the passage of the Gangmasters Licensing Act 2004 in the aftermath of the drowning of at least twenty-one unauthorized cockle pickers at Morecambe Bay in February 2004. The aim of that Act is to ensure compliance with employment and other laws through a licensing system for labour intermediaries involved in agriculture, the gathering of shellfish and related processing activities. For present purposes, what is significant is that the widespread political attention paid to the treatment of migrant workers led to a close interest in the ICRMW.

Non-ratification of the ICRMW

The first question to consider with respect to the Convention in the United Kingdom is the government's refusal to ratify. The government itself has focused on certain detailed provisions with which it has

---

[3] In relation to work permits, see Home Office (2005, Tables 1.4 and 2.2). In relation to agriculture, see House of Commons Select Committee on Home Affairs, Immigration Control (2005–2006, pp. 358–9). In relation to the sectors-based scheme, see Home Office (2006).

[4] For a review of the labour rights issues arising out of contemporary labour migration, see McKay and Rivers (2005).

difficulty. These points are summarized here before going on to consider other possible factors contributing to non-ratification.

Government arguments

Overview

The government's fullest public account of its reasons for non-ratification of the Convention was given in a December 2004 statement to the House of Commons Select Committee on International Development (2003–2004, paragraph 68). This statement is worth setting out in full:

> The rights of migrant workers are already protected in UK legislation and the UK's existing commitments under international law, including the Human Rights Act 1998. Incorporating the full terms of the UN Convention into UK law would mean fundamental changes to legislation, including the Immigration Rules, and would undermine the UK's system of frontier controls as well as having major cost implications for the government and local authorities. We believe that the UK has struck the right balance between the need for immigration control and controlled access to public funds and services on the one hand and the protection of the interests and rights of migrant workers and their families on the other.
>
> For example, at present a work permit holder seeking to enter the UK must not intend to take employment other than as specified on their work permit. If the individual remains in the UK in work permit employment (or in other employment or self-employment categories) for four years, they are eligible to apply for settlement. Those settled in the UK are entitled to claim benefits and access to social housing and public funds in the same way as a British citizen (although state school education and treatment under the NHS are not considered public funds for the purposes of the Immigration Rules and so migrant workers can access these before they are settled). If the UK were to ratify the Convention, we would not be able to restrict the employment that work permit holders can do to that specified on their permit and they would have access to public funds from the date that they entered the UK. Although the UK would retain the right to refuse entry, this would be particularly problematic after entry as the Convention requires that a migrant stays for the length of their latest permission to stay, regardless of whether they subsequently become unemployed. The UN Convention would therefore allow migrant workers to circumvent current immigration controls and remain in the UK even when they are not fulfilling the conditions on which they were granted entry to the UK (pursuing the specified employment).
>
> Giving all migrant workers access to public funds from the date of entry would therefore not only be costly, but also create an unnecessary 'pull factor'. This would be the case if all migrant-receiving countries were

to ratify the Convention, even if the available public funds were equivalent in all migrant-producing and migrant-receiving countries. As above,
the Convention would also allow migrant workers to remain in the UK
and claim benefits for the duration of their period of stay, even when they
are unemployed for some or all of this period. In itself, it would create an
unnecessary 'pull factor'.

In addition to general factors relating to immigration control, the
December 2004 statement identified three specific aspects of the
Convention with which the government had particular difficulty: freedom of employment, the right to remain after employment and equality
of treatment in social benefits. These are examined here in greater detail.

Freedom of employment

Article 52 of the ICRMW requires that migrant workers in a regular
situation have a free choice of employment after not more than two years,
subject to the possibility of national preference for up to five years in
total. In specifying a two-year qualifying period, article 52 is at odds with
immigration policy in the United Kingdom. The general position has
been that persons employed on work permits and successor schemes
have been permitted to work only for a designated employer. In order to
have a free choice of employment, it is necessary that they obtain
'indefinite leave to remain' (permanent residence). The qualifying period
for indefinite leave to remain for those on work permits is now five years,
having been increased from four years in April 2006.[5] It is true that, as a
matter of administrative practice, work permit employees can switch to a
new employer within the same occupation. However, that possibility
depends on the second employer's making an application for a work
permit, and does not cover changes of occupation.

Right to remain after employment

A second difference between the Convention and UK policy identified in
the December 2004 statement concerns the legal right to remain in the
territory, under an immigration permission, after having ceased employment. This factor was elaborated at greater length in a written parliamentary answer given by the Immigration Minister Des Browne on 20
January 2005:

> Most overseas nationals coming to the UK to take employment require a
> work permit. The UK employer applies for a work permit to enable them

---

[5] Immigration Rules, paragraph 134.

to fill a specific vacancy in the UK, following which the worker applies for
leave to enter or remain in the UK. If the migrant worker leaves this
employment they are expected to leave the UK or to apply for a work
permit for their new employment. The Convention, however, would
allow them to remain in the UK for the duration of their leave, whether
or not they were still employed. We consider that unemployed migrants
being able to remain in the UK and claim benefits in these circumstances
would act as an unnecessary 'pull factor' and undermine current immigration controls.[6]

The provision of the Convention that is at issue here is article 51,
according to which:

> Migrant workers who in the state of employment are not permitted freely
> to choose their remunerated activity shall neither be regarded as in an
> irregular situation nor shall they lose their authorization of residence by
> the mere fact of the termination of their remunerated activity prior to the
> expiration of their work permit, *except where the authorization of resi-*
> *dence is expressly dependent upon the specific remunerated activity for*
> *which they were admitted.* Such migrant workers shall have the right to
> seek alternative employment, participation in public work schemes and
> retraining during the remaining period of their authorization to work,
> *subject to such conditions and limitations as are specified in the author-*
> *ization to work* (emphasis added).

This article does, however, seem to go as far as the government believes
in constraining participating states. The approach of the British authorities
is to confer an immigration permission linked to the expected period of
employment, and then, if the work permit employment comes to an end,
to rely on a general power in the Immigration Rules to withdraw immigration permission.[7] While that approach does appear to be ruled out by
Article 51, the italicized passages allow the state to tie an immigration
authorization to continued employment with a particular employer. For
this reason, it is inaccurate to say that the Convention simply permits
migrant workers to stay after their employment comes to an end.

Equality of treatment in social benefits

The third consideration referred to in the December 2004 statement was
migrant workers' access to social benefits. Within the Convention, equality

---

[6] House of Commons Debates, 20 January 2005, column 1088W.
[7] Immigration Rules, paragraph 323: 'A person's leave to enter or remain may be curtailed:…
(ii) if he ceases to meet the requirements of the Rules under which his leave to enter or remain
was granted.'

of treatment in relation to social benefits is set out in particular in article 43. It requires that migrant workers in a regular situation have equality of treatment as regards, *inter alia*, education for their children, housing, social and health services. In addition, article 54 of the Convention provides for equality of treatment, *inter alia*, as regards 'unemployment benefits'.

In the United Kingdom, there are limits to migrant workers' entitlements to social benefits. Migrant workers in a regular situation are entitled, on an equal basis with other residents, to healthcare and to education for themselves and their children. They are also entitled to benefits that derive from their contributions to the national insurance system, including contribution-based jobseekers' allowance (paid for up to six months' unemployment) and the state pension. Regular migrant workers from outside the European Economic Area (EEA) are, however, classed as 'persons subject to immigration control' who are not entitled to non-contributory benefits such as housing benefit, council tax benefit and job-seekers allowance (paid to those who are unemployed).[8] Similarly, A8 workers are ineligible for these benefits when they are out of work.[9] Compliance with articles 43 and 54 would rule out these exclusions of migrant workers from non-contributory benefits.

Since December 2004, the 'public benefits' argument has been the most common specific argument for non-ratification offered by ministers. This can be seen, for example, in the July 2005 submission from the Home Office to the House of Lords Select Committee on the European Union, as part of the latter's inquiry into economic migration:

> The Convention would give migrants the same access to public funds and services as British citizens, regardless of their length of stay in the UK. For example, they would be entitled to equal access to housing, education and social services with UK nationals raising major cost implications.[10]

The same argument was advanced by Baroness Scotland in the debate in the House of Lords that followed the publication of the Select Committee's report.[11]

---

[8] Immigration and Asylum Act 1999, section 115.

[9] This is the effect of changes that came into force on 1 May 2004: see regulation 4(2) of the Accession (Immigration and Worker Registration) Regulations 2004 (SI 2004 No. 1219) and the Social Security (Habitual Residence) Amendment Regulations 2004 (SI 2004 No. 1232).

[10] Supplementary Memorandum from the Home Office, 27 July 2005, published in Select Committee on the European Union, *Economic Migration to the EU*, 2005–06 House of Lords Papers 58, p. 74.

[11] Baroness Scotland's remarks are in House of Lords Debates, 11 May 2006, column 1176.

Other policy considerations

The three policy issues referred to above appear to be the only specific reasons offered by the government for not ratifying the ICRMW. However, at least three other possible conflicts between British law and policy and the Convention can be identified. The first two concern the treatment of irregular workers, while the third concerns the admission of family members of temporary labour migrants.

Irregular workers' employment contracts

Under article 25 of the Convention, *all* migrant workers are to enjoy equal treatment as regards remuneration and other conditions of employment. Article 25(3) states:

> States Parties shall take all appropriate measures to ensure that migrant workers are not deprived of any rights derived from this principle by reason of any irregularity in their stay or employment. In particular, employers shall not be relieved of any legal or contractual obligations, nor shall their obligations be limited in any manner by reason of such irregularity.

This approach is at odds with British law relating to irregular work by migrants. Where a worker knowingly enters an employment relationship, while lacking permission to do so under immigration law, the employment contract is classed as 'illegal'. The result is that the worker can enforce neither the contract itself nor statutory rights relating to it.[12] Ratification of the Convention would require a revision of British law on this point.

Regularization

A second potential difficulty with respect to irregular workers concerns policy on regularization. The Convention's provisions in this area are admittedly ambiguous. On the one hand, Article 35 expressly rules out a *right* to be regularized: 'Nothing in [Part III] of the Convention shall be interpreted as implying the regularization of the situation of migrant workers or members of their families who are non-documented or in an irregular situation or any right to such regularization of their situation.' On the other hand, article 69(1) of the Convention – which is in Part VI – points in a

---

[12] The most recent authority on this question is the decision of the Court of Appeal in July 2004 in *Vakante* v. *Addey and Stanhope School* [2005] ICR 231. For a discussion of the doctrine of illegality in relation to irregular migrant workers, see Ryan (2005*b*, pp. 43–8).

different direction when it provides that 'States Parties shall, when there are migrant workers and members of their families within their territory in an irregular situation, take appropriate measures to ensure that such a situation does not persist.' In cases where unauthorized workers are not to be expelled, article 69(1) arguably requires a state to regularize their situation. That impression is reinforced by article 69(2), which sets out a list of factors to be taken into account 'whenever States Parties...consider the possibility of regularizing the situation of such persons', including 'the circumstances of their entry', 'the duration of their stay' and their 'family situation'.

To the extent that the Convention does place obligations on states with respect to regularization, it may conflict with current UK policy. In recent times, the United Kingdom has made limited standing provision for regularization in two ways. The first is the provision in the Immigration Rules for an individual to obtain indefinite leave to remain after fourteen years' residence, irrespective of legality.[13] The second follows from a Home Office concession that, in cases where a child has been living continuously in the United Kingdom for more than seven years, they and their families are not normally subject to immigration enforcement.[14] In practice, such families can also typically obtain indefinite leave to remain (JCWI, 2006, p. 42). Beyond these policies, there is no recent practice in the United Kingdom of systematic regularization of persons lacking authorization.[15]

Admission of family members of migrant workers

A final aspect of British policy that may be highlighted concerns the admission of family members of temporary migrant workers. The general principle in article 44(2) of the Convention is that contracting states 'shall take measures that they deem appropriate...to facilitate the reunification of migrant workers' with spouses (or equivalents) and minor dependent unmarried children. This article would also present difficulties, as the United Kingdom does not admit the immediate family members of workers on temporary schemes. One such arrangement is for seasonal agricultural workers, who may be employed for up to six months in one year. Article 59 of the Convention confers the rights of regular migrant workers on seasonal workers to the extent that these rights 'are compatible with

---

[13] Immigration Rules, paragraph 276B.
[14] See the statement by Immigration Minister, Mike O'Brien, House of Commons Debates, written answers, 24 February 1999.
[15] For a review of British practice, see Levinson (2005).

their status in that state as seasonal workers, taking into account the fact that they are present in that state for only part of the year'. It is at least arguable that provision for family rights is 'compatible' with the status of seasonal agricultural workers. The other such scheme has been the 'sectors-based scheme' in hospitality and food processing, under which workers are admitted for up to twelve months. While – as we saw above – this scheme was scaled down in 2006, it is significant that the denial of family rights to workers under it is inconsistent with the Convention. In particular, the special provision for 'specified-employment workers' allowed by article 62 does not extend to article 44. If the United Kingdom wished to comply with the Convention, it would have to alter its approach to family reunification for any successor to the sectors-based scheme.

Avoidance of multilateral commitments

It can be seen, therefore, that the ICRMW, if ratified, would have significant implications for British policy on labour migration and migrant workers. While these policy implications are probably sufficient on their own to explain non-ratification, that decision is also consistent with the United Kingdom's general unwillingness to undertake international commitments concerning immigration policy. In other words, even if UK immigration policy was broadly consistent with the Convention, the government would probably still wish to retain flexibility as regards the treatment of immigrants.

Some evidence for this conclusion is to be found in the government's public statements concerning the Convention. To take an example, in its November 2003 written evidence to the House of Commons Select Committee on International Development inquiry on migration and development, the Department for International Development (DFID, 2003–2004, paragraph 38) gave this explanation of the government's reasons for non-ratification:

> The government has no plans to ratify this Convention. The scope is wider than the UK's existing immigration laws. No EU Member States are signatories; and most of the twelve current signatories are countries of origin of migrant workers. The government considers that it has already struck the right balance between the need for immigration control and the protection of the interests and rights of migrant workers.

This passage shows both that the government does not wish to give up its freedom of action in the field of immigration control and that it will be especially reluctant to do so in the absence of support for the Convention from other destination states.

The United Kingdom's reluctance to consider ratification of the ICRMW is consistent with its approach to other instruments. At the international level, the United Kingdom ratified a number of treaties concerning migrant workers in the post-war period: 1949 ILO Convention No. 97 (Convention concerning Migration for Employment) (ratified 22 January 1951), the 1953 European Convention on Medical and Social Assistance (ratified 7 September 1954), the 1955 European Convention on Establishment (ratified 14 October 1969) and the 1961 European Social Charter (ratified 11 July 1962). By contrast, the United Kingdom did not ratify either of the significant instruments on migrant workers adopted in the 1970s: 1975 ILO Convention No. 143 (Convention concerning Migrant Workers (Supplementary Provisions)) and the 1977 ECMW. More recently, the United Kingdom has refused to participate in the Long-Term Residence Directive and the Family Reunification Directive, two EU measures that give non-EU nationals rights of admission and equal treatment.[16] UK reluctance to agree to the Convention is therefore part of a wider policy of refusal to agree to multilateral commitments governing migration policy.

Growing support for the Convention

The opposition of the UK Government to ratification of the ICRMW is not the end of the story, however, given that recent years have seen growing support for the Convention among political actors, both within and outside parliament. There have been frequent calls for ratification, as well as extensive reliance on the text in debates over the detail of public policy. The ICRMW has in fact come to be treated as *the* authoritative statement of international standards concerning migrant workers. Even in the absence of a ratification decision, it is now treated as highly relevant to policy debates concerning immigration in the United Kingdom.

Civil society

The trade unions were probably the first organizations in the United Kingdom to take up the question of ratification of the ICRMW. As early as September 1995, the TUC passed a resolution supporting ratification

---

[16] For a review of the UK approach to EU immigration and asylum policy, see Ryan (2004).

by the EU.[17] The Convention has been more actively promoted since a conference entitled Migrant Workers: Who Benefits?, hosted by the UK office of the United Nations Association (UNA-UK) in London on 10 December 2002.[18] The conference was concerned with various aspects of the treatment of migrant workers, and included a keynote speech by Patrick Taran of the ILO that focused on the Convention. The December 2002 conference led to the formation of a coalition for ratification of the Convention in the United Kingdom, and the ratification coalition subsequently met at UNA-UK offices during 2003 and 2004. The organizations that made up the coalition included the following NGOs: Anti-Slavery International, the Joint Council for the Welfare of Immigrants (JCWI), Kalaayan (an organization representing domestic workers) and Oxfam Great Britain. It also included the TUC, the Transport and General Workers Union (TGWU, the largest private-sector trade union) and UNISON (the largest public-sector trade union).

The creation of the ratification coalition led to greater attention being paid to the ICRMW from 2003 onwards. To mark the entry into force of the Convention in July 2003, the TUC and JCWI organized a joint conference at the TUC building in London, entitled Migrant Workers' Rights – Could We Do More in Britain? The speakers included Frances O'Grady, Deputy General Secretary of the TUC, Patrick Taran of the ILO and Felicity Lawrence, a *Guardian* journalist who has written on migrant labour in agriculture (Lawrence, 2004, Chapter 2). This was also the occasion of the launch of the TUC report *Overworked, Underpaid and Over Here: Migrant Workers in Britain*. Members of the coalition then contributed to a session of the European Social Forum in London in October 2004, with the title Organising for Migrant Workers' Rights – Bringing Trade Unions and Community Organisations Together. Speakers at the session included representatives of Anti-Slavery International, the JCWI and the General Marine and Boilermakers Union (the second-largest private-sector union).

The activities of the ratification coalition appear to have ceased by 2005. This was partly for institutional reasons, as the employee of UNA-UK who had organized the meetings had ceased to work for that organization. More basically, as we shall see, the initial task of the coalition – that of raising awareness of the Convention – had by then been achieved.

---

[17] Information provided to the author by the TUC International Office.

[18] Details of the conference can be found on the United Nations Association website (www.una-uk.org/archive/hr/migrantrights.html [last accessed 23 April 2009]).

Political parties

One sign of the increased recognition given to the ICRMW after 2002 is that ratification has become the policy of two national political parties in the United Kingdom. The more important case is that of the Liberal Democrats, as it is the country's third-largest political party, having obtained 22% of the votes and sixty-two of 645 seats in the 2005 general election for the House of Commons, as well as holding twelve of the United Kingdom's seventy-eight seats in the European Parliament. At their September 2004 annual conference, the Liberal Democrats adopted a resolution on asylum and immigration, which included a commitment to 'The signing and ratification by the UK Government of the UN Convention on the Protection of the Rights of All Migrant Workers and their Families (1990)'. That policy was reaffirmed in the policy documents presented to the party's 2006 annual conference (Liberal Democrats, 2006, p. 14).

The other national political party to support ratification is the Green Party. Although not represented in the House of Commons, the party has two seats in the European Parliament. A commitment to ratify the Convention was included in its 2005 general election manifesto (Green Party, 2005, p. 31).

Parliament

Since 2002, the ICRMW has also come to attract considerable interest and support in parliament. An initial stage in that process was a series of written questions in the House of Commons asking the government about its policy concerning the Convention. Questions of this kind have been asked on at least the following occasions: by Jenny Tonge MP (Liberal Democrat), 9 January 2002; by Vernon Coaker MP (Labour), 4 February 2002; by Lynne Jones MP (Labour), 16 December 2003; and by Michael Wills MP (Labour), 20 and 24 January 2005.[19]

Questions about government policy on ratification have also been raised in two Select Committee reports. As shown above, the government was specifically requested to explain its policy on the Convention in the June 2004 House of Commons Select Committee on International Development report on *Migration and Development*. More recently,

---

[19] House of Commons Debates, 9 January 2002, column 902W; 4 February 2002, column 679W; 16 December 2003, column 865W; 20 January 2005, column 1088W; 24 January 2005, column 134W.

the House of Lords Select Committee on the European Union called attention to the Convention in its report on *Economic Migration to the EU*, published in November 2005.[20] While accepting that the Convention would require the extension of social rights to certain migrant workers, the Select Committee concluded that a full review of ratification should be undertaken. In its words:

> We accept that there are arguments both for and against acceding to the Convention, but it is unsatisfactory that it should simply be left on the shelf. We recommend that the government should commission research into the likely costs and consequences of acceding to it and seek to develop a political consensus towards it, both within the UK and across the EU.[21]

Others in parliament have gone further and expressly called for ratification. In 2004, Tom Brake MP (Liberal Democrat) twice set down a motion in the House of Commons with that objective:

> That this House notes the growing consensus in favour of clearly defined legal rights for migrant workers which is evident in reports and opinions published by bodies as diverse as the World Bank, the United Nations, the European Commission, the Select Committee on International Development and the Trades Union Congress; and calls on the government to provide a robust legal framework for the establishment of rights for migrant workers by ratifying the UN Convention on the Protection of the Rights of All Migrant Workers and their Families (1990).

This motion was first proposed on 14 October 2004 and then again on 20 December 2004 (a different parliamentary session), and in each case the motion attracted extensive support from across political parties.[22] The 14 October 2004 motion attracted forty-six signatures, made up of twenty three Labour MPs, nineteen Liberal Democrat, two Plaid Cymru (Welsh nationalists), one Ulster Unionist (historically aligned with the Conservative Party) and one from the Respect Party. The 20 December 2004 motion was then supported by a total of fifty-seven MPs: thirty-three Labour, twenty-one Liberal Democrat, one Conservative, one Plaid Cymru and one Scottish Nationalist.

There have also been calls for ratification of the Convention in parliamentary debates on specific subjects. The first such reference appears to have been by Lord Hylton (non-party) in the House of Lords on

---

[20] 2005–06 House of Lords Papers 58.   [21] Ibid., para. 97.

[22] Early Day Motion 1741 of the 2003–2004 session and Early Day Motion 430 of the 2004–2005 session.

13 March 2002, when he suggested that ratification could assist in the fight against human trafficking.[23] Similarly, there have been references to the Convention as part of the struggle against contemporary forms of slavery – in the House of Commons on 14 October 2004 by Tom Brake MP (Liberal Democrat) and Oona King MP (Labour), and in the House of Lords on 7 July 2005 by the Earl of Sandwich (non-party).[24] These references to the Convention essentially concern its article 11, which provides that 'no migrant worker or member of his or her family shall be held in slavery or servitude' and that 'no migrant worker or member of his or her family shall be required to perform forced or compulsory labour'.

The Convention has also been relied on in relation to remittances. This concerns article 47 of the Convention, which provides that '[m]igrant workers shall have the right to transfer their earnings and savings, in particular those funds necessary for the support of their families, from the state of employment to their state of origin or any other state', and that contracting states 'shall take appropriate measures to facilitate such transfers'. It was presumably that provision which led David Taylor MP (Labour) to argue in the Commons on 10 November 2004 that the Convention 'would help secure…hugely important remittances to home countries'.[25]

A third aspect of the Convention that has been referred to is the protection it requires for identity or immigration documents. Article 21 of the Convention requires that it be 'unlawful for anyone, other than a public official duly authorized by law, to confiscate, destroy or attempt to destroy identity documents, documents authorizing entry to or stay, residence or establishment in the national territory or work permits'. Chris McCafferty MP (Labour) referred to article 21 in the House of Commons on 9 March 2005, in support of his Bill to make it an offence to control or destroy another person's identification or immigration documents.[26] This is a point on which there has subsequently been government legislation: section 25 of the Identity Cards Act 2006 now includes the offence of possession or control of another person's identity or immigration document 'without reasonable excuse'. Significantly, part

---

[23] House of Lords Debates, 13 March 2002, column 893.
[24] House of Commons Debates, 14 October 2004, columns 157WH and 167WH; House of Lords Debates, 7 July 2005, column 745.
[25] House of Commons Debates, 10 November 2004, column 827.
[26] House of Commons Debates, 9 March 2005, column 1521. See the Control of Identification Documents (Offences) Bill, 2004–05 House of Commons Bills 82.

of the government's justification for this offence was that it would 'serve as a deterrent against…those who traffic illegal or sex workers'.[27]

Finally, the Convention has been referred to in two reports of the House of Commons Select Committee on Foreign Affairs. In its report on *Foreign Policy Aspects of the War against Terrorism*, published on 2 July 2006, the Committee highlighted HRW's criticism that the United Arab Emirates had not ratified the Convention.[28] In addition, the Committee's report on *East Asia*, published on 13 August 2006, directly referred to China's non-ratification of the Convention in its review of the position as regards human rights protection in that country.[29] While these references to the Convention do not concern UK ratification, they show a willingness to use it as a standard for evaluation of other states' respect for human rights. This use of the Convention may have the effect of strengthening the case for ratification by the United Kingdom, or at least for its compliance with its principles.

Conclusion: potential of the Convention in the United Kingdom

One implication of this chapter is that there is little immediate prospect that the United Kingdom will ratify the ICRMW. To do so would have a number of important implications for immigration policy, and would be at odds with the general British desire to avoid multilateral commitments in relation to immigration. At the same time, there is a high degree of support for the Convention among policy actors, including trade unions, NGOs, political parties and members of both Houses of Parliament. This growing support can be attributed to the greater interest consequent upon the entry into force of the Convention on 1 July 2003, and also to the attention paid within the political sphere to the treatment of migrant workers.

The extensive support for the Convention implies that it can have a role in political debate in the United Kingdom, even in the absence of ratification. As we have seen, it is already being cited in a range of specific contexts. It also formed at least part of the background to the 2006 legislation protecting identity and immigration documents. The major points of divergence between current UK policy and the ICRMW principles – the right to change employer, equal treatment to

---

[27] Home Office Minister Andy Burnham, House of Commons Debates, Standing Committee D, 19 July 2005, column 399.

[28] 2005–06 House of Commons Papers 573, paragraph 176.

[29] 2005–06 House of Commons Papers 860–1, paragraph 319.

non-contributory benefits, the legal position of irregular workers, regularization and family rights for temporary workers – are other areas where the Convention might contribute to pressure for change. The general point is that it is accepted as the authoritative statement of the minimum international standards with respect to migrant workers. Political actors can therefore be expected to continue to rely on it in making the case for improvements in their treatment.

References

Anderson, B. and Rogaly, B. 2005. *Forced Labour in the United Kingdom*. Oxford, UK/London, Centre on Migration Policy and Society (COMPAS)/TUC.

Black, R., Collyer, M., Skelton, R. and Waddington, C. 2005. *A Survey of the Illegally Resident Population in Detention in the UK*. (Home Office Online Report 20/05.) Available at www.homeoffice.gov.uk/rds/pdfs05/rdsdr2005. pdf [last accessed 12 May 2005].

CAB. 2004. *Nowhere to Turn: CAB Evidence on the Exploitation of Migrant Workers*. London, Citizens Advice Bureau. Available at www.citizensadvice.org.uk [last accessed 23 April 2009].

DFID. 2003–2004. *House of Commons Select Committee on International Development. Migration and Development: How to Make Migration Work for Poverty Reduction*. London, DFID. (HC Papers 79-II.)

Green Party. 2005. *Real Progress: Real Choice for Real Change*. Manifesto. Available at www.greenparty.org.uk [last accessed 23 April 2009].

Home Office. 2002. *Secure Borders, Safe Haven: Integration with Diversity in Modern Britain*. London, UK Government.

　　2005a. *Controlling Our Borders: Making Migration Work for Britain*. London, UK Government.

　　2005b. *Selective Admission: Making Migration Work for Britain*. London, UK Government.

　　2006. *Working in the UK, Outcome of Review of Sectors Based Scheme*. London, UK Government.

Home Office/Department for Work and Pensions/HM Revenue & Customs/ Department for Communities and Local Government. 2006. *Accession Monitoring Report May 2004–June 2006*. London, UK Government.

House of Commons Select Committee on Home Affairs. 2005–2006. Sixth supplementary memorandum submitted by the Immigration and Nationality Directorate, House of Commons Select Committee on Home Affairs, Immigration Control, 2005–06, pp. 358–59. (HC Papers 775-III.)

House of Commons Select Committee on International Development. 2003–2004. *Migration and Development: How to Make Migration Work for Poverty Reduction*, Vol. I. (HC Papers 79.)

JCWI. 2006. *Recognising Rights, Recognising Political Realities: The Case for Regularising Irregular Migrants*. London, JCWI.

Lawrence, F. 2004. *Not On the Label: What Really Goes Into the Food on Your Plate*. London, Penguin.

Levinson, A. 2005. *Regularisation Programmes in the United Kingdom*. Oxford, UK, University of Oxford/COMPAS.

Liberal Democrats. 2006. *Rights and Responsibilities at Work: Employment and Trade Unions Policy Paper*. Paper for the Federal Conference, March 2005.

McKay, S. and Rivers, A. 2005. Migrant workers and employment law. Ryan (ed.), op. cit., pp. 79–104.

Ryan, B. 2004. *The United Kingdom*. K. Hailbronner and I. Higgins (eds), *Migration and Asylum Law and Policy in the European Union*. Cambridge, UK, Cambridge University Press, pp. 403–26.

   (ed.). 2005a. *Labour Migration and Employment Rights*. Liverpool, UK, Institute of Employment Rights.

   2005b. Legal migration: the right to work in Britain. Ryan (ed.), op. cit., pp. 43–8.

TUC. 2003. *Overworked, Underpaid and Over Here: Migrant Workers in Britain*. London, TUC.

   2004a. *Gone West: Ukrainians at Work in the UK*. London, TUC.

   2004b. *Propping up Rural and Small Town Britain: Migrant Workers from the New Europe*. London, TUC.

12

The French political refusal on Europe's behalf

HÉLÈNE OGER

Introduction

The ICRMW forms part of the charter of human rights for migrants, together with the two ILO conventions on migrant workers. ILO Convention No. 97 covers the whole labour migration continuum from entry to return: conditions of recruitment and equal treatment regarding working conditions, trade unions, collective bargaining, accommodation, social security, employment taxes and legal proceedings. ILO Convention No. 143 is broader, as it deals with irregular migration and with the obligation of states to respect the fundamental rights of migrant workers. The ICRMW has a wider mandate:[1] it clarifies that basic economic, social and cultural rights belong to all migrants (regular and irregular, workers and their family members), although some migrants have more limited rights. The ICRMW reaffirms human rights guaranteed by other general international instruments of human rights but applies them specifically to migrants. Of these three instruments, France has only ratified ILO Convention No. 97.

The ICRMW has two main aims: to eradicate clandestine movements by promoting international cooperation and to ensure equal treatment for migrant workers and their families. It codifies a wide range of rights applicable universally and contains a framework for their effective enjoyment, including the prohibition of any renunciation of these rights. Its approach is based on equal treatment rather than minimal standards. In a regular or irregular situation, all migrants are entitled to a minimum degree of protection, although regular migrants have broader rights. The Convention thus relies on the fundamental notion that all migrants

---

[1] It is also wider than the scope of the ECMW, since the latter is limited to workers who are not seasonal, not frontier workers, not posted workers and not undocumented migrants (article 1). In addition, the ECMW is limited to nationals of the Contracting Parties. Thus, it does not apply to all legally resident migrants, but merely to migrants of the nationals of the ten Parties.

should have access to a minimum degree of protection, in an acknowledgement of their vulnerable status.

As Patrick Taran stated at the UN CHR:

> The ILO conventions and the 1990 Convention represent explicit and comprehensive symbols of a rights-based approach to regulating/managing international migration. These instruments have not yet gathered sufficiently broad ratification. Up to now not enough [advocacy activities have] been generated to facilitate progress in this respect. Migrant and immigrant workers simply do not have large and powerful economic interests willing to advocate in their defense. On the other hand, influential voices and interests are renewing advocacy for restricting migration, and in particular for limiting recognition of human and labor rights of migrants. After all, migrants continue to be seen as a convenient, defenseless and visible scapegoat on which to blame the economic and social costs of globalization.[2]

Additionally, the ICRMW establishes an international framework for cooperation between countries of origin and host countries and encourages complementary regional agreements. It provides for effective implementation of the Convention through the creation of a committee competent to carry out regular monitoring, in cooperation with the ILO, and to deal with state and individual complaints. Nevertheless, sovereignty is maintained, as states retain monopoly on access to their territory and their labour market.

The Convention suffers from several obstacles (see Chapter 1). In France, there has long been a striking lack of awareness, which has, however, decreased significantly since 2004, particularly following the work of NGOs: a campaign was launched in March 2004 by Agir Ici, and a collective for ratification was constituted in October 2004 in order to raise awareness surrounding the compelling importance of ratification. But lack of awareness still continues to prevent mass popular mobilization and involvement of citizens, social actors and politicians.

The Foreign Affairs Minister launched a consultation process for ratification in August 2005,[3] but ministerial answers stated in November 2005 that France cannot independently ratify because of

---

[2] 61st Session of the UN Commission on Human Rights, ILO statement, 'Vulnerable groups: migrant workers', 14 April 2005, p. 2 (see also Chapter 6).

[3] Answer to the CNCDH Advisory Opinion, June 2005, by Philippe Douste-Blazy, Minister for Foreign Affairs, 30 August 2005 (www.commission-droits-homme.fr/binInfoGeneFr/affichageDepeche.cfm?iIdDepeche=159 [last accessed 23 April 2009]).

the transfer of competences to Europe.[4] There are also some legal and financial obstacles in France regarding remittances, cultural rights and family reunification. However, the imprecise rights provided for by the Convention leave states with a wide margin of manoeuvre. Thus, with minor reservations, ratification would be legally compatible. Therefore, the real obstacle in France is the lack of political will in the European framework, and administrative obstacles largely derive from political guidelines. Flexibility, selection and instrumentalization have become a priority for most European governments. A horizontal rights-based approach would imply a risk of undesired immigrants.

Timid but growing awareness of the ICRMW

The first initiative goes back to 29 October 2003 when the Comité Economique et Social (CES)[5] recommended ratifying the ICRMW.[6] According to its opinion on future migrations adopted by eighty-three votes to seventy-eight, France should ratify the Convention as part of an emerging international protection system in order to achieve a successful integration and equal treatment in employment, housing, education, culture, citizenship and social protection. However, this opinion is quasi-unknown and non-binding. A day before the adoption of the opinion during the parliamentary debate for the 2003 Immigration Act, André Gérin, an MP from the Communist Party, recommended ratification of the Convention to ensure a balanced

---

[4] See the two ministerial answers from 1 November and 10 November 2005 to parliamentary questions: 'Pour la mise en œuvre d'une politique commune prévue par le traité, chaque fois que la Communauté a pris des dispositions instaurant, sous quelque forme que ce soit, des règles communes, les États membres ne sont plus en droit, qu'ils agissent individuellement ou même collectivement, de contracter avec des États tiers des obligations affectant ces règles.' ['As far as the implementation of a common policy foreseen by the Treaty is concerned, every time that the Community has taken dispositions that, under whatever form, establish common rules, Member States do not have the right, whether they act individually or even collectively, to engage with third parties in obligations that affect these rules.']

[5] The French Economic and Social Committee is equivalent to the European Economic and Social Committee at the domestic level. It represents professional organizations and delivers opinions, whether compulsory or optional, in the frame of the legislative process on relevant subjects. It may also give opinions where requested by the government.

[6] CES, Opinion les défis de l'immigration future, 29 October 2003, p. 1–30 (www.ces.fr/rapport/doclon/03102922.pdf [last accessed 23 April 2009]).

migration policy,[7] but the then right-wing government remained silent.

It is only from the NGOs campaign onwards (March 2004) that the government has slowly recognized the existence of the Convention. However, it remains largely unknown in France: public opinion is generally ignorant of its existence, and awareness has mostly been rising among NGO members and sympathizers. In other words, the circle of initiates is widening but remains relatively restricted. As a result of the strong NGO campaigning in 2004, the government became more aware and launched a governmental consultation process for ratification.

Late but paramount work of French NGOs

Although the Convention was well known to specialized NGOs in 1990, their commitment quickly evaporated. As a result, it became an almost unknown instrument, even though the precariousness of migrants' rights was growing. With the establishment of December 18 (1998) and of a European network (2002), the movement for global and European ratifications started, especially since the creation in 2000 of International Migrants Day on 18 December. Only in 2004 did interest in the Convention and commitment to it reappear in France.

A major campaign initiated by Agir Ici took place between March and September 2004. The leading co-organizers of the project were three well-known NGOs: Groupe d'information et de soutien des immigrés (GISTI), Service Oecumenique d'Entraide (CIMADE) and the Ligue des droits de l'Homme (LDH, Human Rights League). GISTI, a support and interest group for migrant workers, is the most important association protecting the rights and interests of migrants, and in particular migrant workers and their families. It specializes in migrants' rights and immigration law, especially legal counselling, and legal action, defence, publications and training. CIMADE (an ecumenical mutual-aid service) is a Protestant association supporting international solidarity, legal defence of foreigners, migrants' rights and communication. Finally, the LDH supports legal actions, press releases, information campaigns and individual cases. Apart from the leading NGOs, other bodies have been involved, whether trade unions, lobbies, associations for solidarity and

---

[7] Parliamentary Debates, 28 October 2003, during the general discussion on the Immigration Bill, *Journal Officiel Assemblée Nationale*, 29 October 2003.

development, and associations for human rights for the protection of migrants' rights or for women.[8]

Agir Ici, an NGO that fights for a fairer world, has launched over sixty campaigns on different topics. Since October 2006, it has been the official French affiliate of Oxfam International.[9] Its 2004 campaign in favour of migrants' rights stated that ratification is an emergency in the light of European restrictive policies and the threats migrants are exposed to; the importance of irregular migrants and the violation of their fundamental rights; and the worsening of the rule of law, in the name of the fundamental freedom of movement. It sees the ICRMW as providing a rights-based and balanced approach between North and South interests, which further recognizes the positive role of migrants in host societies. The campaign aims at recognizing the role of migrants in development and at ensuring respect for their rights. It calls on the Ministry of Foreign Affairs to engage in the process of ratification and to stop conditioning cooperation with third countries to migratory clauses.[10] It also calls on

---

[8] The full list of signatories is: ACORT (Assemblée citoyenne des originaires de Turquie); Agir ensemble pour les droits de l'Homme; Aides; Amnesty international – section française; ANAFE (Association nationale d'assistance aux frontières pour les étrangers); ATMF (Association des travailleurs maghrebins de France); ATTAC (Association pour la taxation des transactions financières pour l'aide aux citoyens); CADTM-France (Comité pour l'annulation de la dette du tiers-monde); CARI (Centre d'actions et de réalisations internationales); CATRED (Collectif des accidentés du travail, handicapés et retraités pour l'égalité des droits); CCFD (Comité catholique contre la faim et pour le développement); CEDETIM (Centre d'études et d'initiatives de solidarité internationale); CEDIDELP (Centre de documentation internationale pour le développement, les libertés et la paix); CFSI (Comité français pour la solidarité internationale); COMEDE (Comité médical pour les exilés); Confédération paysanne; CRID (Centre de recherche et d'information pour le développement); FASTI (Fédération des associations de solidarité avec les travailleurs immigrés); Fédération SUD education; Fédération SUD rail; FGTE-CFDT (Fédération des transports et de l'équipement); France Libertés; Franciscain international; FTCR (Fédération des Tunisiens pour une citoyenneté des deux rives); GRDR (Groupe de recherche et de réalisations pour le développement rural); GREF (Groupement des retraités éducateurs sans frontiéres); IDD (Immigration développement démocratie); Ingénieurs sans frontiers; Ligue internationale des femmes pour la paix et la liberté; Médecins du Monde; Peuples solidaires; RITIMO (Réseau des centres de documentation pour le développement et la solidarité internationale); Service civil international – branche française; Service national de la Pastorale des migrants; Survie; Terre des Hommes – France; and Union syndicale G10 solidaires.

[9] Now called Oxfam France – Agir Ici (www.oxfamfrance.org/index.php [last accessed 23 April 2003]).

[10] These are clauses imposed by the EU in association agreements with countries of origin and countries of transit regarding migrants' readmission in order to limit migration to the EU.

the European Commissar for Justice and Home Affairs to urge European states to ratify the Convention and end migratory clauses. Seventy-thousand documents have been distributed; 21,200 citizens have participated; four meetings have been held with the French Government; one press release has been published, along with twelve newspaper articles; and a week of mobilization and forty regional events have been organized.

The campaign mainly targeted the government rather than general French public opinion. As a result, most people in France are not aware of the ICRMW, including politicians and people working in the administration; even those active in administrations dealing specifically with migrant workers, such as social security, are largely unaware of it. This absence of mass mobilization prevents more pressure being brought to bear on the government.

From October 2004 onwards, to continue mobilization around the Convention, a collective for ratification was set up under the supervision of the Association des Travailleurs Maghrebins de France (ATMF, an association of workers from Maghreb countries in France) and GISTI, regrouping French NGOs and campaigns at national level in different areas such as education, environment or migration,[11] while the ATMF, created in 1982 following the extension of the freedom of assembly to non-citizens in 1981,[12] organizes individual support, language courses, training, campaigns and legal aid. The campaign was entitled *Demain le monde – les migrations pour vivre ensemble* (Tomorrow the world – migrations to live together in harmony). It aims at continuing and widening the diffusion of information and the call for ratification in the French and European contexts. It has developed two targeted campaigns: one for public opinion based on the principle of universality of rights, and the other for political actors and trade unions. It stresses the importance of an international convention applying to the entire migratory process for sending and receiving countries, and of an international convention specific to increasingly vulnerable migrants.

---

[11] See www.demain-le-monde.org [last accessed 23 April 2003].

[12] Indeed, the 81-809 Act from 9 October 1981 puts an end to discrimination against foreigners regarding freedom of association. The right to create an association is fully granted to foreigners, as well as their rights to have representative roles in those associations, without any preliminary control. Before, on the basis of a 1939 decree, foreigners were not authorized to create an association, and their actions were preliminarily largely controlled.

The collective for ratification, linked to December 18, organized a major campaign with a petition in favour of ratification. The call for ratification of 17 December 2004 states the importance of the ICRMW, as it recognizes the fundamental rights of both legal and undocumented migrants and protects them as a vulnerable group. It highlights how European governments avoid ratification, despite the increased jeopardy of migrants' situations. It emphasizes the gap between the free movement of European citizens and the exclusion and decreased protection of third-country nationals. Finally, it recalls that many other European NGOs have also called for ratification.[13]

French NGOs have finally been very active in the creation of the EPMWR, which called in April 2005 for the universal ratification of the ICRMW. The Platform further welcomed the reopening of debates on economic migration following the European Commission's 2005 Green Paper, *On An EU Approach to Managing Economic Migration*. However, it stated that the approach must be based on rights of migrants, in contrast to the apparently more utilitarian and unilateral approach chosen by the Commission, in the sense that it takes into account the interests of sending countries only in a very marginal way. In this framework, a first step would be for Europe to encourage Member States to ratify the ICRMW. It stressed that enthusiasm for ratification is strengthened by the opinions of the European Parliament on 24 February 2005, and of the EESC on 30 June 2004. This call has been supported by twenty

---

[13] 'Quatorzième anniversaire d'une convention internationale que la France n'a toujours pas ratifiée: Depuis 1990, la précarisation des droits des migrants est en aggravation constante. L'Union européenne offre la libre circulation aux citoyens des États membres tout en durcissant, pour les autres, les règles de l'asile et du séjour; le principe de non-discrimination inscrit dans le traité d'Amsterdam a pourtant exclu la discrimination fondée sur la nationalité. Face à la dégradation des droits des migrants, les Nations unies ainsi que de nombreuses institutions européennes ou organisations de la société civile rappellent l'importance de la convention des Nations unies. Le gouvernement français qui prône un rôle accru des Nations unies dans les affaires internationales ne doit pas rester sourd à ces appels.' ['Fourteenth anniversary of an international convention that France has still not ratified: Since 1990, the precariousness of migrants' rights is worsening. The European Union offers free movement to the citizens of its Member States, while hardening, for all other people, the rules of asylum and residence; the principle of non-discrimination enshrined in the Treaty of Amsterdam has ruled out discrimination based on nationality. Faced with the degradation of migrants' rights, the United Nations, as well as many European institutions and civil society organizations, recall the importance of the UN Convention. The French government, which advocates a greater role for the UN in international affairs, cannot remain deaf to such appeals'] (www.gisti.org/doc/actions/2004/migrants/dec18.html [last accessed 23 April 2009]).

European associations, among which five are French,[14] demonstrating the proactive stance of French NGOs.

Timid but positive effects of NGO campaigns

Some trade unions and political parties have reacted positively to the NGO campaign. For example, several communist politicians have supported their efforts. On 29 January 2004, the communist MP Robert Bret[15] addressed a written question[16] before the Sénat[17] to the Minister of Foreign Affairs in charge of ratifying international instruments. He stated that the ICRMW should be considered as the seventh international instrument of human rights, specifically protecting rights and equality for both irregular and regular migrants, and France would be proud of ratification. He also wrote to the Ministry of the Interior with the same requirement. There was no ministerial answer.

The communist MP Serge Guichard, head of the National Committee on Discrimination and Human Rights, issued a press release on 18 December 2004, the anniversary of the Convention, supporting the NGO call for ratification.[18] He stated that, for the Communist Party, the migration issue is not marginal and that ratification is necessary. He

---

[14] Organizations that signed the call for ratification by the EPMWR: Agir Ici (French); Amnesty International (European Bureau); ARCI (Associazione Ricreativa e Culturale italiana – Italy); ATMF (France); Catholic Bishops' Conference of England and Wales; CEAR (Comisión Española de Ayuda al Refugiado – Spain); CEME (Commission des Eglises auprès des Migrants en Europe – Europe/Belgium); European Coordination for Migrants' Right to Family Life; December 18 (Belgium); Emmaus International (France); GISTI (Groupe d'information et de soutien des immigrés – France); IMD (IMD Platform Vlaanderen – Belgium); IDHC (Institut de Drets Humans de Catalunya – Spain); JCWI (Joint Council for the Welfare of Immigrants – UK); KMS (Kerkwerk Multicultureel Samen leven – Belgium); Migrant Rights Centre (Ireland); miXeurope (Denmark); MRAP (Mouvement contre le Racisme et pour l'Amitié entre les Peuples – France); PICUM (Platform for International Cooperation on Undocumented Migrants – Europe); and Migrantenweek (Netherlands). In other words, French NGOs, together with Belgian ones, are very active at European level. Of the twenty signatories, five are French, four are Belgian and two are other European countries.

[15] It is interesting to stress that he is Secretary of the parliamentary delegation to the EU and is a member of the Foreign Affairs Commission; in other words, he belongs to the initiated circle.

[16] Robert Bret (Bouches du Rhone – CRC), written question No. 10658 (29 January 2004).

[17] Parliamentary power in France is binary, composed of two assemblies: the Sénat (upper house), elected by regional local representatives, and the Assemblée Nationale (lower house), with directly elected MPs.

[18] 18 décembre Journée Internationale des Migrants, La France doit Ratifier la Convention, press release, 2004 (www.pcf.fr/?iddoc=4127 [last accessed 23 April 2009]).

further stated that the party fully supported the UN initiative on International Migrants Day (18 December). He finally called, in the name of the party, for ratification of the Convention. The Communist Party also invited representatives of the collective for ratification to its annual meeting.

The Green Party has been the one with the strongest and most positive reaction to the NGO campaign. First, Noël Mamère, a well-known MP, called for urgent ratification on behalf of the party.[19] Second, Green MP Boumediene-Thiery asked an oral question[20] concerning ratification before the Sénat on 13 October 2005. Finally, the Green Party launched two petitions supporting ratification in October 2005: one for local and national representatives[21] and one for all citizens.[22] So far, it remains the only political party to have closely followed the NGOs.

There has been no official interest from the Socialist Party. Only two MPs have asked individual written questions. On 25 May 2004,[23] MP Paulette Guinchard-Kunstler questioned France's denial of a convention protecting the rights of migrant workers and essential to the system of international human and fundamental rights. On 8 February 2005, MP Martine Lignière-Cassou[24] recalled the necessity to ratify the ICRMW, because the legal, social and human rights of migrant workers were worsening. Like Bret, she asserted that France would pride itself on ratification. It should even be an obligation, as France is the country of human rights. The other political parties have simply ignored the Convention.

Moreover, there has been no discussion of the Convention within either assembly (or within their committees). Unlike the European Parliament, the French Assemblée Nationale cannot give opinions and does not have any initiative power in practice.[25] Additionally, ratification requires a parliamentary majority, although it is unlikely that a majority could be met without government support.

---

[19] Noel Mamère is a well-known Green Party MP at the Assemblée Nationale.

[20] Question No. 0826S, *Journal Officiel Assemblée Nationale*, p. 2588.

[21] See Petition, 18 October 2005.

[22] See Petition, 22 October 2005.

[23] Question No. 39884, *Journal Officiel Assemblée Nationale*, p. 3751.

[24] Question No. 57336. *Journal Officiel Sénat*, p. 1203.

[25] Its rights are limited by articles 40, 41 and 48 of the French Constitution. Article 40 prevents initiatives concerning the budget. Article 41 gives a governmental right to control and refuse an initiative that has some impact on the executive power to make regulations. Article 48 gives power to the government to control the agenda.

Finally, although some trade unions[26] signed the petition in favour of the Convention, they never directly promoted ratification.

Beyond the timid political engagement, the Commission Nationale Consultative des Droits de l'Homme (CNCDH), the French National Consultative Commission on Human Rights, is the latest and most obvious demonstration of the growing interest in the Convention. This independent body makes non-binding recommendations to the government and regroups a plurality of actors: representatives of NGOs, trade unions, international and national experts, members of parliament, an ombudsman and the representatives of the ministers concerned.[27] It delivered its opinion recommending ratification on 23 June 2005,[28] calling for the promotion and protection of migrants' rights and ratification of the Convention. The Minister of Foreign Affairs answered the opinion on 30 August 2005.[29] He stated that a governmental

---

[26] In particular, Federation SUD Education, Federation SUD Rail and FGTE-CFDT, three trade unions well known at sectoral level, i.e. in education and transport. Union G-10 Solidaires also signed the petition. However, it is not considered as representative in French law.

[27] It also annually reports on racism and xenophobia, awards the annual human rights prize of the French Republic Liberty-Equality-Fraternity given by the French Prime Minister, together with the Rene Cassin medal in secondary schools, and provides training on human rights.

[28] See the website for the French text of the opinion (www.cncdh.fr/article.php3?id_article=152 [last accessed 23 April 2009]).

[29] Réponses du Ministre des Affaires étrangères aux avis de la CNCDH (30 août 2005). M. Philippe Douste-Blazy, Ministre des Affaires étrangères a adressé les courriers suivants au président de la CNCDH. Droits des travailleurs migrants, 'L'avis de la Commission Nationale Consultative des Droits de l'Homme, adopté par l'Assemblée plénière le 23 juin 2005, sur la convention internationale relative à la protection des droits de tous les travailleurs migrants et des membres de leur famille, a retenu mon attention. Ainsi que les représentants du Ministère des Affaires Etrangères ont eu l'occasion de le préciser lors des réunions de la CNCDH consacrées à ce sujet, les pays de l'Union Européenne n'ont pas ratifié ce texte. Certains éléments contenus dans la convention (dispositions fiscales) soulèvent des difficultés techniques. J'ai bien pris note des arguments soulevés par la CNCDH et j'ai souhaité par conséquent de nouvelles consultations internes et interministérielles sur ce texte avant de solliciter l'avis de nos partenaires de l'Union Européenne sur la ratification éventuelle de cette convention. J'ai demandé à mon représentant à la CNCDH, l'Ambassadeur M. Michel Doucin, de vous tenir régulièrement informé des progrès de ce dossier.' [Reply of the Minister of Foreign Affairs on the opinion of the CNCDH (30 August 2005).] Mr Philippe Douste-Blazy, Minister of Foreign Affairs has sent the following letter to the President of the CNCDH. 'Rights of migrant workers. The opinion of the Commission Nationale Consultative des Droits de l'Homme, adopted by the Assembly plenary on 23 June 2005 on the International Convention on the Protection of the Rights of All Migrant Workers and Members of Their Families, has caught my attention. As the representatives of the

consultation process with internal and intergovernmental discussions would be launched before starting another consultation process with all European Member States.

Therefore, the traditional argument of 'unawareness' as an obstacle to ratification has become flawed. The NGO campaigns had an impact on the government, which is now well aware of the Convention but still lacks enthusiasm. In a letter dated February 2005, the Minister of Foreign Affairs even redirected the responsibility for governmental passivity onto the Ministry of Finance. In other words, the obstacles to ratification are no longer based on unawareness but on political (un)willingness.

A political obstacle covered by the European alibi

In a survey of previous research on obstacles to ratification of the Convention, Pécoud and de Gutcheneire (2006) distinguish between administrative, financial, political and legal arguments for not ratifying. Following their study, I divide my analysis between legal, administrative, financial and political obstacles. The reason why the order is changed is because the main obstacle in France is political. Following this framework, I explain the limited impact of the Convention before turning to the four types of obstacle enumerated above.

Limited impact of the ICRMW

While very comprehensive, the Convention would not impose too many obligations on Western states. As noted by de Varennes (2002), it would not result in considerable changes concerning individual rights, which, in France, are already guaranteed to migrants (except for the right to vote and stand for election) – at least theoretically; indeed, there are still important discriminations towards immigrants perpetrated by private individuals in daily life, as well as by the administration. Moreover, in some cases, the documents required in order to enjoy a particular right might in practice be difficult to obtain for foreigners.

> Ministry of Foreign Affairs had the opportunity to state at the meetings of the CNCDH on this matter, no country of the European Union has ratified this treaty. Some elements of the Convention (tax provisions) give rise to technical difficulties. I took note of the arguments raised by the CNCDH and I therefore wish new internal and inter-ministerial consultations on this treaty before seeking the advice of our European Union partners on the possible ratification of this Convention. I asked my representative to the CNCDH, Ambassador Michel Doucin, to keep you regularly informed of the progress of this issue.'] www.cncdh.fr/article.php3?id_article=152.

The rights contained in the ICRMW that would actually require changes if France was to ratify are quite limited. Indeed, economic, social and cultural rights, together with provisions imposing positive obligations on States Parties, do not have a direct effect: it is incumbent on Member States to take the appropriate executive measures, and an individual cannot bring a legal action on the basis of the ICRMW. Furthermore, some provisions only state a general objective, leaving room for manoeuvre and flexibility for states. This is evident in the use of the word *may* in many clauses (i.e. 'states may…'), in expressions such as 'if states consider' or 'if states deem necessary' and in the numerous references to national law (such as 'in accordance with national law'). For example, in the frame of family reunification, article 44(2) says that 'States Parties shall take measures that *they deem appropriate* and that fall *within their competence* to facilitate the reunification of migrant workers' (emphasis added). The right to reunification is thus not a tight legal obligation for states, as it is softened by the vocabulary employed. The same method has been used within the European Community immigration framework, where Member States largely remain in control thanks to flexible clauses. (For a fuller analysis, see Oger and Barbou-des-Places (2004).)

More generally, the rights contained in the ICRMW are limited by respect for state sovereignty: in article 79, the Convention recognizes state sovereignty in terms of entry and residence, as well as access to the labour market, and it often refers to the sovereignty principle (such as in articles 34, 35, 69 and 82). Article 35 thus recalls that the decision regarding regularization belongs to states. Moreover, the Convention does not give any new rights to migrant workers as such, except that of consular protection and assistance (article 65(2)). For example, articles 16(7) and 23 on remittances provide some incentives for states to ease financial transactions, but they have no direct effect despite the novelty of their scope.

A further element limiting the effect of the Convention is the optional nature of inter-state and individual complaints. Indeed, article 77 states:

> A State Party to the present Convention *may* at any time declare under the present article that it recognizes the competence of the Committee to receive and consider communications from or on behalf of individuals subject to its jurisdiction who claim that their individual rights as established by the present Convention have been violated by that State Party (emphasis added).

So far, no state has habilitated the committee for individual complaints. Moreover, there is no formal mechanism to force respect of rights listed by the Convention, as there is no legal court. And states can make reservations (article 91) as long as they are not incompatible with the object and purpose of the Convention (articles 91–92).

In conclusion, the legally binding character of the ICRMW is rather weak, hence limiting the strictly legal obstacles to its ratification in European states. In other words, the few legal obstacles that exist in France are not insurmountable, and in most areas French law complies with the Convention.

Legal obstacles

Pécoud and de Gutcheneire (2006) list a series of legal and political obstacles: conflicting interests of employers, recruitment agencies and government officials; protection of employers rather than migrants; threat to the national welfare state; disadvantaged ethnic minorities; cultural rights; reluctance to provide rights to undocumented migrants; and lack of trust in international law and the UN system in particular. In the French case, there is no evidence of any real obstacle as listed above, except the striking issue of cultural rights. Others might be politically relevant, but not legally so. However, there is an additional obstacle not specifically discussed above but very relevant in France, and that is family reunification.

Thus, the few existing legal obstacles may be grouped into two major areas. If the CNCDH has recognized two (respect for cultural identity (article 31) and transfer of funds (article 47)), only the first is legally relevant. Indeed, the second obstacle appears as more financial than strictly legal. Indeed, while article 32 of the Convention states that migrants 'shall have the right to transfer their earnings and savings' and is echoed by article 47, the latter also provides that 'such transfers shall be made in conformity with procedures established by applicable legislation of the state concerned and in conformity with applicable international agreements'. In other words, the exemption from taxes and the prohibition of double taxing migrants are determined by national law (see below).

GISTI and the collective for ratification stress the other main obstacle to ratification: family reunification. Questions could also be raised concerning the scope of equal treatment in terms of social security. Nevertheless, all these principles are formulated in the Convention with a wide margin of manoeuvre for states, as it only recommends states to facilitate the enjoyment of these rights – it does not order them to do so. To expedite matters, the CNCDH also recommended that France should make some reservations to overcome minor obstacles.

The first of these relates to the right to protect and recognize migrants' culture of origin. According to article 31, states shall ensure respect for cultural identity and shall not prevent migrant workers from maintaining their cultural links. This contradicts the French approach, which views the nation as indivisible, secular and neutral, thus prohibiting any recognition of differences in the public sphere. In the view of the CNCDH, this article, albeit vague, conflicts with these principles and might even conflict with the principle of equality between men and women. The issue is very sensitive in France – the reluctance to open the nation to diversity and cultural heterogeneity is, for example, very visible in political debates on immigration. However, it would be relatively easy to bypass this obstacle by making a reservation.

The second obstacle, as raised by GISTI and the collective for ratification, is the issue of family reunification. According to article 44, States Parties shall take appropriate measures to ensure the protection of the unity of migrants' families and facilitate family reunification; they shall also favourably consider granting equal treatment to other family members of migrant workers. These are fundamental rights, and an important element for migrant integration. However, the opposite political direction has been taken recently by European states in general and the French Government in particular. For states, the right to family reunification is an incentive to a quantitative excess of migration that cannot be controlled. In fact, European states aim at limiting this primary source of migration in order to favour the entry of (qualified) migrant workers.

The 2003 Immigration Act extended the waiting period for reunification, reduced the security of family members of permanent permit holders by providing them with only a temporary card and tightened the conditions of housing and resources for family reunification.[30] Moreover, housing conditions are stricter since the decree of 17 March 2005 (*Journal Officiel*, 19 March 2005). Additionally, *de facto*

---

[30] See Loi N.2003-1119 (26 November 2003) relative à la maîtrise de l'immigration, au séjour des étrangers en France et à la nationalité (known as 'loi Sarkozy'), article 42. Now contained in Livre IV – Regroupement Familial, Code de l'entrée et du Séjour des Etrangers et du Droit d'Asile [Code regarding the entry, stay of foreign nationals and the right to asylum].

reunification for family members living irregularly in the country has been made almost impossible. Indeed, the permit of a sponsor may be withdrawn if he brings his family into the country outwith the family reunification rules. Finally, the 2006 Immigration Act[31] further restricts this right. In other words, government policies do not facilitate family reunification (except for family members of highly skilled migrants).

Finally, a few smaller problems may be mentioned. For example, the possibility of a judge pronouncing a ban from the territory (double penalty) could contradict the principle of equality of migrants before justice, together with the general principle of non-discrimination. Another issue is the political participation of migrants: article 42 states that the host country must facilitate their participation in local decision making, but leaves the right to vote in local elections to the state's sovereignty. If none of the French rules breach article 42, its spirit could, however, be invoked in order to promote migrants' right to vote locally.

In contrast, some legal issues have not been considered as constituting obstacles. Thus, the role and supervision of the UN treaty monitoring body has not been seen as problematic, as France is normally keen to participate in such mechanisms. Furthermore, because the most contentious issues would not have direct effect as they are dependent on national law, direct effect, i.e. the possibility of a migrant basing a claim before national law on the basis of the Convention, seems to have restricted potential.[32]

Additionally, the principle of non-discrimination does not encompass prohibition of discriminatory treatment of third-country nationals as compared with nationals. The non-discrimination principle only prevents states from discriminating between different groups of migrants (article 7). In this context, it might thus be seen as less generous than the ECHR, since the European Court stated in *Gaygusuz*, as confirmed by *Poirrez*, that very weighty reasons should be provided to justify the difference of treatment between a migrant and a national on the exclusive basis of nationality, thanks to a generous interpretation of the right to

---

[31] Loi N.2006-911 (24 July 2006) relative à l'immigration et à l'intégration, *Journal Officiel Assemblée Nationale*, N.170, 25 July 2006, p. 11047. Articles 44–47 modifying different aspects of the legislation on family reunification, as stated in Livre IV – Regroupement Familial, Code de l'Entrée et du Séjour des Etrangers et du Droit d'Asile.

[32] Direct effect is open to rights that are clear and do not need further implementation. Direct effect can also only arise if the state is monist, which is the case in France. Dualist states that distinguish the international and national spheres would not be subject to it.

property enumerated in Protocol 1 of the ECHR.[33] However, an evolution in the interpretation of this article, following the ECHR model, might be possible (Vanheule et al., 2004). A favourable interpretation by the CMW would be a relevant starting point. Additionally, some argue that as the principle of non-discrimination includes non-discrimination on the basis of nationality, it could be used in favour of non-EU citizen migrants. Indeed, the favourable treatment of migrant workers, who are EU citizens, would be discriminatory, and thus non-EU citizens could be entitled to the same rights on the basis of article 7, a use that had been suggested by Cholewinski (1997). However, despite some favourable jurisprudence, such as in *Karakurt* v. *Austria* by the UN Human Rights Committee,[34] the European Court on Human Rights has used European citizenship to justify distinctions between European citizens and third-country nationals.[35] Thus, because the legal position is different, the difference of treatment is not discriminatory, all the more so in that

---

[33] ECHR, *Koua Poirrez* v. *France*, No. 40892/98, 30 September 2003. 'Very weighty reasons would have to be put forward before the court could regard a difference of treatment based exclusively on the ground of nationality as compatible with the Convention' (paragraph 46; see paragraph 42, *Gaygusuz*, 16 September 1996 – breach of article 14 in coordination with article 1, protocol 1).

[34] ECHR, *Karakurt* v. *Austria*, Communication No. 965/2000, 4 April 2002 CCPR/C/74/D/965/2000, paragraph 8.4: 'The question is whether there are reasonable and objective grounds justifying exclusion of the author from a close and natural incident of employment in the State Party otherwise available to EEA nationals: the right to stand for election to the relevant work-council, on the basis of his citizenship alone. Although the Committee had found in one case (N.658/1995, *Van Oord* vs *The Netherlands*) that an international agreement that confers preferential treatment to nationals of a State Party to that agreement might constitute an objective and reasonable ground for differentiation, no general rule can be drawn therefrom to the effect that such an agreement in itself constitutes a sufficient ground with regard to the requirements of article 26 of the Covenant. Rather, it is necessary to judge every case on its own facts. With regard to the case at hand, the Committee has to take into account the function of a member of a work council, i.e., to promote staff interests and to supervise compliance with working conditions (see para. 3.1). In view of this, it is not reasonable to base a distinction between aliens concerning their capacity to stand for election for a work council solely on their different nationality. Accordingly, the Committee finds that the author has been the subject of discrimination in violation of article 26.'

[35] See, for example, ECHR, *Moustaquim* v. *Belgium* [1991] IIHRL 2 (18 February 1991) at 195. If the court concluded to the violation of article 8 of the Convention by the state, it also stated that there could be no discrimination, and thus a breach of article 14 taken with article 8, since Moustaquim could not be compared with either Belgian nationals having the right of abode in their own country or Community nationals whose preferential treatment, deriving from a special legal order to which Belgium belongs, has an objective and reasonable justification.

the Convention does not prevent more favourable treatment for certain groups of migrants.[36]

Nevertheless, this principle has a second limitation: its lack of independence. It is a parasite right, i.e. it can only be used in connection with one of the rights recognized by the Convention, as is the case for article 14 of the ECHR. In other words, the prohibition of discrimination on the basis of nationality seems to have limited scope of action, too limited to threaten existing national and European laws.

In conclusion, there are limited legal obstacles, especially as they can all be easily superseded by reservations. The obstacles are thus more political than legal. The legal changes would be minimal.

Administrative obstacles

Administrative obstacles are linked to political obstacles, because administrative practices stem from government *circulaires*.[37] Moreover, although political obstacles are decisive, administrative hurdles are also relevant with respect to the practical implementation of the Convention. Pécoud and de Guchteneire list two administrative obstacles: the necessary coordination between different actors and a number of ministries; and the possible superfluous character of the Convention due to pre-existing conventions and legislation (Pécoud and de Guchteneire, 2006).

The first of these cannot be seriously raised in France, because coordination between multiple actors has been in place for decades and has been further reinforced with the introduction of European immigration law. Additionally, the French Government constituted in May 2007 has set up a new ministry (Immigration, Integration, National Identity and Co-Development), which regroups all aspects of immigration, borders and nationality. Thus, the Convention would not add any extra complexity, and the grouping under one ministry should simplify matters.

Concerning the superfluous character of the Convention, while it is true that a general body of domestic legislation already exists, France has not ratified ILO Convention No. 143 and is thus not party to any general

---

[36] Article 81(1): 'Nothing in the present Convention shall affect more favourable rights or freedoms granted to migrant workers and members of their families.'

[37] These circulars, which are guidelines for application of administrative decrees, are generally not binding, i.e. not considered as legal documents. They thus cannot be appealed against, unless they contain a new legal element, which gives them a binding nature.

convention for migrants at international level. Obviously, the domestic level is not enough, and France, which considers itself to set an international example, should continue to do so.

However, there is one issue that could be contradictory to administrative practices. Indeed, if French legal protection of irregular migrants is generally in conformity with the Convention, some administrative practices appear to conflict. Irregular migrants have the following rights in France: they can access the universal medical system, they are authorized to visit centres for prevention and detection, and they can abort. They also have a right to marry, to contract a registered partnership (PACS) or to cohabitate. There is a right to education, a right to children's benefits, a right to attend nurseries, as well as a right to maternal and infant protection. In terms of work, they are insured in case of accidents at work, they have the right to a salary, to be paid additional hours, bonuses, paid holidays and recourse in case of breach of contract. However, as irregular migrant workers can be deported, their legal protection is extremely limited in practice. Additionally, they generally hesitate to declare accidents at work because they fear denunciation by social security organs or by employers, although the social security administration is supposed to respect professional confidentiality.

Irregular migrants also have a right to old-age and retirement pensions, emergency housing, social lodgings and public hospitals. Exceptionally, they might also have a right to legal aid, family subsidies[38] or social subsidies.

Furthermore, irregular migrants have had the right to open a bank account since 1998[39] and have discounts for transport. Finally, they have rights during an identity check, and they have the right to join associations and trade unions. In practice, however, any theoretical right can be used as a source of information, thus becoming a threat or danger for the undocumented migrant if the administrative guidance is to localize irregular migrants in order to have them deported. To illustrate these conflicting instructions, I focus on some striking examples.

According to article 28, both regular and irregular migrants have the right to emergency medical care. Yet, in order to receive the Aide Médicale d'État, a foreigner must, since two decrees of 29 July 2005, justify an uninterrupted stay of more than three months, but also all financial

---

[38] There are specific rights when the children are French, and in general are under the CRC.
[39] However, in practice, banks do not readily open an account for a person who cannot prove their address.

resources. Such justifications cause problems. By their very nature, irregular migrants have few documents and are not keen on providing those they do have in case it facilitates their expulsion. Even the Caisse Nationale d'Assurance Maladie des Travailleurs Salariés (CNAMTS, National Employed Workers' Sickness Insurance Fund, an independent body of representatives of employees and employers in charge of the public healthcare service) condemned the proposed measures in its 2004 opinion. In practice, this administrative requirement makes it extremely difficult for irregular migrants to exercise their right to medical treatment. If this does not, strictly speaking, contradict the Convention, it prevents the achievement of its purpose and violates its spirit. Furthermore, the European Committee for Social Rights has declared the required duration of residence illegal for children of irregular migrants, in its interpretation of article 17 of the revised European Social Charter in the light of the UN CRC.[40]

In addition, according to a *circulaire* of 21 February 2006: 'Les procureurs de la République feront procéder chaque fois que nécessaire, en concertation avec les préfets, aux interpellations aux guichets de la préfecture, au domicile ou dans les logements…dans les hôpitaux.' In other words, irregular migrants can be arrested at hospitals as well as at their residence or the local government offices. Following this possibility, the NGO Médecins du Monde recalls that the right to receive health treatment is a fundamental right of every human being and should never be used for means other than medical care.[41] Indeed, the *circulaire* suggests using irregular migrants' fundamental rights in order for the police to localize them and arrest and deport them more quickly.

---

[40] See European Committee of Social Rights, Complaint No. 14/2003 by the *International Federation for Human Rights (FIDH)* v. *France*, Resolution ResCHs(2005)6, paragraph 36. Article 17 of the Revised Charter is further directly inspired by the CRC. It protects in a general manner the right of children and young persons, including unaccompanied minors, to care and assistance. Yet, the Committee notes that: (i) medical assistance to the above target group in France is limited to situations that involve an immediate threat to life; and (ii) children of illegal immigrants are only admitted to the medical assistance scheme after a certain time (paragraph 37). For these reasons, the Committee considers that the situation is not in conformity with article 17 (wcd.coe.int/ViewDoc.jsp? id=856639&BackColorInternet=9999CC&BackColorIntranet=FFBB55&BackColorLog ged=FFAC75 [last accessed 23 April 2009]).

[41] 'Le droit aux soins est inscrit dans le préambule de la Constitution française. C'est un droit fondamental de la personne humaine. Il ne doit jamais être utilisé à d'autres fins que la préservation de la santé.' ['The right to health services is enshrined in the preamble to the French Constitution. It is a fundamental human right. It must never be used for other purposes than the preservation of health.'] Quoted by Veyrinaud (2006, p. 130).

Additionally, although the Convention does not force states to regularize irregular migrants, it recognizes the rights of irregular migrants and discourages undocumented migration. 'States of employment shall take all adequate and effective measures to eliminate employment in their territory of migrant workers in an irregular situation' (article 68(2)) and 'States Parties shall, when there are migrant workers and members of their families within their territory in an irregular situation, take appropriate measures to ensure that such a situation does not persist' (article 69). In the context of regularization, Member States shall take particularly into account the duration of stay and family situation (article 69(2)).

But the French Government has recently taken decisions in three opposite directions. First, it has decreased the amount of the fine for employers employing irregular migrants; second, it has misused the rule on regularization by using information to deport irregular migrants; third, it has sanctioned irregular work by expulsion. However, the aborted European Legislation Oriented Institutes (ELOI) file aimed at reinforcing the surveillance of irregular migrants, together with the fight against the removal of children of undocumented migrants, showed the limit of governmental discretion in this area.

Since a decree of 7 July 2005, the penalty for employers employing irregular migrants has significantly decreased (despite the employment of irregular workers being a crime since 2003). Does this rule follow the principle of article 69 of the Convention, that states 'shall take appropriate measures to ensure that [irregular migration] does not persist'?

Article 86 of the 2003 Act[42] states that for the regularization of a migrant who has been living in France for more than ten years, which can be proven by any means, the duration of stay where the migrant has been residing with falsified documents cannot be taken into consideration in counting the ten-year period.[43] This means that the use of a fake residence permit to obtain regular work is discounted. As a result, although a foreigner is allowed to prove by any means his continuous stay for more than ten years, pay slips are seen as evidence of using fake documents and thus as a reason for refusing a residence permit. Whereas the aim of this measure is to regularize the situation of these people, it

---

[42] Loi No. 2003–1119 (26 November 2003) relative à la maîtrise de l'immigration, au séjour des étrangers en France et à la nationalité.

[43] See, for example, article 86: La loi Sarkozy du 27 novembre 2003: Nier le travail des ouvriers sans papiers pour les priver de tout espoir de regularization. *Plein Droit*, Vols. 65–66 (GISTI, July 2005), pp. 50–2.

instead serves as a means of expelling them. Migrants therefore hesitate to ask for regularization, contradicting the importance of taking into account the duration of stay (article 69). This misuse of French legislation does not directly breach the Convention, as there is no right to work as such, yet it contravenes its spirit.[44] Finally, according to articles 21 and 22 after the 2003 reform, irregular workers, even though they are legally resident, may be expelled. Is this really in conformity with the Convention?

Article 16 of the 2003 Act (relative à la maîtrise de l'immigration, au séjour des étrangers en France et à la nationalité)[45] introduced the possibility of withdrawing a residence permit from migrants who have been exercising a profession without authorization or without a work permit, or to employers employing such workers.

However, two recent developments have highlighted the limitations on administrative action against undocumented migrants. Indeed, the ELOI file created by an *arrêté*[46] of 30 July 2006, aimed at collecting information on irregular migrants with the names of people visiting detention centres or hosting undocumented migrants, was quashed by the Conseil d'État[47] in March 2007.[48] Additionally, following strong protests against the removal of undocumented children and their parents following the children's registration at school,[49] a *circulaire* of 31 October 2005 contained a moratorium against removals until the end of 2006. However, two new *circulaires* of 13 June and 14 June 2006 limit non-removal to children and their parents meeting certain criteria, such as a minimum of one year at school, lack of knowledge of the language of origin and absence of links with countries of origin. This latter criterion has been mainly, and on an exclusive basis, used by *préfectures* as the local representatives of the national administration. Its exclusive use has

---

[44] Articles 52 and 53 refer to access to employment on equal terms with nationals, but these are heavily qualified, and states may always restrict access to some jobs.

[45] This article has been inserted as L313-5 Code de l'Entrée et du Séjour des Etrangers et du Droit d'Asile.

[46] An *arrêté* is an administrative act with low status in the hierarchical scale, the highest being *décret*.

[47] The Supreme Administrative Court in the French system.

[48] The Conseil d'État, on 12 March 2007, quashed the decision on the basis that in order to make such a decision, the government should have enacted a *décret* rather than a mere ministerial *arrêté*.

[49] Mobilization against such removals was organized by the Réseau Éducation Sans Frontières (RESF, Network of Education without Borders), an association grouping parents and teachers.

been criticized by the HALDE (Haute Autorité de Lutte contre les Discriminations),[50] but the non-removal of undocumented migrants with children at school now remains more restricted.

Thus, administrative obstacles, following government guidance, have largely targeted undocumented migrants, and in particular their rights and removals.

Financial obstacles

Pécoud and de Gutcheneire stress that undocumented migration is a source of cheap and flexible labour, a financial discouragement to states to give migrants rights. Although this is certainly a powerful argument for some neighbouring countries, no particular mention has been made in France (Pécoud and de Guchteneire, 2006). In contrast, the main financial obstacle, not mentioned by Pécoud and de Guchteneire, is the remittances issue. The Ministry of Finance seems to be strongly opposed to article 47, which deals with monetary transfers of (regular) migrants to their country of origin. As stated, this appears as a financial obstacle rather than a legal one. As mentioned above, the Ministry of Foreign Affairs informed the collective for ratification that the Convention would cause serious financial difficulties and, unofficially, it is said that the Minister of Finance would oppose ratification.

The argument goes as follows. It would be costly for the French Government to encourage transfers, because this would imply lowering the fees. According to the IOM (2005), the exorbitant fees charged by money transfer agents represent a drain on remittances and mainly affect poor migrants. In order to address this problem adequately, the policies of sending and host countries must be coordinated. Transfers are currently very expensive in France, as banks charge large sums. Beyond bank lobbying of the Ministry of Finance, facilitating the transfer of remittances and reducing their costs would run the risk of major financial outflows from France. However, the 2006 Act has introduced a new type of savings account, the Compte Épargne Co-développement, aimed at facilitating investments in the developing countries of origin.[51] It does,

---

[50] The High Authority to Fight Discrimination and to Promote Equality is a national independent administrative body created in 2006 following two EU directives on non-discrimination. See Veyrinaud (2006, p. 135).

[51] Article L. 221–33 Code Bancaire et Financier (Financial and Monetary Code), introduced by article 1 of Loi No. 2006–911 relative à l'immigration et à l'intégration.

for the first time, officially and legally recognize the existence of regular transfers to countries of origin.[52]

Thus, although remittances remain a serious obstacle, such legal acknowledgement signals the awareness and willingness to create more favourable conditions for migrant workers, as long as they are aimed at investing in the countries of origin. Furthermore, as recommended by the National Human Rights Commission, one simple way to erase this obstacle would be to set reservations. More generally, the Ministry of Finance also seems to consider that ratification would be too expensive. However, this argument is difficult to understand. Ratification would require no new techniques or tools, as even those of sharing information and data with other countries are standard procedures at the European level. In addition, it is difficult to evaluate the extent of the disagreement between the Ministry of Foreign Affairs and the Ministry of Finance, but the global governmental will for greater flexibility and instrumentalism regarding immigration is real and contradicts the spirit of the Convention.

Political obstacles and the European context

Following the two government answers to MP's written questions[53] and the answer to the opinion of the CNCDH,[54] the leading argument used by the government to avoid its responsibility is that preliminary agreement at European level is required.[55]

As underlined by the two ministerial answers, the supposed need for prior discussion with France's European partners is based on the assumption that ratification would no longer be within French competence, but rather European competence, following the Long-Term Residence Directive on the basis of the Accord Européen sur les Transports Routiers (AETR) judgment.[56] As the European Court of Justice asserted in this case:

---

[52] This was initiated by Brard and Godfrain proposing to establish the '*livret d'épargne pour le développement*' in the context of mobilizing savings of migrant workers in France for the development of their home countries and for better productivity (Assemblée Nationale, 12e legislature, No. 1687, 23 June 2004).

[53] See nn. 59 and 60 for details of the two answers to parliamentary questions.

[54] See n. 34 for the exact answer of the ministry to the Commission.

[55] The answer to the CNCDH mentions the need for discussion with European partners, which suggests that European states' agreement is the major obstacle.

[56] Case 22/70, *Commission* v. *Council* (AETR) [1971] ECR 263.

> Each time the Community, with a view to implementing a common policy envisaged by the Treaty, adopts provisions laying down common rules, whatever form these may take, the Member States no longer have the right, acting individually or even collectively, to undertake obligations with third countries which affect those rules.[57]

Building on this jurisprudence, the government argues that, since the European Community has exercised its competence in immigration law, in particular with the enactment of Directive 2003/109 on Third-Country Nationals Long-Term Residents,[58] Member States would no longer be able to independently ratify conventions on the matter, as competence would have been transferred to the European Community.

To be more specific, the Minister of External Affairs answered on November 2005 as follows:

> Il résulte de la jurisprudence AETR de la Cour de justice des Communautés européennes que, pour la mise en œuvre d'une politique commune prévue par le traité, chaque fois que la Communauté a pris des dispositions instaurant, sous quelque forme que ce soit, des règles communes, les États membres ne sont plus en droit, qu'ils agissent individuellement ou même collectivement, de contracter avec des États tiers des obligations affectant ces règles. Par conséquent, les États membres ne seraient plus en droit de participer à la convention en cause que conjointement avec la Communauté, ce qui suppose au préalable une coordination avec celle-ci. À ce jour, aucun pays européen n'a signé cette convention.[59]

A few days later, the Ministry of Cooperation and Development, answering Boumediene-Thiery, similarly argued:

> La France n'a pas signé cette convention pour la simple raison qu'elle recouvre pour partie des compétences communautaires, d'autant que le Traité d'Amsterdam a conféré une compétence à la Communauté dans le domaine des migrations et de l'asile.[60]

Yet a general principle of European Community law, repeated in the Long-Term Residence Directive, is that European rules do not prevent

---

[57] Paragraph 12 of the ECJ judgment.

[58] Council Directive 2003/109/EC of 25 November 2003 concerning the status of third-country nationals who are long-term residents (*Official Journal of the European Union*, L16/44, 2004).

[59] Answer to written question of Martine Lignière-Cassou, *Journal Officiel Assemblée Nationale*, 1 November 2005, p. 10157.

[60] Answer from the Ministry of Cooperation and Development to the question of Alima Boumediene-Thiery, *Journal Officiel Sénat*, 10 November 2005, p. 6854.

Member States from adopting more favourable rules or ratifying more favourable bilateral or international agreements.[61] Thus, the French Government is in no way prevented by European Community law from adopting more favourable measures, and its argument is largely incorrect. This answer illustrates the government's attempt to escape the debate on ratification on Europe's behalf.

However, the European obstacle is real, but in a different way. Coordination and competition between EU Member States make them politically reluctant to ratify any additional instrument beneficial to migrants, fearing an overflow of migrants in their country as a consequence. Whatever its factual (un)realism, this race to the bottom, or at least this race for the instrumental selection of migrants, is a major political obstacle. More generally, the EU approach to migration, which is quite unsupportive of the Convention, has a deep influence on French immigration policies. In a letter to the French NGO Agir Ici in May 2004, António Vitorino[62] stated that ratification is not a European priority,[63] and Franco Frattini[64] argued that ratification would be an obstacle to the fight against irregular migration.[65] As EU states seem to argue that there would be no ratification without an official position being taken by the Council of Ministers, this is an unpromising situation.

European states seem to share a perception of migration issues based on a preoccupation with security. This kind of cooperation results in regulations specifically concentrating on control and exclusion

---

[61] See article 3(3) of Council Directive 2003/109/EC.

[62] Vitorino was a law professor, a judge, a secretary of state of the Macao Government, vice-prime minister of Portugal and chairman of the European Parliament's Civil Liberties Committee before becoming European Commissioner with responsibility for justice and home affairs.

[63] See Commissioner Vitorino's reply to the written question of Ms Miet Smet on 5 March 2004, referred to by Frattini, in his answer to the letter from the EPMWR (www.europarl. europa.eu/sides/getAllAnswers.do?reference=E-2004-0068&language=EN [last accessed 12 May 2009]).

[64] Frattini is Italian, a former law advisor and minister in different ministries, and is currently the Vice-President of the EU and the EU Commissioner responsible for justice, freedom and security.

[65] Frattini's answer to the letter of René Plaetevoet, co-ordinator of the EPMWR from 6 December 2004, Brussels: 'A number of rights have already been recognized by the EU acquis and the European Charter. There is nevertheless a specific problem, as mentioned by Vitorino: there is no distinction between legal residents and irregular migrants. This may constitute a problem in terms of social security and for the credibility of EU policy to prevent illegal migration...I do not consider as a priority the ratification of the ICMW.'

(Guiraudon, 2000). This development is referred to as 'securization' of migration (Cholewinski, 2000), or 'collective restrictivism' (Uçarer, 2001). Common instruments in the field of policy work are elaborated, but no rights and liberties of aliens are put forward (Tholen, 2004). In addition, European policies are based on a largely utilitarist conception of migrants, hierarchizing migrants and their rights on the basis of their (economic) interests for Europe. This objective does not easily fit with the horizontal rights-based approach of the Convention.[66]

In other words, the current objective of the migration policy does not fit with the purpose of the Convention to protect a vulnerable group of people. Expulsion of irregular migrants, security and the objective of instrumental and flexible policy are seen as priorities for the French Government. There is no consideration for the protection of migrants. The trend towards divided and classified migrants with fluctuating rights contradicts the spirit of the Convention. As reflected at European level, states want to keep room for manoeuvre and flexibility, which could be limited by the courts if the Convention was ratified. This trend has been strongly advocated by Nicolas Sarkozy as Minister of the Interior (President of France in May 2007), strongly advocating the evolution towards an *immigration choisie*.[67] The new government and elected president reinforce the belief that resistance to ratification of the Convention will continue in the near future.

Conclusion

Awareness of the ICRMW has come rather late in France and still tends to be found within a circle of initiated people. However, the dynamism of French NGOs, together with the influence and support of some European bodies and institutions, has provided new tools for a better information campaign for ratification. As a result, the government has been forced to recognize its awareness of the Convention, as illustrated in its answer to the CNCDH opinion. Thus, lack of awareness is no longer a sustainable argument for the government.

---

[66] In addition, as stated earlier, the migratory clauses of bilateral and multilateral agreements with neighbouring countries may also contradict the Convention.

[67] *Immigration choisie* (selected migration) has been strongly criticized by NGOs such as GISTI. See, for example, the petition initiated by a network of French NGOs, *Contre l'immigration jetable* (www.contreimmigrationjetable.org/ [last accessed 23 April 2009]).

The obstacles to ratification in France are thus political and strongly linked with Europe. The legal and financial obstacles are rather limited. France could merely request some reservations on family reunification, cultural rights and financial transfers. Furthermore, administrative practices could better take into consideration migrants' interests. The greatest obstacle is political, lying in the discrepancy between the rights-based Convention and the utilitarist and flexible current European and French policies. It is also linked to the European race to the bottom and a refusal to be the first Member State to ratify.

References

Cholewinski, R. 1997. *Migrant Workers in International Human Rights Law: Their Protection in Countries of Employment*. Oxford, UK, Clarendon Press.

——— 2000. The EU acquis on irregular migration: reinforcing security at the expense of rights. *European Journal of Migration and Law*, Vol. 2, Nos. 3–4, p. 361.

de Varennes, F. 2002. *'Strangers in Foreign Lands' – Diversity, Vulnerability and the Rights of Migrants*. Paris, UNESCO. (MOST Working Paper 9.)

Guiraudon, V. 2000. European integration and migration policy: vertical policy-making as venue shopping. *Journal of Common Market Studies*, Vol. 38, p. 251.

IOM. 2005. *World Migration 2005: Costs and Benefits of International Migration*. IOM's biennial flagship publication, No. 882, 22 June 2005. Available at www.iom. int/iomwebsite/Publication/ServletSearchPublication?event=detail&id=4171 [last accessed 23 April 2009].

Oger, H. and Barbou-des-Places, S. 2004. Making the European migration regime: decoding member states' legal strategies. *European Journal of Migration and Law*, Vol. 6, No. 4, p. 353–79.

Pécoud, A. and de Guchteneire, P. 2006. Migration, human rights and the United Nations. An investigation into the obstacles to the UN Convention on Migrant Workers' Rights. *Windsor Yearbook of Access to Justice*, Vol. 24, No. 2, p. 241–66.

Tholen, B. 2004. The Europeanisation of migration policy – the normative issues. *European Journal of Migration and Law*, Vol. 6, No. 4, pp. 323–52.

Uçarer, E. 2001. Managing asylum and European integration: expanding spheres of exclusion? *International Studies Perspectives*, Vol. 2, No. 3, p. 291.

Vanheule, D., Foblets, M.-C., Loones, S. and Bouckaert, S. 2004. The significance of the UN Migrant Workers' Convention of 18 December 1990 in the event of ratification by Belgium. *European Journal of Migration and Law*, Vol. 6, No. 4, pp. 285–321.

Veyrinaud, C. 2006. La politique de l'immigration en 2006: rupture, transition ou continuité? F. Chatillon et al., *La France en 2006: Chronique politique économique et sociale*. Paris, La Documentation Française, pp. 117–35.

13

Migration and human rights in Germany

FELICITAS HILLMANN AND
AMANDA KLEKOWSKI VON KOPPENFELS

Introduction

Today, Germany remains one of the major immigration countries in Europe – even though the country's migrant population is composed mainly of long-term residents. Recent migration flows are limited to highly specialized programmes in certain sectors or to migration for family reunification, and migrants are restricted in their access to the overall labour market. It is estimated that there are a significant number of undocumented migrants in Germany who live and work in the country with an insecure status. Like most European states, Germany has not ratified the ICRMW.

This chapter outlines the reasons for this situation and the ongoing discussion concerning the Convention in Germany. The data were gathered through interviews in 2005, shortly before the September 2005 general election.[1] After the election, the government coalition changed, as did responsibilities within the setting of migration policies.[2] Nonetheless, our interviews indicated that there would not be a significant change in the German Government's position on the Convention, even in the event of a change of government. Indeed, this has been confirmed by the Federal Ministry for Economy and Labour, which is the coordinating ministry for all issues relating to the Convention. The government's objections to the Convention remain the same.

---

[1] The election resulted in only the second Grand Coalition in post-war history: a coalition between the two largest parties, the centre-left SPD and the centre-right CDU. This government replaced the centre-left SPD and left-leaning Greens/B90 government coalition, who had been in power since 1998.

[2] A Federal Commissioner for Migrants (Maria Böhmer) was put in place, for example, marking the first time the post has been held by a member of the CDU. The institutional affiliation of the commissioner also changed: from the Ministry for Family Affairs, Senior Citizens, Women and Youth to the Chancellor's Office. This shift was widely interpreted as a sign that the new government would place high priority on migration and integration.

Our principal findings, broadly speaking, are that, first of all, there is little knowledge about the Convention either within German society or in the political arena. Further, many interviewees, regardless of their affiliation, felt that the Convention would not be ratified in Germany for two reasons, which, indeed, are those mentioned by the German Government: first, that there is a feeling that migrants' rights are adequately protected elsewhere; and, second, that the inclusion of undocumented migrant workers in the Convention makes ratification extremely unlikely, if not impossible, due to the importance placed on the rule of law in Germany. Neither the government nor the trade unions would be likely to make legal migrants and undocumented migrants equal in terms of rights and access to the labour market.

The obstacles to ratification of the Convention in Germany are thus not likely to disappear, regardless of which party is leading the government. Indeed, this has been borne out by the change of government in late 2005. Although German political parties have varied reasons for non-ratification, there is widespread agreement that it would not be possible to ratify the Convention in Germany. At the same time, NGO respondents in particular noted that a high-profile discussion on the topic of undocumented migrant workers' rights was overdue, and that further debate on possible ratification might create an opportunity to have that discussion.

One of our interviewees noted that, while issues of transnational and international labour and migrant work in general have become more prominent, the various actors at national level (i.e. the authorities and, to a certain extent, the trade unions) are still looking for traditional solutions on a national basis, which do not refer to events outside of Germany. In terms of migration, after the Treaty of Amsterdam in 1999, the themes of integration and migration became the responsibility of the Interior and Justice ministries in EU Member States – bringing these issues back to national level. The same interviewee pointed out that the German administration is quite nationally oriented, with considerable concern for the state of affairs within its own borders and little outside. Many of the federal employees in these ministries do not speak another language, thereby limiting their horizon to national issues.

The point was also raised that the whole concept of migration has changed since the ICRMW was negotiated: at the time (mid 1980s), the dominant idea about migration was that it was temporary. However, once it became clear that a significant proportion of migrants remained in the receiving countries, the notion of integration should have been emphasized. Indeed, this point raises an important question, that of the inclusion of integration issues in the Convention. The view was also voiced that there are other – and, in some cases, more recent – conventions that are more likely to be ratified, and hence more attention has been focused on these.

Immigration in Germany

History of German immigration

Prior to the Second World War, Germany was known as a country of emigration, largely sending migrants to the United States, although it also experienced a certain amount of immigration. These migrants included labour migrants as well as refugees; two representative groups were, among others, Polish labour migrants to the industrial Ruhr area in the late nineteenth and early twentieth centuries and French Protestants (Huguenots) in search of religious refuge in the late seventeenth and early eighteenth centuries.

In the post-war 'economic miracle', emerging at the end of the Second World War, it became clear that extra labour was needed, and bilateral recruitment agreements were concluded, starting in 1955, with Italy, Portugal, Turkey, Spain and Yugoslavia. The increased participation of German women in the labour market, which would also have helped to ease the shortage of labour, was rejected at the political level. These agreements led to the recruitment of 3 to 4 million workers altogether, with the one-millionth migrant, Portuguese worker Armando Rodrigues, receiving a festive welcome, including a bouquet of flowers and a moped as a welcome present, in September 1964.

With the oil crisis of 1973, however, official labour recruitment was terminated, with the intention that the foreign workers then in Germany should return home to rejoin their families. Instead, the opposite occurred, with family members joining workers in Germany. As a result, the number of migrant workers and their families living in Germany rose. Following the ban on labour recruitment, labour migrants did continue to work in Germany, although never again to the extent of the period from 1955 to 1974. Indeed, the system shifted to one of selective, mainly short-term, migration, which continues today. Seasonal work and short-term contracts in the agriculture, hotel and restaurant, construction and IT sectors are still granted to migrant workers, and new programmes are being developed. These contracts are limited in numbers and in duration. Both immigration and work – whether carried out by foreigners or by Germans – are very closely regulated in Germany. Throughout the years, with respect to immigration, the themes of control, regulation and acceptability to the German population have been emphasized.

Indeed, until 1998, Germany did not see itself as an immigration country, a position that was supported by government statements – irrespective of the political party in office. The statement *Deutschland ist kein Einwanderungsland* (Germany is not an immigration country) was meant to express that Germany was not a classical immigration country of the United States-Canada-Australia model, but was rather an accidental and temporary country of immigration. At the same time, however, this statement expressed the political and public attitude towards migration and immigrants. There was no coherent integration policy, whether at federal level, the state (*Länder*) or local level; although, today, important first steps have been made, there is, as in many immigration countries, still no coherent overall policy.

Following this situation, there have been two significant sources of tension in Germany with respect to migration: first, for some sectors of society a feeling of a certain cultural distance between Germans and migrants has caused social tensions, xenophobia and even violence against migrants, still felt today. Second, with unemployment high among Germans, and even higher among some groups such as Turkish citizens, people have also resisted further immigration and, occasionally, have even shown anger towards migrants already in Germany.

However, since 2000, the concept of immigration to Germany has entered the public and political arena. A new citizenship law entered into force on 1 January 2000 and an independent Immigration Commission was called into existence that same year. This Commission recommended a number of steps to bring political action into line with reality, resulting in an Immigration Law that took many of the Commission's recommendations into account and which entered into force on 1 January 2005. Additionally, by this point, demographic issues were relevant: an ageing and shrinking population had become a visible reality. Some sectors showed labour shortages and, thus, in 1999 the so-called Green Card programme was created, which permitted up to 20,000 IT workers to come to Germany for up to five years (about 16,000 came in total).[3] This programme established once and for all that

---

[3] The programme ended in January 2005 – when the Immigration Law took effect.

although unemployment in Germany was high, targeted recruitment in certain sectors was nonetheless necessary. Other sectors, in particular the care sector, are also now discussed as areas in which migrant workers may need to be recruited.

The major provisions of the 2005 Immigration Law (Zuwander-ungsgesetz – in full: Gesetz zur Steuerung und Begrenzung der Zuwanderung und zur Regelung des Aufenthalts und der Integration von Unionsbürgern und Ausländern (Law for Management and Limitation of Immigration and for the Regulation of Residence and the Integration of EU Citizens and Foreigners)) are as follows: first, admin-istrative changes have been made, which simplifies the process of acquir-ing residence permits. Second, highly skilled workers may now come to work in Germany, accompanied by their family members. With an investment of €1 million, anyone can establish a small business in Germany, as long as they also create at least ten jobs. Foreign students are now permitted to stay up to one year after graduation in order to search for a job. The ban on recruitment for unskilled or low-skilled workers, on the other hand, was maintained, with certain exceptions for specific types of workers. Third, humanitarian migration (asylum and temporary protected status, or *Duldung*) is maintained in the new law, as is family reunification. The concept of integration, the introduction of which has been encouraged by the European Commission,[4] is new, while security aspects have also been included.

Non-citizens living in Germany have various legal statuses. The most common is the residence permit, either unlimited or limited (*Aufenthaltserlaubnis*). The most stable legal status, the unlimited resi-dence permit, is granted after five years of legal presence. There are several other less-stable legal forms of residence granted to non-citizens living in Germany: about 230,000 have a *Duldung*, a form of subsidiary protection, or protection from deportation, similar to temporary pro-tected status in the United States. The majority of non-citizens holding a *Duldung* come from developing countries and Turkey (Beauftragte, 2005). There are some 7.3 million non-citizens living in Germany, and a further estimated 1 million undocumented migrants.

---

[4] See, for example, Communication from the Commission, *A Common Agenda for Integration – Framework for the Integration of Third-Country Nationals in the European Union*, COM(2005) 0389 final (http://ec.europa.eu/justice_home/doc_centre/ immigration/integration/doc_immigration_ integration_en.htm [last accessed 23 April 2009]).

While the exact number of undocumented migrants is not clear, there is a broad consensus on the existence of this marginalized group. The estimated number of undocumented migrants has not increased in recent years; meanwhile, however, public debate on this topic has gained ground, with various initiatives raising the issue. A substantial body of research and literature now exists (see, for an overview, Schönwälder et al., 2004; Alt, 2003). The problem of exploitative situations persists, with the public attitude seeming to be that this is a problem of the immigrants themselves, but it does not represent a more significant social concern or widespread unsatisfactory conditions in the labour market. The country report of the ILO (Cyrus, 2005), which is based on qualitative research methods (given the lack of other more quantitative data), concludes that a considerable number of undocumented migrants work in exploitative conditions or forced labour (*Zwangsarbeit*). Migrants working in certain branches are especially susceptible to exploitation. These include the agricultural sector, the entertainment industry, the care sector (see Hillmann, 2005), domestic work, hotels/restaurants and, rarely, sweatshops.

Immigrants in Germany today

General features

Since the 1960s, the non-citizen proportion of the German population has grown steadily: in 1960, 686,000 (1.2%) of the total population were non-citizens. The official statistics refer only to the registered population not holding a German passport, but do not represent naturalized persons with an immigrant background. Unlike the British census-based system, there are no representative data on the minority population, only on citizenship status. The non-citizen population reached a high point in 1997, at 9% of the overall population, and since then has hovered around 8.9%. The absolute numbers (around 7.35 million for 1997 to 2003) dropped slightly, to 7.28 million in 2004 (Bundeszentrale für politische Bildung, 2004; Destatis, 2004),[5] possibly reflecting increased naturalization figures (in 2002 there were some 150,000 naturalizations, and in 2003 there were 140,000). A recent micro-census report estimates

---

[5] Other figures (Beauftragte, 2005) reflect a much greater drop, from 7.3 million in 2003 to 6.7 million in 2004 (Sonderauswertung AZR, 2004). This change, however, resulted after a clean-up of the data, and the drop of 600,000 is probably not accurate.

that around 15% of the total population living in Germany are either migrants themselves or have at least one migrant parent.

The majority of migrants to Germany originate from European countries (79.08%), of whom 25.22% are EU nationals (Beauftragte, 2005). The most significant immigrant group are the Turks (1.87 million), followed by those from the former Yugoslavia (865,829 from Croatia, Serbia, Montenegro and Macedonia), Italians (601,258) and Poles (326,882). Some 4.2% (310,943) originate from Africa and 3.11% (228,499) are from the Americas. Migrants with an Asian background represent 12.43% (911,995). The gender ratio is slightly unbalanced (46.9% of all foreigners are female). The vast majority of non-citizens (61%) have lived for at least ten years in Germany, and nearly one-fifth for more than thirty years.

Migrant work in Germany: forms and patterns

There are considerable differences between the labour market participation rate (*Erwerbsquote*) of the non-citizen and of the German populations in Germany. The rate is, overall, higher among the non-citizen population (in 2003 the rate for non-citizens was 51.7%, and for natives, 49.2%), especially among men (non-citizens at 60.8%; natives at 55.6%), but lower among the female population (non-citizens at 41.7%; natives at 43.2%) (Beauftragte, 2005).

Despite the higher participation, the non-citizens' position in the labour market is more vulnerable: they earn less than the comparable native population, their qualification levels are lower and they more often work in lower-level jobs. Of all employed non-citizens, 36.3% are employees, 52.7% workers and 9.5% are self-employed. The share of self-employed has risen in the past decade or so (from 6.7% in 1991) while the proliferation of forms of ethnic economies in urban areas is generally interpreted as one outcome of high unemployment among foreigners.

The number of non-citizens employed within the social security system (*Sozialversicherungspflichtig Beschäftigte*), i.e. in legal employment with social security benefits, including health and unemployment insurance, has dropped since 2001 and reached 1.7 million in 2003. The official unemployment rate among non-citizens is 20% on average for the whole of Germany, but particular groups show unemployment rates up to 40% within their national reference group (Beauftragte, 2005; Gesemann, 2001).

The ICRMW in Germany

History of the Convention

Germany became part of the development process of the ICRMW during the early 1980s,[6] when the first working group on the proposed Convention was held. Germany's position in the political process of developing the Convention is essential to understanding its contemporary position. It participated in the open-ended working group drafting the Convention (although other countries were not present during this initial phase). Germany's participation was ultimately the result of a decision by the Foreign Ministry, which urged the Ministry of Labour and Social Affairs to participate in the process. Although many receiving countries took part in the discussions, our informant said that it was widely believed that the end result would favour the G-77.[7]

In the discussions during the second reading of the Convention, which started in 1985, Germany followed what became known as the 'German formula'. At many points of discussion, Germany proposed alternative wordings to points which it (as well as many other countries) found objectionable. Some of these alternatives were accepted, but many were not. If the alternative wording was not accepted, Germany formally withdrew the proposal and asked to have Germany's position noted in the protocol. This strategy meant that while Germany formally supported the text of the Convention, it could refer to the criticisms on record and thus maintain its somewhat hesitant position, not wanting to be bound too much by the Convention.

The working group was divided into regional groups, among them the so-called MESCA faction, made up of Mediterranean and Scandinavian countries (originally Italy, France, Finland and Sweden, but also Greece, Portugal, Spain and later Norway). The former wanted to protect their countrymen living in former colonies while the latter were interested in a humanitarian agenda. Apart from this historical moment, a general divide between the interests of the developing countries (and thus mainly sending countries) and the industrialized countries (mainly receiving

---

[6] The following is based on an interview with a former German civil servant who participated in the process.

[7] G-77 stands for 'The Group of 77 at the United Nations', established in 1964 by seventy-seven developing countries who were signatories of the 'joint declaration of the Seventy-Seven Countries' issued at the end of the first session of the UNCTAD. The group lobbies in favour of the economic interests of the developing countries (www.g77.org).

countries) existed from the outset, including the selection of venue: Geneva, as the seat of the ILO, was viewed suspiciously by the developing countries, and thus meetings took place in New York. At the same time, the very flexible timeframe made decisions difficult (the working group was 'open-ended'). The developed countries would have preferred to leave the theme of migrant workers within the purview of the ILO, while the developing countries were in favour of it being addressed by the UN more broadly (Köhler, 2004, p. 85).

During the years of negotiation, Germany maintained the same three objections:

(1) Rights for migrant workers are already covered by the two UN covenants (civil and political rights – ICCPR; economic, social and cultural rights – ICESCR), so that further codification is not needed. Moreover, the mistaken impression could be given that the countries that ratified these instruments were not respecting the migrant workers' rights they laid out.
(2) The Convention touches on basic human rights that are covered elsewhere and, again, therefore do not need to be repeated. Likewise, basic rights (most importantly, human rights) and technical rights (such as potential migrants' right to complete information on the receiving countries and the intended work (article 37)) are equal in importance, which should not be the case.
(3) Irregular migrants are given a position that is much too strong in terms of the protection of their rights.

Activities concerning the Convention

Activities concerning the Convention in Germany have been limited to NGOs, and even then are not widespread, while a lengthy report published in January 2007 by the German Institute for Human Rights (Spiess, 2007) represents the most in-depth study of the Convention to date. One NGO, the Komitee für Grundrechte und Demokratie (Committee for Basic Rights and Democracy, CBRD), was asked to publicize the Convention in Germany by the NGO December 18, which has coordinated the European campaign for ratification. The CBRD accordingly carried out a campaign in 2004, collecting 1,500 to 1,600 signatures to a petition calling for ratification of the Convention, and holding a press conference to announce the delivery of the petition to the federal government, which delivered an official response (see below).

Prior to the publication of the German Institute for Human Rights' report, CBRD publicity had been the most significant activity concerning the Convention.

The CBRD's promotion of the petition was accompanied by the distribution of leaflets on the difficult situation of migrant workers in Germany as well as the benefits they would receive under the Convention, in the hope that if the extremely poor working conditions of migrant workers were known, there would be more widespread support for the Convention. Following this line of logic, more publicity could have positive results (some interviewees felt otherwise, see below). Today, the CBRD notes that it does not expect ratification of the Convention – nor was it expected at the time of the campaign – but wanted to raise public awareness of the poor situation of migrant workers, including undocumented workers. According to the CBRD, the campaign was successful in so far as the left-leaning, open-minded segment of society is now more familiar with the Convention. The publication of the German Institute for Human Rights' report does indicate that the cause has been taken up by others.

Awareness of the Convention

Overall, awareness of the Convention in Germany is extremely low. Apart from several activist NGOs, academics and politicians, it is virtually unknown – a Convention that 'blooms in obscurity', as one parliamentarian put it. In the last few years, since the entry into force of the Convention, knowledge of it has increased, probably due to the CBRD publicity campaign as much as the entry into force itself.

Even among NGOs, the existence of the Convention is not well known, and then only among highly specialized NGOs dealing with topics such as human trafficking. Social workers are, for the most part, not aware of the Convention. We spoke with five NGOs dealing with migrants or human rights who were unwilling to grant interviews for the simple reason that they knew nothing of the Convention and, at the same time, were unwilling to go on record as unfamiliar with it.

Among government officials with whom we spoke, only those whose portfolio includes the Convention have more than a passing familiarity with it. All indications – including comments by interviewees – seem to be that this situation is widespread. Even those politicians and parliamentarians who are well informed in the field of human rights and migration are unaware of the Convention, while the same holds true for academics and NGOs.[8]

For a long time, protection of human rights for migrant workers was simply not a problem in Germany; there was no awareness of human rights violations in the labour market, whether towards Germans or migrant workers. It was widely believed that the standards in Germany were higher than elsewhere – both for German workers and for legal non-citizen residents. Germany's system of co-determination, in which workers and trade union representatives have a seat on company boards, exemplifies the high standards of the German labour system. Neoliberal groups were also not in favour of additional laws regulating working conditions.

Work in the underground economy was moreover not seen in the broader setting of 'decent work'; in other words, guidelines regulating minimum standards for work in the informal sector were not seen as necessary or, indeed, even considered.

There are also structural reasons for the lack of awareness of the Convention in Germany: it was completed in 1990, the year in which East and West Germany unified. Unification led to a focus on internal politics, although a major overhaul of asylum policy was negotiated to take effect in 1993.

Trade unions, a group quite likely to be affected by ratification of the Convention, have a somewhat ambivalent relationship to it. While, on the one hand, at the institutional level there is an awareness of the Convention and even a certain fear of it, individual union members have essentially no knowledge of it. One respondent estimated, for example, that within all German trade unions, there are about 100 individuals who know that the Convention exists, about fifty who have read it and twenty who have a political interpretation of it; in other words, a very small minority given the estimated 7 million union members in Germany. This is due to the domestic, rather than international, orientation of the trade unions. Indeed, the Convention was initially interpreted as infringing upon the national trade unions.

Although the rights of migrants to form or to join trade unions are specifically mentioned in the Convention (articles 26 and 33), the issue of

---

[8] Indeed, one interviewee noted that he had known little about the Convention until we asked for an interview, at which point his staff briefed him, while another noted that he had worked on the Convention in earlier years but had little to do with it since, and was again briefed.

its ratification is simply not on the agenda for trade unions, whether as an internal point or for discussion with government representatives. Nonetheless, trade unions have begun to show some interest in the Convention; there have been some recently organized workshops on irregular migration. Other unions, in particular IG Metall, have launched a discussion more specifically targeted at looking at clandestine migration and human rights. This development supports the contention of NGOs that, even in the absence of ratification of the Convention, important issues, most significantly the protection of migrant workers, are nonetheless raised and discussed.

Reasons for non-ratification

German Government

One of the key obstacles to ratification of the ICRMW for the German Government is the inclusion of irregular migrant workers in the protections outlined. Germany, perhaps more than other receiving countries, particularly values the rule of law. As such, a Convention explicitly providing rights above and beyond basic human rights to individuals who do not have a legal residence status will not be ratified by any German Government, regardless of the party leading the government. Migration in Germany is, as in many countries, a highly politicized debate. In Germany, given its respect for the law, the question of irregular migration is even more contentious. Consequently, from a structural standpoint, it is not in any political party's interest to support a Convention that advocates granting rights to irregular migrants.

Nonetheless, the debate over the Convention does serve to bring certain issues into the public sphere, as noted above. Although the chances of its ratification are slim at best, it still has the potential to increase protection for migrant workers, despite its unratified status in Germany.

The second broad reason for non-ratification in Germany – and the one more often quoted by the German Government – is that the rights it seeks to protect are already addressed elsewhere; the Convention is therefore superfluous. These objections have been maintained since 1990, repeated in various communications from the government, regardless of which party was in power.

We contacted a number of federal ministries in Germany, seeking to have a number of government responses for the purpose of comparison, but we repeatedly received the response that the Federal Ministry for Economy and Labour was responsible for this Convention and was the only source of statements on the subject. The German Government maintains a unified position on the Convention. Indeed, the government's official answer in 2005 came from the Ministry for Economy and Labour and may be summarized as follows.

The federal government does not see a need to ratify the ICRMW. The reasons for this include:

- Basic human rights are already covered in the ICESR, which entered into force in 1976 and to which Germany is a signatory. This Covenant refers to all human beings in Germany, irrespective of their legal status. Germany signed and ratified the Covenant in 1976. Fair wages and safe and healthy working conditions are guaranteed in this Covenant, as well as in the ICCPR. These rights are extended to migrants as well as citizens.

- There would only be a need to renew these rights for migrant workers if the international community felt that the parties to the Covenant were withholding these rights from migrant workers. This is not, as a general rule, the case.

- The concept of 'migrant worker' is not defined clearly enough. Irregular workers are included as well, and rights are extended to them which, in the German federal government's opinion, go far beyond what is needed in order to guarantee their basic human rights. These rights could create a situation where irregular workers would choose to go to Germany. Particularly given the passage of the new immigration law (which came into force in 2005), in which combating clandestine migration is a goal, the federal government does not intend to ratify this Convention.

- Other groups are included in the Convention, such as independent migrant workers, project-tied workers and frontier workers, for whom it is simply not appropriate that these rights be extended.

- The position of the federal government is supported by the fact that the international recognition of this Convention, despite its having been agreed upon in 1990 and taking effect in 2003, is quite low. Of the twenty-seven (in 2005; there are now forty-one) States Parties, not a single one is primarily a receiving country, nor are there any EU Member States. There is also no sign that any EU Member State plans to ratify the Convention. A one-sided move to support the Convention would isolate Germany.

Following the 2005 change of government, we inquired of the ministry if the same objections remained; they do.

Both the Convention itself and the broader issues it touches on have been addressed by the German Government in various official documents. As noted, the position of Chancellor Merkel's government, in power since November 2005, is not notably different from that of her predecessors.

The 2005 Coalition Agreement, a lengthy document outlining the intentions of the Grand Coalition (of the centre-right CDU, its sister party the CSU and centre-left SPD) government,[9] gives some clear indications as to a possible attitude towards the Convention, although it is not mentioned. In section 2.8, entitled 'Measures against illegal work: "black" work and the shadow economy', the Merkel Government outlines its general philosophy: illegal work, working outside the tax code and working in the shadow economy are 'not small peccadilloes, but harm our country'. The coalition partners state that they intend to restrict the shadow economy severely, with increased raids and controls (Koalitionsvertrag, 2005, p. 39).

At the same time, elsewhere in the coalition treaty, the new German Government states that, although it supports the development of a Europe-wide asylum policy, the entry of new EU citizens to each Member State must be able to be individually regulated (Koalitionsvertrag, 2005, p. 40). The document further notes (p. 151) that Germany will maintain a seven-year prohibition on individuals from the new EU Member States working in Germany, and that Germany's borders with these states will continue to be strictly watched until these states adhere to the regulations of the Schengen area. Both migration control and control of the shadow economy are to be strengthened.

Specific reference to the Convention, although notably lacking in the Coalition Agreement, has been expressed publicly by the German Government at least twice before: two parliamentary questions were put to the government, one in 1999 and one in 2006 – during the previous and the current administrations. In 1999, responding to a series of questions by a member of the Bundestag Petra Pau and the PDS party[10] on the situation of migrant workers in Germany in 1999,[11] and

---

[9] See Koalitionsvertrag, 2005.

[10] The PDS (Party of Democratic Socialism), absorbed into the 'Left Party' (Die Linke) as of June 2007, was the successor to the SED (Socialist Unity Party) of the former German Democratic Republic, and was positioned at the far left of the political spectrum.

[11] Printed matter [*Drucksache*] 14/1181, 17 June 1999.

again in response to a request from a Bundestag member, the former Minister of Justice, Herta Däubler-Gmelin, an SPD (centre-left) parliamentarian in May 2006, the government issued comprehensive statements.[12]

In both 1999 and in 2006, the government maintains the same objections. Indeed, in May 2006, the government representative explicitly noted that its objections to the Convention were laid out in 1990 at the UN General Assembly and that they 'remain unchanged'.[13] These responses echo the response we received from the Ministry for Economy and Labour. The 2006 response again draws on the fact that, of the then thirty-four signatories to the Convention, none is primarily a country of destination, and that no EU Member State has signed it. The 2006 response also notes that in 2002, the German Government was urged by the Green and SPD parties to ratify various UN conventions, noting that 'The migrant workers' Convention was not included in that listing.'[14] However, the 2002 document does call for Germany to 'work toward the ratification of other conventions and protocols relevant for human rights, as well as for the withdrawal of reservations'.[15]

The Ministry for Foreign Affairs issues a regular report on human rights, commenting both on Germany and on other countries.[16] The 2005 report does not mention the Convention, but says: 'Germany will continue to work in the United Nations for the strengthening of the protection of human rights for migrants. It is convinced that this protection is thoroughly guaranteed by the implementation of the basic human rights agreements.'[17]

The conclusion to be drawn from official documents, then, is that ratification of the Convention in Germany is unlikely, but that the protections included in it – with the exception of those extended to persons without a legal residence document – are taken seriously in the country.

---

[12] Printed matter [Drucksache] 16/1737, Antwort des Parlamentarischen Staatssekretärs Gerd Andres vom 22. Mai 2007.

[13] Ibid.   [14] Ibid., p. 3.

[15] Printed matter [Drucksache] 15/136, Antrag der Fraktionen SPD und Bündnis 90/die Grünen. Menschenrechte als Leitlinie der deutschen Politik, p. 8.

[16] Bericht der Bundesregierung über ihre Menschenrechtspolitik in den auswärtigen Beziehungen und in anderen Politikbereichen, 2005 (www.auswaertiges-amt.de/diplo/de/Infoservice/Broschueren/Menschenrechte7.pdf [last accessed 23 April 2009]).

[17] Ibid., p. 169.

Non-governmental attitudes towards ratification

Other interviewees– non-governmental, parliamentary and academic – largely reinforced the government statements, either noting that the ICRMW is extremely unlikely to be ratified or that the protections laid out therein are guaranteed elsewhere.

From the perspective of an FDP (Liberal) Party MP, ratification of the Convention would be 'tautological'. In his view, the majority of the human rights it calls for are covered in other conventions and agreements, as well as the German *Grundgesetz* (basic law, i.e. the Constitution). As for labour market rights, when pressed he agreed that, indeed, they were not covered. At the same time, he did not see this as a particularly vital area of concern. While other interviewees had mentioned their concerns about irregular migration, this interviewee did not – although he noted that other political parties (particularly the CDU/CSU) might have that concern.

Among NGOs familiar with the Convention (as noted above, they are a minority), only a few reluctantly give it priority, feeling that their efforts would be better used elsewhere, given the improbability of ratification. One NGO noted that it would be strategically unwise to give the impression that migrants' human rights in Germany are not protected – a backlash might develop in which certain segments of society might protest against non-citizens having access to various rights and protections. The emphasis should be on the areas in which migrants do have rights. This is perceived as a very sensitive topic in Germany.

On the other hand, as one NGO noted, not all the available legal possibilities for migrant protection are taken advantage of, and there should therefore be stronger awareness-raising activities. From an NGO perspective, the knowledge of existing regulations among German local, state and federal offices seems to be limited, while these offices also often seem to be reluctant to even discuss the Convention – largely because of the fear that this might result in more administrative work: reports, forms to be filled out, etc.

NGOs note that the legal situation concerning the authorities' interaction with irregular migrants if the Convention were to be ratified is not completely clear. Under current legislation,[18] 'public offices' are required to report an individual's irregular status if, in the course of official duties,

---

[18] Gesetz über den Aufenthalt, die Erwerbstätigkeit und die Integration von Ausländern im Bundesgebiet (Aufenthaltsgesetz – AufenthG) (Law on Residence, Work and Integration of Foreigners in Germany (Residence Law)), § 87.

such as registration for schooling, such status is discovered. However, if an official working in one of these offices 'happens' to discover that a person has irregular status, they are not required to report it. 'Public offices' include police stations, courts, embassies, unemployment offices, welfare offices, offices for youth in the areas of education and science, as well as those who make decisions about admittance to social or medical establishments.[19]

Irregular migrants are guaranteed basic medical care by § 1 Abs. 1 Nr. 5 of the Federal Law on Asylum Seekers' Social Benefits, which defines as eligible those who 'are required to leave the country, even if a deportation order has not yet been or is no longer able to be carried out'. These benefits include care (including dental care) in the case of acute illness or acute pain, care in the case of pregnancy and other benefits, as necessitated in individual cases.[20] This right to medical care is somewhat compromised by the reporting requirement as discussed above.

There are, however, an increasing number of medical establishments that do treat irregular migrants and do not report them to the authorities. The Malteser International has established three centres in Germany (in Cologne, Berlin and Darmstadt) in which migrants without health insurance can be treated.[21] As healthcare is free in these centres, official documents on the part of individuals are not needed, thereby avoiding the requirement of reporting persons with irregular status to the authorities.

The NGOs with whom we spoke noted the complexity of the reporting situation, remarking that, in some cases, women in an irregular status are afraid to go to a hospital, and children are consequently born at home. The birth is then not reported officially, which creates problems later in life, as that child then has no official documents. The NGOs further noted that, in most large German cities, there are networks that assist people in such cases to register their children, at least on an informal and

[19] Illegal aufhältige Migranten in Deutschland Datenlage, Rechtslage, Handlungsoptionen Bericht des Bundesministeriums des Innern zum Prüfauftrag 'Illegalität' aus der Koalitionsvereinbarung vom 11. November 2005, February 2007, p. 95, paragraph 87.1.1 (www.emhosting.de/kunden/fluechtlingsrat-nrw.de/system/upload/download_1232.pdf [last accessed 23 April 2009]).
[20] Ibid., p. 23.
[21] See www.greenpeace-magazin.de/magazin/reportage.php?repid=2558; http://www.marienhospital-darmstadt.de/dokumente/MIM1-07.pdf [last accessed 23 April 2009].

short-term basis. In other words, as in the provision of healthcare, individuals find ways to work around the situation.

The 'added value' of the Convention is therefore difficult for some interviewees to determine. There are some concerns that its detailed nature would make it even more difficult to ensure that migrants have access to the rights they are, in principle, guaranteed. A further concern that was expressed is that migrant workers legally resident in Germany would be economically affected by the Convention – the increase in available migrant workers can be assumed to lead to higher competition for jobs, possibly having a negative effect on wages. There are fears that nobody knows exactly what repercussions and/or costs ratification of the Convention might mean.

The labour market situation in Germany, with 5 million unemployed as of 2007, makes 'selling' the Convention difficult. The government wishes to promote its new Immigration Law as well as further promoting policies combating xenophobia, but ratifying a Convention that expressly grants rights to irregular migrants would greatly complicate this task.

Despite the government's argument that the rights and protections contained in the Convention are adequately covered elsewhere, one of our interviewees noted that certain groups of migrants, such as those with a so-called *Duldung* ('tolerated' status) or those migrating for family reunification, are not exhaustively addressed under Germany's Law on Foreigners/Immigration Law, so the Convention could be politically helpful. There is, therefore, interest in a debate on these topics.

Immigration legislation – and legislation affecting migrants – is quite complex in Germany, meaning that knowledge of regulations and the question of which regulation applies to which group of migrants is not an easy matter, nor is it accessible to migrants or to those working on their behalf.

Perspectives

The chances of ratification, then, are rather small in Germany. In general, NGOs, along with academics focusing on undocumented populations, felt that more widespread discussion of the topic of extended rights for migrant workers, including the undocumented population, would be beneficial. The German Institute for Human Rights in particular com-missioned its own report on the Convention, feeling that it would be of interest to know more about it. The general feeling was that there should be a strengthening of the human rights system and of personal rights in areas where irregular migrants do not enjoy protection. Others noted that there is a high informational value in discussing the Convention, which would be even greater if the focus were not only on migrant workers.

EU perspective

As expressed by a number of interviewees, it is unlikely that a number of EU countries will agree that the ICCRMW is necessary and work together for ratification. All European countries seem to share the opinion that there would be little point in ratifying the Convention, yet there is no cooperation among governments on points such as this.

At the EU level, the question of labour migration is certain to be raised again, at which point the Convention might once again be addressed. If former Commissioner Frattini (responsible for Justice and Home Affairs) had recommended ratification, it might have made a difference to Germany's attitude. If a non-EU country were to ratify the Convention, however, it would make no difference.

If the Convention were addressed from an EU perspective, according to an anonymous source, issues that should be dealt with in Germany, such as minimum standards for undocumented workers, could be portrayed as issues common to all EU countries, which would make German agreement on these points easier.

Summary

Of the countries that have ratified or signed the ICRMW, most are sending countries, while some could be classified to some degree as both sending and receiving. No primarily receiving country has ratified the Convention. This shows its intrinsic complexity: national debate is set against the need for international regulation and protection of migrant workers. The discussion on the Convention reflects the contradictory reality of migration in times of globalization and the ambiguous re-regulation of the different geographical levels (local, national and global).

To extend the closely guarded rights of native Germans and resident legal migrant workers (cf. Coalition Agreement, the will to reduce the shadow economy and numbers of Germans working clandestinely) to others, even if they have no legal status in Germany, would be opening a debate in Germany that is simply before its time.

Germany still has much higher standards concerning the world of work and, at the moment, a much more privileged worker protection scheme (for Germans as well as for legal residents) than other European countries – while there is also a segment of informal and sometimes irregular work(ers). These two realities (a situation that is not unique to Germany) are perceived as separate, and there is an interest in maintaining high standards. The authorities are convinced that general human rights are granted to all migrant workers, but migrant advocate NGOs and an academic focus on the rights of undocumented workers state that the rights may exist, but that access is limited.

Various lobby groups seem to use the Convention as a tool for opening a debate on sensitive issues within the migratory setting, rather than being convinced of the need for the Convention itself.

International standards are required at a time when the definitions of sending, receiving and transit countries and of globalized migration networks are growing increasingly blurred. Minimal standards for migrant protection should be supported by some form of international lobbying.

Conclusion

We might conclude that a broad debate on topics touched on by the Convention is yet to come. Even if unlikely to be ratified soon, it could be a starting point for a new debate on the 'ranking of rights', i.e. to make human rights as much a priority for national legal regimes as 'law and order' (Bielefeldt, 2006).

The basic situation in Germany remains that government control of the labour sector is fairly closely regulated and, while quite expensive for employers, it offers employees, including resident non-citizens, a good deal. In the event of illness, unemployment or retirement, the social security scheme is quite generous. The generosity of the system is one reason that entry into it is so closely regulated. It cannot, however, function without social security contributions from its participants – one very significant reason for the crackdown on employment outside the system. At the same time, the rule of law in Germany is very highly regarded. These two factors, together with the long-term distrust or even fear of irregular immigration in Germany (immigration has been very closely regulated), create a situation in which ratification of the Convention is unlikely.

References

Alt, J. 2003. *Leben in der Schattenwelt: Problemkomplex Illegale Migration.* Karlsruhe, Germany, Loeper Literaturverlag.

Beauftragte der Bundesregierung für Migration, Flüchtlinge und Integration. 2005. Bericht der Beauftragten der Bundesregierung für Migration, Flüchtlinge und Integration über die Lage der Ausländerinnen und Ausländer in Deutschland. Berlin, German Government.

Bielefeldt, H. 2006. Menschenrechte 'irregulärer Migrantinnen und Migranten'. J. Alt and M. Bommes (eds), *Illegalität. Grenzen und Möglichkeiten der Migrationspolitik.* Wiesbaden, Germany, Verlag für Sozialwissenschaften, pp. 81–93.

Bundeszentrale für politische Bildung. 2004. *Datenreport.* Bonn, Germany, German Government.

Cyrus, N. 2005. *Menschenhandel und Arbeitsausbeutung in Deutschland. Sonderaktionsprogramm zur Bekämpfung der Zwangsarbeit.* Geneva, Switzerland, ILO.

Destatis. 2004. Bevölkerung am 31.12.2004 nach Geschlecht und Staatsangehörigkeit. Wiesbaden/Bonn/Berlin, Federal Statistical Office. Available at www.destatis. de/basis/d/bevoe/bevoetab4.php [last accessed 23 April 2009].

Gesemann, F. 2001. *Migration und Integration in Berlin.* Opladen, Germany, Leske und Budrich.

Hillmann, F. 2005. Migrants' care work in private households, or the strength of bilocal and transnational ties as a last(ing) resource in global migration. B. Pfau-Effinger and B. Geissler (eds), *Care and Social Integration in European Countries.* Bristol, UK Policy Press, pp. 93–114.

Koalitionsvertrag. 2005. Available at www.cducsu.de/upload/koavertrag0509.pdf [last accessed 23 April 2009].

Köhler, P. A. 2004. Staatliche Souveränität und Schutz der Arbeitsmigranten. Nach dem Inkrafttreten der Konvention zum Schutz der Rechte aller Wanderarbeitnehmer. *Vereinte Nationen*, Vol. 3, pp. 83–8.

Schönwälder, K., Vogel, D. and Sciortino, G. 2004. *Migration und Illegalität in Deutschland. AKI-Forschungsbilanz.* Berlin, Wissenschaftszentrum Berlin für Sozialforschung.

Spiess, K. 2007. *Die Wanderarbeitnehmerkonvention der Vereinten Nationen Ein Instrument zur Stärkung der Rechte von Migrantinnen und Migranten in Deutschland.* Berlin, German Institute for Human Rights.

14

Migration and human rights in Italy: prospects for the ICRMW

KRISTINA TOUZENIS[1]

Introduction

This chapter aims at highlighting why Italy has not yet ratified the ICRMW, on the basis of interviews with various representatives of Italian society who in one way or another have dealings with migrants' rights: trade unions, NGOs, politicians and academics. It focuses on different kinds of possible obstacles (cultural, social, legal and political) and aims to show what role each of these categories plays in the non-ratification of the Convention. The research is largely based on interviews, as the Convention does not receive a great deal of attention from the academic community in Italy and thus very few sources are available on this subject.

Italy, as with many other developed countries faced with the absence of a willing domestic workforce, increasingly looks outside its borders for low-skilled workers. Migrant workers and irregular migrants from poorer countries have stepped in to fill the demand. In addition, receiving countries concerned with deregulating the labour market and making it more flexible have made it easier for cost-conscious and competition-minded employers to exploit migrant workers – at the expense of formal employment and human rights protections. This is especially true as the informal sector or 'underground economy' has expanded in wealthy countries, providing increased risks and rewards for immigrants (Cholewinski, 2005). As shown below, the underground economy is rather significant in Italy, and this has been identified during this research as one motive for not putting into place a legal framework granting rights to irregular migrants. As also noted, there is a link between cheap irregular workforces and

---

[1] The views expressed in this chapter do not necessarily express the views of the IOM. This research has been done in the author's own capacity.

migration policies, as the irregular workforces to a certain extent benefit society as a whole – at least economically.

Italy has ratified 1948 ILO Convention No. 97 (in 1952), 1975 ILO Convention No. 143 (in 1981), the European Social Charter (in 1965), the European Social Charter (Revised) (in 1999) and the European Convention on the Legal Status of Migrant Workers (in 1995), as well as the ICCPR and ICESCR (both in 1978), the CEDAW in 1985, the CAT in 1989 and the CRC in 1991. But it still has not ratified the ICRMW. Given the willingness to ratify other instruments relating to the protection of migrants, this seems strange, as it may seem that, having ratified the ILO and EU instruments, there is not much that is new in the Convention. However, it is worth noting that Italy ratified the two ILO conventions more than twenty years ago – in the 1950s Italy was still a country of emigration, and even in the early 1980s the climate surrounding the discourse on migration was different to what it is today, as Italy has only fairly recently become a country of destination.

Foreigners in Italy and violations of human rights

Temporary workers represent a major component of the immigrants present in Italy, especially in agriculture in the south (Caritas di Roma, 2005, p. 304). These workers can find it difficult or even impossible to change their employers or employment, bring over their families, gain secure residence status and access the full range of social benefits (Cholewinski, 2005). In 2004, a total of 983,499 visas was granted; of these, most were family reunification visas, followed by visas to employees. In 2005, that number had risen to 1,076,080, of which 35.3% were visas to employees and 40.1% were family reunification visas. Another relatively large group was that of visas for study (11%) (Caritas di Roma, 2006, p. 80). The migrants coming to Italy are mainly people with primary education (32.9%), followed closely by a group with secondary education (27.8%) (Caritas di Roma, 2005, p. 103). In 2005, there were more than 3 million foreigners resident in Italy, compared with 2.6 million in 2003 (Caritas di Roma, 2006, p. 13). There is a noteworthy presence of minors in Italy, 19.3% in 2005 (compared with 15.6% in 2003). Most migrants have a residence permit based on their work in Italy (62.6% in 2005, 66.1% in 2003) and about one-third have a permit based on family reunification (Caritas di Roma, 2006, p. 13). (These numbers refer only to regular migrants.) In 2005, the total number of visas with a view to a longer stay in Italy (excluding transit, tourism, business visits, medical cures, etc. – all short stay) was 224,080 (Caritas di Roma, 2006, p. 80).

These numbers can be put into perspective by considering the immigration flux in the 1990s. Throughout the 1990 to 1999 period, 217,718 permits for work purposes were issued and 220,080 were issued for family reunification. The immigration population increased by around 80,000 per annum in the 1990s, and since then it has been increasing by around four times as much per annum (Caritas di Roma, 2006, p. 85). The four main nationalities in the immigration population are Romanians, Albanians, Americans (United States) and Moroccans (Caritas di Roma, 2006, p. 84). Immigrants mainly seek to establish themselves in the north of the country, but the south probably has more irregular migrants (Caritas di Roma, 2005, pp. 50–4).

It is obviously difficult to find statistical evidence of the number of irregular migrants present in Italy. However, there are some indicators. In 2005, 16,163 persons were present in the Centri di Permanenza Temporanea e Assistanze (CPTAs, Centres for Temporary Stay and Assistance) and 119,923 were subject to expulsion orders (Caritas di Roma, 2006, p. 89). Further, there is always a very high number of applicants for the so-called 'regularizations' (over half a million), which gives an idea of the number of irregular migrants present on Italian territory. In the last regularization in 2002, 705,404 persons applied, and of these, 634,728 were granted a regular permit.[2]

The presence of vast numbers of irregular migrants is perhaps more tolerated, or even accepted, in Italy than in other countries. It goes without saying that they work in unregulated work situations and basically sustain a large part of the Italian economy. This fits well into the general context of the labour market, which is characterized by insecurity, precariousness and irregularities for national workers also. Any fight against irregular migration in Italy is futile unless there is some control of irregular work situations. As already mentioned, almost 650,000 migrants were regularized in 2002 by the Bossi-Fini Law,[3] but about 250,000 irregulars were prevented from being regularized. Dependent on their employers to

---

[2] See www.interno.it/mininterno/export/sites/default/it [last accessed 24 April 2009].

[3] Law 189/2002, named after the ministers who promoted it. Umberto Bossi is the founder of the 'Lega Nord' Party, which works for the independence of the northern Italian regions and is known for its fight against irregular migration, its fight against Islamism, its Eurosceptism and its opposition to the entry of Turkey into the EU. Gianfranco Fini is head of the Alleanza Nazionale Party, which has the Italian Fascist Party as its forerunner.

apply on their behalf, in many cases they were warned not to make any attempt to regularize their situation (Pezzota, 2004, pp. 36–8).

The 'black market' and irregular migration are strongly connected, and while the state seems to be fighting the latter, it has made it almost impossible to immigrate legally, thus favouring both irregular labour and irregular migration. Both are implicitly accepted, as they are needed and somehow 'fit' into the currently precarious labour market. A low-cost workforce is necessary to close the financial gap in the country's economy.

A 2004 survey on the Italian attitude towards immigrants revealed that 72% of the sample expressed negative attitudes towards immigrants, agreeing (or agreeing strongly) that 'the economic situation in Italy means that we cannot take any more migrants'; 21.8% agreed slightly with this statement and only 7% were totally against it. There is a direct relationship between hostility to immigrants and a low level of education, as 40.5% of those who strongly agreed with the proposition had only completed primary education. The prevailing view, accepted by 83%, was that Italy should support the countries of origin through aid rather than by accepting immigrants, but the majority (51.5%) accepted the proposition that 'the immigrants who are working in Italy contribute to the wealth of our country' (Caritas di Roma, 2003, p. 72).

In March 2005, Médecins sans Frontières (MSF) Italy published a report on the conditions in which immigrants work in agriculture (MSF, 2005). The report concludes that young men and women who have come to Italy for security are, even if they are a necessity for the economy, living in appalling situations not worthy of a civilized country, mainly because they are 'invisible' and ignored and thus cannot avail themselves of their rights. The research showed that out of 770 migrants interviewed (of an estimated total of 12,000 agricultural workers in the south of Italy), 23.4% were asylum seekers; that is, with a residence permit that does not allow them to work – they should be receiving financial support from social services but only 6 to 7% were. Those recognized as refugees amounted to 6.3%; 18.9% had a residence permit for a motivation different from seasonal work (study, family reunification, other types of work); and 51.4% did not have a residence permit, and none of them had the contract provided for in the law concerning seasonal work (MSF, 2005, p. 2).

MSF concludes that a large majority of these persons are living in conditions that do not even fulfil the UNHCR minimum standards for camps in times of crisis: 40% live in abandoned buildings, 36% in over-crowded housing; 30% share a mattress; more than 50% have no running water, 30% have no electricity and 43.2% have no sanitation; and most eat only once a day, even when they work eight to twelve hours, and their diet is poor. According to Italian law, the employer is responsible for housing for seasonal workers, but only 3.4% benefit from this. Those earning €25 or less a day amount to 48%, and they have to pay for transport from the place where they live to where they work – on average €5 per day. Almost a third declare they have suffered some sort of abuse, violence or maltreatment during the past six months; in 82.5% of cases the aggressor was an Italian (MSF, 2005, p. 3). Obviously this creates serious health problems for the immigrants: of the 770 persons interviewed, MSF could only declare forty-one to be in 'good health', even though they are all young people around 30 years of age; in the Italian population, 70.7% of that age group are in 'good health'. The situation gets worse the longer the immigrant stays in Italy (MSF, 2005, p. 4).

Italian legislation

The first real sign that immigrants were increasingly in demand to carry out the lowliest and most unpleasant jobs in the Italian labour market can be found in the Martelli Law of 1990 (Law 39/1990). By then it had become clear that comprehensive legislation was needed on immigration. At this point there were less than half a million foreigners in Italy with a valid residence permit. The deputy PM Claudio Martelli, of the Italian Socialist Party, had decided to push for new legislation that would be tolerant and European in its approach, including a wide range of elements such as entry and residence, work, housing, welfare and foreign students. The debate was heated and the initiative was accused of being too 'soft'. The law, approved on 28 February 1990, attempted a balance between the reforms put forward by social movements and the restrictions proposed by the Republican Party (Caritas di Roma, 2003, pp. 145–6).

However, it lacked adequate measures for the integration of immigrants, and insufficient funds were set aside for this purpose. In 1992, Bill No. 5353, which contained a series of measures concerning health, schooling, housing, vocational training and recognition of qualifications, was drawn up but was not approved before Italy had a change of government. However, the left-wing Ciampi Government built on the proposal and established a Commission to draft a comprehensive new law on the legal position of immigrants, including their rights and obligations and appropriate administrative measures to give substance to them. The final document was at the time more progressive than the EU approach – the EU still described the entry of foreigners as 'exceptional', feeding the myth of zero immigration. However, the legislation was not passed during the 1990s, as the centre-right governments led by the then PM Silvio Berlusconi held a more restrictive view of what was necessary in the migration field. All in all, the decade saw the creation of a rather confusing range of documents, decrees and laws (Caritas di Roma, 2003, pp. 147–8).

By 1998, the number of regularly resident immigrants had risen to 1,240,721 (2.2% of the population), and Italy had become the fourth-largest receiving country in the EU. Between 1986 and 1998, the foreign population had almost tripled. A comprehensive law on immigration was urgently needed. Law 286/1998, on immigration and the status of foreigners,[4] answered this need, acknowledging that immigration had become a structural, stable phenomenon in Italy that required planning at the highest level with the collaboration of sending countries. Immigration flows were to be planned over a three-year period, by annual decrees.

This comprehensive policy deals with the following aspects of immigration:

- General principles: fundamental rights granted to all foreign citizens, and legally resident foreigners enjoy the same civil rights as Italians, except the right to vote. Every year, the government is to issue a programme of measures in relation to entry, economic and social policies for integration and criteria for determining entry quotas (this may be changed to regulation on a three-year basis). Proposed regional councils for immigration have been established.
- Entry, residence and deportation.
- The labour market.
- Right to family reunification.
- Health (urgent or essential care is offered free to irregular migrants), education (irregular migrants' children should attend school), housing and social integration (any form of discrimination, even indirect, in relation to access to services, housing, training courses and economic activity is prohibited).
- Regulations concerning EU citizens (Caritas di Roma, 2003, pp. 148–9, 153–7).

The government did take into account the proposals from the various commissions and social organizations – such as trade unions and NGOs working in the field of migration – that had also been heard earlier in

---

[4] Popularly known as the Turco-Napolitano Law, after the then presiding Minister for Social Affairs Livia Turco and the Minister of Internal Affairs Giorgio Napolitano.

the 1990s, but the need to avoid legal obstacles and to include the EU Schengen obligations prevented it from fully accepting these recommendations. The legislation omitted asylum seekers and people in need of temporary protection (Italy still has no asylum law). As well as facilitating access to work and integration, other great improvements included guaranteed healthcare and primary education, access to the legal process and the right of appeal for undocumented immigrants. But criticisms were still received both from opposition parties and civil society, in particular the trade unions, especially regarding refusal of entry to those who arrive at the border without the necessary documents, deportations, the right of appeal, the provisions that allow detention for up to thirty days in CPTAs and the requirement for a minimum income in order to renew residence permits. One of the most innovative aspects of the law was that job-seekers could enter the country simply to look for work, but that was abolished by an amendment of 2002. The 1998 legislation was also amended the following year to regularize the situation of immigrants resident in Italy before March 1998 – further regularizations have, however, taken place subsequently, a sign that the current immigration law is not exactly a success, although it had become the *testo unico* – the definitive text on immigration law (Caritas di Roma, 2003, pp. 149–50).

In October 2001, the then centre-right administration approved a new immigration Bill (Bossi-Fini), which contained more restrictive measures on some points, modifying the Turco-Napolitano. These concerned particularly the conditions for obtaining work permits and family reunification and the appeals procedure against refusal of entry and deportation, with an increased maximum period of detention. It introduced a *contratto di soggiorno* (contract of residence), which ties entry and residence to work. Regular foreign workers (except seasonal workers) who lose their jobs may register as unemployed and look for work for the remaining time of their permit, up to a maximum of six months. All work permit holders must apply for renewal of their permit three months before the expiry of the previous permit, the maximum duration of a work permit being two years. The Bossi-Fini Law is based on the principle that job-seekers can only enter the country after a job offer has been made, and reinstating the possibility of entry to search for work, as under the 1998 legislation, is now one of the primary objectives of many NGOs and unions.

Italian immigration law as it stands does not follow the spirit of the ICRMW, but reduces the immigrant to a mere mercantile concept, functioning only in relation to the labour market. There is a serious underestimation of the importance of the social aspect of immigration, regarding not only rights and conditions but also meeting public expectations on reception and integration – questions of identity, occupation, public order and personal safety.

Under the 2002 legislation, several cases have been brought before the Constitutional Court (on family reunification and CPTAs – which have become prisons curtailing the freedom of foreign citizens – the evaluation of refugee status and expulsion procedures). The law has been judged unconstitutional where it establishes that expulsion can be effected without due process or where it sanctions obligatory arrest where a foreigner has not left the country within five days after he or she has been instructed to do so.[5] It has been characterized as discriminatory with regard to expulsion, the taking of fingerprints and making a residence permit conditional on the duration of a work contract. Further, as mentioned above, some 250,000 irregulars have been prevented by their employers from being regularized (Pezzota, 2004, pp. 36–8).

In late April 2007, the Council of Ministers approved a *disegno di legge delega* (DDL, authorization to draw up legislation) for the government to reform the migration law. The DDL established that the government should adopt, within twelve months (but in any case not before January 2008), a new law modifying the existing text. The details were extremely vague but it appeared that some of the Bossi-Fini restrictions on labour migration would have been modified; for example, the possibility of entering the country to seek work will be reintroduced and the CPTAs will be modified based on proposals from the De Mistura Commission (named after Staffan De Mistura, in charge of the study), which produced its anticipated report in January 2007. It concluded that the system does not reflect, nor does it correspond to, the complexities of the migration phenomenon; it does not permit effective management of irregular migration; it requires improvements with respect to migrants' rights; it leads to difficulties for the police as well as those in detention; and its costs are disproportionately high. The Commission proposed diversification in the treatment of different categories of persons, gradualism and proportionality in interventions, incentives to collaboration between migrants and authorities and more involvement of civil society in

---

[5] Sentences 222/2004 and 223/2004 have judged unconstitutional the lack of judicial guarantees for expulsion, and sentence 78/2007 (March) established that articles 5, 5-bis, 9 and 13, which provide for obligatory expulsion in case of lack of residence permit, are in violation of the Italian Constitution.

management (De Mistura, 2007, paragraph 5.1). In any case, the change of government in 2008 interrupted this process. Yet, in spring 2009, a new DDL was introduced and discussed at parliament and could have an influence over migration issues, notably by criminalizing irregular entry.

Obstacles to ratification of the ICRMW

In Italy, as in many other countries, there is a 'culture of citizenship' problem in that policies are not only geared towards protecting only Italian citizens, but they are based on the notion that non-citizens do not deserve or need protection and may actually be seen as potential dangers to citizens. The problem manifests itself in the form of phobias and worry about the future in a context of migration. This 'non-culture', which may be considered an international phenomenon, produces policies spurred on by fear of public opinion, which in many cases can seem utilitarian and demagogical, that have vote-seeking as their main goal. Such policies are, however, counterproductive, or at least unproductive, as immigration is a necessity if the national economy is to be kept going (INCMR, 2003, p. 4). In fact, it is generally held that such policies are out of touch with public opinion and that people have by now understood that immigration is necessary for the country.

Administrative/financial obstacles

The *contratto di residenza* (the residence permit based on a contract, mentioned above), which requires the migrant to have a permanent work contract (thus putting the legal status of the immigrant in the hands of the employer), obviously requires stability in the work situation. This is in complete contrast with the 2003 legislation governing contracts, which relies on considerable 'flexibility' and thus creates insecurity. It has become difficult to obtain a long-term contract in Italy (not only for immigrants) on the basis of which a residence permit can be issued. Relying on a contractual system that is more or less obsolete, migrant workers – as one of the most vulnerable groups – are under pressure, and there is a real possibility that irregular migration and irregular work situations will increase and that migrants with regular status will lose that status even if they have been resident in Italy for years (Pastore, 2004).[6]

---

[6] The trade unions have been active in denouncing this flexibility and insecurity (see, e.g., www.ihf-hr.org/viewbinary/viewdocument.php?doc_id=5524 [last accessed 24 April 2009]). The Ministry of Work also shows that time-limited contracts have become more frequent (see www.lavoro.gov.it [last accessed 24 April 2009]).

The administrative provisions in article 42 of the Convention (especially article 42(1)) may create a certain fear that ratification will be a financial burden, but this is probably not a major reason for non-ratification, especially as a similar provision is present in Italian law (article 42 of the 2002 legislation). With respect to article 42(2) (representation of migrants in local communities), there are already a number of such representatives and consultants at municipal level, as first established by the 1998 legislation. Finally, the ICRMW provisions regarding the state's obligation to inform migrants of their rights, laws, duties, etc. (especially article 65(d)) might also be considered a financial burden in order to achieve an adequate level of information in a bureaucratic context.

Legal obstacles

The ICRMW articles relating only to regular migrants are of interest not so much because they grant rights specifically connected to the status of these migrants, but because conceptually they bring them rather close to the figure of the citizen (in the context of the 'culture of citizenship' mentioned above, this becomes relevant). Note, however, that the 1998 legislation (certain points of which were modified by the 2002 Bossi-Fini Law) actually follows the standard proposed in the Convention on this point. Considering that many aspects of the 1998 law remain in force, the reluctance to ratify seems odd, but considering that ratification would be useful internally in order to secure future legislation according to the mood of the political debate (Pittau, 1999), one might conclude that this is precisely one of the major obstacles to ratification – the fact that it would take future legislation 'out of the hands' of the national government. The idea of having their hands tied on migration policy goes against the ideology of most governments. Obviously, the restrictions in the 2002 amendment affect migrants' chances of actually enjoying the rights that have been left unaltered from 1998 (and thus follow the standards of the Convention), as many of these depend on legal status (Pastore, 2004).

The term 'members of the family' used in the ICRMW is much broader than that intended in current Italian national law. Whereas the Convention includes not only spouses and those who have a 'relationship that, according to applicable law, produces effects equivalent to marriage' but also 'dependent children and other dependent persons who are recognized as members of the family by applicable legislation or applicable bilateral or multilateral agreements between the states concerned' (article 4), Italian law restricts family reunification to spouses and children under the age of 18 (or over 18 in the case of physical disability) who are economically dependent on their parents. Parents can achieve reunification only if they are economically dependent and have no other children in their home country. Family reunification has, in fact, been mentioned as a probable formal obstacle by several of the interviewees who contributed to this research. This obstacle is not present in ILO Convention No. 143, which is apparently conceived as more in line with Italian legislation.

However, Legislative Decree No. 5 of 8 January 2007 grants entry permits for various reasons, including family reunification. A foreigner with a residence card or a permit for more than one year may apply for family reunification for spouses, minors (children under 18 at the time the application is filed), as well as those born out of wedlock once the other parent has consented. Further, children over 18 who for health reasons depend on their parents, and parents dependent on the applicant who do not have adequate support in the country of origin, may benefit. As can be seen, the definition of eligible family members has been extended compared with Law 189/2002 and is now more in line with the Convention.

In fact, the consequences for national legislation if the Convention were to be ratified would not be too significant, even considering such provisions as those regulating foreign migrant workers' entry into Italy (Baratta, 2004, p. 27) – which have been the object of serious criticism – or those protecting the fundamental rights of undocumented migrant workers.

Fundamental human rights are already guaranteed by national legislation (Baratta, 2004, p. 23), thus the Convention would not have any significant impact on these – at least not from a strictly legal point of view. Further, the Convention's section regarding irregulars is not particularly innovative – irregulars have basic human rights, which should already be respected on the basis of the ICCPR and the ICESCR. Obviously, the principle of non-discrimination is also respected in national legislation and thus applies to irregulars, even if the explicit right to equal treatment is reserved for regular migrants[7] – and even if rights such as decent conditions of work, health (which is actually better protected in Italian law than under the Convention), education of children (also guaranteed by national law) and union rights are strongly conditioned by the actual situation of 'clandestine' migrants (Baratta, 2004, p. 30).

[7] Article 3, paragraph 3 of Law 286/1998 – modified by Law 189/2002.

The differentiation/discrimination between regular and irregular migrants in national legislation should thus not be underestimated. For example, the MSF research mentioned above shows that even if irregular migrants also have the right to medical care (anonymously), 75% of refugees, 85.3% of asylum seekers and 88.6% of irregulars did not benefit from any kind of health services (MSF, 2005, p. 4). Thus the legal distinction/discrimination between irregulars and regulars does effectively deprive irregulars of even their basic human rights – ratification would create an obligation to *effectively* 'grant' these rights to irregulars too. This does not seem to be an immediate politico-economic goal.

One important point is that, even if the different parts of the Convention are not in themselves controversial, as many are covered by other instruments, when they are all brought together in one unified text and applied to migrants, they have a very strong symbolic value. Ratification would obviously require some revision of the law on immigration, but the strictly legal obstacles are not impossible to deal with (Baratta, 2004, pp. 40–1). Although the legal framework may not pose a significant problem on paper, however, the lack of will to implement protective norms should not be overlooked.

In terms of norms against discrimination (article 7 of the Convention) based on racism, national legislation leaves something to be desired: even if the 1998 legislation establishes that regional observatories against racism should be created, this has never been effected, and Decrees 215/2003 and 216/2003 have the serious defect that they do not establish the inversion of the burden of proof in cases of presumed racism. Further, a clause in these decrees establishes that national legislation on the legal condition of migrants is not challengeable on the grounds of presumed discriminatory provisions – even if this is directly or indirectly discriminatory. The Ufficio per la Promozione della Parità di Trattamento e la Rimozione delle Discriminazioni (Office for the Promotion of Equity in Treatment and the Elimination of Discrimination), not being an independent institution, cannot fulfil its role of impartially ensuring equity in treatment and evaluating the effectiveness of norms enacted to combat racism.

Political and cultural obstacles

Irregular migration

The MSF report notes how it seems to be silently accepted, if not approved, that migrants should live in more 'modest' conditions than Italians. However, as the report also shows, migrant agricultural workers often live not modestly but in conditions near degradation. To accept that they live according to UNCHR refugee camp standards would be difficult, as these are conditioned by specific emergency situations, but conditions here are even worse, and there is no emergency. Obviously the 'invisibility' and lack of legal recognition of these people contribute to the substandard conditions. The MSF concludes that there is a specific and urgent need for political will to recognize migrant workers' rights, and that notable evidence of this lack of political will is the non-ratification of the ICRMW. A thorough respect for the Convention would include revision of social and labour norms (not only those relating to migration), but this is not in line with current policies.

Ignorance of the ICRMW

Awareness of the Convention and its contents is generally very low, except among the restricted number of persons working in the field. This general lack of knowledge has been attributed to two main factors: (i) it is not on the political agenda to create awareness – rather the opposite; and (ii) even if NGOs, trade unions and the Italian National Committee for Migrants' Rights (INCMR)[8] intend to address this lack of awareness, they often have difficulty in doing so, partly due to lack of funding but also because they have to deal with emergencies. In academic research, not much attention is paid to the Convention either – again there are a few individuals familiar with it, but little general awareness. One suggested motive is that, as long as ratification remains a hypothesis rather than hard fact, academia will pay it little attention.

---

[8] The INCMR was formed on 17 December 2002. Its main goal is to raise awareness of the Convention and promote its ratification. It includes various representatives from civil society and international organizations present in Italy: the IOM, the ILO, the Federation of Evangelic Churches, the Migrantes Foundation, Caritas Italiana, la Casa dei Diritti Sociali and three large union organizations: Confederazione Generale Italiana del Lavoro (CGIL), Confederazione Italiana Sindacati dei Lavoratori (CISL) and Unione Italiana del Lavoro (UIL). The INCMR is not exclusively focused on lobbying institutions that may ratify the Convention, but campaigns on the theme of the human rights of migrant workers and their families in Italy, as in the rest of Europe, bearing in mind the political debate already under way. However, it has encountered difficulties, not because of lack of goodwill but rather because of the heterogeneous nature of its members, and more importantly its limited resources. One example of how the membership constituted an obstacle was when it tried to promote a television 'spot' about the Convention. The spot should have been created by students of communication science, and national television (RAI) had expressed an interest, but internal discussion blocked the initiative and the opportunity was lost.

There seems to be a general consensus, from government to government – left or right, as the case may be – that this subject is not discussed, which may be seen as a bureaucratic way of not doing anything. If the Convention is mentioned, there seems to be an unwillingness to say that Italy should not ratify it, but on the other hand, no one seems prepared to initiate formal procedures to set the process in motion. Ratification would probably even pass unobserved by the general population. In fact, ratifying would not mean loss of votes, even if such fears may be one of the motives behind the lack of political will. Because of the silence surrounding the Convention, there is no context in which to insert a qualified discussion (outwith the groups working to promote it) – there might even be confusion between the ILO and the UN conventions. The lack of understanding of the ICRMW provisions means that it is seen as more in conflict with national law or interests than it actually is. The fear that ratifying the Convention would to a certain extent imply opening up the borders or losing control over who should be regularized, due to lack of knowledge of its contents, also conditions the movements of the current political opposition. There may even be a specific fear that the Convention includes the right to *enter* a state.

Migration seen as an emergency

The theme 'immigration' is surrounded by political prejudice and is discussed in terms of emergencies; irregularities and actions are promoted that are not at all relevant to integration. All political parties have a rather strong social policy. The ICRMW falls outside the logic of 'emergencies', which seems to be the framework in which immigration is inserted. In Europe, immigration is a stable and ordinary reality, but it is treated as an emergency. In this context of clashing views and philosophies, it is clear that focusing on particular articles as legal obstacles can be used as an excuse for non-ratification, whereas the true reasons are political or ideological.

In this context, it is opportune to note that many states, including Italy, wish to appear as countries where it is possible to stay for a determined period rather than countries of long-term immigration. Any Convention that proposes a rights-based approach to immigrants will have little appeal to such states (Baratta, 2004, pp. 126–7). The very title of the Convention could be seen as a problem (granting rights to *all* migrant workers gives the impression that new rights are being given in abundance to migrants), and in the current political climate, this is not seen in a positive light. The fear is that the public might think that migrants were receiving a series of additional rights, and political opinion is that the public would be against this.

Culture of rights

Ratification of the ICRMW would mean changing the whole debate and instituting general 'popular education' on rights and integration, thus facing up to changes in cultural and, especially, political attitudes. Protecting irregular migrants would favour the politics of inclusion and regularization. Combined with the general silence on all aspects of migration, the problem is not so much the Convention itself, but the fact that there is no political will to face the migration debate, other than the rhetoric of problems and emergencies and the reluctance to strengthen the protection of rights. In this context, and the fact that the welfare system is in crisis (the exploitation of irregular workers can be defined as a necessity), the populist belief that immigrants abuse already scarce resources is very convenient.

Lastly, it has been noted that the Convention is perhaps outdated – that the past fifteen years have seen so much change in migration movements and characteristics that it should be updated. Exactly how this should be done has not been elaborated, but at least it would draw attention to the subject – even if the result was a set-back in migrants' protection, considering the current political environment. The international environment has been identified as an obstacle in itself – multilateralism is in crisis in general, and there is no real wish to enter into this type of agreement. States want to make these decisions at national level, and entering into international agreements, such as the ICRMW, is not in line with the present neoliberal ideology of maximum flexibility. Consequently, all types of protection for individuals suffer. What does seem to be accepted at the political level is ad hoc collaboration agreements between countries, which can be controlled and are practical solutions to specific 'problems'.

Conclusion

Many provisions of the ICRMW find analogous national ones. Italy's 1998 immigration law is considered to be in conformity with the Convention – the restrictions from 2002 may raise some problems, but these could be overcome. This is not to say that, in practice, the current legislation affecting migrants does not create significant problems. Studies focused exclusively on the legal aspects do not explain the surrounding climate – and they are not intended to. Indeed, such studies are useful to demonstrate that ratification will not require much modification of existing legislation, and to prove people wrong who may say so. However, even if the legal debate does not create serious problems, the surrounding discourse and the spirit in which laws are created and applied do. In fact, the legislation – even the 1998 law – has in practice not prevented the serious abuse and exploitation of migrant workers.

The Convention would be an attack on the absurdity of the current system, which, on the one hand, seems to fight irregular migration but, on the other, needs it. It is culturally opposed to a system that systematically violates – hidden behind rhetoric – labour market security. The fact that various groups, politicians, organized crime and ordinary citizens have a common economic interest in having one group with less rights than others is a serious obstacle.

The very philosophy of the ICRMW is to view the migrant as a full person with rights, not just as a cog in the wheels of the economy, and even if national legislation is not contrary to the letter of the Convention, the spirit of its conception and application may be so.[9] True respect for the Convention would mean not only changing the migration law but reviewing many welfare norms. And, as mentioned above, the notion that national legislation does protect fundamental rights of irregular migrants is doubtful.

The main political obstacles to ratification are that granting rights to irregular migrants does not serve the national economy, and it might be unpopular with the public. Further, it would be completely opposed to the current debate, which considers migration a 'problem' to be 'dealt with' by applying restrictive measures. Even if favouring migrants' rights may no longer effectively lose a political party votes, as migration is useful, there is a need for a change of mindset in a society that does not consider migrants' rights to be a matter of concern.

References

Baratta, R. 2004. *La Convenzione sui diritti dei migranti e la normativa italiana sull'immigrazione*. Rome, Urbaniana University Press, Quaderni SIMI. (Studi Emigrazione 153.)

Caritas di Roma. 2003. *Dossier Statistico Immigrazione. Contemporary Immigration in Italy – Current Trends and Future Prospects*. Rome, Caritas.

---

[9] As noted by CISL, CGIL and UIL in November 2003 in a statement before the event on 18 December (www.uil.it/pol_territoriali/man_migranti.htm [last accessed 24 April 2009]).

2005. *Dossier Statistico Immigrazione. Contemporary Immigration in Italy – Current Trends and Future Prospects.* Rome, Caritas.

2006. *Dossier Statistico Immigrazione. Contemporary Immigration in Italy – Current Trends and Future Prospects.* Rome, Caritas.

Cholewinski, R. 2005. Protecting migrant workers in a globalized world. *Migration Information Source.* Available at www.migrationinformation.org/Feature/display.cfm?ID=293 [last accessed 24 April 2009].

De Mistura, S. 2007. *2007 Report of the De Mistura Commission.* Available at http://detention-in-europe.org/images/stories/2007%20il%20rapporto.pdf [last accessed 24 April 2009].

INCMR. 2003. Proc. Seminario di Approfondimento Giuridico sulla Convenzione internazionale sulla protezione dei diritti dei lavoratori migranti e dei membri delle loro famiglie, adottata dall'Assemblea Generale delle Nazioni Unite il 18 dicembre 1990, 6 May 2003, organized by the Italian National Committee for Migrants' Rights in collaboration with La Sapienza University, Rome.

MSF. 2005. *I Frutti dell'ipocrazia. Storia di chi l'agricultura la fa. Di nascosto.* Geneva, Switzerland, Médecins sans Frontières.

Pastore, M. 2004. Statement alla 33° sessione del Comitato delle Nazioni Unite per i diritti economici, sociali e culturali, 8 to 26 November. Geneva, Switzerland, Sub-Commission on the Promotion and Protection of Human Rights.

Pezzota, S. 2004. Proc. 7th Meeting Internazionale Migrazioni Loreto, 25 July–1 August 2004.

Pittau, F. 1999. La Convenzione dell'ONU sui lavoratori migranti: prospettive d'impegno a 10 anni di distanza. *Affari sociali internazionali*, Vol. 27, No. 4, pp. 97–108.

15

The ICRMW and the European Union

EUAN MACDONALD AND RYSZARD CHOLEWINSKI

Introduction

Conceived in the 1970s, drafted in the 1980s and opened for ratification in the 1990s, paraphrasing Pécoud and de Guchteneire (2006, p. 252), the ICRMW finally entered into force on 1 July 2003. Despite the fact that it is viewed by the OHCHR as one of the eight core international human rights treaties, to date it boasts only forty-one States Parties – by some distance the lowest ratification level of any instrument in this category currently in force. This lack of support for the Convention from the international community becomes even more striking on consideration of the fact that not one single major labour destination country has yet ratified it[1] – even those that have otherwise exemplary records (on paper at least) of support for international and regional human rights instruments, especially the Member States of the EU.

This chapter draws heavily on a report, commissioned by UNESCO and written by the present authors,[2] which focuses on the reasons for non-ratification of the ICRMW, and the prospects for rectifying this, in seven countries of the European Economic Area (EEA):[3] six EU Member

---

[1] However, this is changing, as one of the latest countries to have ratified the Convention is Argentina, which is generally viewed as a destination country in South America. Moreover, Mexico, Morocco and the Libyan Arab Jamahiriya are also destination countries for migrant workers, as well as significant transit countries in their respective regions.

[2] See MacDonald and Cholewinski (2007), in particular Part 5. The report was based on a series of detailed individual studies carried out in the states involved, and those concerning the four largest EU Member States have been revised and published as contributions to the present volume: see chapters by Hillmann and Klekowski von Koppenfels (Germany), Oger (France), Ryan (United Kingdom) and Touzenis (Italy).

[3] The EEA comprises, as of June 2009, thirty states: the twenty-seven EU members (Austria, Belgium, Bulgaria, Cyprus, Czech Republic, Denmark, Estonia, Finland, France, Germany, Greece, Hungary, Ireland, Italy, Latvia, Lithuania, Luxembourg, Malta, Poland, Portugal, Romania, Slovakia, Slovenia, Spain, Sweden, the Netherlands and the United Kingdom) plus Iceland, Lichtenstein and Norway.

States (France, Germany, Italy, Poland, Spain and the United Kingdom) and Norway. To put things in perspective, all the above states have ratified the other seven core international human-rights treaties currently in force and are, of course, parties to the ECHR. This general record becomes a little more uneven, however, when international and regional instruments specifically aimed at migrants, in particular ILO Conventions Nos. 97 and 143[4] and the ECMW, are taken into consideration: while some states, such as Italy and Norway, have indeed ratified all three, both Germany and the United Kingdom are party only to ILO Convention No. 97 (which, crucially, does not deal with irregular migrants), and Poland is not bound by any of these migrant-specific agreements. It would seem, therefore, that there is something that makes even those states that view themselves as leaders in the human rights field decidedly reticent when it comes to the rights of migrants in general, and irregular migrants in particular, as the complete absence of ratifications of the ICRMW by any country in the EU/EEA bears out.

This chapter first provides an overview of the principal obstacles to ratification of the Convention in the seven EU/EEA countries examined in the above-cited report. It then considers the EU context and the validity of the arguments in a number of these countries that ratification is dependent on the EU taking a lead. The compatibility of the developing EU migration policy with the Convention's provisions is then examined, with a view to ascertaining how this policy might better comply with the Convention. Finally, the importance of forthcoming EU law and policy making in the field of legal migration is emphasized, and the impact it is likely to have on the success of the ICRMW in terms of future ratification by EU Member States is assessed.

Obstacles to ratification in EU/EEA Member States

The reasons behind the non-ratification of the ICRMW are manifold and relate in complex ways to general attitudes towards migration, certain Convention-specific objections and the manner in which these interact. Given the widely varying historical, demographic and economic realities

---

[4] See, respectively, 1949 ILO Convention No. 97 (Convention concerning Migration for Employment (Revised)) and 1975 ILO convention No. 143 (Convention concerning Migrant Workers (Supplementary Provisions)). The texts of these instruments are available from the ILO International Labour Standards website (www.ilo.org/public/english/standards/norm/index.htm [last accessed 24 April 2009]).

of the countries in the region, it is perhaps unsurprising that many of the obstacles to ratification are particular to individual states. Neither Poland nor Norway, for example, have had much experience with the regulation of high levels of immigration, and thus lack the developed institutional framework and infrastructure for dealing with this issue that the Convention often seems to presuppose (MacDonald and Cholewinski, 2007, p. 58, n. 4), while the long-standing French objection to the recognition of minorities on its territory has created some difficulties.[5] Despite these differences, however, recent research carried out into individual EU/EEA states suggests that by far the most important obstacles to ratification are largely shared between the countries of the region. These can be divided into three different sets of issues: low levels of awareness of the Convention (MacDonald and Cholewinski, 2007, Part 3, n. 4); legal objections (Part 4.1.1); and political concerns (Part 4.1.1).[6]

Lack of awareness

While lack of awareness of the Convention is clearly a problem in all European states, it seems evident that in two at least, France and the United Kingdom, successful civil society action has done much to alleviate this problem. In both cases, the actors involved did not attempt to campaign individually, but instead pooled resources in order to achieve a stronger and more sustained campaign. The civil society networks in both countries were structured around 'coalitions for ratification', made up of prominent NGOs and trade unions, who then combined various activities, such as the organization of conferences, leafleting campaigns, petitions, etc., in order to both inform the public and put pressure on politicians to act. Other states, such as Italy and Spain, have followed a similar, if considerably more rudimentary, pattern, also achieving some significant results. In a number of states, however, such as Poland and Germany, civil society awareness-raising campaigns have been almost entirely absent.

---

[5] MacDonald and Cholewinski (2007, p. 54); see also Hélène Oger's contribution to the present volume (Chapter 12).

[6] A fourth set of issues, that of 'financial or administrative' obstacles, is often referred to in the academic literature on this subject. However, the individual country studies carried out for the UNESCO report made clear that these were, where they were raised at all by politicians or civil society actors, largely viewed as minor issues. One exception is France, where the Convention provisions relating to the facilitation of remittances (article 47(1)) have caused real concern. See MacDonald and Cholewinski (2007, Part 4.2).

Perhaps unsurprisingly, recent studies also suggest a strong correlation between the extent and success of the civil society awareness-raising campaigns and the levels of political party endorsement of the ICRMW (MacDonald and Cholewinski, 2007, pp. 45–6). In France and the United Kingdom, a number of significant political parties have made ratification a central policy goal, perhaps most strikingly in the United Kingdom with the Liberal Democrats, the third-largest party in the country. In both countries, the Green Parties have also officially endorsed the Convention, while in Italy the far-left parliamentary grouping has adopted a positive stance, as has the Spanish leftist group, the United Left (Izquierda Unida), which includes both Greens and Communists. No significant political party in Poland or Germany has endorsed the Convention in any way. Similarly, there is a high degree of correlation between relatively successful civil society campaigns and parliamentary activity in the respective countries (MacDonald and Cholewinski, 2007, pp. 46–9). In both France and the United Kingdom, a number of parliamentary questions have been asked on the issue of the ICRMW; in the United Kingdom, Liberal Democrat MPs have tabled motions calling for ratification, whereas in France the CES and the CNCDH have both issued opinions recommending ratification.[7] There have also been a number of questions before the Spanish Parliament on this issue, although in this respect by far the most significant progress has been made at regional level, where the Catalan Parliament (representing, incidentally, the region in which the civil society campaign in favour of the ICRMW has been concentrated) has adopted a number of resolutions urging ratification (MacDonald and Cholewinski, 2007, p. 49, n. 4). Again, there has been little or no parliamentary activity in respect of the Convention in Germany, Norway or Poland.

It is also clear, however, that simply raising awareness of the *existence* of the ICRMW is insufficient; more must be done to familiarize both publics and political elites with its *content*, particularly as a number of prevalent objections are based on simple misconceptions (or misrepresentations) of the substance of certain provisions. Moreover, it is also readily evident that awareness raising alone cannot dispel a number of important obstacles to ratification, as these are founded not on

---

[7] See CES, Avis adopté par le Conseil économique et social au cours de sa séance du mercredi 29 octobre 2003 sur 'les defis de l'immigration future' (October 2003); and CNCDH, Avis sur la convention internationale sur la protection des droits de tous les travailleurs migrants et des membres de leur familles (23 June 2005), respectively.

misunderstandings but rather on scepticism over the necessity of the Convention and to the effect on migration that it may have. Mere knowledge of Convention provisions here is insufficient; rather, a difficult task of persuasion remains to be accomplished. This distinction maps neatly on to the two remaining sets of obstacles, termed here the 'legal' and the 'political'.[8]

Legal objections

The legal obstacles of general concern, which fall squarely into the 'misconception' category of perceived obstacles to ratification, are, essentially, twofold: first, the common claim that the Convention would limit the sovereign rights of states to decide who can enter their territory and for how long they can remain; and second, the equally ubiquitous fear that the Convention would provide for a robust right of family reunification to all migrant workers present in a regular situation in the territory of a state. Neither of these objections, however, stands up to close reading of the text: regarding the former, for example, article 79 provides that 'Nothing in the present Convention shall affect the right of each State Party to establish the criteria governing admission of migrant workers and members of their families', whereas states' responsibilities in terms of family reunification under article 44 are limited to taking such measures 'as they deem appropriate to facilitate the reunification of migrant workers with their spouses...as well with their minor dependent unmarried children'. In language as heavily qualified as this, leaving to states such a wide margin of discretion, it is difficult to see any obligation of any sort, let alone one that could present a serious obstacle to ratification.

Political concerns

Perhaps the most important obstacles facing ratification of the ICRMW, however, are political. These can be grouped into three different basic claims: first, that the Convention is entirely superfluous in the context of international human rights law; second, and relatedly, that the rights it prescribes are already largely guaranteed, on paper at least, by national

---

[8] It is worth bearing in mind that this categorization is in many ways an artificial one; there are strong political aspects to the first group, just as there are some decidedly legal elements present in the second. This distinction remains, however, useful for analytical purposes.

laws of the states concerned; and third (and perhaps slightly incoherently, when read in the light of the previous two), that the Convention endows irregular migrants with too many rights, and as a result would hinder both processes of social integration and the struggle against irregular movements of people. These three objections to the ICRMW appear to be perhaps the most common general objections from the governments of EU Member States, and each represents a real challenge to the prospects of its ratification. None, however, can be reduced to mere 'misunderstandings' in the manner of the two other general legal obstacles described above; rather, the hard task of persuasion remains in large part to be accomplished – for both the governing elites and the populations to which they answer. In terms of the last of these, for example, while there can be no doubt – as is often pointed out – that the Convention *intends* to contribute to the struggle against irregular migration, the issue of whether its 'rights-based' approach to doing so will, in fact, play out in this manner, or whether it will instead be counterproductive, remains deeply controversial. These issues can only be resolved by a combination of in-depth analyses into the legal, social and politico-economic effects of ratification on the one hand, and by a successful public information campaign, based on the results of the foregoing, on the other. If this does not prove possible, it seems doubtful whether the governing elites of many EU Member States will ever be persuaded to take the Convention seriously.

Appraisal

The task of overcoming these practical, legal and political obstacles, then, be it through awareness raising, myth dispelling or persuasive argument, must be viewed as central to any attempt to promote ratification of the ICRMW. In the European context, however, there is another factor of huge importance that sets it apart from any other region. The EU, by far the most developed supranational polity in the world, is in many respects an entity *sui generis*: both the breadth and the depth of integration that it has achieved, and the manifold complexities of its functioning, render it quite unique among regional political, social and economic unions. In no other setting have so many states agreed to cede so much decision-making power over such a wide range of topics to an 'international' body; and no other such entity can, in turn, boast the political, economic and legal influence over the domestic systems of its members – including, perhaps most notably in the international context, a regional court with compulsory jurisdiction over all matters within EU competence: the European Court of Justice.

It is perhaps unsurprising, then, that the set of studies carried out in countries of the region unanimously suggest that national government positions on the ICRMW, which seem to range at the moment from the largely indifferent to the openly hostile, could be profoundly affected by concentrated, positive action at the EU level on this issue. Indeed, in some states, in particular Germany, this appeared as perhaps the only option for making substantial progress on the issue of ratification in the foreseeable future (see, e.g., MacDonald and Cholewinski, 2007, p. 69, n. 4), whereas in others, such as France, the claim has been made that the recent transfer of powers in terms of immigration policy to the EU means that individual states no longer have the capacity to unilaterally ratify the Convention (see MacDonald and Cholewinski, 2007, p. 54; also n. 25 and related text). The EU thus represents one – perhaps *the* – crucial battleground for the ICRMW, not only regionally but globally. Success in that forum will mean that twenty-seven states ratify the Convention, in one of the most significant migrant-destination regions in the world, with a strong potential for a positive knock-on effect given the EU's influence worldwide. Failure, on the other hand, seems likely to simply entrench the negative positions already adopted by the vast majority of states, both within the EU's boundaries and beyond. The remainder of this chapter, then, is devoted to an analysis of the past and potential role of the ICRMW within the developing EU common migration policy.

The EU context

While the EU could undoubtedly have had an important part to play in encouraging ratification of the ICRMW in the years immediately following its adoption by the UN General Assembly in December 1990, certain more recent developments in both the composition and the competencies of the EU have meant that it will almost inevitably play a vital role in either the success or the failure of the Convention, both within the region itself and beyond. Chief among these, and in a real sense the basis of all the others, was the decision to adopt Title IV of Part III of the Treaty Establishing the European Communities (EC Treaty),[9] introduced as an amendment by the Treaty of Amsterdam in 1997,[10] which transfers

---

[9] *Official Journal of the European Union*, C325/5, 2002.
[10] *Official Journal of the European Union*, C340/1, 1997.

asylum and immigration matters to Community competence.[11] That these new powers will not lie dormant was signalled by the EU Presidency Conclusions to the Tampere Summit, Finland, in October 1999:[12] recalling that '[f]rom its very beginning European integration has been firmly rooted in a shared commitment to freedom based on human rights, democratic institutions and the rule of law'.[13] The Conclusions went on to proclaim the objective of creating a common EU asylum and migration policy within the framework of the area of freedom, security and justice, on the basis that:

> [t]his freedom should not…be regarded as the exclusive preserve of the Union's own citizens. Its very existence acts as a draw to many others world-wide who cannot enjoy the freedom Union citizens take for granted. It would be in contradiction with Europe's traditions to deny such freedom to those whose circumstances lead them justifiably to seek access to our territory.[14]

The EU, then, has since the Treaty of Amsterdam seen its powers increased to include, in theory, all aspects of immigration law and policy; and it has, both in the Tampere Conclusions and in subsequent legislative action (discussed in more detail below), signalled its intent to use them.

Certainly, the potential importance of the EU in terms of the prospects for ratification of the ICRMW in the countries of the region was manifested slightly differently in different national settings. Perhaps the strongest formulation is to be found in the claim of the French Government, outlined above, that the transfer of competence in the field of immigration effected by the Treaty of Amsterdam means that France would be acting unlawfully if it unilaterally ratified the Convention: that, since the famous judgment by the Court of Justice of the European Communities in the AETR case in 1971, once common

---

[11] It is worth noting here that the United Kingdom, Ireland and Denmark all negotiated the possibility to opt out of any Community action in this field during the adoption of the Treaty of Amsterdam. Although Ireland and the United Kingdom (and Denmark if the measure builds on the Schengen acquis) have chosen to participate in many of the measures in the fields of asylum and the struggle against irregular immigration, they have been significantly less keen to opt-in to measures concerning legal migration. The United Kingdom in particular has chosen not to participate in any of the Community measures in this field.

[12] Presidency Conclusions, Tampere European Council, 15 to 16 October 1999, *Bulletin EU*, pp. 10–99 (www.europarl.europa.eu/summits/tam_en.htm [last accessed 24 April 2009]).

[13] Ibid., Conclusion 1.   [14] Ibid., Conclusion 3.

Community rules on a certain issue have been established, Member States no longer have the power to undertake unilateral commitments with third countries in that field.[15] This argument, as a point of law, seems suspect: Community legislation in this area represents a minimum standard; it does not prevent Member States from adopting national (or international) provisions more favourable than those laid down at the regional level.

Politically, however, there does seem to be a view, in some states at least, that having formally transferred competence on migration matters to the EU, states should not proceed unilaterally in this respect. This was the opinion very clearly expressed by the former French Minister for Foreign Affairs, Philippe Douste-Blazy, in his response to the CNCDH *Avis* calling for ratification of the ICRMW, noted above.[16] Moreover, the lack of a common EU position on the Convention was the reason perhaps most frequently cited by Spanish Government officials (and, indeed, members of other political parties and civil society groups) for Spain's non-ratification; there seems to be a very general belief within that country that the correct course of action politically is to wait for the EU institutions to take the lead on the issue. While few other governments have been as explicit as the French and the Spanish in looking to defer responsibility for ratification of the Convention onto the EU, the general view to emerge is unmistakeably that EU action in this respect could make an important difference in altering the prevailing negative attitudes towards the Convention.

Of course, it would be naive to read into this nothing other than a genuine expression of regional solidarity. Although this may be present to some degree, the use of the EU in this manner seems to be just as much, if not more, about finding a convenient alibi to help to evade awkward questions about the non-ratification of a core international

---

[15] Case 22/70, *Commission* v. *Council* [1971] ECR 263 (the AETR judgment), in which the Court held that the decision by the European Community to implement a common transport policy meant that Member States no longer had the right to unilaterally conclude other agreements with third parties on that issue. The government has relied on this view in two written responses to parliamentary questions on the issue: the first in a response to a question by the Socialist Deputy Martine Lignière-Cassou on 1 November 2005 (*Journal Officiel Assemblée Nationale*, 1 November 2005, p. 10157), and the second in response to a question by the Green Party Senator Alima Boumediene-Thiery on 10 November 2005 (*Journal Officiel Sénat*, 10 November 2005, p. 6854).

[16] See n. 7, above. The response from the Minister for Foreign Affairs, given on 30 August 2005, is available in its original French (www.cncdh.fr/article.php3?id_article=152 [last accessed 24 April 2009]).

human rights treaty. Most importantly, it must be recalled that it will not be possible to make any serious headway in terms of forging a strong regional position on ratification without the active consent and participation of the Member States themselves; and their general lack of activity in this respect at regional level makes the appeal for EU guidance seem more than a little disingenuous. Nonetheless, such rhetorical strategies do serve to underline the considerable potential that exists in terms of the EU encouraging ratification by its members, and also points to one way in which governments can seek to minimize the perceived political risk of being seen to support the Convention, discussed in the previous section. It is important to recall that the 'EU alibi' can, and frequently does, work both ways: there can scarcely be a government in the EU that does not know full well the benefits of displacing responsibility for politically sensitive decisions onto European institutions. While this is a strategy that raises significant issues in terms of democratic accountability, its potential usefulness in terms of encouraging ratification of the ICRMW in the face of the distortions and sensationalism introduced into the debate on immigration by a capricious and often hostile media should not be underestimated.

The ICRMW and EU migration law

Having established that EU action in this respect is of paramount and growing importance to the prospects for ratification of the ICRMW in EU Member States and beyond, it is worth taking a little time to consider what regional legislation on migration has been passed in this field, before going on to outline the contours of its interaction, present and future, with the provisions of the Convention. One thing should, however, be noted at the outset: the fact that EU law in general provides migrant nationals of EU Member States with a catalogue of rights that goes far beyond the minimum standards laid down in the ICRMW. In examining EU migration legislation in terms of the Convention, then, we are concerned in very large degree with the treatment of third-country nationals and members of their families present on, or looking to enter, EU territory.

Community migration legislation

As noted above, the transfer of competence in migration matters to EU institutions is a relatively recent phenomenon (in terms of the development of EU law), beginning with the introduction of Title IV to Part III of the EC Treaty by the Treaty of Amsterdam in 1997, which aimed at the creation of an area of freedom, security and justice. The starting point for the practical realization of that goal was provided by the Tampere Conclusions of 1999, which set out the target of achieving a common asylum and migration policy among the Member States of the EU. The most relevant Conclusions come under heading III, 'Fair treatment of third country nationals':[17]

> 18. The European Union must ensure fair treatment of third country nationals who reside legally on the territory of its Member States. A more vigorous integration policy should aim at granting them rights and obligations comparable to those of EU citizens. It should also enhance non-discrimination in economic, social and cultural life and develop measures against racism and xenophobia.
>
> ...
>
> 21. The legal status of third country nationals should be approximated to that of Member States' nationals. A person, who has resided legally in a Member State for a period of time to be determined and who holds a long-term residence permit, should be granted in that Member State a set of uniform rights which are as near as possible to those enjoyed by EU citizens; e.g. the right to reside, receive education, and work as an employee or self-employed person, as well as the principle of non-discrimination vis-à-vis the citizens of the state of residence. The European Council endorses the objective that long-term legally resident third country nationals be offered the opportunity to obtain the nationality of the Member State in which they are resident.

Note that this 'fair treatment' goal represents only one dimension of the common migration policy; the next subheading of the Conclusions, also devoted to the same topic, is entitled 'Management of migration flows'. It thus seems evident that the EU common migration policy and the ICRMW are structured, in broad outline at least, along similar lines; that is, an attempt to encourage regulation of transboundary movements of people while also guaranteeing a set of fundamental rights to all those who cross international borders. What is less clear, however, is whether the manner in which the balance between these two often competing imperatives is being struck by Community legislation in practice is in accord with the Convention's approach to that issue. This is considered in more detail in the next section.

---

[17] Presidency Conclusions (see n. 12).

In general, however, progress on the elaboration of the common migration policy has been neither as swift nor as comprehensive as that on the related issue of asylum (see, e.g., Cholewinski, 2004, pp. 4–5). Ten major instruments have been adopted in the field of immigration since the Tampere Summit, although there are considerable grounds for doubt over the extent to which they can be viewed as contributing to a 'common' migration policy, even in those limited areas that they do cover.[18] Moreover, an ambitious proposal advanced by the Commission in 2001 – and the one that would have had been most clearly relevant to the issues covered by the ICRMW – was withdrawn due to the hostility it generated from some Member States, namely the draft directive on the conditions of entry and residence of third-country nationals for the purpose of paid employment and self-employed economic activities.[19] In its *Policy Plan on Legal Migration*, issued in December 2005, the Commission outlines its intentions to introduce five more specific directives dealing with economic migration in the period 2007 to 2009: two in 2007 (on admission of highly skilled workers, which was adopted in May 2009, and on a general framework on the status of all persons admitted for the purposes of employment); one in 2008 (on seasonal workers); and the remaining two in 2009 (on intra-corporate transferees and remunerated trainees).[20] The first two proposals were introduced in October 2007 and the draft general framework directive is discussed in the concluding part of this chapter.

Of those Community instruments in the field of migration that are in force, many focus to a large degree on the conditions of admission or permission to remain for certain categories of people, such as highly skilled workers and students,[21] scientific researchers[22] or victims of

---

[18] For both a listing and a detailed critical analysis of nine of the instruments, and of the future prospects for a common EU migration policy, see De Bruycker (2007, pp. 329–48). The tenth instrument, adopted in May 2009, is the 'Blue Card' Directive. See Council Directive 2009/50/EC of 25 May 2009 on the conditions of entry and residence of third-country nationals for the purposes of highly qualified employment (*Official Journal of the European Union*, L155/17, 2009).

[19] COM(2001) 386, 11 July 2001.

[20] See *Commission Policy Plan on Legal Migration*, COM(2005) 669, 21 December 2005; more generally, see Peers (2006, p. 111).

[21] See respectively the 'Blue Card' Directive, n. 18 above, and Council Directive 2004/114/EC of 13 December 2004 on the conditions of admission of third-country nationals for the purposes of studies, pupil exchange, unremunerated training or voluntary service (*Official Journal of the European Union*, L375/12, 2004).

[22] Council Directive 2005/71/EC of 12 October 2005 on a specific procedure for admitting third-country nationals for the purposes of scientific research (*Official Journal of the European Union*, L289/15, 2005).

trafficking,[23] or they deal with cooperation between Member States in the execution of removal orders;[24] as such, they largely fall outside the immediate scope of the ICRMW, although where they contain provisions regulating certain rights of the specific groups concerned after entry to the host state, they may be brought back within its ambit – and the same can even be said of certain measures adopted within the framework of the common asylum policy to regulate asylum seekers' access to employment (see, e.g. Cholewinski, 2004, pp. 5–6, n. 28). By far the two most important instruments adopted in this field in terms of the human rights of migrants, however, are the Directive on the right to family reunification[25] and the Directive concerning the status of third-country nationals who are long-term residents,[26] which were to have been transposed into the laws of twenty-two Member States by 3 October 2005 and 23 January 2006, respectively. Denmark, Ireland and the United Kingdom are not participating in these measures, having negotiated opt-outs during the adoption of the Treaty of Amsterdam.

The first of these, the Family Reunification Directive, provides that all third-country nationals with a residence permit valid for one year or more, and who have 'reasonable prospects of obtaining the right of permanent residence'[27] have the right to bring their spouse and minor dependent children.[28] This, of course, speaks directly to article 44 of the ICRMW, which provides only that states should 'facilitate' as 'they deem appropriate' such reunification; there can be little doubt that Community legislation in this area goes some distance beyond the Convention in terms of the right that it affords third-country nationals. Moreover, the Directive provides, in its article 14, for certain economic and social rights of family members who enter through exercising this right, in particular to access to education,

---

[23] Council Directive 2004/81/EC of 29 April 2004 on the residence permits issued to third-country nationals who are victims of trafficking in human beings or who have been the subject of an action to facilitate illegal immigration, who cooperate with competent authorities (*Official Journal of the European Union*, L261/19, 2004).

[24] See, for example, Council Directive 2001/40/EC of 28 May 2001 on the mutual recognition of decisions on the expulsion of third-country nationals (*Official Journal of the European Union*, L149/34, 2001); Council Directive 2003/110/EC of 25 November 2003 on assistance in case of transit for the purposes of removal by air (*Official Journal of the European Union*, L321/26, 2003).

[25] Council Directive 2003/86/EC of 22 September 2003 on the right to family reunification (*Official Journal of the European Union*, L251/12, 2003).

[26] Council Directive 2003/109/EC of 25 November 2003 concerning the status of third-country nationals who are long-term residents (*Official Journal of the European Union*, L16/44, 2004).

[27] Family Reunification Directive (see n. 25), article 2.   [28] Ibid., article 3.

employment and vocational guidance (although these provisions are subsequently weakened by limiting references to national legislation).[29] It is
noteworthy, however, that these rights are provided only to the same extent
as they are enjoyed by the sponsor, not on a par with nationals of the host
state as they would have to be according to article 45(1) of the Convention;
and this does seem to be one area in which the Directive lags behind the
provisions of the Convention. On the whole, despite the fact that this
Directive has been much criticized (and, indeed, was the subject of a failed
challenge brought by the European Parliament before the European Court
of Justice on the grounds that certain provisions it contained violated article
8 of the ECHR,[30] which has been ratified by all thirty EEA countries[31]), it
nonetheless provides for a *right* to family reunification that is, even without
taking into consideration the extremely favourable regime applicable to EU
citizens working in other Member States, unrivalled by any other international instrument, and certainly goes beyond the very weak obligation
contained in article 44 of the Convention.[32]

In many respects, the basic subject matter of the Long-Term Residents
Directive itself falls outside the scope of the ICRMW, concerned as it is
with the conditions under which migrants who have resided legally for a
particular length of time in an EU Member State should be granted the
right to a secure residence status imprinted with an EU component.
However, the Directive also contains a number of provisions that lay
down the rights to which those accorded long-term resident status are
entitled. Most important here is the equal treatment provision contained
in its article 11, which provides that long-term residents shall be afforded
treatment equal to nationals of the host state in relation, *inter alia*, to
access to employment, vocational training, social security and tax benefits, and to freedom of association, although it is worth noting that article
11(4) immediately allows Member States to restrict equal treatment to

---

[29] For a critique of the introduction of references to national legislation in this Directive,
and in others in this field more generally, see De Bruycker (2007, pp. 334–5, n. 29).

[30] Case C-540/03, *Parliament v. Council, Official Journal of the European Union*, C47/21,
2004. The ECJ judgment of 12 August 2006 (*Official Journal of the European Union*,
C190/1, 2006) is available from the Court's website (http://curia.europa.eu/en/content/
juris/index.htm [last accessed 24 April 2009]).

[31] 4 November 1950, European Treaty Series (ETS) No. 5. The Convention has been ratified
by all forty-seven Council of Europe Member States.

[32] The right to family reunification under Community law is, in fact, significantly more
complex than this brief outline suggests, drawing as it does on no less than three separate
legal bases, of which the Family Reunification Directive is only one. For a detailed
discussion of this right, see Groenendijk (2006).

certain largely undefined 'core benefits'.[33] These rights, it must be said, compare in many respects rather badly with the equivalent provisions in the ICRMW: article 45 of the Convention provides for equal treatment with nationals in relation to access to educational institutions, vocational guidance, social and health services – and only the last of these is subject to any sort of caveat or restriction ('provided the requirements for participation in the scheme are met'). More importantly, however, the relevant provision in the Convention applies to *all* migrants in a regular situation; the clear implication of the Long-Term Residents Directive, by proclaiming these rights as a benefit of that status, is that those migrants who do not fall under its terms are not entitled to these rights, at least to the same extent, regardless of the regularity of their stay. By thus allowing core social benefits to be attached to a particular privileged status (that of long-term residence), EU law leaves little or no conceptual space at all for the social rights of other regular migrants – not to mention those that the ICRMW insists should be enjoyed by all, regardless of status.

EU legislation adopted in the field of migration to date, then, appears, in so far as it directly concerns issues also dealt with by the ICRMW, to have been of mixed quality, with some rights granted exceeding those laid out in the Convention and others not even measuring up to that proposed minimum standard. Again, it should be stressed that this is in terms of migrants who are third-country nationals; the catalogue of rights afforded to EU citizens goes far beyond anything envisaged by the Convention. In general, however, EU action in this field has focused less on the actual rights of migrants present on the territory of the EU and more on the regulation of those seeking to enter; in this manner, what is perhaps most striking is that there is relatively little material with which direct comparisons between the provisions of the ICRMW and Community law, of the type carried out in the last two paragraphs, can be made. This suggests that the two bodies of law, though looking to regulate, ostensibly at least, the same broad subject matter, are driven by

---

[33] The term 'core benefits' receives no further elaboration in the operative provisions of the Directive; however, Recital 13 of the Preamble does note that it should be understood as including 'at least minimum income support, assistance in case of illness, pregnancy, parental assistance and long-term care'. This, however, leaves a considerable degree of ambiguity, not just as to the content and scope of the rights concerned, but also as to the formal legal status of the definition, contained as it is in the Preamble and not the substantive provisions of the text. For a critique of this legislative technique, used with some regularity in Community instruments in the field of migration, see De Bruycker (2007, pp. 335–6, n. 29).

two very different logics: while the Convention adopts an overwhelmingly rights-based approach, Community action has, to a large degree, been guided by labour market and security issues.

The ICRMW and development of EU common migration policy

As noted above, the Tampere Conclusions lay down a dual approach to the creation of the EU common migration policy, the strands of which may, in practice, introduce competing imperatives: the 'fair treatment of third-country nationals' on the one hand, and the 'management of migration flows' on the other. The drafting history of the ICRMW, as led by the MESCA group, displays the same dual concern;[34] however, with four of the six substantive sections clearly devoted to the enunciation and definition of the human rights of migrants, and only one – Part VI on the 'promotion of sound, equitable, humane and lawful conditions in connection with international migration of workers and members of their families' – overtly concerned with the regulation of migration flows themselves, the structural bias of the latter instrument is abundantly clear. It seems equally clear that, if anything, the basic logic that has to date driven Community legislative action in the construction of the common migration policy has been structured in the opposite manner, with considerably more attention being paid to the regulation of migration flows, both regular and irregular, than with the rights of those that constitute them (see, generally, Cholewinski, 2004, pp. 7–14, n. 28).

While it is undoubtedly true that the EU is, in general, firmly committed to the principle of respect for fundamental human rights as they are laid down in the ECHR,[35] this commitment has not, to date, been fully transposed into the action taken in terms of the creation of the common migration policy. The focus instead has been on regulating the entry and movement of third-country nationals to the EU, through, for example, the EU common visa list[36] and, much more recently, the

---

[34] The Mediterranean and Scandinavian (MESCA) countries took a leading role in the proceedings of the UN working group drafting the ICRMW, among them Spain, Italy, Greece, Portugal, Sweden, and, at a slightly later stage, Norway. See Lönnroth (1991, p. 731).

[35] Article 6(2) of the Treaty on the European Union states that the ECHR is to be considered part of the EU/EC *acquis*.

[36] Council Regulation 539/2001 of 15 March 2001 listing the third countries whose nationals must be in possession of visas when crossing the external borders and those whose nationals are exempt from that requirement (*Official Journal of the European Union*, L81/1, 2001 (as amended)).

development of an EU Borders Code.[37] While it is not normally claimed that these measures, and others like them, actually themselves violate the human rights of migrants (although it has been argued that such measures, or their application, may amount to unlawful discrimination) (see, generally, Cholewinski, 2002), the practical relegation of rights discourse in this field to a status below that of the technical regulation of labour markets or national security will almost inevitably lead to policies and laws that conflict with the provisions laid down in the ICRMW. This can, perhaps, be seen most clearly in two areas in which the developing EU common migration policy and the Convention diverge: (i) on the principle of equal treatment between migrants and nationals; and (ii) on the treatment of irregular migrants.

As noted above, the former consideration, although representing one of the very basic principles on which the ICRMW rests, is fairly heavily truncated in both the Family Reunification and the Long-Term Residents Directives. Even the now-redundant proposal for a Directive on the admission of third-country nationals for the purpose of paid employment and self-employed economic activities displays the same dilution of rights discourse as the others, despite the fact that it was eventually rejected. The Commission's original proposal contained a provision guaranteeing equal treatment between national and lawfully resident third-country migrant workers in the sphere of social rights, and ended with the insertion of an additional clause in the last available version of the Council's amended text, granting Member States a significant margin of discretion in limiting and undermining these rights.[38]

This considerable dilution of the principle of equal treatment in the construction of the EU common migration policy was not, however, an aberration only introduced at the level of binding legislative instruments; rather, its roots are quite clear in the basic aspirational rhetoric of Community endeavour in this field. The Tampere Conclusions were welcomed by many in civil society as constituting a balanced and ambitious document that laid a sound foundation for the improvement of the living and working conditions of third-country nationals within the borders of the EU; indeed, some who are now sharply critical of the

---

[37] Regulation 562/2006/EC of the European Parliament and of the Council of 15 March 2006 establishing a Community Code governing the movement of persons across borders (Schengen Borders Code) (*Official Journal of the European Union*, L105/1, 2006). For a detailed analysis of the Borders Code, see Peers (2007, n. 29).

[38] Compare article 11 of the Commission proposal (see n. 19), with the same provision in Council Doc. 13954/03 (25 November 2003). See also Cholewinski (2002, p. 11, n. 28).

progress that has been made to date in terms of the common migration policy, such as the EESC,[39] prefer to read the legislative developments outlined above as a move away from sound objectives contained in the Conclusions, rather than a continuation of the logic of flawed ones.

That a robust version of the equal treatment principle, so central to the ICRMW, was never envisaged in the EU context is confirmed by nothing more than a superficial engagement with the text of the Tampere Conclusions, in particular the sections thereof quoted at length above. Everywhere, the rhetoric of equality is qualified: after stating that the EU must ensure the 'fair' treatment of third-country nationals *who are legally resident*, this is clarified by the goal of providing them with rights 'comparable' to those of nationals, coupled with efforts to 'enhance' non-discrimination. Further on, the goal is stated as 'approximating' the rights of third-country nationals and those of Member States; indeed, even those of the former group who are long-term residents in Member States should only be guaranteed rights 'as near as possible' to those of EU citizens. It is not, then, surprising that the binding legislative measures adopted in this field by the Community institutions, often the result of lengthy negotiating processes and dealing with topics that are highly sensitive politically, should display a marked lack of commitment to the principle of equal treatment.

It is, however, important not to overstate this point. The EU Member States guarantee a wide range of social and economic rights to their citizens, and it is far from clear that claiming all these entitlements as *human* rights is not stretching that concept further than is helpful. A lack of a robust commitment to a principle of equal treatment with nationals is, then, on its own insufficient to constitute a human rights violation, particularly as the equal treatment principle itself allows for distinctions based on nationality if these are prescribed by law and can be objectively and proportionately justified in pursuance of a legitimate and pressing social concern in a democratic society.[40] What it does bring usefully to the fore, however, is the difference in the basic driving philosophies behind the ICRMW on the one hand, and Community legislation in this field on the other. It is this difference, moreover, that can best explain those areas in which EU law actually does (or will) stand in stark

---

[39] The EESC is a consultative body representing the social partners and other civil society organizations set up under the EC Treaty (Part 5, Title I, Ch. 3). See EESC Opinion on the International Convention on Migrants (own-initiative opinion), Brussels, 30 June 2004, Doc. SOC/173.

[40] For example, this is the standard approach taken to the application of the equality principle in the jurisprudence of the ECHR.

contradiction to the rights laid out in the Convention. The area in which this is most evident is in the Community treatment of irregular migrants.

One of the most obvious incongruities here relates to a document that, for the moment, is only declaratory: the Charter of Fundamental Rights of the European Union,[41] which has not yet acquired legally binding force because of the rejection in the 2005 French and Dutch referenda of the now defunct EU Constitutional Treaty, although it will become binding in most Member States once the less ambitious version of this instrument, the Treaty of Lisbon, amending the EC and EU treaties, is ratified by them and enters into force.[42] The Charter makes a threefold distinction between EU citizens, regular migrants and all other migrants, including irregular migrants. Most rights contained therein are afforded either to the first or the last of these categories, and in this respect the instrument does (or will, if and when it becomes legally binding) provide many protections to all those present on EU territory, regardless of the regularity of their presence. Most notable, perhaps, is the strength and universality with which the right to healthcare is formulated: '*Everyone* has the right of access to preventive health care and the right to benefit from medical treatment under the conditions established by national laws and practices.'[43] This is certainly considerably more than the right to emergency medical care proclaimed in article 28 of the ICRMW. The Charter, however, only makes the limitation of access to all social security rights to 'everyone *residing and moving legally* within the European Union';[44] that is, to *regular* migrants only – this stands in contrast to article 27 of the Convention, which provides for (albeit qualified) access to social security rights for all migrant workers and members of their families.[45]

---

[41] Charter of Fundamental Rights of the European Union (*Official Journal of the European Union*, C341/1, 2000).

[42] See, respectively, the Treaty Establishing a Constitution for Europe (*Official Journal of the European Union*, C310/1, 2004) and the Treaty of Lisbon amending the Treaty on the European Union and the Treaty establishing the European Community, Lisbon, 13 December 2007 (*Official Journal of the European Union*, C206/1, 2007). However, exceptions regarding the Charter's application by the European Court of Justice and national courts, as well as the justiciability of economic and social rights, have been agreed in respect of two EU Member States. See Protocol on the Application of the Charter of Fundamental Rights of the European Union to Poland and to the United Kingdom (*Official Journal of the European Union*, C206/156, 2007).

[43] Charter of Fundamental Rights, article 35 (emphasis added).

[44] Ibid., article 34(2) (emphasis added).

[45] It is also worth noting that a number of Association Agreements, concluded between the EU and third states, contain provisions explicitly removing certain rights in respect of

That a lack of focus on the human rights element of the common migration policy can lead to the unwarranted erosion of those rights in the name of either migration regulation or national security is best brought out by the EU treatment of irregular migrants more generally. First, it is worth noting that, without having ratified the ICRMW, the only regional human rights treaty that is clearly applicable to all migrants, regular and otherwise, on EU/EEA territory is the ECHR; the other Council of Europe instruments, such as the European Social Charter, the Revised Charter, and the ECMW,[46] in principle apply only to those present lawfully, and even then only to nationals of Contracting Parties.[47] While migrant workers have in the past used the provisions of the ECHR to secure effective protection of certain rights (such as, e.g., extension of the right to respect for family and private life (article 8) or to peaceful enjoyment of one's possessions, contained in article 1 of Protocol No. 1 to the ECHR to encompass certain social security entitlements),[48] the ECHR does not contain the full range of economic, social and cultural rights that are guaranteed by the core UN human rights instruments.

The Tampere Conclusions adopted an explicitly security-based approach to irregular migration, proclaiming that 'the European Council is determined to tackle at its source illegal immigration, especially by combating those who engage in trafficking in human beings and economic exploitation of migrants'.[49] It was expected at the time, however, that this legitimate aim would be complemented by measures designed to protect the human rights of the irregular migrants concerned; this, however, has not materialized.

---

employment conditions and social security from migrant nationals of that third state who are present irregularly on the territory of the EU. See, for example, the Euro-Mediterranean Association Agreement with Morocco (*Official Journal of the European Union*, L70/2, 2000), article 66; more generally, see Cholewinski (2001, pp. 371–2).

[46] See, respectively, the European Social Charter (18 October 1961; ETS No. 35), the European Social Charter (Revised) (3 May 1996; ETS No. 163) and the ECMW (24 November 1977; ETS No. 93).

[47] However, this formal position has been questioned by the European Committee of Social Rights, which monitors the application of the Charter and Revised Charter and administers the Collective Complaints Protocol (9 November 1995; ETS No. 158), and under which certain trade unions and NGOs can bring complaints against those Contracting Parties accepting the procedure under the Protocol. In a case against France, decided in September 2004, the Committee found a violation of article 17 of the Charter concerning protection and assistance to children and young persons in respect of national measures limiting the access of the children of irregular migrants to healthcare provisions. See Complaint No. 14/2003, *International Federation for Human Rights (FIDH) v. France.*

[48] In terms of the latter, see, in particular, *Gaygusuz v. Austria* (1996) 23 EHRR 364 and *Poirrez v. France*, Eur. Ct. H. R. judgment of 30 September 2003.

[49] Presidency Conclusions (see n. 12) Conclusion 23.

Indeed, in 1994, the Commission itself made a strong plea for enacting such safeguards. In a landmark Communication on immigration and asylum policies, it argued that the credibility of a restrictive policy to prevent irregular migration would be undermined without the adoption of measures to define minimum standards for the treatment of this vulnerable group.[50] Instead, however, the focus has been on criminalization and penalization – often not merely of those involved in facilitating human trafficking and smuggling, but also, to a certain extent, of irregular migrants themselves;[51] and legislation to protect the rights of the migrants thus criminalized has not been forthcoming. Indeed, even the provisions of the ECHR are limited in this respect to prohibition of the collective expulsion of aliens (mirrored in article 22 of the ICRMW)[52] and the safeguards in articles 3 (freedom from degrading treatment and right of *non-refoulement*), 5(1)(f) (detention of migrants is only permissible either to prevent unauthorized entry or for those subject to removal or deportation) and 8 (respect for family life) (see Cholewinski, 2005, pp. 241–2).

The issue of the criminalization of irregular migrants provides one further illustration of the differing philosophies behind the ICRMW and Community legislation in this field to date. The latter endorsed this practice by its Member States with the incorporation into the *acquis* of article 3(2) of the Schengen Implementation Agreement,[53] under which states undertake to 'introduce penalties for the unauthorised crossing of external borders at places other than crossing points or at times other than the fixed opening hours'. The former, on the other hand, although not expressly ruling out the imposition of criminal penalties on those who seek to enter or remain in the territory of a state without the proper authorization, equally does not explicitly sanction it, focusing instead on providing for penalties for employers, migrant smugglers and traffickers; and it is worth noting that, in this, it follows the example set by ILO

---

[50] European Commission, *Communication to the Council and the European Parliament on Immigration and Asylum Policies*, COM(1994) 23, 23 February 1994, p. 29, paragraph 109.

[51] On this point generally, see Cholewinski (2001, n. 59, esp. pp. 376–82). The EU has also recently adopted a Directive with a view to the establishment of a uniform system of employer sanctions in the EU. Directive 2009/52/EC of the European Parliament and of the Council of 18 June 2009 providing for minimum standards on sanctions and measures against employers of illegally staying third-country nationals (*Official Journal of the European Union*, L168/24, 2009).

[52] Protocol No. 4 to the ECHR (16 September 1963, ETS No. 46), article 4.

[53] Agreement on the Implementation of the Schengen Agreement of 14 June 1985 concerning the Gradual Abolition of Checks at their Common Borders, 19 June 1990 (*International Legal Materials*, Vol. 30, 1991, p. 84).

Convention No. 143.[54] In 1999, the ILO Committee of Experts on the Application of Conventions and Recommendations went so far as to suggest that sanctions against irregular migrant workers are 'contrary to the spirit of the [ILO] instruments'.[55]

It would probably be going too far to suggest that laws criminalizing irregular migrants are actually contrary to the provisions of the ICRMW; the Convention does, at points, seem to imply that some such practices are acceptable.[56] Its overwhelming preoccupation, however, is with proclaiming and protecting the fundamental rights of those concerned; and, as the discussion above illustrates, the emphasis of Community action in this field is entirely elsewhere. This alternative focus is even manifest at the level of public rhetoric. Among the various major institutions and organizations dealing with migration at the international (regional or global) levels, almost all have begun to use terms such as 'irregular' or 'undocumented' to refer to those entering or remaining on the territory of a state without authorization. The EU, on the other hand, is almost unique in retaining the vocabulary of 'illegality' in this respect, even, on occasion, to the extent of using the derogatory contraction 'illegals' in official documents.[57] One effect of this terminology is to deflect attention away from the image of the irregular migrant as first and foremost a bearer of rights – precisely the image that the ICRMW seeks to both recapture and to foreground.

The subordination of the rights of irregular migrants to issues of security and labour market regulation is itself both symptom and cause of what is perhaps the biggest difference between the approach pursued

---

[54] See n. 4 (above), article 6(1).

[55] International Labour Conference, 87th Session, Geneva, June 1999, Report III (1B), *Migrant Workers: General Survey on the Reports on the Migration for Employment Convention (Revised) (No. 97), and Recommendation (Revised) (No. 86), 1949, and the Migrant Workers (Supplementary Provisions) Convention (No. 143), and Recommendation (No. 151), 1975,* at paragraph 338. See also Cholewinski (2001, p. 379, n. 59).

[56] The ICRMW does appear to implicitly acknowledge that irregular migrants may face criminal or administrative penalties when it provides, for example in article 17(3), that any migrant detained by state authorities for violation of migration-related provisions should be held, as far as is practicable, separately from convicted persons or those awaiting trial. See Cholewinski (2001, n. 91).

[57] See Council Conclusions on the development of the Visa Information System (VIS), Doc. 6534/04 (20 February 2004), one purpose of which is to 'assist in the identification and documentation of undocumented *illegals* and simplify the administrative procedures for returning citizens of third countries' (emphasis added). For a critique of the use of this terminology, see Cholewinski (2001, pp. 13–14, n. 28).

in the developing EU common migration policy and that of the ICRMW: even in those areas where the former looks to lay down rights for third-country nationals living and working on the territory of the EU, there is often little or no sense that *human* rights are involved. Consider, for example, the Commission's 2005 Green Paper on economic migration, which aimed to 'identify the main issues at stake...for an EU legislative framework on economic migration' by laying out 'the basic foundations upon which any action in this field must be built'. The discourse of rights features only peripherally in the paper, and even then there is no sense that such entitlements inhere in each and every human being. Rather, 'the EU must...take account of the fact that the main world regions are already competing to attract migrants to meet the needs of their econo-mies. This highlights the importance of ensuring that an EU economic migration policy delivers a secure legal status and a guaranteed set of rights.'[58]

This basic idea of 'migrant-as-consumer' is carried on in the Commission's *Policy Plan on Legal Migration*, which grew out of the Green Paper. It sets out the important project of a General Framework Directive covering the rights of all economic migrants who are in a regular situation but who are not yet entitled to long-term residence status, and in this sense may go some way to addressing the imbalance in Community legislation to date on this issue. Again, however, the idea of *human* rights is conspicuous by its absence from the text of the *Policy Plan*; instead, providing rights to such migrants is justified in economic terms: 'This would not only be fair toward persons contributing with their work and tax payments to our economies, but would also contribute to establishing a level playing field within the EU.'[59]

When such understandings of the role and function of rights are allowed to dominate, it is easy to see how the entitlements guaranteed by international human rights instruments come to be truncated or, in the case of irregular migrants, almost entirely neglected. There is no guarantee that the logic of economics and that of human rights will lead to exactly the same protections and to exactly the same degree; indeed, where one is systematically subordinated to the other, such convergence seems unlikely. Perhaps more importantly, however, the economic logic

---

[58] See the Commission Green Paper, *On an EU Approach to Managing Economic Migration*, COM(2004) 811 final, 11 January 2005, p. 4.
[59] See *Commission Policy Plan* (see n. 20), p. 6, paragraph 2.1.

that is used to justify a set of rights in the context of *legal* migration pulls largely in the opposite direction when confronted with the issue of how to deal with irregular migrants; neither 'rights-as-incentive' nor 'rights-as-just-desserts' leave any conceptual space for a robust protection regime of that vulnerable group of people (as current EU legislation in this field amply demonstrates). It is important to note here that the proposed General Framework Directive (discussed below) only sets out rights for those in a regular situation; the *Policy Plan* makes reference to 'illegal' immigration only to exclude it from consideration.[60] It seems unlikely, therefore, that irregular migrants will have the benefit of having their human rights laid out clearly in binding Community legislation in the foreseeable future.

Community institutions and the ICRMW

There can therefore be little doubt that the EU could play an important role in promoting and encouraging ratification of the ICRMW, both among its own Member States and in the world more generally. It seems equally clear, however, that, from a human rights standpoint at least, Community legislation could only benefit from an explicit endorsement of the Convention, in such a manner as to allow its provisions and basic philosophy to inform the development of the common migration policy. This section examines the prospects of such a shift occurring, by looking briefly at the position of various EU institutions *vis-à-vis* the Convention.

As noted above, the need to respect the rights of migrants while regulating the phenomenon of migration, both regular and irregular, has long been present in EU rhetoric on this issue, even if this has not always been effectively translated into practice as regards the treatment of third-country nationals. Despite the fact, however, that rights

---

[60] Ibid., p. 4. The *Policy Plan* states that the issue of 'illegal' immigration will be dealt with in a separate Communication. This Communication, released in July 2006, entitled *On Policy Priorities in the Fight against Illegal Immigration of Third-Country Nationals*, COM(2006) 402, 19 July 2006, does make a number of references to the need to observe fundamental rights, as laid down in, *inter alia*, the ECHR and the Charter of Fundamental Rights, when legislating in this field. It does not, however, contain any specific guidance on what these rights might be in the particular context of irregular migration; as already noted, both the ECHR and the Charter provide for significantly lower levels of protection in many respects than does the ICRMW (p. 3, paragraph 8).

in general, and human rights in particular, have often been lacking from the approach pursued by the EU in this field, the ICRMW has received a degree of support from some of the major institutional players. Worth mentioning first among these is the European Commission Communication of 1994, noted above, which explicitly recognized the importance of a rights-based approach in the construction of a credible and effective migration policy, particularly in terms of restricting irregular migration, and which called upon Member States to ratify the ICRMW as a means of giving practical expression to this goal.[61] Of course, this early endorsement by one of the most important Community institutions has not proved as significant as it might have, in that none of the Member States have followed the course of action recommended; moreover, it represents the one and only time that the Commission has engaged in any serious manner with the Convention.[62] It receives absolutely no mention in any of the major Commission documents on the common migration policy of the last few years, from the draft Directive on migration for employment,[63] through the Green Paper on economic migration[64] to its most recent *Policy Plan on Legal Migration*.[65] While there were some signs, briefly, that the Commission was planning to undertake a more systematic study of the provisions of the Convention and their compatibility with the developing Community law and policy in this field,[66] this has not, to date, materialized; and a more recent response from the former Commissioner for Freedom, Security and

---

[61] European Commission (see n. 50), p. 29, paragraphs 109–110.

[62] The only other occasion on which the Commission mentioned the ICRMW in an official communication was a matter-of-fact reference in the Communication containing the *Proposal for a Council Directive Concerning the Status of Third-Country Nationals Who are Long-Term Residents*, COM (2001), 127 final, 13 March 2001, which notes, at p. 4, paragraph 2.1, that '[i]n 1990 the United Nations adopted an International Convention on the Protection of the Rights of all Migrant Workers and Members of their Families, which is not yet in force. It has not yet been ratified by any of the Union Member States'. See also Cholewinski (2001, p. 4, n. 28).

[63] See n. 19, above.   [64] Commission Green Paper (see n. 58).

[65] *Commission Policy Plan* (see n. 20).

[66] See the answer given by the former Justice and Home Affairs Commissioner, António Vitorino, on behalf of the Commission (written question E-0068/04 by MEP Miet Smet (PPD-PE) on the International Convention on the Protection of the Rights of All Migrant Workers and Their Families) (5 March 2004), in which he notes that 'the Commission intends to launch a study on the points in common with – and those on which it differs from – common immigration policy as it has developed at EU level since the entry into force of the Treaty of Amsterdam' (www.europarl.europa.eu/omk/sipade3?L=EN&OBJID=71667& LEVEL=4&SAME_LEVEL=1&NAV=S& LSTDOC=Y [last accessed 24 April 2009]).

Justice, Franco Frattini, to a letter from the EPMWR, suggests that the Commission itself has adopted a negative stance on the ICRMW.[67]

The Convention does, however, enjoy stronger and more recent support from two other EU institutions, the European Parliament and the EESC, which, although significantly less powerful in terms of actual legislative and decision-making competences, may nonetheless prove to be allies of considerable importance. The European Parliament adopted, on 18 February 1998, a resolution on human rights in the EU, in which it deplored the fact that no Member State had ratified the Convention, and called upon them to do so;[68] perhaps more importantly, however, it has since repeated this call on several occasions and in various contexts. Thus, the European Parliament resolution on EU priorities and recommendations for the 61st Session of the UN CHR from 2005 makes the now-familiar (from that institution, at least) call 'on the Member States to ratify the UN Migrant Workers' Convention and to support the universal ratification thereof';[69] while an even more recent resolution on women's immigration makes a number of references to the

---

[67] See Commissioner Frattini's response to the letter from the EPMWR, 25 February 2005 (www.coordeurop.org/sito/0com/pdf07_euplat_Frattini _rep.pdf [last accessed 24 April 2009]). Frattini himself refers to Vitorino's response, outlined above, in noting the 'specific problem raised by this Convention [the ICRMW]': that 'there is no clear distinction between third-country workers who are legally residing in a Member State and those whose position is not regular'; one important difference, however, is that Vitorino's answer was framed in terms of what the obstacles to ratification may be, given how Member States perceive the Convention – indeed, he begins by noting that '[t]he Member States are [probably] better placed than the Commission to explain their reasons for not ratifying'. In Frattini's letter, on the other hand, this lack of clear distinction between regular and irregular migrants is presented both as objective fact and as the position of the Commission itself. In any event, this argument seems more than a little disingenuous: the ICRMW does make a very clear distinction between the rights that must be granted to all migrants and those that need be afforded only to those in a regular situation. This objection thus seems to collapse, upon closer inspection, into the political objection, outlined earlier, that the former category is simply too broad and will thus be more of a hindrance than a help in efforts to prevent or reduce irregular migration.

[68] The text of the resolution is available in French on the GISTI website (www.gisti.org/doc/plein-droit/38/europe.html [last accessed 24 April 2009]).

[69] European Parliament Resolution on EU priorities and recommendations for the 61st Session of the UN Commission on Human Rights in Geneva (14 March–22 April 2005), 24 February 2005, P6_TA-PROV(2005)0051, paragraph 22. This call is repeated on an annual basis in the same context; more resolutions in a similar vein are listed on the website of the NGO, December 18 (www.december18.net/web/general/page.php?pageID=79&menuID=36&lang=EN [last accessed 24 April 2009]).

Convention, calling on Member States to act in accordance with its provisions.[70]

Moreover, as noted above, in June 2004 the EESC adopted an own-initiative opinion on the ICRMW in which it calls strongly for ratification. The motivation behind the opinion seems to be a sense of dissatisfaction with the development of the EU common migration policy since the Tampere Conclusions of 1999, and in particular with the lack of a robust rights-based approach in the legislative action taken in this field to date:

> The Commission has drawn up numerous legislative proposals which have, however, met with considerable resistance within the Council. Four years on, the results are meagre: the legislation that has been adopted is disappointing and has moved away considerably from the Tampere objectives, the proposals of the Commission, the opinion of the Parliament and the stance of the EESC. The current system used within the Council to adopt agreements allows proposals to be blocked. This, coupled with the attitudes of some governments, makes it very difficult to achieve consensus.[71]

The EESC goes on to note that 'Europe is an area of freedom, democracy and respect for the human rights of all people. In order to strengthen these values in the future, all the Member States of the EU must ratify the international conventions that protect these basic human rights and their legal precepts must be incorporated into both Community and national legislation.'[72] In this respect, the EESC opinion concludes not merely by encouraging Member States to ratify the ICRMW,[73] and urging the Presidency of the Council to 'undertake the necessary initiatives' to ensure that they do so within a period of two years following the release of the opinion, but also suggests that the EU itself should ratify the Convention, if and when it acquires the power to enter into international agreements.[74]

Conclusion

The EU thus not only has the potential to play a crucial positive role in encouraging ratifications of the ICRMW in its own Member States and,

---

[70] European Parliament Resolution on women's immigration: the role and place of immigrant women in the European Union, 24 October 2006, P6_TA-PROV(2006)0437, at, for example, paragraph 8.

[71] EESC Opinion on the International Convention on Migrants (see n. 39), paragraph 4.4.

[72] Ibid., paragraph 5.6.   [73] Ibid., paragraph 6.1.

[74] Ibid., paragraph 6.2. The EU will acquire this general power once the Treaty of Lisbon (see n. 42), is ratified by all Member States and enters into force.

by example, in the world more generally, through its highly developed legal order capable of enforcing policy changes on EU Member State national governments (and providing them with a useful alibi when confronted with sceptical publics); it also boasts by far the highest level of sustained institutional support for the Convention of any polity in the region. If this constitutes grounds for renewed optimism, however, it must be approached with great caution: those bodies that have come out in favour of ratification (the European Parliament and the EESC) can play only a very limited role in the enactment of measures in the field of legal migration, while those with the real legislative power (the Commission and the Council) clearly remain less than convinced of the benefits that the ICRMW could bring to the developing common migration policy. It is clear that many of the general political obstacles outlined above still constitute powerful barriers at Community level, and this is hardly surprising given the dominant role that national government representatives still play in the Council. There is no real prospect, then, of positive EU action in this respect without the active support of, at the very least, a handful of influential Member States.

It is also important to recall that, although the Treaty of Amsterdam transferred asylum and immigration matters to European Community law (under Title IV of the EC Treaty), the competence of the European Parliament on legal migration is still limited to a consultative role; it does not yet have the ability, as it does in the fields of asylum, border control or irregular migration, as well as in other areas within the Community Pillar, to co-legislate with the Council on the basis of proposals advanced by the Commission.[75] This is a significant limitation on the strength of the parliament's voice, and will make it more likely that the ICRMW will not feature in the planned directives on legal migration, unless the Treaty of Lisbon, which will give the Parliament a co-legislative power in this field, is ratified by all EU Member States and enters into force. Of these directives, by far the most important for the purposes of this study is the proposed General Framework Directive,[76] which, as noted above, seeks to lay down a set of rights to be enjoyed by third-country nationals present in a regular situation on the territory of the EU, who have not

---

[75] Treaty establishing the European Community (*Official Journal of the European Union*, C325/1, 2002), article 67, as amended.

[76] European Commission, *Proposal for a Council Directive on a Single Application Procedure for a Single Permit for Third-Country Nationals to Reside and Work in the Territory of a Member State and On a Common Set of Rights for Third-Country Workers Legally Residing in a Member State*, COM(2007) 638, 23 October 2007.

yet qualified for long-term resident status. Chapter III of the proposed directive, entitled 'Right to equal treatment', lays out in article 12(1) a range of rights that third-country nationals who are workers may enjoy on an equal basis with nationals.[77] While the *Policy Plan on Legal Migration*, which signalled the proposal for the General Framework Directive, was largely silent on the issue of which rights would be recognized in this measure, it was, however, substantially clearer on the issue of who the beneficiaries would be when it stated that the purpose of the instrument would be 'to guarantee a common framework of rights to all third-country nationals *in legal employment* already admitted in a Member State'.[78] The proposed General Framework Directive confirms this approach. Article 2(b) defines a 'third-country worker' as 'any third-country national who has been admitted to the territory of a Member State and is allowed to work legally in that Member State'. Here, the absence of the ICRMW's approach, of guaranteeing human rights to all, is readily evident. While this does not, of course, rule out the possibility that the human rights of irregular migrants will be dealt with satisfactorily in other instruments, the Community track record here provides little ground for assuming that this will be the case.

A second issue of interest concerns the basis on which the rights contained in the General Framework Directive will be afforded to their beneficiaries – on an equal footing with those of Member State nationals, or according to some minimum standard? Again, while the *Policy Plan* was silent on this issue, the Green Paper on economic migration, from which the *Policy Plan* was developed, contained some guidance. In its (very brief) section on rights, it notes simply that 'third-country workers should enjoy the same treatment as EU citizens in particular with regard to certain basic economic and social rights before they obtain long-term resident status'.[79] Although this formulation seems to contain a more robust idea of equal treatment even than that expressed in the Tampere Conclusions, it remains extremely vague both on the nature and specific

---

[77] Article 12(1) lists the following rights: working conditions, including pay and dismissal as well as health and safety at the workplace; freedom of association in workers', employers' or occupational organizations; education or vocational training; recognition of diplomas, certificates and other professional qualifications; social security; payment of acquired pensions when moving to a third country; tax benefits; and access to goods and services and the supply of goods and services made available to the public, including procedures for obtaining housing and the assistance afforded by employment offices.

[78] *Commission Policy Plan* (see n. 20), p. 6, Section 2.1 (emphasis added).

[79] Commission Green Paper (see n. 58), p. 10, Section 6.1.

content of the rights it concerns. This ambiguity is further compounded by the fact that, although long-term residents are to be entitled to a broader catalogue of rights 'in line with the principle of the differentiation of rights according to the length of stay',[80] even those rights in respect of which they are entitled to equal treatment with nationals can be restricted to core economic and social rights. The relation between these two categories, the 'basic' rights that the Green Paper suggests should be ensured to all regular migrants, and the 'core' rights that the Long-Term Resident Directive protects from restrictions as to equal treatment, is complicated further in the proposed General Framework Directive, which only grants a set of rights to third-country *workers*. While this category includes persons that are not in actual employment at a given time or who were not necessarily admitted to the Member State for the purpose of employment (e.g. students who have since been permitted to switch their status, family members or researchers), nonetheless the employment context remains the governing factor for enjoyment of the rights in question. Furthermore, Article 12(2) of the draft directive follows to some degree the approach taken in the Long-Term Residents Directive by affording Member States discretion to restrict the application of the principle of equal treatment with nationals in respect of a number of rights. For example, certain rights (working conditions, freedom of association, tax benefits and social security, except for unemployment benefits) may be restricted to third-country workers who are actually in employment, whereas access to public housing may be limited to those cases where third-country nationals have been staying or who have a right to stay in the territory of the Member State concerned for at least three years.[81] It is clear therefore that the notion of equal treatment in the proposed measure does not receive as strong a formulation as it could have done had the ICRMW been taken more fully into consideration.

The limitation of the European Parliament's input to a purely consultative role thus makes it likely, though not unavoidable, that Community legislation in this field will continue to be at odds with, if

---

[80] Ibid.

[81] Commission, *Proposal for a Council Directive on a Single Application Procedure for a Single Permit for Third-Country Nationals to Reside and Work in the Territory of a Member State and on a Common Set of Rights for Third-Country Workers Legally Residing in a Member State* (see n. 76), draft article 12(2)(d), (e) and (c), respectively.

not always actually contrary to, certain fundamental premises of the ICRMW – which, it should be recalled, is recognized by the OHCHR as one of eight core international human rights instruments currently in force. This is perhaps clearest in terms of the two issues outlined above: (i) the erosion of the equal treatment principle and (ii) the general absence of explicit recognition of the importance of the human rights of irregular migrants in the development of the EU common migration policy. The proposed General Framework Directive is, however, still in the process of being negotiated, and it is not impossible that the EU Council and Member State delegations could be persuaded to address some of these concerns in the measure that is eventually adopted.[82]

The period in which the EU negotiates and lays down the rights of all regular migrant workers present on its territory could be crucial in defining the future attitudes towards the ICRMW within Community institutions; and these, in turn, will have a major impact on the prospects for ratification of the Convention within individual Member States. Importantly, however, the proposed General Framework Directive, as currently drafted, contains a clause that expressly enables Member States to adopt or maintain provisions that are more favourable to third-country nationals lawfully resident and working within their territories and is without prejudice to more favourable provisions of Community legislation (including Community agreements with third countries) and 'bilateral or multilateral agreements between one or more Member States and one or more third countries'.[83] The detailed explanatory memorandum accompanying the draft directive does not specifically refer to the ICRMW in this regard, although the Convention would clearly qualify as a 'multilateral agreement';[84] consequently, the existence of this clause effectively undermines the arguments of those Member States that claim

---

[82] However, indications are that the provisions of the draft Directive are being subject to further restrictions during the negotiations in the Council. See Doc. 9860/09 (14 May 2009).

[83] Ibid., article 13.

[84] The explanatory memorandum refers specifically to the European Social Charter and Revised Charter, the ECMW and the ICESCR, although it observes that a list of other treaties is provided in Annex 5 of the Commission Staff Working Paper accompanying the proposal. The sole reference to the ICRMW can be found in this secondary document. See European Commission, Staff Working Document, accompanying document to proposal for a Council Directive on a single application procedure for a single permit for third-country nationals to reside and work in the territory of a Member State and on a common set of rights for third-country workers legally residing in a Member State, Impact Assessment, Vol. II – Annexes, SEC(2007) 1408/3, pp. 113–17.

that it is not possible to ratify the ICRMW in the absence of a consensus on this question in the EU as a whole.

Thus, although at present it seems that the main holders of legislative power in this field of EU action retain a predominantly negative stance on the Convention, there is nonetheless a real window of opportunity to change this, bearing in mind that it enjoys both a higher profile and a higher degree of institutional support at the regional level than it does in any of the individual EU Member States. This means that, despite the obvious reticence of both the Commission and the Council, the EU remains at one and the same time the most efficient focus for lobbyists (in terms of the potential power it has in promoting ratification of the Convention in the region) and the forum in which such efforts are most likely to succeed.

References

Cholewinski, R. 2001. The EU *acquis* on irregular migration: reinforcing security at the expense of rights. *European Journal of Migration and Law*, Vol. 2, pp. 361–405.

  2002. *Borders and Discrimination in the European Union*. Brussels/London, Migration Policy Group/Immigration Law Practitioners' Association.

  2004. The UN Convention on Migrant Workers as a rights-based framework for the EU's common immigration policy: a preliminary assessment. (Unpublished paper on file with authors.)

  2005. The need for effective individual legal protection in immigration matters. *European Journal of Migration and Law*, Vol. 7, pp. 237–62.

Cholewinski, R., Perruchoud, R. and MacDonald, E. (eds). 2007. *International Migration Law: Developing Paradigms and Key Challenges*. The Hague, Netherlands, T. M. C. Asser Press.

De Bruycker, P. 2007. Legislative harmonization in European immigration policy. Cholewinski et al. (eds), op. cit., pp. 329–48.

Groenendijk, K. 2006. Family reunification as a right under community law. *European Journal of Migration and Law*, Vol. 8, pp. 215–30.

Lönnroth, J. 1991. The International Convention on the Rights of All Migrant Workers and Members of Their Families in the context of international migration policies. *International Migration Review*, Vol. 25, No. 4, pp. 710–36.

MacDonald, E. and Cholewinski, R. 2007. *The Migrant Workers Convention in Europe. Obstacles to the Ratification of the International Convention on the Protection of the Rights of All Migrant Workers and Members of Their Families: EU/EEA Perspectives*. Paris, UNESCO. (Migration Studies 1.)

Pécoud, A. and de Guchteneire, P. 2006. Migration, human rights and the United Nations: an investigation into the obstacles to the UN Convention on Migrant Workers' Rights. *Windsor Yearbook of Access to Justice*, Vol. 24, No. 2, pp. 241–66.

Peers, S. 2006. Key legislative developments on migration in the European Union. *European Journal of Migration and Law*, Vol. 8, pp. 97–114.

    2007. Enhancing cooperation on border controls in the European Union. Cholewinski et al. (eds), op. cit., pp. 447–63.

Annex 1

International Convention on the Protection of the Rights of All Migrant Workers and Members of Their Families Adopted by General Assembly Resolution 45/158 of 18 December 1990

Preamble

The States Parties to the present Convention,

Taking into account the principles embodied in the basic instruments of the United Nations concerning human rights, in particular the Universal Declaration of Human Rights, the International Covenant on Economic, Social and Cultural Rights, the International Covenant on Civil and Political Rights, the International Convention on the Elimination of All Forms of Racial Discrimination, the Convention on the Elimination of All Forms of Discrimination against Women and the Convention on the Rights of the Child,

Taking into account also the principles and standards set forth in the relevant instruments elaborated within the framework of the International Labour Organisation, especially the Convention concerning Migration for Employment (No. 97), the Convention concerning Migrations in Abusive Conditions and the Promotion of Equality of Opportunity and Treatment of Migrant Workers (No. 143), the Recommendation concerning Migration for Employment (No. 86), the Recommendation concerning Migrant Workers (No. 151), the Convention concerning Forced or Compulsory Labour (No. 29) and the Convention concerning Abolition of Forced Labour (No. 105), Reaffirming the importance of the principles contained in the Convention against Discrimination in Education of the United Nations Educational, Scientific and Cultural Organization,

Recalling the Convention against Torture and Other Cruel, Inhuman or Degrading Treatment or Punishment, the Declaration of the Fourth United Nations Congress on the Prevention of Crime and the Treatment of Offenders, the Code of Conduct for Law Enforcement Officials, and the Slavery Conventions,

Recalling that one of the objectives of the International Labour Organisation, as stated in its Constitution, is the protection of the interests of workers when employed in countries other than their own, and bearing in mind the expertise and experience of that organization in matters related to migrant workers and members of their families,

Recognizing the importance of the work done in connection with migrant workers and members of their families in various organs of the United Nations, in particular in the Commission on Human Rights and the Commission for Social Development, and in the Food and Agriculture Organization of the United Nations, the United Nations Educational, Scientific and Cultural Organization and the World Health Organization, as well as in other international organizations,

Recognizing also the progress made by certain States on a regional or bilateral basis towards the protection of the rights of migrant workers and members of their families, as well as the importance and usefulness of bilateral and multilateral agreements in this field,

Realizing the importance and extent of the migration phenomenon, which involves millions of people and affects a large number of States in the international community,

Aware of the impact of the flows of migrant workers on States and people concerned, and desiring to establish norms which may contribute to the harmonization of the attitudes of States through the acceptance of basic principles concerning the treatment of migrant workers and members of their families,

Considering the situation of vulnerability in which migrant workers and members of their families frequently find themselves owing, among other things, to their absence from their State of origin and to the difficulties they may encounter arising from their presence in the State of employment,

Convinced that the rights of migrant workers and members of their families have not been sufficiently recognized everywhere and therefore require appropriate international protection,

Taking into account the fact that migration is often the cause of serious problems for the members of the families of migrant workers as well as for the workers themselves, in particular because of the scattering of the family,

Bearing in mind that the human problems involved in migration are even more serious in the case of irregular migration and convinced therefore that appropriate action should be encouraged in order to prevent and eliminate clandestine movements and trafficking in migrant workers, while at the same time assuring the protection of their fundamental human rights,

Considering that workers who are non-documented or in an irregular situation are frequently employed under less favourable conditions of work than other workers and that certain employers find this an inducement to seek such labour in order to reap the benefits of unfair competition,

Considering also that recourse to the employment of migrant workers who are in an irregular situation will be discouraged if the fundamental human rights of all migrant workers are more widely recognized and, moreover, that granting certain additional rights to migrant workers and members of their families in a regular situation will encourage all migrants and employers to respect and comply with the laws and procedures established by the States concerned,

Convinced, therefore, of the need to bring about the international protection of the rights of all migrant workers and members of their families, reaffirming and establishing basic norms in a comprehensive convention which could be applied universally,

Have agreed as follows:

Part I: Scope and definitions

Article 1

1. The present Convention is applicable, except as otherwise provided hereafter, to all migrant workers and members of their families without distinction of any kind such as sex, race, colour, language, religion or conviction, political or other opinion, national, ethnic or social origin, nationality, age, economic position, property, marital status, birth or other status.

2. The present Convention shall apply during the entire migration process of migrant workers and members of their families, which comprises preparation for migration, departure, transit and the entire period of stay and remunerated activity in the State of employment as well as return to the State of origin or the State of habitual residence.

Article 2

For the purposes of the present Convention:

1. The term 'migrant worker' refers to a person who is to be engaged, is engaged or has been engaged in a remunerated activity in a State of which he or she is not a national.

2.
   (a) The term 'frontier worker' refers to a migrant worker who retains his or her habitual residence in a neighbouring State to which he or she normally returns every day or at least once a week;
   (b) The term 'seasonal worker' refers to a migrant worker whose work by its character is dependent on seasonal conditions and is performed only during part of the year;
   (c) The term 'seafarer', which includes a fisherman, refers to a migrant worker employed on board a vessel registered in a State of which he or she is not a national;
   (d) The term 'worker on an offshore installation' refers to a migrant worker employed on an offshore installation that is under the jurisdiction of a State of which he or she is not a national;
   (e) The term 'itinerant worker' refers to a migrant worker who, having his or her habitual residence in one State, has to travel to another State or States for short periods, owing to the nature of his or her occupation;
   (f) The term 'project-tied worker' refers to a migrant worker admitted to a State of employment for a defined period to work solely on a specific project being carried out in that State by his or her employer;
   (g) The term 'specified-employment worker' refers to a migrant worker:
      (i) Who has been sent by his or her employer for a restricted and defined period of time to a State of employment to undertake a specific assignment or duty; or
      (ii) Who engages for a restricted and defined period of time in work that requires professional, commercial, technical or other highly specialized skill; or
      (iii) Who, upon the request of his or her employer in the State of employment, engages for a restricted and defined period of time in work whose nature is transitory or brief; and who is required to depart from the State of employment either at

the expiration of his or her authorized period of stay, or earlier if he or she no longer undertakes that specific assignment or duty or engages in that work;

(h) The term 'self-employed worker' refers to a migrant worker who is engaged in a remunerated activity otherwise than under a contract of employment and who earns his or her living through this activity normally working alone or together with members of his or her family, and to any other migrant worker recognized as self-employed by applicable legislation of the State of employment or bilateral or multilateral agreements.

Article 3

The present Convention shall not apply to:

(a) Persons sent or employed by international organizations and agencies or persons sent or employed by a State outside its territory to perform official functions, whose admission and status are regulated by general international law or by specific international agreements or conventions;

(b) Persons sent or employed by a State or on its behalf outside its territory who participate in development programmes and other co-operation programmes, whose admission and status are regulated by agreement with the State of employment and who, in accordance with that agreement, are not considered migrant workers;

(c) Persons taking up residence in a State different from their State of origin as investors;

(d) Refugees and stateless persons, unless such application is provided for in the relevant national legislation of, or international instruments in force for, the State Party concerned;

(e) Students and trainees;

(f) Seafarers and workers on an offshore installation who have not been admitted to take up residence and engage in a remunerated activity in the State of employment.

Article 4

For the purposes of the present Convention the term 'members of the family' refers to persons married to migrant workers or having with them a relationship that, according to applicable law, produces effects equivalent to marriage, as well as their dependent children and other dependent persons who are recognized as members of the family by applicable legislation or applicable bilateral or multilateral agreements between the States concerned.

Article 5

For the purposes of the present Convention, migrant workers and members of their families:

(a) Are considered as documented or in a regular situation if they are authorized to enter, to stay and to engage in a remunerated activity in the State of employment pursuant to the law of that State and to international agreements to which that State is a party;

(b) Are considered as non-documented or in an irregular situation if they do not comply with the conditions provided for in subparagraph (a) of the present article.

Article 6

For the purposes of the present Convention:

(a) The term 'State of origin' means the State of which the person concerned is a national;

(b) The term 'State of employment' means a State where the migrant worker is to be engaged, is engaged or has been engaged in a remunerated activity, as the case may be;

(c) The term 'State of transit,' means any State through which the person concerned passes on any journey to the State of employment or from the State of employment to the State of origin or the State of habitual residence.

Part II: Non-discrimination with respect to rights

Article 7

States Parties undertake, in accordance with the international instruments concerning human rights, to respect and to ensure to all migrant workers and members of their families within their territory or subject to their jurisdiction the rights provided for in the present Convention without distinction of any kind such as to sex, race, colour, language, religion or conviction, political or other opinion, national, ethnic or social origin, nationality, age, economic position, property, marital status, birth or other status.

Part III: Human rights of all migrant workers and members of their families

Article 8

1. Migrant workers and members of their families shall be free to leave any State, including their State of origin. This right shall not be subject to any restrictions except those that are provided by law, are necessary to protect national security, public order (ordre public), public health or morals or the rights and freedoms of others and are consistent with the other rights recognized in the present part of the Convention.
2. Migrant workers and members of their families shall have the right at any time to enter and remain in their State of origin.

Article 9

The right to life of migrant workers and members of their families shall be protected by law.

Article 10

No migrant worker or member of his or her family shall be subjected to torture or to cruel, inhuman or degrading treatment or punishment.

Article 11

1. No migrant worker or member of his or her family shall be held in slavery or servitude.
2. No migrant worker or member of his or her family shall be required to perform forced or compulsory labour.
3. Paragraph 2 of the present article shall not be held to preclude, in States where imprisonment with hard labour may be imposed as a punishment for a crime, the performance of hard labour in pursuance of a sentence to such punishment by a competent court.
4. For the purpose of the present article the term 'forced or compulsory labour' shall not include:
   (a) Any work or service not referred to in paragraph 3 of the present article normally required of a person who is under detention in

consequence of a lawful order of a court or of a person during conditional release from such detention;

(b) Any service exacted in cases of emergency or calamity threatening the life or well-being of the community;

(c) Any work or service that forms part of normal civil obligations so far as it is imposed also on citizens of the State concerned.

Article 12

1. Migrant workers and members of their families shall have the right to freedom of thought, conscience and religion. This right shall include freedom to have or to adopt a religion or belief of their choice and freedom either individually or in community with others and in public or private to manifest their religion or belief in worship, observance, practice and teaching.

2. Migrant workers and members of their families shall not be subject to coercion that would impair their freedom to have or to adopt a religion or belief of their choice.

3. Freedom to manifest one's religion or belief may be subject only to such limitations as are prescribed by law and are necessary to protect public safety, order, health or morals or the fundamental rights and freedoms of others.

4. States Parties to the present Convention undertake to have respect for the liberty of parents, at least one of whom is a migrant worker, and, when applicable, legal guardians to ensure the religious and moral education of their children in conformity with their own convictions.

Article 13

1. Migrant workers and members of their families shall have the right to hold opinions without interference.

2. Migrant workers and members of their families shall have the right to freedom of expression; this right shall include freedom to seek, receive and impart information and ideas of all kinds, regardless of frontiers, either orally, in writing or in print, in the form of art or through any other media of their choice.

3. The exercise of the right provided for in paragraph 2 of the present article carries with it special duties and responsibilities. It may therefore be subject to certain restrictions, but these shall only be such as are provided by law and are necessary:

(a) For respect of the rights or reputation of others;
(b) For the protection of the national security of the States concerned or of public order (ordre public) or of public health or morals;
(c) For the purpose of preventing any propaganda for war;
(d) For the purpose of preventing any advocacy of national, racial or religious hatred that constitutes incitement to discrimination, hostility or violence.

Article 14

No migrant worker or member of his or her family shall be subjected to arbitrary or unlawful interference with his or her privacy, family, home, correspondence or other communications, or to unlawful attacks on his or her honour and reputation. Each migrant worker and member of his or her family shall have the right to the protection of the law against such interference or attacks.

Article 15

No migrant worker or member of his or her family shall be arbitrarily deprived of property, whether owned individually or in association with others. Where, under the legislation in force in the State of employment, the assets of a migrant worker or a member of his or her family are expropriated in whole or in part, the person concerned shall have the right to fair and adequate compensation.

Article 16

1. Migrant workers and members of their families shall have the right to liberty and security of person.
2. Migrant workers and members of their families shall be entitled to effective protection by the State against violence, physical injury, threats and intimidation, whether by public officials or by private individuals, groups or institutions.
3. Any verification by law enforcement officials of the identity of migrant workers or members of their families shall be carried out in accordance with procedure established by law.
4. Migrant workers and members of their families shall not be subjected individually or collectively to arbitrary arrest or detention; they shall not be deprived of their liberty except on such grounds and in accordance with such procedures as are established by law.

5. Migrant workers and members of their families who are arrested shall be informed at the time of arrest as far as possible in a language they understand of the reasons for their arrest and they shall be promptly informed in a language they understand of any charges against them.

6. Migrant workers and members of their families who are arrested or detained on a criminal charge shall be brought promptly before a judge or other officer authorized by law to exercise judicial power and shall be entitled to trial within a reasonable time or to release. It shall not be the general rule that while awaiting trial they shall be detained in custody, but release may be subject to guarantees to appear for trial, at any other stage of the judicial proceedings and, should the occasion arise, for the execution of the judgement.

7. When a migrant worker or a member of his or her family is arrested or committed to prison or custody pending trial or is detained in any other manner:

   (a) The consular or diplomatic authorities of his or her State of origin or of a State representing the interests of that State shall, if he or she so requests, be informed without delay of his or her arrest or detention and of the reasons therefor;

   (b) The person concerned shall have the right to communicate with the said authorities. Any communication by the person concerned to the said authorities shall be forwarded without delay, and he or she shall also have the right to receive communications sent by the said authorities without delay;

   (c) The person concerned shall be informed without delay of this right and of rights deriving from relevant treaties, if any, applicable between the States concerned, to correspond and to meet with representatives of the said authorities and to make arrangements with them for his or her legal representation.

8. Migrant workers and members of their families who are deprived of their liberty by arrest or detention shall be entitled to take proceedings before a court, in order that that court may decide without delay on the lawfulness of their detention and order their release if the detention is not lawful. When they attend such proceedings, they shall have the assistance, if necessary without cost to them, of an interpreter, if they cannot understand or speak the language used.

9. Migrant workers and members of their families who have been victims of unlawful arrest or detention shall have an enforceable right to compensation.

Article 17

1. Migrant workers and members of their families who are deprived of their liberty shall be treated with humanity and with respect for the inherent dignity of the human person and for their cultural identity.
2. Accused migrant workers and members of their families shall, save in exceptional circumstances, be separated from convicted persons and shall be subject to separate treatment appropriate to their status as unconvicted persons. Accused juvenile persons shall be separated from adults and brought as speedily as possible for adjudication.
3. Any migrant worker or member of his or her family who is detained in a State of transit or in a State of employment for violation of provisions relating to migration shall be held, in so far as practicable, separately from convicted persons or persons detained pending trial.
4. During any period of imprisonment in pursuance of a sentence imposed by a court of law, the essential aim of the treatment of a migrant worker or a member of his or her family shall be his or her reformation and social rehabilitation. Juvenile offenders shall be separated from adults and be accorded treatment appropriate to their age and legal status.
5. During detention or imprisonment, migrant workers and members of their families shall enjoy the same rights as nationals to visits by members of their families.
6. Whenever a migrant worker is deprived of his or her liberty, the competent authorities of the State concerned shall pay attention to the problems that may be posed for members of his or her family, in particular for spouses and minor children.
7. Migrant workers and members of their families who are subjected to any form of detention or imprisonment in accordance with the law in force in the State of employment or in the State of transit shall enjoy the same rights as nationals of those States who are in the same situation.
8. If a migrant worker or a member of his or her family is detained for the purpose of verifying any infraction of provisions related to migration, he or she shall not bear any costs arising therefrom.

Article 18

1. Migrant workers and members of their families shall have the right to equality with nationals of the State concerned before the courts and

tribunals. In the determination of any criminal charge against them
or of their rights and obligations in a suit of law, they shall be entitled
to a fair and public hearing by a competent, independent and impartial tribunal established by law.

2. Migrant workers and members of their families who are charged with
   a criminal offence shall have the right to be presumed innocent until
   proven guilty according to law.

3. In the determination of any criminal charge against them, migrant
   workers and members of their families shall be entitled to the following minimum guarantees:

   (a) To be informed promptly and in detail in a language they under-
       stand of the nature and cause of the charge against them;

   (b) To have adequate time and facilities for the preparation of their
       defence and to communicate with counsel of their own choosing;

   (c) To be tried without undue delay;

   (d) To be tried in their presence and to defend themselves in
       person or through legal assistance of their own choosing; to be
       informed, if they do not have legal assistance, of this right; and to
       have legal assistance assigned to them, in any case where the
       interests of justice so require and without payment by them in
       any such case if they do not have sufficient means to pay;

   (e) To examine or have examined the witnesses against them and to
       obtain the attendance and examination of witnesses on their
       behalf under the same conditions as witnesses against them;

   (f) To have the free assistance of an interpreter if they cannot under-
       stand or speak the language used in court;

   (g) Not to be compelled to testify against themselves or to confess
       guilt.

4. In the case of juvenile persons, the procedure shall be such as will take
   account of their age and the desirability of promoting their
   rehabilitation.

5. Migrant workers and members of their families convicted of a crime
   shall have the right to their conviction and sentence being reviewed by
   a higher tribunal according to law.

6. When a migrant worker or a member of his or her family has, by a
   final decision, been convicted of a criminal offence and when subsequently his or her conviction has been reversed or he or she has been
   pardoned on the ground that a new or newly discovered fact shows
   conclusively that there has been a miscarriage of justice, the person
   who has suffered punishment as a result of such conviction shall be

compensated according to law, unless it is proved that the non-disclosure of the unknown fact in time is wholly or partly attributable to that person.

7. No migrant worker or member of his or her family shall be liable to be tried or punished again for an offence for which he or she has already been finally convicted or acquitted in accordance with the law and penal procedure of the State concerned.

Article 19

1. No migrant worker or member of his or her family shall be held guilty of any criminal offence on account of any act or omission that did not constitute a criminal offence under national or international law at the time when the criminal offence was committed, nor shall a heavier penalty be imposed than the one that was applicable at the time when it was committed. If, subsequent to the commission of the offence, provision is made by law for the imposition of a lighter penalty, he or she shall benefit thereby.

2. Humanitarian considerations related to the status of a migrant worker, in particular with respect to his or her right of residence or work, should be taken into account in imposing a sentence for a criminal offence committed by a migrant worker or a member of his or her family.

Article 20

1. No migrant worker or member of his or her family shall be imprisoned merely on the ground of failure to fulfil a contractual obligation.

2. No migrant worker or member of his or her family shall be deprived of his or her authorization of residence or work permit or expelled merely on the ground of failure to fulfil an obligation arising out of a work contract unless fulfilment of that obligation constitutes a condition for such authorization or permit.

Article 21

It shall be unlawful for anyone, other than a public official duly authorized by law, to confiscate, destroy or attempt to destroy identity documents, documents authorizing entry to or stay, residence or establishment in the national territory or work permits. No authorized confiscation of such documents shall take place without delivery of a detailed receipt. In no case shall it be permitted to destroy the passport or equivalent document of a migrant worker or a member of his or her family.

Article 22

1. Migrant workers and members of their families shall not be subject to measures of collective expulsion. Each case of expulsion shall be examined and decided individually.
2. Migrant workers and members of their families may be expelled from the territory of a State Party only in pursuance of a decision taken by the competent authority in accordance with law.
3. The decision shall be communicated to them in a language they understand. Upon their request where not otherwise mandatory, the decision shall be communicated to them in writing and, save in exceptional circumstances on account of national security, the reasons for the decision likewise stated. The persons concerned shall be informed of these rights before or at the latest at the time the decision is rendered.
4. Except where a final decision is pronounced by a judicial authority, the person concerned shall have the right to submit the reason he or she should not be expelled and to have his or her case reviewed by the competent authority, unless compelling reasons of national security require otherwise. Pending such review, the person concerned shall have the right to seek a stay of the decision of expulsion.
5. If a decision of expulsion that has already been executed is subsequently annulled, the person concerned shall have the right to seek compensation according to law and the earlier decision shall not be used to prevent him or her from re-entering the State concerned.
6. In case of expulsion, the person concerned shall have a reasonable opportunity before or after departure to settle any claims for wages and other entitlements due to him or her and any pending liabilities.
7. Without prejudice to the execution of a decision of expulsion, a migrant worker or a member of his or her family who is subject to such a decision may seek entry into a State other than his or her State of origin.
8. In case of expulsion of a migrant worker or a member of his or her family the costs of expulsion shall not be borne by him or her. The person concerned may be required to pay his or her own travel costs.
9. Expulsion from the State of employment shall not in itself prejudice any rights of a migrant worker or a member of his or her family

acquired in accordance with the law of that State, including the right to receive wages and other entitlements due to him or her.

Article 23

Migrant workers and members of their families shall have the right to have recourse to the protection and assistance of the consular or diplomatic authorities of their State of origin or of a State representing the interests of that State whenever the rights recognized in the present Convention are impaired. In particular, in case of expulsion, the person concerned shall be informed of this right without delay and the authorities of the expelling State shall facilitate the exercise of such right.

Article 24

Every migrant worker and every member of his or her family shall have the right to recognition everywhere as a person before the law.

Article 25

1. Migrant workers shall enjoy treatment not less favourable than that which applies to nationals of the State of employment in respect of remuneration and:
   (a) Other conditions of work, that is to say, overtime, hours of work, weekly rest, holidays with pay, safety, health, termination of the employment relationship and any other conditions of work which, according to national law and practice, are covered by these terms;
   (b) Other terms of employment, that is to say, minimum age of employment, restriction on home work and any other matters which, according to national law and practice, are considered a term of employment.
2. It shall not be lawful to derogate in private contracts of employment from the principle of equality of treatment referred to in paragraph 1 of the present article.
3. States Parties shall take all appropriate measures to ensure that migrant workers are not deprived of any rights derived from this principle by reason of any irregularity in their stay or employment. In particular, employers shall not be relieved of any legal or contractual obligations, nor shall their obligations be limited in any manner by reason of such irregularity.

Article 26

1. States Parties recognize the right of migrant workers and members of their families:
   (a) To take part in meetings and activities of trade unions and of any other associations established in accordance with law, with a view to protecting their economic, social, cultural and other interests, subject only to the rules of the organization concerned;
   (b) To join freely any trade union and any such association as aforesaid, subject only to the rules of the organization concerned;
   (c) To seek the aid and assistance of any trade union and of any such association as aforesaid.
2. No restrictions may be placed on the exercise of these rights other than those that are prescribed by law and which are necessary in a democratic society in the interests of national security, public order (ordre public) or the protection of the rights and freedoms of others.

Article 27

1. With respect to social security, migrant workers and members of their families shall enjoy in the State of employment the same treatment granted to nationals in so far as they fulfil the requirements provided for by the applicable legislation of that State and the applicable bilateral and multilateral treaties. The competent authorities of the State of origin and the State of employment can at any time establish the necessary arrangements to determine the modalities of application of this norm.
2. Where the applicable legislation does not allow migrant workers and members of their families a benefit, the States concerned shall examine the possibility of reimbursing interested persons the amount of contributions made by them with respect to that benefit on the basis of the treatment granted to nationals who are in similar circumstances.

Article 28

Migrant workers and members of their families shall have the right to receive any medical care that is urgently required for the preservation of their life or the avoidance of irreparable harm to their health on the basis of equality of treatment with nationals of the State concerned. Such emergency medical care shall not be refused them by reason of any irregularity with regard to stay or employment.

Article 29

Each child of a migrant worker shall have the right to a name, to registration of birth and to a nationality.

Article 30

Each child of a migrant worker shall have the basic right of access to education on the basis of equality of treatment with nationals of the State concerned. Access to public pre-school educational institutions or schools shall not be refused or limited by reason of the irregular situation with respect to stay or employment of either parent or by reason of the irregularity of the child's stay in the State of employment.

Article 31

1. States Parties shall ensure respect for the cultural identity of migrant workers and members of their families and shall not prevent them from maintaining their cultural links with their State of origin.
2. States Parties may take appropriate measures to assist and encourage efforts in this respect.

Article 32

Upon the termination of their stay in the State of employment, migrant workers and members of their families shall have the right to transfer their earnings and savings and, in accordance with the applicable legislation of the States concerned, their personal effects and belongings.

Article 33

1. Migrant workers and members of their families shall have the right to be informed by the State of origin, the State of employment or the State of transit as the case may be concerning:
   (a) Their rights arising out of the present Convention;
   (b) The conditions of their admission, their rights and obligations under the law and practice of the State concerned and such other

matters as will enable them to comply with administrative or other formalities in that State.

2. States Parties shall take all measures they deem appropriate to disseminate the said information or to ensure that it is provided by employers, trade unions or other appropriate bodies or institutions. As appropriate, they shall co-operate with other States concerned.

3. Such adequate information shall be provided upon request to migrant workers and members of their families, free of charge, and, as far as possible, in a language they are able to understand.

Article 34

Nothing in the present part of the Convention shall have the effect of relieving migrant workers and the members of their families from either the obligation to comply with the laws and regulations of any State of transit and the State of employment or the obligation to respect the cultural identity of the inhabitants of such States.

Article 35

Nothing in the present part of the Convention shall be interpreted as implying the regularization of the situation of migrant workers or members of their families who are non-documented or in an irregular situation or any right to such regularization of their situation, nor shall it prejudice the measures intended to ensure sound and equitable conditions for international migration as provided in part VI of the present Convention.

Part IV: Other rights of migrant workers and members of their families who are documented or in a regular situation

Article 36

Migrant workers and members of their families who are documented or in a regular situation in the State of employment shall enjoy the rights set forth in the present part of the Convention in addition to those set forth in part III.

Article 37

Before their departure, or at the latest at the time of their admission to the State of employment, migrant workers and members of their families shall have the right to be fully informed by the State of origin or the State of employment, as appropriate, of all conditions applicable to their admission and particularly those concerning their stay and the remunerated activities in which they may engage as well as of the requirements they must satisfy in the State of employment and the authority to which they must address themselves for any modification of those conditions.

Article 38

1. States of employment shall make every effort to authorize migrant workers and members of their families to be temporarily absent without effect upon their authorization to stay or to work, as the case may be. In doing so, States of employment shall take into account the special needs and obligations of migrant workers and members of their families, in particular in their States of origin.
2. Migrant workers and members of their families shall have the right to be fully informed of the terms on which such temporary absences are authorized.

Article 39

1. Migrant workers and members of their families shall have the right to liberty of movement in the territory of the State of employment and freedom to choose their residence there.
2. The rights mentioned in paragraph 1 of the present article shall not be subject to any restrictions except those that are provided by law, are necessary to protect national security, public order (ordre public), public health or morals, or the rights and freedoms of others and are consistent with the other rights recognized in the present Convention.

Article 40

1. Migrant workers and members of their families shall have the right to form associations and trade unions in the State of employment for the promotion and protection of their economic, social, cultural and other interests.
2. No restrictions may be placed on the exercise of this right other than those that are prescribed by law and are necessary in a democratic society in the interests of national security, public order (ordre public) or the protection of the rights and freedoms of others.

Article 41

1. Migrant workers and members of their families shall have the right to participate in public affairs of their State of origin and to vote and to be elected at elections of that State, in accordance with its legislation.
2. The States concerned shall, as appropriate and in accordance with their legislation, facilitate the exercise of these rights.

Article 42

1. States Parties shall consider the establishment of procedures or institutions through which account may be taken, both in States of origin and in States of employment, of special needs, aspirations and obligations of migrant workers and members of their families and shall envisage, as appropriate, the possibility for migrant workers and members of their families to have their freely chosen representatives in those institutions.
2. States of employment shall facilitate, in accordance with their national legislation, the consultation or participation of migrant workers and members of their families in decisions concerning the life and administration of local communities.
3. Migrant workers may enjoy political rights in the State of employment if that State, in the exercise of its sovereignty, grants them such rights.

Article 43

1. Migrant workers shall enjoy equality of treatment with nationals of the State of employment in relation to:
   (a) Access to educational institutions and services subject to the admission requirements and other regulations of the institutions and services concerned;
   (b) Access to vocational guidance and placement services;
   (c) Access to vocational training and retraining facilities and institutions;
   (d) Access to housing, including social housing schemes, and protection against exploitation in respect of rents;
   (e) Access to social and health services, provided that the requirements for participation in the respective schemes are met;

    (f) Access to co-operatives and self-managed enterprises, which shall not imply a change of their migration status and shall be subject to the rules and regulations of the bodies concerned;

    (g) Access to and participation in cultural life.

2. States Parties shall promote conditions to ensure effective equality of treatment to enable migrant workers to enjoy the rights mentioned in paragraph 1 of the present article whenever the terms of their stay, as authorized by the State of employment, meet the appropriate requirements.

3. States of employment shall not prevent an employer of migrant workers from establishing housing or social or cultural facilities for them. Subject to article 70 of the present Convention, a State of employment may make the establishment of such facilities subject to the requirements generally applied in that State concerning their installation.

Article 44

1. States Parties, recognizing that the family is the natural and fundamental group unit of society and is entitled to protection by society and the State, shall take appropriate measures to ensure the protection of the unity of the families of migrant workers.

2. States Parties shall take measures that they deem appropriate and that fall within their competence to facilitate the reunification of migrant workers with their spouses or persons who have with the migrant worker a relationship that, according to applicable law, produces effects equivalent to marriage, as well as with their minor dependent unmarried children.

3. States of employment, on humanitarian grounds, shall favourably consider granting equal treatment, as set forth in paragraph 2 of the present article, to other family members of migrant workers.

Article 45

1. Members of the families of migrant workers shall, in the State of employment, enjoy equality of treatment with nationals of that State in relation to:

    (a) Access to educational institutions and services, subject to the admission requirements and other regulations of the institutions and services concerned;

    (b) Access to vocational guidance and training institutions and services, provided that requirements for participation are met;

    (c) Access to social and health services, provided that requirements for participation in the respective schemes are met;

    (d) Access to and participation in cultural life.

2. States of employment shall pursue a policy, where appropriate in collaboration with the States of origin, aimed at facilitating the integration of children of migrant workers in the local school system, particularly in respect of teaching them the local language.

3. States of employment shall endeavour to facilitate for the children of migrant workers the teaching of their mother tongue and culture and, in this regard, States of origin shall collaborate whenever appropriate.

4. States of employment may provide special schemes of education in the mother tongue of children of migrant workers, if necessary in collaboration with the States of origin.

Article 46

Migrant workers and members of their families shall, subject to the applicable legislation of the States concerned, as well as relevant international agreements and the obligations of the States concerned arising out of their participation in customs unions, enjoy exemption from import and export duties and taxes in respect of their personal and household effects as well as the equipment necessary to engage in the remunerated activity for which they were admitted to the State of employment:

(a) Upon departure from the State of origin or State of habitual residence;

(b) Upon initial admission to the State of employment;

(c) Upon final departure from the State of employment;

(d) Upon final return to the State of origin or State of habitual residence.

Article 47

1. Migrant workers shall have the right to transfer their earnings and savings, in particular those funds necessary for the support of their families, from the State of employment to their State of origin or any other State. Such transfers shall be made in conformity with procedures established by applicable legislation of the State concerned and in conformity with applicable international agreements.

2. States concerned shall take appropriate measures to facilitate such transfers.

Article 48

1. Without prejudice to applicable double taxation agreements, migrant workers and members of their families shall, in the matter of earnings in the State of employment:
   (a) Not be liable to taxes, duties or charges of any description higher or more onerous than those imposed on nationals in similar circumstances;
   (b) Be entitled to deductions or exemptions from taxes of any description and to any tax allowances applicable to nationals in similar circumstances, including tax allowances for dependent members of their families.
2. States Parties shall endeavour to adopt appropriate measures to avoid double taxation of the earnings and savings of migrant workers and members of their families.

Article 49

1. Where separate authorizations to reside and to engage in employment are required by national legislation, the States of employment shall issue to migrant workers authorization of residence for at least the same period of time as their authorization to engage in remunerated activity.
2. Migrant workers who in the State of employment are allowed freely to choose their remunerated activity shall neither be regarded as in an irregular situation nor shall they lose their authorization of residence by the mere fact of the termination of their remunerated activity prior to the expiration of their work permits or similar authorizations.
3. In order to allow migrant workers referred to in paragraph 2 of the present article sufficient time to find alternative remunerated activities, the authorization of residence shall not be withdrawn at least for a period corresponding to that during which they may be entitled to unemployment benefits.

Article 50

1. In the case of death of a migrant worker or dissolution of marriage, the State of employment shall favourably consider granting family members of that migrant worker residing in that State on the basis of family reunion an authorization to stay; the State of employment

shall take into account the length of time they have already resided in that State.

2. Members of the family to whom such authorization is not granted shall be allowed before departure a reasonable period of time in order to enable them to settle their affairs in the State of employment.

3. The provisions of paragraphs 1 and 2 of the present article may not be interpreted as adversely affecting any right to stay and work otherwise granted to such family members by the legislation of the State of employment or by bilateral and multilateral treaties applicable to that State.

Article 51

Migrant workers who in the State of employment are not permitted freely to choose their remunerated activity shall neither be regarded as in an irregular situation nor shall they lose their authorization of residence by the mere fact of the termination of their remunerated activity prior to the expiration of their work permit, except where the authorization of residence is expressly dependent upon the specific remunerated activity for which they were admitted. Such migrant workers shall have the right to seek alternative employment, participation in public work schemes and retraining during the remaining period of their authorization to work, subject to such conditions and limitations as are specified in the authorization to work.

Article 52

1. Migrant workers in the State of employment shall have the right freely to choose their remunerated activity, subject to the following restrictions or conditions.

2. For any migrant worker a State of employment may:
   (a) Restrict access to limited categories of employment, functions, services or activities where this is necessary in the interests of this State and provided for by national legislation;
   (b) Restrict free choice of remunerated activity in accordance with its legislation concerning recognition of occupational qualifications acquired outside its territory. However, States Parties concerned shall endeavour to provide for recognition of such qualifications.

3. For migrant workers whose permission to work is limited in time, a State of employment may also:

(a) Make the right freely to choose their remunerated activities subject to the condition that the migrant worker has resided lawfully in its territory for the purpose of remunerated activity for a period of time prescribed in its national legislation that should not exceed two years;

(b) Limit access by a migrant worker to remunerated activities in pursuance of a policy of granting priority to its nationals or to persons who are assimilated to them for these purposes by virtue of legislation or bilateral or multilateral agreements. Any such limitation shall cease to apply to a migrant worker who has resided lawfully in its territory for the purpose of remunerated activity for a period of time prescribed in its national legislation that should not exceed five years.

4. States of employment shall prescribe the conditions under which a migrant worker who has been admitted to take up employment may be authorized to engage in work on his or her own account. Account shall be taken of the period during which the worker has already been lawfully in the State of employment.

Article 53

1. Members of a migrant worker's family who have themselves an authorization of residence or admission that is without limit of time or is automatically renewable shall be permitted freely to choose their remunerated activity under the same conditions as are applicable to the said migrant worker in accordance with article 52 of the present Convention.

2. With respect to members of a migrant worker's family who are not permitted freely to choose their remunerated activity, States Parties shall consider favourably granting them priority in obtaining permission to engage in a remunerated activity over other workers who seek admission to the State of employment, subject to applicable bilateral and multilateral agreements.

Article 54

1. Without prejudice to the terms of their authorization of residence or their permission to work and the rights provided for in articles 25 and 27 of the present Convention, migrant workers shall enjoy equality of treatment with nationals of the State of employment in respect of:

(a) Protection against dismissal;
(b) Unemployment benefits;
(c) Access to public work schemes intended to combat unemployment;
(d) Access to alternative employment in the event of loss of work or termination of other remunerated activity, subject to article 52 of the present Convention.

2. If a migrant worker claims that the terms of his or her work contract have been violated by his or her employer, he or she shall have the right to address his or her case to the competent authorities of the State of employment, on terms provided for in article 18, paragraph 1, of the present Convention.

Article 55

Migrant workers who have been granted permission to engage in a remunerated activity, subject to the conditions attached to such permission, shall be entitled to equality of treatment with nationals of the State of employment in the exercise of that remunerated activity.

Article 56

1. Migrant workers and members of their families referred to in the present part of the Convention may not be expelled from a State of employment, except for reasons defined in the national legislation of that State, and subject to the safeguards established in part III.
2. Expulsion shall not be resorted to for the purpose of depriving a migrant worker or a member of his or her family of the rights arising out of the authorization of residence and the work permit.
3. In considering whether to expel a migrant worker or a member of his or her family, account should be taken of humanitarian considerations and of the length of time that the person concerned has already resided in the State of employment.

Part V: Provisions applicable to particular categories of migrant workers and members of their families

Article 57

The particular categories of migrant workers and members of their families specified in the present part of the Convention who are documented or in a regular situation shall enjoy the rights set forth in part III and, except as modified below, the rights set forth in part IV.

Article 58

1. Frontier workers, as defined in article 2, paragraph 2 (a), of the present Convention, shall be entitled to the rights provided for in part IV that can be applied to them by reason of their presence and work in the territory of the State of employment, taking into account that they do not have their habitual residence in that State.
2. States of employment shall consider favourably granting frontier workers the right freely to choose their remunerated activity after a specified period of time. The granting of that right shall not affect their status as frontier workers.

Article 59

1. Seasonal workers, as defined in article 2, paragraph 2 (b), of the present Convention, shall be entitled to the rights provided for in part IV that can be applied to them by reason of their presence and work in the territory of the State of employment and that are compatible with their status in that State as seasonal workers, taking into account the fact that they are present in that State for only part of the year.
2. The State of employment shall, subject to paragraph 1 of the present article, consider granting seasonal workers who have been employed in its territory for a significant period of time the possibility of taking up other remunerated activities and giving them priority over other workers who seek admission to that State, subject to applicable bilateral and multilateral agreements.

Article 60

Itinerant workers, as defined in article 2, paragraph 2 (A), of the present Convention, shall be entitled to the rights provided for in part IV that can be granted to them by reason of their presence and work in the territory of the State of employment and that are compatible with their status as itinerant workers in that State.

Article 61

1. Project-tied workers, as defined in article 2, paragraph 2 (of the present Convention, and members of their families shall be entitled to the rights provided for in part IV except the provisions of article 43, paragraphs 1 (b) and (c), article 43, paragraph 1 (d), as it pertains to social housing schemes, article 45, paragraph 1 (b), and articles 52 to 55.
2. If a project-tied worker claims that the terms of his or her work contract have been violated by his or her employer, he or she shall have the right to address his or her case to the competent authorities of the State which has jurisdiction over that employer, on terms provided for in article 18, paragraph 1, of the present Convention.
3. Subject to bilateral or multilateral agreements in force for them, the States Parties concerned shall endeavour to enable project-tied workers to remain adequately protected by the social security systems of their States of origin or habitual residence during their engagement in the project. States Parties concerned shall take appropriate measures with the aim of avoiding any denial of rights or duplication of payments in this respect.
4. Without prejudice to the provisions of article 47 of the present Convention and to relevant bilateral or multilateral agreements, States Parties concerned shall permit payment of the earnings of project-tied workers in their State of origin or habitual residence.

Article 62

1. Specified-employment workers as defined in article 2, paragraph 2 (g), of the present Convention, shall be entitled to the rights provided for in part IV, except the provisions of article 43, paragraphs 1 (b) and (c), article 43, paragraph 1 (d), as it pertains to social housing schemes, article 52, and article 54, paragraph 1 (d).
2. Members of the families of specified-employment workers shall be entitled to the rights relating to family members of migrant workers provided for in part IV of the present Convention, except the provisions of article 53.

Article 63

1. Self-employed workers, as defined in article 2, paragraph 2 (h), of the present Convention, shall be entitled to the rights provided for in part

IV with the exception of those rights which are exclusively applicable to workers having a contract of employment.

2. Without prejudice to articles 52 and 79 of the present Convention, the termination of the economic activity of the self-employed workers shall not in itself imply the withdrawal of the authorization for them or for the members of their families to stay or to engage in a remunerated activity in the State of employment except where the authorization of residence is expressly dependent upon the specific remunerated activity for which they were admitted.

Part VI: Promotion of sound, equitable, humane and lawful conditions in connection with international migration of workers and members of their families

Article 64

1. Without prejudice to article 79 of the present Convention, the States Parties concerned shall as appropriate consult and co-operate with a view to promoting sound, equitable and humane conditions in connection with international migration of workers and members of their families.

2. In this respect, due regard shall be paid not only to labour needs and resources, but also to the social, economic, cultural and other needs of migrant workers and members of their families involved, as well as to the consequences of such migration for the communities concerned.

Article 65

1. States Parties shall maintain appropriate services to deal with questions concerning international migration of workers and members of their families. Their functions shall include, *inter alia*:

   (a) The formulation and implementation of policies regarding such migration;

   (b) An exchange of information, consultation and co-operation with the competent authorities of other States Parties involved in such migration;

   (c) The provision of appropriate information, particularly to employers, workers and their organizations on policies, laws and regulations relating to migration and employment, on agreements concluded with other States concerning migration and on other relevant matters;

    (d) The provision of information and appropriate assistance to migrant workers and members of their families regarding requisite authorizations and formalities and arrangements for departure, travel, arrival, stay, remunerated activities, exit and return, as well as on conditions of work and life in the State of employment and on customs, currency, tax and other relevant laws and regulations.

2. States Parties shall facilitate as appropriate the provision of adequate consular and other services that are necessary to meet the social, cultural and other needs of migrant workers and members of their families.

Article 66

1. Subject to paragraph 2 of the present article, the right to undertake operations with a view to the recruitment of workers for employment in another State shall be restricted to:
    (a) Public services or bodies of the State in which such operations take place;
    (b) Public services or bodies of the State of employment on the basis of agreement between the States concerned;
    (c) A body established by virtue of a bilateral or multilateral agreement.

2. Subject to any authorization, approval and supervision by the public authorities of the States Parties concerned as may be established pursuant to the legislation and practice of those States, agencies, prospective employers or persons acting on their behalf may also be permitted to undertake the said operations.

Article 67

1. States Parties concerned shall co-operate as appropriate in the adoption of measures regarding the orderly return of migrant workers and members of their families to the State of origin when they decide to return or their authorization of residence or employment expires or when they are in the State of employment in an irregular situation.

2. Concerning migrant workers and members of their families in a regular situation, States Parties concerned shall co-operate as appropriate, on terms agreed upon by those States, with a view to promoting adequate economic conditions for their resettlement and to

facilitating their durable social and cultural reintegration in the State of origin.

Article 68

1. States Parties, including States of transit, shall collaborate with a view to preventing and eliminating illegal or clandestine movements and employment of migrant workers in an irregular situation. The measures to be taken to this end within the jurisdiction of each State concerned shall include:
   (a) Appropriate measures against the dissemination of misleading information relating to emigration and immigration;
   (b) Measures to detect and eradicate illegal or clandestine movements of migrant workers and members of their families and to impose effective sanctions on persons, groups or entities which organize, operate or assist in organizing or operating such movements;
   (c) Measures to impose effective sanctions on persons, groups or entities which use violence, threats or intimidation against migrant workers or members of their families in an irregular situation.

2. States of employment shall take all adequate and effective measures to eliminate employment in their territory of migrant workers in an irregular situation, including, whenever appropriate, sanctions on employers of such workers. The rights of migrant workers vis-à-vis their employer arising from employment shall not be impaired by these measures.

Article 69

1. States Parties shall, when there are migrant workers and members of their families within their territory in an irregular situation, take appropriate measures to ensure that such a situation does not persist.

2. Whenever States Parties concerned consider the possibility of regularizing the situation of such persons in accordance with applicable national legislation and bilateral or multilateral agreements, appropriate account shall be taken of the circumstances of their entry, the duration of their stay in the States of employment and other relevant considerations, in particular those relating to their family situation.

Article 70

States Parties shall take measures not less favourable than those applied to nationals to ensure that working and living conditions of migrant workers and members of their families in a regular situation are in keeping with the standards of fitness, safety, health and principles of human dignity.

Article 71

1. States Parties shall facilitate, whenever necessary, the repatriation to the State of origin of the bodies of deceased migrant workers or members of their families.

2. As regards compensation matters relating to the death of a migrant worker or a member of his or her family, States Parties shall, as appropriate, provide assistance to the persons concerned with a view to the prompt settlement of such matters. Settlement of these matters shall be carried out on the basis of applicable national law in accordance with the provisions of the present Convention and any relevant bilateral or multilateral agreements.

Part VII: Application of the Convention

Article 72

1.

   (a) For the purpose of reviewing the application of the present Convention, there shall be established a Committee on the Protection of the Rights of All Migrant Workers and Members of Their Families (hereinafter referred to as 'the Committee');

   (b) The Committee shall consist, at the time of entry into force of the present Convention, of ten and, after the entry into force of the Convention for the forty-first State Party, of fourteen experts of high moral standing, impartiality and recognized competence in the field covered by the Convention.

2.

   (a) Members of the Committee shall be elected by secret ballot by the States Parties from a list of persons nominated by the States Parties, due consideration being given to equitable geographical distribution, including both States of origin and States of employment, and to the representation of the principal legal systems. Each State Party may nominate one person from among its own nationals;

(b) Members shall be elected and shall serve in their personal capacity.

3. The initial election shall be held no later than six months after the date of the entry into force of the present Convention and subsequent elections every second year. At least four months before the date of each election, the Secretary-General of the United Nations shall address a letter to all States Parties inviting them to submit their nominations within two months. The Secretary-General shall prepare a list in alphabetical order of all persons thus nominated, indicating the States Parties that have nominated them, and shall submit it to the States Parties not later than one month before the date of the corresponding election, together with the curricula vitae of the persons thus nominated.

4. Elections of members of the Committee shall be held at a meeting of States Parties convened by the Secretary-General at United Nations Headquarters. At that meeting, for which two thirds of the States Parties shall constitute a quorum, the persons elected to the Committee shall be those nominees who obtain the largest number of votes and an absolute majority of the votes of the States Parties present and voting.

5.

(a) The members of the Committee shall serve for a term of four years. However, the terms of five of the members elected in the first election shall expire at the end of two years; immediately after the first election, the names of these five members shall be chosen by lot by the Chairman of the meeting of States Parties;

(b) The election of the four additional members of the Committee shall be held in accordance with the provisions of paragraphs 2, 3 and 4 of the present article, following the entry into force of the Convention for the forty-first State Party. The term of two of the additional members elected on this occasion shall expire at the end of two years; the names of these members shall be chosen by lot by the Chairman of the meeting of States Parties;

(c) The members of the Committee shall be eligible for re-election if renominated.

6. If a member of the Committee dies or resigns or declares that for any other cause he or she can no longer perform the duties of the Committee,

the State Party that nominated the expert shall appoint another expert from among its own nationals for the remaining part of the term. The new appointment is subject to the approval of the Committee.

7. The Secretary-General of the United Nations shall provide the necessary staff and facilities for the effective performance of the functions of the Committee.

8. The members of the Committee shall receive emoluments from United Nations resources on such terms and conditions as the General Assembly may decide.

9. The members of the Committee shall be entitled to the facilities, privileges and immunities of experts on mission for the United Nations as laid down in the relevant sections of the Convention on the Privileges and Immunities of the United Nations.

Article 73

1. States Parties undertake to submit to the Secretary-General of the United Nations for consideration by the Committee a report on the legislative, judicial, administrative and other measures they have taken to give effect to the provisions of the present Convention:
   (a) Within one year after the entry into force of the Convention for the State Party concerned;
   (b) Thereafter every five years and whenever the Committee so requests.

2. Reports prepared under the present article shall also indicate factors and difficulties, if any, affecting the implementation of the Convention and shall include information on the characteristics of migration flows in which the State Party concerned is involved.

3. The Committee shall decide any further guidelines applicable to the content of the reports.

4. States Parties shall make their reports widely available to the public in their own countries.

Article 74

1. The Committee shall examine the reports submitted by each State Party and shall transmit such comments as it may consider appropriate to the State Party concerned. This State Party may submit to the Committee observations on any comment made by the Committee in accordance with the present article. The Committee may request

supplementary information from States Parties when considering these reports.

2. The Secretary-General of the United Nations shall, in due time before the opening of each regular session of the Committee, transmit to the Director-General of the International Labour Office copies of the reports submitted by States Parties concerned and information relevant to the consideration of these reports, in order to enable the Office to assist the Committee with the expertise the Office may provide regarding those matters dealt with by the present Convention that fall within the sphere of competence of the International Labour Organisation. The Committee shall consider in its deliberations such comments and materials as the Office may provide.

3. The Secretary-General of the United Nations may also, after consultation with the Committee, transmit to other specialized agencies as well as to intergovernmental organizations, copies of such parts of these reports as may fall within their competence.

4. The Committee may invite the specialized agencies and organs of the United Nations, as well as intergovernmental organizations and other concerned bodies to submit, for consideration by the Committee, written information on such matters dealt with in the present Convention as fall within the scope of their activities.

5. The International Labour Office shall be invited by the Committee to appoint representatives to participate, in a consultative capacity, in the meetings of the Committee.

6. The Committee may invite representatives of other specialized agencies and organs of the United Nations, as well as of intergovernmental organizations, to be present and to be heard in its meetings whenever matters falling within their field of competence are considered.

7. The Committee shall present an annual report to the General Assembly of the United Nations on the implementation of the present Convention, containing its own considerations and recommendations, based, in particular, on the examination of the reports and any observations presented by States Parties.

8. The Secretary-General of the United Nations shall transmit the annual reports of the Committee to the States Parties to the present Convention, the Economic and Social Council, the Commission on Human Rights of the United Nations, the Director-General of the International Labour Office and other relevant organizations.

Article 75

1. The Committee shall adopt its own rules of procedure.
2. The Committee shall elect its officers for a term of two years.
3. The Committee shall normally meet annually.
4. The meetings of the Committee shall normally be held at United Nations Headquarters.

Article 76

1. A State Party to the present Convention may at any time declare under this article that it recognizes the competence of the Committee to receive and consider communications to the effect that a State Party claims that another State Party is not fulfilling its obligations under the present Convention. Communications under this article may be received and considered only if submitted by a State Party that has made a declaration recognizing in regard to itself the competence of the Committee. No communication shall be received by the Committee if it concerns a State Party which has not made such a declaration. Communications received under this article shall be dealt with in accordance with the following procedure:

   (a) If a State Party to the present Convention considers that another State Party is not fulfilling its obligations under the present Convention, it may, by written communication, bring the matter to the attention of that State Party. The State Party may also inform the Committee of the matter. Within three months after the receipt of the communication the receiving State shall afford the State that sent the communication an explanation, or any other statement in writing clarifying the matter which should include, to the extent possible and pertinent, reference to domestic procedures and remedies taken, pending or available in the matter;

   (b) If the matter is not adjusted to the satisfaction of both States Parties concerned within six months after the receipt by the receiving State of the initial communication, either State shall have the right to refer the matter to the Committee, by notice given to the Committee and to the other State;

   (c) The Committee shall deal with a matter referred to it only after it has ascertained that all available domestic remedies have been invoked and exhausted in the matter, in conformity with the generally recognized principles of international law. This shall not be the rule where, in the view of the Committee, the application of the remedies is unreasonably prolonged;

(d) Subject to the provisions of subparagraph (c) of the present paragraph, the Committee shall make available its good offices to the States Parties concerned with a view to a friendly solution of the matter on the basis of the respect for the obligations set forth in the present Convention;

(e) The Committee shall hold closed meetings when examining communications under the present article;

(f) In any matter referred to it in accordance with subparagraph (b) of the present paragraph, the Committee may call upon the States Parties concerned, referred to in subparagraph (b), to supply any relevant information;

(g) The States Parties concerned, referred to in subparagraph (b) of the present paragraph, shall have the right to be represented when the matter is being considered by the Committee and to make submissions orally and/or in writing;

(h) The Committee shall, within twelve months after the date of receipt of notice under subparagraph (b) of the present paragraph, submit a report, as follows:

(i) If a solution within the terms of subparagraph (d) of the present paragraph is reached, the Committee shall confine its report to a brief statement of the facts and of the solution reached;

(ii) If a solution within the terms of subparagraph (d) is not reached, the Committee shall, in its report, set forth the relevant facts concerning the issue between the States Parties concerned. The written submissions and record of the oral submissions made by the States Parties concerned shall be attached to the report. The Committee may also communicate only to the States Parties concerned any views that it may consider relevant to the issue between them. In every matter, the report shall be communicated to the States Parties concerned.

2. The provisions of the present article shall come into force when ten States Parties to the present Convention have made a declaration under paragraph 1 of the present article. Such declarations shall be deposited by the States Parties with the Secretary-General of the United Nations, who shall transmit copies thereof to the other

States Parties. A declaration may be withdrawn at any time by notification to the Secretary-General. Such a withdrawal shall not prejudice the consideration of any matter that is the subject of a communication already transmitted under the present article; no further communication by any State Party shall be received under the present article after the notification of withdrawal of the declaration has been received by the Secretary-General, unless the State Party concerned has made a new declaration.

Article 77

1. A State Party to the present Convention may at any time declare under the present article that it recognizes the competence of the Committee to receive and consider communications from or on behalf of individuals subject to its jurisdiction who claim that their individual rights as established by the present Convention have been violated by that State Party. No communication shall be received by the Committee if it concerns a State Party that has not made such a declaration.

2. The Committee shall consider inadmissible any communication under the present article which is anonymous or which it considers to be an abuse of the right of submission of such communications or to be incompatible with the provisions of the present Convention.

3. The Committee shall not consider any communication from an individual under the present article unless it has ascertained that:
   (a) The same matter has not been, and is not being, examined under another procedure of international investigation or settlement;
   (b) The individual has exhausted all available domestic remedies; this shall not be the rule where, in the view of the Committee, the application of the remedies is unreasonably prolonged or is unlikely to bring effective relief to that individual.

4. Subject to the provisions of paragraph 2 of the present article, the Committee shall bring any communications submitted to it under this article to the attention of the State Party to the present Convention that has made a declaration under paragraph 1 and is alleged to be violating any provisions of the Convention. Within six months, the receiving State shall submit to the Committee written explanations or statements clarifying the matter and the remedy, if any, that may have been taken by that State.

5. The Committee shall consider communications received under the present article in the light of all information made available to it by or on behalf of the individual and by the State Party concerned.
6. The Committee shall hold closed meetings when examining communications under the present article.
7. The Committee shall forward its views to the State Party concerned and to the individual.
8. The provisions of the present article shall come into force when ten States Parties to the present Convention have made declarations under paragraph 1 of the present article. Such declarations shall be deposited by the States Parties with the Secretary-General of the United Nations, who shall transmit copies thereof to the other States Parties. A declaration may be withdrawn at any time by notification to the Secretary-General. Such a withdrawal shall not prejudice the consideration of any matter that is the subject of a communication already transmitted under the present article; no further communication by or on behalf of an individual shall be received under the present article after the notification of withdrawal of the declaration has been received by the Secretary-General, unless the State Party has made a new declaration.

Article 78

The provisions of article 76 of the present Convention shall be applied without prejudice to any procedures for settling disputes or complaints in the field covered by the present Convention laid down in the constituent instruments of, or in conventions adopted by, the United Nations and the specialized agencies and shall not prevent the States Parties from having recourse to any procedures for settling a dispute in accordance with international agreements in force between them.

Part VIII: General provisions

Article 79

Nothing in the present Convention shall affect the right of each State Party to establish the criteria governing admission of migrant workers and members of their families. Concerning other matters related to their legal situation and treatment as migrant workers and members of their families, States Parties shall be subject to the limitations set forth in the present Convention.

Article 80

Nothing in the present Convention shall be interpreted as impairing the provisions of the Charter of the United Nations and of the constitutions of the specialized agencies which define the respective responsibilities of the various organs of the United Nations and of the specialized agencies in regard to the matters dealt with in the present Convention.

Article 81

1. Nothing in the present Convention shall affect more favourable rights or freedoms granted to migrant workers and members of their families by virtue of:
   (a) The law or practice of a State Party; or
   (b) Any bilateral or multilateral treaty in force for the State Party concerned.
2. Nothing in the present Convention may be interpreted as implying for any State, group or person any right to engage in any activity or perform any act that would impair any of the rights and freedoms as set forth in the present Convention.

Article 82

The rights of migrant workers and members of their families provided for in the present Convention may not be renounced. It shall not be permissible to exert any form of pressure upon migrant workers and members of their families with a view to their relinquishing or foregoing any of the said rights. It shall not be possible to derogate by contract from rights recognized in the present Convention. States Parties shall take appropriate measures to ensure that these principles are respected.

Article 83

Each State Party to the present Convention undertakes:

(a) To ensure that any person whose rights or freedoms as herein recognized are violated shall have an effective remedy, notwithstanding that the violation has been committed by persons acting in an official capacity;
(b) To ensure that any persons seeking such a remedy shall have his or her claim reviewed and decided by competent judicial, administrative or

legislative authorities, or by any other competent authority provided for by the legal system of the State, and to develop the possibilities of judicial remedy;

(c) To ensure that the competent authorities shall enforce such remedies when granted.

Article 84

Each State Party undertakes to adopt the legislative and other measures that are necessary to implement the provisions of the present Convention.

Part IX: Final provisions

Article 85

The Secretary-General of the United Nations is designated as the depositary of the present Convention.

Article 86

1. The present Convention shall be open for signature by all States. It is subject to ratification.
2. The present Convention shall be open to accession by any State.
3. Instruments of ratification or accession shall be deposited with the Secretary-General of the United Nations.

Article 87

1. The present Convention shall enter into force on the first day of the month following a period of three months after the date of the deposit of the twentieth instrument of ratification or accession.
2. For each State ratifying or acceding to the present Convention after its entry into force, the Convention shall enter into force on the first day of the month following a period of three months after the date of the deposit of its own instrument of ratification or accession.

Article 88

A State ratifying or acceding to the present Convention may not exclude the application of any part of it, or, without prejudice to article 3, exclude any particular category of migrant workers from its application.

Article 89

1. Any State Party may denounce the present Convention, not earlier than five years after the Convention has entered into force for the State concerned, by means of a notification in writing addressed to the Secretary-General of the United Nations.
2. Such denunciation shall become effective on the first day of the month following the expiration of a period of twelve months after the date of the receipt of the notification by the Secretary-General of the United Nations.
3. Such a denunciation shall not have the effect of releasing the State Party from its obligations under the present Convention in regard to any act or omission which occurs prior to the date at which the denunciation becomes effective, nor shall denunciation prejudice in any way the continued consideration of any matter which is already under consideration by the Committee prior to the date at which the denunciation becomes effective.
4. Following the date at which the denunciation of a State Party becomes effective, the Committee shall not commence consideration of any new matter regarding that State.

Article 90

1. After five years from the entry into force of the Convention a request for the revision of the Convention may be made at any time by any State Party by means of a notification in writing addressed to the Secretary-General of the United Nations. The Secretary-General shall thereupon communicate any proposed amendments to the States Parties with a request that they notify him whether they favour a conference of States Parties for the purpose of considering and voting upon the proposals. In the event that within four months from the date of such communication at least one third of the States Parties favours such a conference, the Secretary-General shall convene the conference under the auspices of the United Nations. Any amendment adopted by a majority of the States Parties present and voting shall be submitted to the General Assembly for approval.
2. Amendments shall come into force when they have been approved by the General Assembly of the United Nations and accepted by a

two-thirds majority of the States Parties in accordance with their respective constitutional processes.

3. When amendments come into force, they shall be binding on those States Parties that have accepted them, other States Parties still being bound by the provisions of the present Convention and any earlier amendment that they have accepted.

Article 91

1. The Secretary-General of the United Nations shall receive and circulate to all States the text of reservations made by States at the time of signature, ratification or accession.

2. A reservation incompatible with the object and purpose of the present Convention shall not be permitted.

3. Reservations may be withdrawn at any time by notification to this effect addressed to the Secretary-General of the United Nations, who shall then inform all States thereof. Such notification shall take effect on the date on which it is received.

Article 92

1. Any dispute between two or more States Parties concerning the interpretation or application of the present Convention that is not settled by negotiation shall, at the request of one of them, be submitted to arbitration. If within six months from the date of the request for arbitration the Parties are unable to agree on the organization of the arbitration, any one of those Parties may refer the dispute to the International Court of Justice by request in conformity with the Statute of the Court.

2. Each State Party may at the time of signature or ratification of the present Convention or accession thereto declare that it does not consider itself bound by paragraph 1 of the present article. The other States Parties shall not be bound by that paragraph with respect to any State Party that has made such a declaration.

3. Any State Party that has made a declaration in accordance with paragraph 2 of the present article may at any time withdraw that declaration by notification to the Secretary-General of the United Nations.

Article 93

1. The present Convention, of which the Arabic, Chinese, English, French, Russian and Spanish texts are equally authentic, shall be deposited with the Secretary-General of the United Nations.
2. The Secretary-General of the United Nations shall transmit certified copies of the present Convention to all States.

In witness whereof the undersigned plenipotentiaries, being duly authorized thereto by their respective Governments, have signed the present Convention.

Annex 2

Ratifications of ILO Conventions 97 and 143 and of ICRMW as at June 2009

State	Ratification ILO C-97	Ratification ILO C-143	Ratification ICRMW	Signature ICRMW
Albania	2 Mar. 2005	12 Sept. 2006	5 June 2007	
Algeria	19 Oct. 1962		21 Apr. 2005	
Argentina			23 Feb. 2007	10 Aug. 2004
Armenia	27 Jan. 2006	27 Jan. 2006		
Azerbaijan			11 Jan. 1999	
Bahamas	25 May 1976			
Bangladesh				7 Oct. 1998
Barbados	8 May 1967			
Belgium	27 July 1953			
Belize	15 Dec. 1983		14 Nov. 2001	
Benin		11 June 1980		15 Sept. 2005
Bolivia			12 Oct. 2000	
Bosnia and Herzegovina	2 June 1993	2 June 1993	13 Dec. 1996	
Brazil	18 June 1965			
Burkina Faso	9 June 1961	9 Dec. 1977	26 Nov. 2003	16 Nov. 2001
Cambodia				27 Sept. 2004
Cameroon	3 Sept. 1962	4 July 1978		
Cape Verde			16 Sept. 1997	
Chile			21 Mar. 2005	24 Sept. 1993
Colombia			24 May 1995	
Comoros				22 Sept. 2000
Congo				29 Sept. 2008
Cuba	29 Apr. 1952			
Cyprus	23 Sept. 1960	28 June 1977		
Dominica	28 Feb. 1983			
Ecuador	5 Apr. 1978		6 Feb. 2002	

State	Ratification ILO C-97	Ratification ILO C-143	Ratification ICRMW	Signature ICRMW
Egypt			19 Feb. 1993	
El Salvador			14 Mar. 2003	13 Sept. 2002
France	29 Mar. 1954			
Gabon				15 Dec. 2004
Germany	22 June 1959			
Ghana			8 Sept. 2000	8 Sept. 2000
Grenada	9 July 1979			
Guatemala	13 Feb. 1952		14 Mar. 2003	7 Sept. 2000
Guinea		5 June 1978	8 Sept. 2000	
Guinea-Bissau				12 Sept. 2000
Guyana	8 June 1966			15 Sept. 2005
Honduras			11 Aug. 2005	
Indonesia				22 Sept. 2004
Israel	30 Mar. 1953			
Italy	22 Oct. 1952	23 June 1981		
Jamaica	22 Dec. 1962		25 Sept. 2008	25 Sept. 2008
Kenya	30 Nov. 1965	9 Apr. 1979		
Kyrgyzstan	10 Sept. 2008		29 Sept. 2003	
Lesotho			16 Sept. 2005	24 Sept. 2004
Liberia				22 Sept. 2004
Libyan Arab Jamahiriya			18 June 2004	
Madagascar	14 June 2001			
Malawi	22 Mar. 1965			
Malaysia (Sabah)	3 Mar. 1964			
Mali			6 June 2003	
Mauritania			22 Jan. 2007	
Mauritius	2 Dec. 1969			
Mexico			8 Mar. 1999	22 May 1991
Montenegro	3 June 2006	3 June 2006		23 Oct. 2006
Morocco			21 June 1993	15 Aug. 1991
Netherlands	20 May 1952			
New Zealand	10 Nov. 1950			
Nicaragua			26 Oct. 2005	
Niger			18 Mar. 2009	
Nigeria	17 Oct. 1960			
Norway	17 Feb. 1955	24 Jan. 1979		
Paraguay			23 Sept. 2008	13 Sept. 2000
Peru			14 Sept. 2005	22 Sept. 2004

State	Ratification ILO C-97	Ratification ILO C-143	Ratification ICRMW	Signature ICRMW
Philippines	21 Apr. 2009	14 Sept. 2006	5 July 1995	15 Nov. 1993
Portugal	12 Dec. 1978	12 Dec. 1978		
Rep. of Moldova	12 Dec. 2005			
Rwanda			15 Dec. 2008	
Saint Lucia	14 May 1980			
San Marino		23 May 1985		
Sao Tome and Principe				6 Sept. 2000
Senegal			9 June 1999	
Serbia	24 Nov. 2000	24 Nov. 2000		11 Nov. 2004
Seychelles			15 Dec. 1994	
Sierra Leone				15 Sept. 2000
Slovenia	29 May 1992	29 May 1992		
Spain	21 Mar. 1967			
Sri Lanka			11 Mar. 1996	
Sweden		28 Dec. 1982		
Syrian Arab Rep.			2 June 2005	
Tajikistan	10 Apr. 2007	10 Apr. 2007	8 Jan. 2002	7 Sept. 2000
The former Yugoslav Republic of Macedonia	17 Nov. 1991	17 Nov. 1991		
Timor-Leste			30 Jan. 2004	
Togo		8 Nov. 1983		15 Nov. 2001
Trinidad and Tobago	24 May 1963			
Turkey			27 Sept. 2004	13 Jan. 1999
Uganda		31 Mar. 1978	14 Nov. 1995	
United Kingdom	22 Jan. 1951			
United Rep. of Tanzania (Zanzibar)	22 June 1964			
Uruguay	18 Mar. 1954		15 Feb. 2001	
Venezuela	9 June 1983	17 Aug. 1983		
Zambia	2 Dec. 1964			

INDEX